D1710755

MOUNTAIN MEASURES

A SECOND SERVING

A COLLECTION OF WEST VIRGINIA RECIPES

"The purpose of the Junior League is exclusively educational and charitable and is to promote voluntarism, to develop the potential of its members for voluntary participation in community affairs, and to demonstrate the effectiveness of trained volunteers."

Mountain Measures

and

Mountain Measures: A Second Serving

Published by
Junior League of Charleston, West Virginia, Inc.

ISBN No. 0-9606232-1-3

Library of Congress Catalog Card Number 83083047

First Printing, 1984 — 20,000 copies

While the recipes in this book may not all be original, they were
donated as favorites by the contributors.

Proceeds from the sale of **MOUNTAIN MEASURES: A SECOND
SERVING** will go to all community projects of the Junior League
of Charleston, West Virginia, Inc.

Preface and historical writings by Paul D. Marshall.

Art work by Mrs. Robert M. Chilton.

Cover design by Patricia Cahape, Two Rivers Design Group.

Cover photograph by Garnett D. Brown, Brown Photographics.

"Schoolhouse", the quilt pattern chosen for the cover is a variation
of the traditional schoolhouse design. It was created and made by
Cabin Creek Quilts, Box 383, Cabin Creek, WV 25035.

Information on Fairs and Festivals mentioned in this book may be
obtained by writing: Governor's Office of E.C.D., 1900 Washington
Street East, Charleston, West Virginia 25311.

Copies may be obtained by addressing **MOUNTAIN MEASURES:
A SECOND SERVING,** The Junior League of Charleston, P.O. Box
1924, Charleston, West Virginia 25327. Price $11.95 plus $1.50 per
copy mailing costs. West Virginia residents please add 5% sales tax.
Order blanks in back of book.

KANSAS CITY
PRESS, INC.

Printed by
Kansas City Press
Olathe, Kansas

CONTENTS

Each section is keyed by a traditional quilt pattern. The quilt pattern next to a recipe indicates a regional dish.

ACKNOWLEDGEMENTS

COOKBOOK COMMITTEE

Mrs. John M. Slack, III,
Co-Chairman
Mrs. Robert F. Goldsmith,
Co-Chairman
Mrs. Bruce Berry
Mrs. Rodney D. Dean
Mrs. Steven Doty
Mrs. Charles Q. Gage
Mrs. C. Page Hamrick, III

Mrs. Richard E. Hardison
Mrs. John R. Hoblitzell
Mrs. William Huffman
Mrs. C. William Kim
Mrs. J.K. Lilly, III
Mrs. John C. Palmer, IV
Mrs. James W. Shuman
Mrs. Richard C. Sinclair

TYPISTS

Mrs. Malcolm Chaney
Mrs. John D. McCue, Jr.
Miss Lucy Moore

With special gratitude to the original **MOUNTAIN MEASURES** cookbook committee without whose hardwork and dedication this book would not have been possible.

With thanks to Mrs. James D. Bartsch, Mrs. Michael Cox, Mrs. William F. Dobbs, Jr., Mrs. Michael Foster, Dr. Linda S. Geronilla, Mrs. J. Crawford Goldman, Miss Carolanne Griffith, Mrs. Charles Isbell, Mrs. William B. McElroy, Mrs. Harold Selinger, Mr. and Mrs. William Wykle, and to all those Junior League members and their families who researched, tested, evaluated and provided invaluable assistance.

Paul D. Marshall, architect and preservationist, is a native of Charleston, West Virginia. Since 1976 a large percentage of his firm's work has been in the field of historic preservation. Commissions have included historical and architectural surveys, adaptive use of historic buildings, restoration, reconstruction and stabilization of historic structures. Mr. Marshall is a member of the American Institute of Architects and its national committees on Regional Development and Natural Resources, and Historic Resources. During 1982-83 and 1983-84 he was president of the Kanawha Valley Historic and Preservation Society and is a board member of the Preservation Alliance of West Virginia, a statewide historic preservation organization. He is also a member and the State Preservation Coordinator for the West Virginia Society of Architects.

BIBLIOGRAPHY

West Virginia Department of Culture and History
Historic Preservation Unit

Commission of Archives and History of
The United Methodist Church

Dr. and Mrs. John A. Washington
Harewood, Charles Town, West Virginia

State of West Virginia
Department of Natural Resources
Division of Parks and Recreation

Harpers Ferry National Historical Park
National Park Service
U.S. Department of the Interior

The Frontiersman by Allan W. Eckert
Bantam Books/Little, Brown and Company, Inc.
Boston, Massachusetts, 1967

Historic America, Buildings, Structures, and Sites
Historic American Buildings Survey/Historic American
   Engineering Record
National Park Service
U.S. Department of the Interior
Library of Congress, Washington, D.C., 1983

New River Gorge National River, West Virginia
A Cultural Research Project
Volume 2: History, Architecture and Community
Paul D. Marshall & Associates, Inc.
Allen Blueprint Co./Dunbar Printing Co., 1981

PREFACE

Lord Dunmore, the royal governor of Virginia wrote:

"I have learnt from experience that the established authority of any government in America and the policy of government at home are both insufficient to restrain the Americans; and that they acquire no attachment to place; but wandering about seems engrafted in their nature; and it is a weakness incident to it, that they should ever imagine the lands further off are still better than those upon which they are already settled."

This description of Americans is valid even today, when one views the transient society in which we live, and new pioneers shuttle into today's frontier - space. But in the eighteenth century a new breed of American was spilling into the Valley of Virginia and crossing the formidable Appalachian barrier. The land they entered was equally as strange and challenging as the shore line appeared to the first Europeans who came to America. This new breed was the frontiersman, for the most part unlettered men, a group which included hunters, disappointed farmers from Europe and the East, trappers, military veterans, adventurers, and a nucleus of sturdy, honorable men who took along with them Daniel Boone's three essentials: "A good gun, a good horse, and a good wife."

The frontiersman and his family tamed the wilderness, forging new settlements in the beautiful mountains and valleys of what we now call West Virginia. Settlements grew, roads improved, and civilization's amenities gradually caught up with the pioneers who had outrun them. Schools and churches were built and local governments were formed. Generation upon generation built upon the solid foundations laid by their forefathers but, gradually, the early pioneer slipped from memory. The conscience of America was stirred during our 1976 Bi-Centennial celebration. For many Americans it was the first awareness of a rich heritage. It is good to reflect on the nature of our heritage and traditions, for to forget is to cut ourselves off from our roots. To remember is to maintain the heritage for those who follow.

Through the medium of *Mountain Measures: A Second Serving* we seek to recall and honor those who courageously pioneered the hostile frontier, and also those who have nurtured the heritage. We remember the citizen soldier, the farmer, the miner, the railroader, the landowner, the business man, the industrialist, and the builder. Of course, the excellent collection of recipes recalls the pioneer woman who created, used, and passed on from generation to generation her knowledge and ingenuity.

Photographs of fourteen West Virginia historic sites have been selected for this edition representing several widely scattered regions of the state. The architectural styles vary from the rugged vernacular of a hewed log farm house to the Georgian elegance of the state Executive Mansion, and from pioneer meeting houses to a downtown stone Gothic church. The examples chosen span two hundred years of West

Virginia settlement history and symbolize the faith, vision and hard work which have been the essence of our heritage.

You are invited, then, to take a mental walk back into history. Listen for the ring of an ax through forested hills, the joy expressed in a simple hymn tune, or the lonely sound of a steam locomotive whistle. Imagine a stagecoach driver struggling with his team over rutted roads, picture a frontier barn raising, or recall a joyful reunion at the train station.

It is good to remember.

Paul D. Marshall

HARPERS FERRY

Robert Harper arrived at this beautiful and now historic site in 1747, purchasing a primitive ferry service from the area's first settler, Peter Stephens, who had claimed the land in 1733. Robert Harper was a millwright and soon built a grist mill, taking advantage of the excellent waterpower resources.

The town clings to a steep point of land at the confluence of the Shenandoah and Potomac rivers which have carved their way through the Blue Ridge Mountains on their way to the sea. In 1783, Thomas Jefferson claimed the view of the cleft in the mountains "worth a voyage across the Atlantic."

George Washington persuaded Congress to establish a U.S. Army Armory at Harpers Ferry because of its access to water power and raw materials, its secure position, and proximity to Washington, D.C. The armory was producing its first weapons in 1801 and remained in service until destroyed in 1861 to keep it from falling into Confederate hands.

The armory attracted the attention of ardent abolitionist John Brown who, in October, 1859, selected the area as the starting point for an insurrection the object of which was to establish a free-Negro stronghold. The raid was quickly quelled and John Brown was executed for treason.

The combined tragedies of the John Brown raid, the Civil War, and a series of terrible floods in the late 19th century wrecked the town's economy and many of the downtown buildings were abandoned for years.

Today Harpers Ferry is a National Historic Park. Most of the downtown buildings have been restored and furnished to interpret life in the mid-19th century. Millions of tourists visit each year to see Jefferson's spectacular view and experience a part of West Virginia which puts history on display.

The photograph shows St. Peters Catholic Church (1830's) as seen above the historic buildings along Shenandoah Street.

Photo by Governor's Office of E.C.D.

APPETIZERS

Rising Star

ANTIPASTO SPREAD

1 pound mushrooms, sliced
2 large green peppers, cut into strips
¼ cup olive oil
1 (6 ounce) can tomato paste
1 tablespoon red wine vinegar
1 teaspoon sugar
¼ teaspoon oregano
1 teaspoon salt
Dash of pepper

2 tablespoons capers
¼ cup ripe pitted olives, sliced
¼ cup green olives, sliced
1 (4 ounce) jar pickled tiny white onions
1 (3½ ounce) can tuna, drained
Garlic powder to taste
Optional: sliced cauliflower, green beans, carrots or celery

Sauté mushrooms, peppers and optionals in olive oil for 5 minutes. Add next 6 ingredients and simmer 15 minutes. Add rest of ingredients and remove from heat. Store in refrigerator in glass container until serving. Serve on crackers. Serves 8.

Barbara Morgan, M.D.

ARTICHOKE BAKE

2 (14 ounces each) cans artichoke hearts
1 cup Parmesan cheese
½ cup mayonnaise
½ cup sour cream

Dash of Worcestershire sauce
¼ teaspoon seasoned salt
Dash of onion powder
Dash of pepper

Drain artichokes thoroughly, pressing to remove excess liquid. Finely chop artichoke hearts. Combine all ingredients in mixing bowl. Place in shallow baking dish. Bake at 350° for 15 to 20 minutes or until bubbly and brown around the edges. Serve with crackers. Yield: 3 cups.

Variation: Add 1 (4 ounce) can chopped green chilies or 1 (8 ounce) can water chestnuts, chopped.

Mary Jean Davis (Mrs. K. Paul)

BACON CHIPS

2 cups brown sugar
2 tablespoons dry mustard

1 pound thick sliced bacon

Mix mustard and brown sugar together. Spread bacon on a cookie sheet. Sprinkle the dry mixture over the bacon. Use it all! Bake at 250° for 1 hour. Remove from oven and drain on a brown paper bag. Cut or break into "chips" for a sweet, finger hors d'oeuvre. May be served at a brunch. This can be kept in the refrigerator for one week. Serves 12 to 14.

Bonnie W. Bartsch (Mrs. James)

BACON ROLL UPS

1 pound bacon
1 (8 ounce) package
    Pepperidge Farm
    stuffing

1 egg, beaten
1 cup water
½ cup margarine

Cut each bacon strip into three short pieces. Make stuffing as directed on package, using egg, water and margarine. Place 1 rounded teaspoon of stuffing on each piece of bacon, roll up and secure with a toothpick. Place on rack in pan. Bake at 425° for 6 to 8 minutes on each side, turning once. Can be frozen before or after baking. If freezing after baking, undercook slightly and reheat. Serves 6 to 8.

Jean G. Campe (Mrs. Robert, Jr.)

BRIE EN CROUTE

1 (3 ounce) package cream
    cheese
¼ cup butter

¾ cup flour
1 small round of Brie cheese

Allow butter and cheese to come to room temperature. Add flour. Mix together with a pastry cutter. Form a ball with the dough and place in aluminum foil. Refrigerate for three hours. Split in half. Roll into 2 flat circles. Place Brie in the middle of one and place the other circle on top. Pinch the sides together. Bake at 350° for 15 to 20 minutes or until golden brown. Let set 10 to 20 minutes before serving. Serves 4 to 6.

Betsy C. Peterson

HOT BRIE

1 whole Brie cheese
   (2 pounds)

¾ cup brown sugar
1 cup slivered almonds

Place cheese in an ovenproof serving dish. Sprinkle brown sugar first and then almonds over top. Bake at 300° for 20 minutes until cheese is soft and almonds and sugar are brown. May need to place under broiler for last minute. Serve with crackers. Serves 16 to 20.

Betsy G. Wyant (Mrs. David)

ALMONDS-IN-A-HAYSTACK

4 cups finely chopped ham
⅓ cup sliced green onions
¼ cup pickle relish
¾ cup salad dressing,
   divided

1 (8 ounce) package cream
   cheese, softened
1 to 2 cups slivered almonds,
   toasted

Combine ham, onions and relish with half of cream cheese, ½ cup salad dressing and ½ cup almonds. Mix well and chill. Shape into 1 large or 2 small mounds. Combine ¼ cup salad dressing and remaining cream cheese. Mix well. Frost mound with cream cheese mixture. Chill slightly. Cover with toasted almonds. Serve with crackers or party rye bread.

Sandra W. Mantz (Mrs. Eric)

BLUE CHEESE BALL

3 (8 ounces each) packages
   cream cheese
4 ounces Blue cheese
8 ounces yellow crock
   cheese

2 medium onions, grated
   Garlic powder
   Parsley or chopped pecans

Allow cheeses to soften. Blend together cheeses, onion and garlic powder. Chill one hour or until firm. Roll into 1 large or 2 medium balls. Roll ball in parsley or chopped pecans.

Victoria G. Hardy (Mrs. Waller C., III)

BLUE CHEESE CHEESECAKE

¼ cup bread crumbs
¼ cup Parmesan cheese
2 (8 ounces each) packages
   cream cheese,
   softened
⅓ cup heavy cream
4 eggs

2 to 3 drops Tabasco sauce
½ pound country bacon
1 medium onion, finely
   chopped
½ pound Blue cheese,
   crumbled

Mix bread crumbs and Parmesan cheese. Shake in 8" or 9" buttered springform pan*. Remove excess. Beat until smooth cream cheese, cream, eggs and Tabasco. Cook bacon, drain and crumble. Saute onion in 1 tablespoon of the bacon grease. Fold bacon, onion and Blue cheese into cream cheese mixture. Pour into springform pan, shaking to settle. Place pan in larger pan in 2" of boiling water. Cook at 325° for 1 hour and 40 minutes. Turn off oven and leave in 1 hour longer. Before cooling, tilt pan so that all the water that has seeped in will drain out. To serve: turn over and remove bottom of pan so that crumb mixture makes the top. Cut in wedges. Serve with crackers. Freezes well. Serves 10 to 12.

*If 9" pan is used, decrease cooking time 10 minutes.

Kay M. Davis (Mrs. Sidney P., Jr.)

LIVER CHEESE BALL

1 (8 ounce) package cream
   cheese, softened
½ pound liver sausage
1 tablespoon grated onion
2 teaspoons lemon juice
1 teaspoon Worcestershire
   sauce

½ to 1 teaspoon salt
⅛ teaspoon pepper
½ cup chopped cashews,
   pecans or peanuts
   (optional)
Chopped parsley

Combine all ingredients except parsley. Chill. Shape into a ball. Roll in parsley. Serve with crackers. Yield: 2 cups.

Elizabeth Beury

OLIVE CHEESE BALL

1 (8 ounce) package cream cheese, softened
1½ cups grated Cheddar cheese
1 (5 ounce) jar smoked flavored process cheese spread

1 teaspoon Worcestershire sauce
½ teaspoon dry mustard
1 (6 ounce) can pitted ripe olives, sliced
Parsley or pecans

Mix all ingredients except olives and parsley until smooth and creamy. Add olives. Chill. Shape into a ball. Roll in parsley or pecans. Refrigerate several hours before serving. Serves 10 to 12.

Janice H. Flannery (Mrs. David)

PINEAPPLE CHEESE BALL

2 (8 ounces each) packages cream cheese, softened
2 cups chopped pecans, divided

1 (13½ ounce) can crushed pineapple, drained
¼ cup diced green pepper
2 tablespoons diced onion
1 teaspoon seasoned salt

Beat cream cheese until smooth. Mix 1 cup pecans with all other ingredients. Form into ball. Chill. Roll in remaining pecans. Place in freezer for 6 hours, then store in refrigerator. Serve with crackers.

Nancy S. Dodson (Mrs. Raymond)

CHEESE BLINTZES

2 loaves soft texture sandwich bread, crusts removed
2 (8 ounces each) packages cream cheese, softened
⅓ cup sugar

2 egg yolks
1¼ cups margarine
Cinnamon sugar - enough to coat each roll*
2 (16 ounces each) cartons sour cream

Roll each bread slice until flat. Mix cream cheese, sugar and egg yolks. Spread mixture on each slice of bread and roll up. Melt margarine and coat each roll. Coat each bread roll with cinnamon sugar. Can be frozen at this point. Cut each roll in half and place on cookie sheet. Bake at 350° for 15 minutes. Serve with sour cream in a bowl to dip. Yield: 7 dozen.

*Editor's note: to make cinnamon sugar mix 1 cup sugar with 2 tablespoons cinnamon.

Barbara S. Moore (Mrs. James D., Jr.)

DEVILED HAM CHEESE BALL

2 (3 ounces each) cans
  deviled ham
1 (8 ounce) package cream
  cheese, softened
½ cup minced onion
½ cup chopped green olives
  Chopped pecans

Combine all ingredients. Shape into ball and roll in chopped pecans. Refrigerate at least one hour before serving. Serve with crackers. Serves 6 to 8.

Victoria R. Frisk (Mrs. Fred M., Jr.)

CHEESE PUFFS
Must sit overnight

4 ounces Feta cheese
1 cup small curd cottage
  cheese
1 (3 ounce) package cream
  cheese, softened
5 tablespoons cornstarch
1 egg
1 teaspoon white pepper
  Phyllo dough
1 cup butter, melted

Combine first 6 ingredients. Cut phyllo into 2″ strips. Layer phyllo, butter, phyllo, butter, applying butter with a pastry brush. Layer 4 to 5 strips of dough for each cheese puff. Place filling in top corner of each pile of strips. Fold like a flag: on a diagonal to make a triangle, over and over. Cover with butter. Place on a buttered pan. Refrigerate overnight. Bake at 375° for 20 to 25 minutes. Can be frozen before baking. Serves 8 to 10.

Mary Lu MacCorkle (Mrs. John)

GOLDEN CHICKEN NUGGETS

4 to 6 whole chicken
  breasts, boned and
  skinned
1 cup unseasoned bread
  crumbs
1 cup grated Parmesan
  cheese
½ teaspoon salt
2 teaspoons thyme,
  crumbled
2 teaspoons basil, crumbled
1 cup margarine, melted

Cut each boneless breast into 6 to 8 nuggets about 1½″ square. Combine bread crumbs, cheese and seasonings in a pie plate. Dip each nugget in butter and roll in crumb mixture until coated. Place nuggets in a single layer on foil-lined baking sheet; do not crowd. Bake at 400° for 10 minutes per side, turning once during cooking. Can be made a day ahead and refrigerated. To serve, reheat at 350° for 3 to 5 minutes. Place while hot into a chafing dish. Serves 8 to 10.

Gina H. Rugeley (Mrs. Edward W., Jr.)

CHICKEN OLIVE TURNOVERS
Must be made day ahead

½ cup margarine, softened
1 (3 ounce) package
   cream cheese
1 cup sifted flour
1½ to 2 cups cooked,
   chopped chicken

1 (10½ ounce) can cream of
   mushroom soup
¼ teaspoon seasoned salt
¼ teaspoon onion powder
   Sliced olives

Mix margarine and cream cheese. Combine with flour. Roll in ball and refrigerate overnight. Roll dough out and cut with a 3½″ round cutter. Combine chicken, soup, salt and onion powder to make filling. Place 2 tablespoons of filling onto each circle with 2 to 3 sliced olives. Fold over and seal edges. Place on a greased cookie sheet. Bake at 400° for 20 minutes. Yield: 2 dozen.

Beverly S. McElroy (Mrs. William)

CUCUMBER SANDWICHES

2 large cucumbers
1 tablespoon salt
1 rounded tablespoon
   mayonnaise
1 rounded tablespoon
   sour cream
1 rounded tablespoon
   softened cream cheese

⅛ teaspoon green onion
   flakes
⅛ teaspoon dill weed
   Dash of pepper
1 small onion, finely chopped
1 loaf white bread, crusts
   removed

Peel cucumbers and grate into very thin slices. Add salt to cucumbers and refrigerate for a few hours. Wring moisture from cucumbers with hands, removing as much juice as possible. Chop cucumbers. Mix mayonnaise, sour cream and cream cheese with cucumber. Add seasonings and onion. Slice bread into quarters. Spread the cucumber mixture on each quarter to make an open face sandwich.

Bonnie W. Bartsch (Mrs. James)

GREEN ONION CANAPES

6 to 8 slices very thin
   white bread, crust
   removed
2 bunches green onions

2 cups shredded extra sharp
   Cheddar cheese
2 tablespoons mayonnaise

Slice bread into quarters. Place on cookie sheet. Bake at 350° for 5 minutes to toast on one side. Slice green onions into rounds. Mix onions, cheese and mayonnaise. Add more mayonnaise if needed to bind mixture together. Turn bread over. Place a well rounded teaspoon on each piece. Bake at 350° for 15 minutes or until bubbly. Serves 8 to 10.

Lynn H. Goldsmith (Mrs. Robert F.)

HANKIE PANKIES

1 pound Velveeta cheese
1 pound ground round
1 pound hot pork sausage
½ teaspoon garlic powder
3 tablespoons Worcester-
   shire sauce

½ teaspoon pepper
2 teaspoons oregano
½ teaspoon crushed hot
   pepper (optional)
1 loaf cocktail rye bread

Cube cheese and set aside to soften. Brown meats in large skillet. Drain well. Add seasonings to meat mixture. While meat is still hot, add cheese, mixing until cheese is melted. Place mixture in refrigerator to cool for 1 hour. Spread a well rounded teaspoon on each slice of bread. Place on a cookie sheet. Bake at 375° for 8 to 10 minutes. May be frozen on cookie sheet. When frozen, place in plastic bags for easy storage. To serve bake at 350° for 15 minutes. Sprinkle with parsley before serving. Serves 10 to 12.

Yolan Williams (Mrs. Paul)

JUDY'S APPETIZER

1 cup Monterey Jack
   cheese, shredded
1 cup Cheddar cheese,
   shredded
1 cup chopped fresh
   mushrooms

½ cup chopped green onion
1 (4 ounce) can pitted ripe
   olives, chopped
   Mayonnaise
   Party rye bread

Mix cheeses, mushrooms, onions and olives. Add just enough mayonnaise to hold together. Spread on party rye bread. Bake at 400° for 5 minutes or until cheese melts. Serves 15.

Judy Bockstahler (Mrs. Fred)

TANGY MEAT BALLS

1 pound ground pork
1 pound ground chuck
2 cups soft bread crumbs
2 eggs, slightly beaten
½ cup chopped onion
2 tablespoons chopped
  parsley

1 teaspoon salt
2 tablespoons margarine
1 (10 ounce) jar apricot
  preserves
½ cup barbecue sauce

Combine first 7 ingredients. Shape into 1" balls. Brown in margarine. Drain. Place in casserole. Combine preserves and sauce. Pour over meatballs. Bake at 350° for 40 minutes. Serve in chafing dish. Yields 4 to 5 dozen.

Karen W. Gage (Mrs. Charles)

HAM FILLED MUSHROOMS

2 pounds large fresh
  mushrooms
¼ cup margarine
1½ pounds cooked ham,
  ground

½ cup sour cream
3 tablespoons chopped chives
6 to 8 pimento stuffed
  green olives, sliced

Wash and separate the mushroom caps from stems. Chop the stems to make 1 cup. Briefly saute caps in margarine, removing from heat just when beginning to wilt. Add ham, sour cream and chives to stems. Mound mixture in caps. Place on buttered pan. Bake at 350° for 10 minutes. Garnish each with a slice of olive. Serve hot. Makes 25 to 35 depending on size of mushrooms.

Sue Hancock Miller

PARTY MUSHROOMS

1 pound fresh mushroom
  caps
8 ounces Braunschweiger

1 package Stouffer frozen
  spinach soufflé, cooked
Parmesan cheese to taste

Wash and pat dry mushroom caps. Stuff each cap with Braunschweiger. Top each with soufflé. Sprinkle with cheese. Bake at 425° for 10 to 15 minutes. Serves 8 to 10.

Rebecca K. Palmer (Mrs. John C., IV)

MINI QUICHES

Pastry for a 2 crust pie
¾ cup chopped cooked
   shrimp, ham or
   mushrooms
¼ cup sliced green onions
4 ounces shredded Swiss
   cheese

½ cup mayonnaise
2 eggs
⅓ cup milk
¼ teaspoon salt
¼ teaspoon dried dill weed

On floured surface roll half of pastry into 12″ circle. Cut six 4″ circles. Repeat with remaining pastry. Fit into twelve 2½″ muffin pan cups. Fill each with a few shrimp, onion and cheese. Beat remaining ingredients, pour over cheese. Bake at 400° for 15 to 20 minutes or until browned. Serves 6 to 8.

Mrs. Charles Wilson

EASY PIZZA APPETIZERS

1 (2¼ ounce) can chopped
   pitted ripe olives
½ cup drained cooked
   tomatoes, finely
   chopped
1 cup grated sharp
   Cheddar or Mozzarella
   cheese

½ cup grated Parmesan
   cheese
1 tablespoon grated onion
½ teaspoon basil
⅛ teaspoon oregano
¼ teaspoon garlic powder
7 slices very thin bread,
   toasted and buttered

Combine all ingredients except bread. Spread mixture on toast. Cut into fourths. Bake at 400° for 10 to 12 minutes. May be frozen and baked at 350° for 10 to 15 minutes. Serves 4 to 6.

Therese S. Cox (Mrs. Michael L.)

TOASTED PECANS

½ pound pecan halves
1 teaspoon Worcestershire
   sauce

2 teaspoons butter, melted
¼ teaspoon salt
   Additional salt to taste

Mix Worcestershire sauce, ¼ teaspoon salt and butter. Place pecans on baking sheet. Pour butter mixture over. Stir. Bake at 400° for 5 minutes. Salt to taste. Stir. Bake until browned. Allow to cool completely, at least 6 hours, before serving.

Donald Kesterson

EASY POTATO SKINS

4 raw potatoes	Optional: Parmesan or
½ cup margarine, melted	grated Cheddar cheese,
Salt to taste	crumbled bacon and/or
	sour cream

Peel potatoes in ¼″ thick strips. Toss peels and margarine together. Sprinkle lightly with salt and any optionals. Place on a greased cookie sheet, skin side up. Bake at 475° for 8 minutes or until crisp.

Lynn H. Goldsmith (Mrs. Robert F.)

PUMPKIN POPPINGS

Seeds from 1 pumpkin	2 tablespoons margarine
Water	Salt to taste
2 tablespoons salt	

Clean pumpkin seeds. Cover with water in a bowl. Add salt and soak overnight. Drain. Stir fry in margarine until seeds pop. Cook 5 minutes longer. Salt to taste. Serve as snacks.

Allison Bibbee
Michael Rice

SAUSAGE SWIRL

2 pounds hot bulk sausage	¼ cup corn meal
4 cups flour	2 tablespoons baking powder
¼ cup sugar	⅔ cup cooking oil
1 teaspoon salt	⅔ to 1 cup milk

Allow sausage to come to room temperature. Blend together dry ingredients. Stir in oil and milk to make a stiff dough. Divide dough into 2 pieces. Roll each piece into a thin 10″ x 18″ rectangle on a floured surface. Spread with sausage. Roll up lengthwise. Chill 4 hours or longer. Slice into ½″ thick pieces. Bake at 350° for 20 to 25 minutes until golden brown. Serve hot. May be prepared ahead, frozen, thawed and baked. Yield: 6 dozen.

Judy H. Kim (Mrs. William)

SNAILS 'N' MUSHROOMS

½ cup butter, divided
1¼ teaspoons minced
   shallots
1 clove garlic, minced
1½ tablespoons minced
   parsley

½ tablespoon grated
   celery
¼ teaspoon salt
   Dash of pepper
16 mushroom caps, hollowed
   out
16 canned snails, drained

Cream 6 tablespoons of butter with shallots, garlic, parsley, celery, salt and pepper. Place mushrooms on greased baking sheet with caps up. Place a dot of butter on each cap, add a snail, top with a little butter mixture. Bake at 375° for 15 minutes.

Ann A. Hlusko (Mrs. G. Paul, Jr.)

WONDERFUL SPINACH SQUARES

4 tablespoons butter
3 eggs
1 cup flour
1 cup milk
1 teaspoon salt
1 teaspoon baking powder

⅓ cup chopped onion
1 pound mild Cheddar
   cheese, grated
2 (10 ounces each) packages
   frozen chopped spinach,
   thawed and drained

Preheat oven to 350°. Place butter in 9" x 13" baking pan. Melt in oven. Remove pan and set aside. In a large bowl, beat eggs. Beat in flour, milk, salt and baking powder. Fold in onion, cheese and spinach. Spread evenly in pan. Bake at 350° for 35 minutes. Cool 45 minutes. (When finished baking, spinach will look like it is swimming in butter, but as it cools, butter is absorbed.) Cut into pieces. Can be frozen at this point. To serve, defrost and reheat at 325° for 12 minutes. Serves 12.

Marilou P. Morton (Mrs. Gordon)

SAUERKRAUT BALLS

½ pound each: ground
   ham, ground lean
   pork, ground corned
   beef
1 medium onion, finely
   chopped
½ cup minced parsley
2 tablespoons cooking oil
3 cups flour, divided

2 cups milk
1 teaspoon salt
1 teaspoon dry mustard
2 pounds sauerkraut, well
   drained
3 eggs, well beaten
1 cup bread crumbs
   Additional oil for frying

In a large skillet brown in oil the meats, onion and parsley. Stir in 2 cups flour, milk, salt and mustard. Cook on low heat, stirring constantly, until thick. Cut in sauerkraut using a sharp knife, or put in food processor until well mixed. Refrigerate for 1 hour. Roll into walnut size balls. Coat each with remaining flour, then egg, then bread crumbs. Deep fry at 375° until slightly brown. Serve hot with Hot Mustard Sauce. Can be cooked ahead, frozen, then baked at 350° for 20 minutes. Yield: 7 to 9 dozen.

Therese S. Cox (Mrs. Michael L.)

SPINACH BALLS

2 (10 ounces each) pack-
   ages frozen chopped
   spinach
2 cups herb stuffing mix
1 large onion, chopped
4 eggs, beaten

¾ cup margarine, melted
1 teaspoon garlic powder
½ teaspoon thyme
1 teaspoon pepper
½ cup Parmesan cheese

Thaw spinach and squeeze dry. Mix all ingredients. Shape into small bite sized balls. May be frozen at this point. Bake at 350° for 10 to 15 minutes until light brown. To serve, use a thin pretzel instead of a toothpick. Serve with Hot Mustard Sauce.

Julia H. Wise (Mrs. Fritz)

HOT MUSTARD SAUCE

½ cup dry mustard
½ cup white vinegar
¼ cup sugar

1 egg yolk
⅛ teaspoon salt
1 tablespoon white wine
   (optional)

Mix mustard and vinegar. Set aside for 3 hours at room temperature. Mix sugar and egg yolk in saucepan over low heat. Add mustard mixture, salt, and wine. Cook, stirring constantly, until slightly thickened. Cover and store in refrigerator. Serve cold. Will keep in refrigerator 3 to 4 weeks.

Sara Z. Hoblitzell (Mrs. John)

SWEET AND SOUR WATER CHESTNUTS

1 (8 ounce) can water
   chestnuts
1 pound bacon
1 (14 ounce) bottle ketchup

8 tablespoons sugar
1 (4½ ounce) jar strained
   baby peaches

Cut each water chestnut in half. Wrap ½ slice of bacon around each one and secure with a toothpick. Place on baking pan. Bake at 350° for 35 minutes. Drain off grease. Combine ketchup, sugar and fruit. Dip each in sauce. Rebake at 350° for 30 minutes. May be frozen after dipping and then reheated. Serves 8 to 10.

Janet T. Hovious (Mrs. Joseph C.)

ZUCCHINI SQUARES

3 cups thinly sliced
   zucchini
1 cup buttermilk baking
   mix
½ cup finely chopped onion
½ cup grated Parmesan
   cheese
2 tablespoons parsley

1 teaspoon seasoning salt
1 tablespoon oregano
   Dash of pepper
1 clove garlic, chopped fine
¼ cup cooking oil
4 eggs, beaten slightly
½ teaspoon Italian seasoning

Mix all ingredients, except zucchini in bowl. Fold in zucchini. Place in a greased 9" x 13" baking dish. Bake at 350° for 20 to 25 minutes or until golden. Cut in squares when slightly cooled. Serve warm. Freezes well. To serve: defrost and reheat. Serves 14 to 20.

Lynn H. Goldsmith (Mrs. Robert F.)

COCKTAIL DELIGHT

2 (1 pound each) packages
   Kielbasa

2 cups brown sugar

Slice sausage into bite size pieces. Place in an electric skillet. Sprinkle brown sugar over sausage until sausage is completely covered. Cook covered at 300° for 30 minutes, stirring after 10 minutes. Serve in a chafing dish.

Mary Jean M. Davis (Mrs. K. Paul)

ANGELS ON HORSEBACK

2 pints medium size fresh
  oysters
2 tablespoons Worcester-
  shire sauce
1 cup chili sauce

2 cups chopped green
  pepper
12 slices uncooked bacon
¾ cup grated Parmesan
  cheese

Drain oysters and place in an ovenproof dish. Combine Worcestershire and chili sauce. Cover oysters. Sprinkle with green peppers. Bake at 350° for 10 to 15 minutes or until oysters begin to puff. Remove and sprinkle with finely diced bacon and cheese. Return to oven and bake 10 to 12 minutes. Keep hot while serving. Serve with crackers or rye bread. Serves 6 to 8.

Mary T. Karr (Mrs. George)

CRAB BITES

PASTRY

1 (8 ounce) package cream
  cheese

½ cup butter
1½ cups flour

Cream all ingredients. Chill for 1 to 2 hours. Roll dough out very thin. Cut into 2″ rounds. Press into miniature muffin tins, stretching to come up sides. Bake at 350° for 7 to 8 minutes.

FILLING

4 tablespoons margarine
¼ cup flour
1½ cups milk
1 cup grated sharp Cheddar
  cheese
2 (7½ ounces each) cans
  crabmeat, rinsed, boned
  and crumbled

1 scallion, minced
¼ teaspoon paprika
2 tablespoons fresh minced
  parsley
3 drops hot sauce
1 teaspoon lemon juice
¼ teaspoon celery salt

Melt margarine in saucepan. Add flour and cook, stirring over medium heat for 2 minutes. Be careful and do not let burn. Slowly add milk, stirring constantly. Cook to medium thickness. Add cheese; cook, stirring, until melted. Add remainder of ingredients. Fill each pastry cup with mixture. Bake at 375° for 12 to 15 minutes until bubbly. Serve immediately. May be frozen before baking. Freeze on cookie sheets; then store in freezer cartons. Bake an additional 10 to 15 minutes when taking directly from freezer. Makes 5 to 6 dozen.

Sara Z. Hoblitzell (Mrs. John R.)

EASY CRAB SWISS BITES

1 (12 count) package refrigerator butterflake biscuits
1 (7½ ounce) can crabmeat, drained and flaked
1 (6 ounce) can water chestnuts, drained and diced
1 tablespoon minced green onion, tops and bottoms
½ cup mayonnaise
¼ teaspoon curry powder
1 teaspoon lemon juice
Salt and pepper to taste

Separate each biscuit into three rounds. Place on baking sheet sprayed with non-stick spray. Mix all other ingredients. Spoon on top of each roll. Bake at 350° for 15 minutes. May freeze before or after cooking. Serves 12 to 14.

Katherine M. Swingle (Mrs. Gary)

SEA CRABBIES

½ cup margarine, softened
1½ tablespoons mayonnaise
1 (5½ to 7 ounce) can crabmeat (or frozen crabmeat)
½ teaspoon garlic powder
1 (5 ounce) jar Old English cheese
1 package English muffins

Blend all ingredients and spread on muffins. Cut crabbies into quarters. Freeze on cookie sheet. May be stored in plastic bag in freezer at this point. While still frozen, put under broiler for a few minutes until bubbly. Serves 10 to 12.

Mrs. James Seibert

SEVICHE

1½ pounds white fish
12 to 18 limes (enough juice to cover fish)
¾ cup chopped green olives
¾ cup finely chopped celery
¾ cup finely chopped onion
¼ teaspoon garlic powder
¼ teaspoon Accent
¼ teaspoon thyme
Dash of Tabasco sauce
Dash of Worcestershire sauce
Salt to taste
Pepper to taste
Cracked coriander seeds, bay leaves and hot pickled jalapeno peppers, optional

Slice fish into small pieces, ¾" to 1½" wide, removing all dark meat. Squeeze limes. Soak fish in lime juice in glass container for 4 hours in refrigerator. Stir and rearrange every 30 minutes. Reserving juice, remove fish and rinse in colander with cold water. Add rest of ingredients to juice and mix. Add fish and refrigerate overnight or up to 2 days. Serve with crackers or on a bed of lettuce as appetizer.

Paul M. Bruun

SHRIMP AND ARTICHOKES

1 egg yolk
½ cup vegetable oil
½ cup olive oil
½ cup wine vinegar
2 tablespoons Dijon
   mustard
1 (2 ounce) jar pimento,
   chopped
2 tablespoons minced
   parsley

2 tablespoons minced
   chives
¼ teaspoon salt
2 (10 ounces each) packages
   frozen artichoke hearts;
   cooked, drained and
   chilled
1½ pounds medium shrimp,
   cooked and chilled

Place egg yolk in a bowl. Beat in oils, vinegar and mustard. Add herbs, salt, and pimento. Beat again. Pour over shrimp and artichoke hearts. Marinate at least 2 hours. May be prepared 2 days in advance. Serve with toothpicks as an appetizer, or at a ladies' luncheon on a bed of lettuce. Serves 10.

Deborah L. Sutton (Mrs. James)

CHILI CON QUESO

½ pound Velveeta cheese
½ pound Monterey Jack
   cheese with jalapeno
   peppers
1 to 2 teaspoons flour
1 tablespoon chili powder
1 medium onion, chopped

1 clove garlic, minced
1 tablespoon cooking oil
1 (10 ounce) can tomatoes
   and chopped green
   chilies
Jalapeno pepper, chopped
(optional)

Cube the cheeses and toss with flour and chili powder. Saute onion and garlic in oil in saucepan. Add cheeses and tomatoes and green chilies. Cook until cheese has melted and flavors have blended. Serve hot in chafing dish with tortilla chips. Can be reheated in microwave. Regular Jack cheese can be used for milder flavor.

Donna L. Dean (Mrs. Rodney D.)

CHRISTMAS CHEESE SPREAD

1½ pounds medium or sharp
    Cheddar cheese
1½ cups mayonnaise
1   cup diced sweet pickle

2   tablespoons finely minced
    onion
1   (2 ounce) jar pimento,
    drained and diced

Bring cheese to room temperature. Mix in large bowl until smooth. Add mayonnaise and onion. Continue mixing until fluffy. Fold in pickle and pimento. Chill. Serve with party rye rounds. Serves 20.

Lucille W. Watkins (Mrs. Ralph)

HERBED CHEESE SPREAD

1   (8 ounce) package cream
    cheese, softened
¼   cup butter, softened
½   teaspoon Beau Monde
    dressing
¼   teaspoon Fines Herbes
    seasoning
¼   teaspoon finely chopped
    chives

¼   teaspoon garlic powder
½   teaspoon parsley, finely
    chopped
1   teaspoon water
¼   teaspoon red wine vinegar
¼   teaspoon Worcestershire
    sauce

Combine all ingredients with an electric mixer. Pack into a small crock. Refrigerate overnight or longer to allow flavors to blend. Remove and serve at room temperature with crackers. Yield: 1½ cups.

Sara Z. Hoblitzell (Mrs. John R.)

CURRIED CHUTNEY SPREAD

2   (8 ounces each) packages
    cream cheese
½   cup chutney, chopped
½   cup chopped toasted
    almonds

1   teaspoon curry powder
    (or more to taste)
½   teaspoon dry mustard

Bring cream cheese to room temperature. Mix all ingredients together. Pack in crock and chill. Serve with crackers. Yield: 3 cups.

Barbara W. Rose (Mrs. Ned)

LOW CALORIE CURRY DIP

1½ cups Weight Watcher's mayonnaise
2 teaspoons curry powder
1 tablespoon grated onion
1 teaspoon dry mustard
½ teaspoon salt
Dash of pepper
Dash of Tabasco sauce
Dash of Worcestershire sauce

Blend all ingredients. Refrigerate. Serve with raw vegetables. Yield: 1½ cups.

Gina H. Rugeley (Mrs. Edward)

DILL DIP

⅔ cup mayonnaise
⅔ cup sour cream
1 tablespoon parsley flakes
1 tablespoon dried minced onion
1 tablespoon dill weed
1 teaspoon Beau Monde dressing

Mix all ingredients. Chill overnight. Serve with crackers or raw vegetables. Yield: 2 cups.

Taunja W. Miller (Mrs. Perry F.)

HOT CRAB MEAT DIP

2 (6½ ounces each) cans crab meat
1 teaspoon lemon juice
6 tablespoons margarine, melted
6 tablespoons flour
1½ cups chicken broth
1½ cups evaporated milk
1 medium onion, chopped
1 teaspoon Accent
3 tablespoons chopped pimento (optional)
⅓ pound Gruyere or Swiss cheese, grated
¼ pound grated Parmesan cheese

Drain and flake crab meat. Sprinkle lemon juice on crab and toss thoroughly. Set aside. Combine margarine and flour, cooking over low heat until blended and smooth. Slowly stir in chicken broth and milk. Cook, stirring, until thickened. Add onion, Accent, pimento, and cheeses. Stir until cheese is melted. Add crab meat Heat thoroughly and serve in a chafing dish. Serve with crackers or fresh vegetables. Serves 20 to 25.

Susan B. Halonen (Mrs. Robert)

UNCLE MART'S DELUXE CRAB SPREAD

3 (8 ounce) packages cream
  cheese
1½ cups heavy cream
1½ cups mayonnaise
1 (8 ounce) can mushrooms,
  stems and pieces
3 tablespoons grated onion
3 tablespoons chives, finely
  chopped
¼ cup fresh parsley,
  chopped
1 pound lump crab meat
  Tabasco to taste
3 tablespoons Blue cheese
3 tablespoons fresh lemon
  juice
1 clove garlic, pressed

Stir all ingredients until well blended in a large bowl. Do not mix in blender. Chill. Serve with crackers. Shrimp may be substituted for crab meat. Serves 25.

May also be served in patty shells as a first course or as a main course at a luncheon.

Helen Young (Mrs. Ed)

CUCUMBER DIP
Must be made ahead.

2 large unpeeled
  cucumbers
½ cup vinegar
2 teaspoons salt
½ teaspoon garlic salt
2 (8 ounces each) packages
  cream cheese
¾ cup mayonnaise

Grate cucumbers in food processor or on grater with ½ inch holes. Add vinegar and salt. Stir, cover and allow to stand overnight in refrigerator. Next day squeeze out liquid and discard. Blend all other ingredients. Combine cream cheese mixture with cucumbers. Serve with potato chips. Best if made several days in advance. Yield: 2½ cups.

Betsie M. Dobbs (Mrs. William F., Jr.)

HERRING DIP

1 (8 ounce) jar herring in
  wine sauce
½ cup mayonnaise
1 cup sour cream
1 tablespoon sugar
1 tablespoon lemon juice
½ teaspoon celery seed
1 medium green pepper,
  chopped
6 chopped green onions

Drain liquid from herring. Remove onion and seeds and discard. Cut the herring into small chunks. Mix with remaining ingredients. Refrigerate at least 24 hours before using. Serve with crackers or party rye bread. Keeps well. Yield: 2½ cups.

Judith H. McJunkin (Mrs. Brittain)

HOMOS WITH TAHINI
A Lebanese Chick Pea Dip

½ cup (scant) tahini
2 small cloves garlic, crushed
½ teaspoon salt
Dash of pepper
½ cup water
Juice of 2 lemons (4 tablespoons)

1 (15 ounce) can chick peas (garbanzos), drained
1 to 2 tablespoons cooking oil
Paprika
Cumin
Fresh parsley or mint

Place tahini, garlic, salt, pepper and water in food processor or blender. While blending, gradually add lemon juice. Add chick peas and purée until a thick consistency. Spread oil over top and garnish with paprika, cumin and parsley. A few of the chick peas may be saved as garnish. Serve with crackers or fresh vegetables. May also be used as part of the main course.

Eleanor K. Rashid (Mrs. Richard)

JAZEBEL

1 (18 ounce) jar apple jelly
1 (16 ounce) jar pineapple preserves

1 (5 ounce) jar horseradish
1¾ ounces dry mustard
1 (8 ounce) package cream cheese

Mix first 4 ingredients. Store covered in refrigerator. Pour generously over a block of cream cheese. Serve with crackers. Yield: 4½ cups.

Gene Hodges

MEXICAN SALSA

1 (3 ounce) can pitted black olives, chopped
1 (4 ounce) can chopped green chilies
1 medium onion, chopped

1 large tomato, chopped
1½ tablespoons vinegar
3 tablespoons cooking oil
1 teaspoon garlic salt

Combine first four ingredients. Combine remaining ingredients and pour over vegetable mixture. Chill at least two hours. Serve with Nacho flavored or corn chips. Yield: 2 cups.

Sharon H. Hall (Mrs. William)

BAKED MEXICAN DIP

2 (10 ounces each) cans bean dip
1 pound ground chuck
1 package taco seasoning mix
1 cup shredded Monterey Jack cheese
½ to 1 (4 ounce) can chopped green chilies
2 to 4 tablespoons hot taco sauce

1 cup shredded sharp Cheddar cheese
¼ cup chopped green onions
1 (3¼ ounce) can pitted black olives, chopped
½ cup finely chopped tomatoes
1 avocado, finely chopped
Jalapeno peppers, chopped (optional)
1 cup (or more) sour cream

Spread bean dip in a 9" x 13" baking dish. Cook ground chuck with taco seasoning as directed on package. Spread over bean dip. Layer Monterey Jack cheese over meat. Spread chilies (to taste) over cheese. Drizzle hot taco sauce (to taste) over all. Layer Cheddar cheese over taco sauce. Bake at 350° for 20 to 30 minutes. Remove from oven and cool slightly. Sprinkle green onions, olives, tomatoes and avocado over the top. Add jalapeno peppers if desired. Mound the sour cream in the middle. Serve hot with tortilla chips. Can also be served as a main dish casserole.

Diane S. Doty (Mrs. Steven)

TEX MEX DIP

2 (10½ ounces each) cans bean dip
3 medium ripe avocados
2 tablespoons lemon juice
¼ teaspoon pepper
¼ teaspoon salt
1 cup sour cream
½ cup mayonnaise
½ package taco seasoning mix

2 cups chopped tomatoes
1 (6 ounce) can pitted black olives, chopped
1 cup chopped green onions
1 (8 ounce) package grated sharp Cheddar cheese
2 (8 ounce) packages round tostitos

Spread the bean dip on a large round tray. Place avocados, lemon juice, salt, and pepper in food processor or blender. Blend. Spread the puréed avocado over the bean dip leaving a little space around the edges to show the bean dip. Mix together sour cream, mayonnaise, and taco seasoning. Spread over avocado layer. Sprinkle with tomatoes, olives and onions. Top with shredded cheese. Serve cold or at room temperature with chips. Serves 12.

Alice G. Abernethy (Mrs. Michael D.)

OLIVE SPREAD
Must be made ahead

2 (3 ounces each) packages
    cream cheese, softened
½ cup mayonnaise
    Dash of pepper
1 cup chopped salad olives

½ cup pecans, chopped
2 tablespoons olive liquid
1 loaf very thin sliced white
    bread, crusts removed

Mix all ingredients except bread. Chill at least 2 days. Layer bread on a baking pan. Toast in oven at 250° for 30 minutes. Turn and toast 30 more minutes. Serve with spread. Spread may also be served with crackers.

Ann A. Hlusko (Mrs. G. Paul, Jr.)

PINK SQUIRREL FONDUE

1 (7 or 10 ounce) jar
    marshmallow cream
3 tablespoons créme
    d'almond
1 tablespoon white créme
    de cacao
1 teaspoon lemon juice

Angel food cake pieces
Assorted fruit - bananas
    or apples preserved
    with lemon juice,
    strawberries, pineapple
    chunks, mandarin
    oranges, nuts

Combine all liquid ingredients in a saucepan. Stir over low heat until smooth and warm. Transfer to fondue pot over low heat. Spear dippers with toothpick, swivel to coat. Additional liqueurs may be added to taste. Serves 15 to 20.

Therese S. Cox (Mrs. Michael L.)

RAW VEGETABLE DIP

½ cup mayonnaise
½ cup sour cream
2 teaspoons tarragon
    vinegar
½ teaspoon onion salt
2 tablespoons chili sauce
⅛ teaspoon thyme

2 tablespoons grated onion
¼ teaspoon curry powder
    Dash of Tabasco sauce
1 teaspoon chopped parsley
1 teaspoon chopped green
    pepper
½ teaspoon Accent

Mix all ingredients together. Dip should be quite thick. Serve as a dip for raw vegetables or as a dressing for tossed salad. If you like curry, the ¼ teaspoon can be increased. Yield: 1½ cups.

Nina A. Ratrie (Mrs. Turner R., Jr.)

SHRIMP DIP

1 (8 ounce) package cream
   cheese
½ cup unsalted sweet butter
2 (4½ ounces each) cans
   baby shrimp

3 green onions, chopped
3 dashes hot sauce
7 dashes Worcestershire
   sauce

Melt butter and cream cheese together. Mixture must be stirred for a long time before it will mix together well. Drain shrimp and add to mixture. Stir in onions, hot sauce, and Worcestershire sauce. Refrigerate. Serve with crackers.

June L. Marlowe (Mrs. L. Gilbert)

ELEGANT SHRIMP POTATO CHIP DIP

1 (4½ ounce) can shrimp,
   drained
1 (8 ounce) package cream
   cheese
2 tablespoons milk

½ teaspoon Worcestershire
   sauce
½ pint whipping cream
1 tablespoon grated onion

Clean and cut shrimp into small pieces. Set aside. Soften cream cheese. Add milk, mixing with an electric mixer until smooth. Add Worcestershire sauce. In a separate bowl whip cream just until stiff. Beat into cream cheese mixture on low speed. Fold in shrimp and onion. Refrigerate. May also be served with fresh vegetables. Yield: 3½ cups.

Bonnie W. Bartsch (Mrs. James D.)

HOT SPINACH DIP

1 (10 ounce) package frozen
   chopped spinach
1 (8 ounce) package cream
   cheese
3 tablespoons milk

2 tablespoons margarine
⅛ teaspoon nutmeg
6 slices crisp, cooked bacon,
   crumbled and divided
1 tablespoon lemon juice

Cook spinach according to package directions. Drain well. Heat cream cheese, milk, margarine, and nutmeg, stirring until smooth. Stir in spinach, half of bacon and lemon juice. Garnish with remaining bacon. Serve warm in a chafing dish surrounded by fresh vegetables. May be served chilled as spread for crackers. Freezes well. Thaw at room temperature and then heat. Yield: 2½ cups.

Susan B. Halonen (Mrs. Robert)

MOTHER'S SPINACH DIP
Must be made a day ahead

1 (10 ounce) package frozen
   chopped spinach
1 cup mayonnaise
1 cup sour cream

¼ cup chopped onion
1 box Knorr Swiss
   vegetable soup mix

Thaw and squeeze dry spinach. Combine all ingredients. Refrigerate overnight. Serve with crackers or fresh raw vegetables. Yield: 3 cups.

Margaret C. Harkins (Mrs. Frank S., Sr.)

HAREWOOD

In 1752 Lawrence Washington willed 230 acres of his Shenandoah Valley land to Samuel Washington, his half-brother and George's full brother. Samuel's house, Harewood, was built in the last years of the 1760's by 18th century builder John Arliss, and occupied by the family in 1770.

Harewood was one of the first houses in the Shenandoah Valley to be constructed of locally-quarried limestone and is the oldest of eight Washington family houses still standing in Jefferson County. It is the only one still occupied by Washington family members.

Samuel was an important landowner in the county and a public servant. He was a justice of the peace in Stafford County before he moved to Harewood, and continued as a justice in the new county. He also served as colonel of the militia and sheriff and county lieutenant. He died in 1781 at the early age of 47.

Many famous people have visited Harewood including Louis Philippe, later king of France, Generals Gates, Lee, Stephens and, of course, George Washington, who visited frequently. In 1794, James Madison and Dolly Payne Todd were married in the beautifully paneled drawing room. Dolly Madison was the sister of Lucy, George Washington's (son of Samuel) wife. George had inherited the house at his father's death.

Harewood is of Georgian style, consisting of two stories and five bays. The entrance is marked by a wooden pedimented portico resting on paired, freestanding round columns. The cornice is wood, dentiled below the gutter line. The roof is hipped. The original plan had a separate kitchen building, also of native limestone. The main house interior is elegant in its simplicity and dignity. All rooms contain fine 18th century detailing but the most important space is the drawing room with its beautiful native-pine paneling which still has its original paint. Family tradition says the exquisite marble parlor mantelpiece was a gift from the Marquis de Lafayette.

Photo by Gerald S. Ratliff

SOUPS AND SANDWICHES

Duck Paddle

ASPARAGUS POTATO CREAM SOUP

1 (13¾ ounce) can chicken
   broth
3 medium potatoes, peeled
   and chopped
⅓ cup chopped onion
1 teaspoon salt
⅛ teaspoon nutmeg
1 (8 ounce) package frozen
   cut asparagus

1½ cups light cream, or one
   (10 ounce) can cream of
   chicken soup
1 (5 ounce) jar Neufchatel
   cheese spread with
   pimento, or one (4
   ounce) carton whipped
   cream cheese with
   pimento
1 cup milk, optional

Combine first 4 ingredients in large saucepan. Bring to boil. Simmer, covered, until potatoes are tender. Add asparagus, nutmeg and cream. Cook over low heat until asparagus is tender. Add cheese. Cook, stirring until well blended. Do not boil. If soup is used, milk may be added at this point for thinning. Serves 6 to 8.

Jane S. McEldowney (Mrs. Robert E., III)

BEAN SOUP

½ pound navy beans
½ pound pinto beans
2 quarts water
1 pound pork pieces (pork
   roast or ham)
1 teaspoon salt

½ cup chopped celery
3 chopped carrots
1 medium onion, chopped
1 bay leaf
   Pepper to taste

Soak beans overnight in water to cover. Rinse and drain. Combine all ingredients. Bring to a boil, reduce heat and simmer 3 to 4 hours, adding more water if necessary. Yield: 2½ quarts.

Patricia H. Frazier (Mrs. Jerry L.)

CREAM OF BROCCOLI SOUP

1 bunch fresh broccoli,
   chopped
1 cup chopped ham
2½ cups water
1 (10 ounce) can chicken
   broth
1 medium onion, chopped
2 medium potatoes, chopped

4 tablespoons butter
1 teaspoon thyme
1 teaspoon basil
1 teaspoon pepper
1 teaspoon salt
1 cup milk or light cream
   Parsley for garnish

Combine all ingredients except milk and parsley in a large saucepan. Bring to a boil, reduce heat and simmer 30 to 40 minutes until broccoli is tender. In several batches, blend mixture in blender until smooth. Return to pot and add milk. Simmer 15 to 20 minutes. Serve, garnished with parsley. Can be made ahead and reheated. Serves 6.

Sara Z. Hoblitzell (Mrs. John R.)

BROCCOLI POTATO SOUP

4 tablespoons butter
1 large leek, chopped
6 cups chicken broth,
   divided
1 bunch broccoli

6 medium potatoes, peeled
   and diced
   Salt and pepper to taste
1 cup heavy cream
   Shredded sharp Cheddar
   cheese

Melt butter in large, heavy pan. Add leek. Simmer until soft. Add 4 cups chicken broth, potatoes and chopped broccoli stems (reserve flowerets). Season with salt and pepper. Simmer until vegetables are soft. With slotted spoon, remove vegetables from broth and purée in food processor or blender. Return purée to broth, mixing well. Add remaining 2 cups of chicken broth and chopped broccoli flowerets. Simmer until broccoli is tender. Add cream. Season with additional salt and pepper to taste. Serve topped with shredded cheese. Serves 6 to 8.

Diane S. Doty (Mrs. Steven E.)

CAULIFLOWER SOUP

1 small onion, chopped
1 head cauliflower, broken
   into flowerets
5 carrots, diced
½ cup butter
½ tablespoon sugar
¾ cup sherry, divided
¾ teaspoon dry mustard

½ teaspoon nutmeg
½ teaspoon salt
⅛ teaspoon pepper
4 cups chicken stock
1 cup mashed potatoes
1 cup grated Cheddar
   cheese

Cook onions, cauliflower and carrots in butter until soft in large saucepan. Add sugar, ¼ cup sherry and seasonings. Simmer covered for 45 minutes. Add remaining ½ cup sherry, chicken stock, mashed potatoes and cheese. Purée in a blender or food processor. Return mixture to a saucepan and simmer over low heat for 15 minutes, stirring occasionally. Yield: 2 quarts.

Patty W. Bowers

OLD ENGLISH CHEESE SOUP

¾ cup margarine, divided
½ cup finely chopped celery
½ cup finely chopped carrot
½ cup finely chopped green
   pepper
½ cup finely chopped onion
6 tablespoons flour

4¼ cups milk
1 teaspoon salt
2½ cups shredded sharp
   processed American
   cheese
2 cups chicken broth

Melt ¼ cup butter in skillet, add vegetables and sauté until tender. Set aside. Melt ½ cup butter in Dutch oven over low heat. Stir in flour, cooking until smooth and bubbly. Gradually stir in milk; cook and stir constantly until mixture is thickened and smooth. Add sautéed vegetables, salt, cheese and broth. Cook, stirring frequently, until cheese melts and soup is heated through. Serves 6 to 8.

Constance H. Toma (Mrs. George E.)

MIKE MOWERY'S CHILI
This will separate the men from the boys.

6 pounds sirloin tip or round roast, cut in 1" cubes
Cooking oil
2 pounds onions, sliced
1 whole garlic bulb, diced
1 green pepper, chopped
2 fresh jalapeno peppers or 1 (3 ounce) can jalapeno relish
2 quarts beer
1 fresh cayenne pepper, chopped or 1 tablespoon ground cayenne pepper
4 tablespoons chili powder
2 (3 ounces each) cans chopped green chilies
2 tablespoons Tabasco sauce
2 tablespoons dark molasses
1 tablespoon thyme
2 tablespoons lime juice
2 tablespoons Hungarian paprika
1 tablespoon ground cumin
1 tablespoon whole cumin seed
1 tablespoon ground coriander
2 bay leaves
2 teaspoons dry mustard
1 tablespoon Worcestershire sauce
2 tablespoons Masa Harina flour
Salt to taste
Optional:
1 (6 ounce) can tomato paste
1 small can refried beans

Brown beef cubes in oil. Remove with slotted spoon. Sauté onions, garlic and green pepper in drippings. In large ovenproof pan, combine all ingredients except flour and optional items. Stir and cook until mixture simmers. Place in oven and bake at 350° for 2 hours. Remove. Combine flour with 2 tablespoons water in a separate dish to make a thin paste. Stir into chili. Thin with more beer if needed. Add refried beans or tomato paste if desired and heat through. Freezing enhances flavor. Serves 12 to 16.

Mary Lu MacCorkle (Mrs. John)

CLAM AND CHICKEN BISQUE

1½ cups clam juice
2 tablespoons chopped onion
¼ cup diced celery
1 small bay leaf
2 cups chicken stock
2 tablespoons butter
3 tablespoons flour
½ cup minced clams
1 cup half and half
1 cup finely chopped cooked, chicken
Salt and pepper to taste

Simmer clam juice with onion, celery and bay leaf for 30 minutes. Add chicken stock and bring to boil. Strain stock, discarding vegetables and bay leaf. Melt butter in large saucepan. Blend in flour. Add hot stock all at once, stirring vigorously until smooth. Add remaining ingredients. Simmer 20 minutes, stirring occasionally. Do not allow bisque to boil. Serves 4 to 6.

Gina H. Rugeley (Mrs. Edward W., Jr.)

CURRIED CLAM CHOWDER
Must be prepared ahead

2 to 4 cups butter clams
1 cup chicken broth
1 teaspoon each: thyme, celery, salt, paprika and pepper
2 large potatoes, peeled and diced
3 medium onions, chopped

5 slices uncooked bacon, chopped
½ cup white wine
2 to 3 cups milk
1 teaspoon Madras curry Pinch of cayenne pepper
1 dozen saltine crackers

Combine clam juice, broth and seasonings in a large saucepan over low heat. Add potatoes and simmer until potatoes are tender. Sauté in separate pan onions, bacon and chopped clam necks. Do not brown. Add to broth mixture. Stir in wine and remove from heat. Add whole clams, milk, curry and cayenne pepper. Let stand 2 hours. Crumble saltines into mixture, gently reheat and serve. Serves 6 generously.

Mary Lee W. Lilly (Mrs. J.K., III)

EASY CRAB BISQUE

1 (10½ ounce) can cream of mushroom soup
1 (10½ ounce) can cream of asparagus soup
1½ soup cans milk

1 cup light cream
1 (6½ ounce) can crab meat, drained
¼ cup sherry
Paprika

Blend soups in medium saucepan. Stir in milk and cream. Heat to boiling; add crab and heat through. Add sherry before serving. For each serving sprinkle with paprika and add a small amount of butter. Serves 6.

Paula W. Flaherty (Mrs. Thomas V.)

MARY LEE'S CUCUMBER SOUP

1 cup chicken bouillon
1 cup sour cream
1 large cucumber, minced
1 tablespoon instant onion
   soup mix

1 teaspoon dried chives
1 tablespoon diced parsley
½ teaspoon salt
1 tablespoon paprika
   Parsley for garnish

Combine all ingredients, blending well. Chill 4 hours or longer before serving. Serve in chilled cups. Top with parsley as garnish. Serves 4.

Mary Lee W. Lilly (Mrs. J.K., III)

FISH CHOWDER

8 slices bacon
3 medium onions, chopped
2 cloves garlic, minced
2 stalks celery, chopped
2 large carrots, sliced
2 large potatoes, cubed
2 (6½ ounces each) cans
   minced clams
1½ cups water

2 chicken bouillon cubes
1 bay leaf
1 pound frozen fish fillets
   (cod, flounder or
   haddock)
2 cups half and half
¼ cup chopped parsley
   Pepper

Fry bacon and drain, reserving 2 tablespoons drippings. Set bacon aside. In a Dutch oven sauté onion, garlic and celery in drippings until tender. Add carrots, potatoes, juice from clams, water, bouillon cubes and bay leaf. Simmer 15 to 20 minutes. Cut partially thawed fish fillets into 1″ cubes. Add to pot. Simmer covered for 6 to 8 minutes until fish is cooked. Add bacon, half and half, clams, parsley and pepper. Stir gently and heat through. Do not boil. Serves 6.

Nelle Dickinson Chilton

THE BEST GAZPACHO

3 medium bell peppers,
   chopped
3 medium cucumbers,
   peeled and chopped
5 medium tomatoes,
   peeled and chopped
2 medium red onions,
   chopped
½ teaspoon garlic powder
2 (10 ounces each) cans
   Snap-E-Tom or V-8
   juice

2 tablespoons lemon juice
3 teaspoons salt
½ teaspoon oregano
½ teaspoon basil
½ teaspoon Tabasco sauce
1 tablespoon Worcester-
   shire sauce
½ cup cooking oil
½ cup red wine vinegar
   Garnishes: Sour cream
   and garlic croutons

Combine all ingredients, except garnishes. Refrigerate 2 hours. Purée 2 cups of mixture in blender or food processor, then return to balance of ingredients. Chill thoroughly. Serve with dollop of sour cream, topped with croutons. Serves 8.

Ellen S. Field (Mrs. John A., III)

JEAN'S QUICK DIET GAZPACHO

4 cups tomato juice
½ cup Catalina salad
   dressing (regular or
   reduced calorie)

1 medium cucumber,
   chopped
1 medium green pepper,
   chopped
1 medium onion, chopped

Combine all ingredients. Chill several hours before serving. Serves 4 to 6.

Catherine Bradford

GREEN PEPPER SOUP

½ pound leftover beef roast,
   cut in bite size pieces
⅓ to ½ cup uncooked rice
2 to 3 tablespoons grated
   onion
2 large green peppers,
   chopped

¼ cup chopped celery tops
3 (10½ ounces each) cans
   beef broth
2 beef bouillon cubes
   Water as needed
   Parsley, optional

Combine all ingredients except parsley in a saucepan. Cover and simmer 30 to 40 minutes to blend flavors, adding water if needed. Browned ground sirloin may be substituted for roast. Garnish with parsley. Serves 6.

Esther Heath (Mrs. George R.)

MINESTRONE SOUP

1 (28 ounce) can tomatoes, chopped
1 (8 ounce) can tomato sauce
2 beef bouillon cubes
1 medium onion
1 teaspoon salt
1 bay leaf
5 cups water

¼ teaspoon each: pepper, cumin, oregano and basil
2 cups chopped cabbage
1 (16 ounce) can pinto beans, drained
1 zucchini, chopped
1 cup elbow macaroni
Parmesan cheese

Combine tomatoes, tomato sauce, bouillon, onion and seasonings with 5 cups water in large pot. Simmer ½ hour. Add beans, zucchini and cabbage, cooking until vegetables are tender. Just before serving add macaroni and cook until just tender. Serve topped with Parmesan cheese. Yield: 3 quarts.

Sharon H. Hall (Mrs. William R.)

OYSTER SOUP
A very rich soup

½ cup butter
¼ cup flour
1 cup half and half
2 egg yolks
4 cups fish stock or clam juice

Juice of ½ lemon
½ cup white wine
2 (12 ounces each) cans oysters
Cayenne and white pepper

Melt butter in large saucepan. Blend in flour. Add all ingredients except oysters and pepper. Simmer without boiling until heated through. Add oysters and seasonings at serving time. Serves 6 to 8.

Paula S. McKenney (Mrs. Ronald A.)

GOLDEN CREAM OF POTATO SOUP

6 cups chopped potatoes
2 cups water
1 cup sliced celery
½ cup chopped onion
2 teaspoons parsley flakes
1 cup carrot slices
2 chicken bouillon cubes

1 teaspoon salt
Dash of pepper
4 tablespoons flour
3 cups milk, divided
¾ pound Velveeta cheese, cubed

Combine first 9 ingredients in large saucepan. Simmer covered until tender. In a separate cup combine flour and 4 tablespoons milk to make a thin paste. Stir into soup. Add cheese and remainder of milk. Simmer until thick and smooth.

Marsha Hanna

SIMPLE SENEGALESE SOUP

1 (10½ ounce) can cream of chicken soup
1 (10½ ounce) can beef bouillon
1 (10½ ounce) can cream of asparagus soup

1 (8 ounce) carton sour cream
Dash of curry powder
Salt and pepper to taste
Paprika
Parsley or chives

Combine first 6 ingredients in a blender or food processor. Cover and chill. Serve cold or hot. Top with paprika and parsley or chives. Serves 6.

Caroline C. Nelson

SUMMER SQUASH SOUP

2 pounds yellow squash, cubed
1 onion, chopped
2 tablespoons butter
2 teaspoons curry

4 cups chicken broth
2 medium potatoes, cubed
½ cup cream
Salt and pepper
Croutons

Sauté onion and squash in butter until tender. Add curry. Cook 1 minute, stirring often. In medium saucepan cook potatoes in broth until tender. Add squash mixture to broth. Cook 10 minutes. Purée in batches in blender or food processor. Return to pan, add cream and seasonings and heat. Sprinkle with croutons. Serves 6 to 8.

Barbara H. Slack (Mrs. John M., III)

CURRIED PEANUT BUTTER SQUASH SOUP
Surprisingly different

1 medium butternut
   squash, peeled and cut
4 cups chicken broth
1 peeled apple, chopped
1 large onion, chopped

½ cup peanut butter
1½ teaspoons curry
1 teaspoon salt
Pepper to taste
½ cup cream or milk

Cook squash, apple and onion in chicken broth until soft in a large saucepan. Add peanut butter, curry and seasonings. Purée in blender in batches. Return to pot. Thin with cream and heat through. Serves 4 to 6.

Katherine Rose (Mrs. Stanley H., Jr.)

HEARTY VEGETABLE SOUP

3 to 4 pounds soup bones
2½ quarts cold water
1 (28 ounce) can whole
   tomatoes
1 (12 ounce) can tomato
   paste
1 (20 ounce) package frozen
   mixed vegetables

1 large onion, chopped
1 tablespoon parsley flakes
4 stalks celery, chopped
Salt and pepper to taste
1 small handful vermicelli

In stockpot simmer soup bones in water for 2 hours. Remove bones, cool and cut off meat. Skim fat from stock and add meat. Add remaining ingredients except vermicelli. Simmer 30 to 40 minutes. Break vermicelli into thirds, add to pot and simmer 10 to 15 minutes. Yield: 3 to 4 quarts.

Sara Z. Hoblitzell (Mrs. John R.)

HOMEMADE VEGETABLE SOUP

1 (46 ounce) can V-8 juice
6 cups water
2 pounds beef shanks
4 carrots, chopped
1 large onion, chopped
2 potatoes, chopped
4 celery stalks, chopped
1 to 2 cups shredded
   cabbage

2 teaspoons Worcestershire
   sauce
2 teaspoons garlic powder
1 vegetable bouillon cube
1 beef bouillon cube
1 (10 ounce) package frozen
   mixed vegetables

In large pot combine V-8 juice, water and shanks. Bring to boil, reduce heat and simmer for 2 hours. Remove shanks and cut off lean part of meat. Return meat to pot. Add all ingredients except frozen vegetables. Simmer until vegetables are tender. Add frozen vegetables and cook 30 minutes longer. Yield: 4 quarts.

Mary Elizabeth Goodwin

WATERCRESS SOUP
An elegant soup for a dinner party.

8 tablespoons butter, divided	1 cup milk
	Salt and pepper to taste
2½ tablespoons flour	3 green onions, chopped
2½ cups chicken stock	2 bunches watercress

Melt 6 tablespoons butter. Stir in flour, cooking 2 to 3 minutes until smooth and bubbly. Slowly add stock and milk, cooking over low heat until thickened. Simmer 3 minutes. Season with salt and pepper. Sauté onion in a separate pan in 2 tablespoons butter until soft. Wash and trim watercress leaving some of stem. Add to onion, cover and cook 4 minutes. Stir vegetables into sauce. Place in blender. Blend on low until smooth. Chill overnight. Makes 4 cups.

Mrs. T. Roland L. Sinclair

ZUCCHINI SOUP

1 pound zucchini, sliced	Salt and pepper to taste
¼ cup chopped onion	1 cup cream of chicken soup
1⅓ cups water	
2 chicken bouillon cubes	¼ to ½ cup white wine
¼ teaspoon rosemary	

Simmer all ingredients except soup and wine 10 minutes until vegetables are tender. Purée in blender or food processor until smooth. Return to saucepan. Add soup and wine. Simmer 5 to 10 minutes on low heat. Serves 4 to 6.

Eliza M. Smith (Mrs. I. Noyes, Sr.)

LENTIL SOUP

2 cups lentils	1 (16 ounce) can tomatoes
½ pound mild sausage	2½ teaspoons salt
½ pound hot sausage	½ teaspoon oregano
8 ounces pepperoni, cut in bite size pieces	¼ teaspoon sage
	¼ teaspoon red pepper
8 cups water	2 medium carrots, sliced
2 cups chicken broth	2 stalks celery, diced
1 cup chopped onion	

Wash lentils. Cut sausage into small pieces, fry and drain. Boil pepperoni; drain off grease. Place all ingredients except carrots and celery in large pot. Bring to boil. Reduce heat, cover and simmer 30 minutes, stirring occasionally. Add carrots and celery. Simmer covered for 40 minutes. Serves 8.

Karen Potesta

BEEF BUNYA
An old Hungarian recipe.

5 pound rump roast	1 green pepper, finely chopped
2 cloves garlic	2 stalks celery, thinly sliced
2 (14½ ounces each) cans beef broth	1 pound fresh mushrooms, sliced
2 onions, thinly sliced	Horseradish

Bury garlic cloves in roast (one in each end). Roast covered at 300° for 3 hours. Reserve juice and refrigerate both overnight. Slice beef thinly with electric knife. Heat juices from roast with beef broth. Add vegetables and cook until tender. Add sliced beef and heat through. Serve on semi-hard buns with horseradish. Reserve sauce for dipping. Enough for 12 sandwiches.

Carol Gaujot (Mrs. Phillip D.)

CRAB MEAT SANDWICH

1 (6½ ounce) can crab meat, drained
½ cup shredded sharp American cheese
½ cup chopped celery
2 tablespoons drained relish
2 tablespoons chopped green onions
1 hard boiled egg, chopped
3 tablespoons salad dressing
½ teaspoon lemon juice
½ teaspoon horseradish
10 slices buttered bread
5 slices tomato
Salt and pepper to taste

Combine first 9 ingredients. Spread on 5 slices of bread. Top with tomato. Season with salt and pepper. Top with remaining bread slices. Grill until golden brown. Serves 5.

Mrs. Paul F. Saylor

BROILED CRAB MEAT SANDWICH

1 (7½ ounce) can crab meat, drained
2 cups grated Cheddar cheese
2 minced green onions
⅓ cup mayonnaise
6 English muffins, halved
2 tomatoes, optional

Mix together first 4 ingredients. Spread on muffins. Top with tomato slice. Broil until bubbly. Yield: 12 halves or 6 servings.

Diane Minsker (Mrs. Michael)

HAM SANDWICH FILLING

½ pound Velveeta cheese
½ cup smoked, pressed ham
4 hard boiled eggs, chopped
½ cup diced celery
½ cup chopped onion
2 tablespoons vinegar
2 tablespoons mayonnaise
1 tablespoon sugar

Coarsely dice ham and cheese. Add eggs, celery and onion, tossing well. Add remaining ingredients. Refrigerate covered several hours. Spread generously on hamburger buns or onion rolls. Place on baking sheet. Brown at 350° for 10 minutes until bubbly. Serves 4 to 6.

Vicki H. Duncan (Mrs. C. Ronald)

OVEN DIVAN SANDWICHES

6 slices toast
6 slices cheese
¾ pound sliced chicken
1 (10 ounce) package frozen
    broccoli, thawed
¾ cup mayonnaise

¼ cup grated Parmesan
    cheese
1 teaspoon dry mustard
2 to 3 tablespoons milk
¼ cup chopped red onion

Arrange toast in 9" x 13" baking pan. Layer with sliced cheese, chicken and broccoli. Combine next 4 ingredients. Spoon over sandwiches. Sprinkle with onion. Bake uncovered at 400° for 15 to 20 minutes. Serves 6.

Charlotte R. Lane (Mrs. J. Thomas)

PEPPERONI CHEESE LOAF
Kathy's original featured in Southern Living.

1 loaf frozen bread dough
1 egg, beaten
½ cup Parmesan cheese
2 (3½ ounces each) pack-
    ages sliced pepperoni:
    use 3" rounds if
    available

2 cups shredded Mozzarella
    cheese
½ teaspoon dried oregano

Thaw dough and allow to rise according to package directions. Roll out dough into a large circle on a lightly greased baking sheet. Brush egg over dough. Sprinkle with Parmesan cheese. Layer pepperoni and Mozzarella cheese on top. Sprinkle with oregano. Roll up jellyroll fashion, sealing edges and tucking under ends. Can be refrigerated at this point until ready to bake. Bake, seam side down, at 375° for 30 minutes. Slice to serve. Serves 6.

Kathy S. Chaney (Mrs. Malcolm)

PIZZA
An original developed over 6 years of testing.
Sauce and dough can easily be doubled.

SAUCE

2 tablespoons olive oil
½ to ⅔ cup chopped onion
2 cloves garlic, minced
1 (28 ounce) can tomatoes, mashed
2 (6 ounces each) cans tomato paste
1½ cups water
2 teaspoons sugar

1 teaspoon Italian seasoning (or blend of oregano and basil)
2 tablespoons Italian dressing
1 teaspoon salt
¼ teaspoon fennel seed
½ cup Italian peppers in sauce (Oliverio); if not available add green pepper to sauce

Sauté onion and garlic in oil. Place all ingredients in large pot and simmer 2 hours. May be prepared ahead. Freezes.

DOUGH

½ cup warm water
1 package yeast
1 teaspoon sugar
2 tablespoons margarine

½ cup boiling water
1 teaspoon salt
3 cups flour

Combine first 3 ingredients in a small glass dish. Stir. Set aside for 5 minutes. In mixing bowl or food processor pour boiling water over margarine. Cool. Add flour, salt and yeast mixture. Mix. Place in a large oiled bowl and let rise 45 minutes. Punch down and divide for assembly. Makes enough dough for 1 large or two 12″ pizzas.

TOPPINGS AND ASSEMBLY

Grated Mozzarella cheese
Sliced green pepper
Sliced mushrooms
Italian or mild sausage, fried and drained

Slices of pepperoni
Anchovies
Chopped olives
Chopped hot peppers
Thinly sliced onion rings

Grease pizza pans. Roll dough on floured surface to desired thickness. Fit dough in pizza pans. Spread with sauce. Top with generous amount of grated Mozzarella cheese and desired toppings. Bake at 350° for 10 minutes, then at 425° for 15 minutes or until browned.

Donna L. Dean (Mrs. Rodney D.)

REUBEN WRAP UPS

1 (8 count) package
    refrigerated crescent
    rolls
1 (8 ounce) can sauerkraut,
    well drained

2 tablespoons Thousand
    Island salad dressing
8 thin slices cooked
    corned beef
2 slices Swiss cheese, cut in
    ½" strips

Unroll dough and separate into 8 triangles. Chop sauerkraut and combine with salad dressing. Place one slice corned beef across wide end of triangle. Spread 2 tablespoons sauerkraut on corned beef. Top with 2 strips of cheese. Roll up, beginning at wide end of triangle. Bake on ungreased baking sheet at 375° for 10 to 15 minutes until golden brown. Serve hot. Makes 8.

Mary Ann Cody

SATURDAY AFTERNOON SANDWICH

1 bunch fresh broccoli
    or asparagus
    Salt and pepper to taste
4 slices crusty bread or
    English muffin halves
4 slices ham

4 thin slices onion
4 slices tomato
3 to 4 hard boiled eggs,
    sliced
4 slices Swiss cheese

Steam broccoli until crisp tender. Drain, pat dry and season with salt and pepper. To assemble sandwich: toast bread, top with ham, broccoli, onion, tomato, sliced eggs, and then cheese. Place under broiler until cheese melts. Top with dressing. Makes 4 sandwiches

DRESSING

½ cup buttermilk
1½ cups mayonnaise
½ cup finely chopped
    parsley
1 cup finely chopped
    carrots

1 tablespoon chopped onion
½ cup finely chopped celery
1 teaspoon garlic powder
¼ teaspoon salt

Blend buttermilk and mayonnaise. Add remaining ingredients. Refrigerate overnight.

Barbara H. Slack (Mrs. John M., III)

SLOPPY JOES

2 pounds ground chuck
1 medium onion, chopped
3 stalks celery, diced
6 tablespoons Worcester-
   shire sauce
2 tablespoons mustard

1 (14 ounce) bottle ketchup
2 (15 ounces each) cans
   tomato sauce
1 medium green pepper,
   diced

Cook ground chuck, onion and celery until tender. Drain. Add remaining ingredients. Cook uncovered on low heat for 1 hour. Serve on hamburger buns. Serves 15.

Patricia W. Berry (Mrs. Bruce)

SKILLET BURGERS
Great for picnics - can be cooked over an open fire.

1½ pounds ground chuck
1   green pepper, chopped
1   onion, chopped
1   tablespoon mustard

¾ cup ketchup
1 tablespoon sugar
1 teaspoon salt
8 hamburger buns

Brown chuck, onion and green pepper in skillet. Add remaining ingredients. Simmer for 30 minutes. Spoon on hamburger buns. Serves 8.

Linda K. Meckfessel (Mrs. Richard R.)

PORK BARBEQUE

4 to 5 pound pork roast,
   cooked and shredded
2 tablespoons butter
¼ cup chopped onion
¼ cup chopped green
   pepper
1 clove garlic, minced
1 cup ketchup
½ cup chili sauce
½ cup water
¼ cup wine vinegar

¼ cup sugar
1 tablespoon Worcester-
   shire sauce
2 teaspoons spicy mustard
½ teaspoon horseradish
½ teaspoon salt
¼ teaspoon each: paprika,
   chili powder and black
   pepper
½ teaspoon Tabasco sauce,
   optional

Melt butter and sauté onion and green pepper in medium saucepan. Add all remaining ingredients for sauce. Simmer 30 minutes. Combine pork and sauce in a casserole. Bake at 300° for 1 hour. Serve on buns with slaw. May be frozen. Place barbeque mixture on buns. Wrap individually in waxed paper. Reheat in microwave. Serves 12 to 15.

Donna L. Dean (Mrs. Rodney D.)

58

REHOBOTH CHURCH

"For now the Lord has made a broad place (Rehoboth) for us, and we shall be fruitful in the land." Genesis 26:22.

The Methodist Society in America was founded in 1784 and appointed Francis Asbury its first Bishop. A Methodist Society was formed on the western Virginia frontier in what was then known as the "Sinks" of Greenbrier County (Monroe County, West Virginia today).

A young clergyman, William Phoebus, was the first full-time Methodist Minister in the new regional Society. The first meetings were held in cabins and a few widely scattered schoolhouses. The Society, under William Phoebus' leadership soon outgrew the "cabin ministry" and a meeting house became a necessity.

Edward Keenan, a Methodist convert from Catholicism, gave the land on which Rehoboth Church still stands "for us long as grass grows and water flows." The church was built in 1786 and tradition says that Bishop Asbury dedicated the building. The church was pleasantly sited in a broad sink made free of hiding places for the Indians.

Bishop Asbury did hold sessions of the Greenbrier Conference at Rehoboth in 1792, 1793 and 1796, and the centennial celebration of the founding of the Methodist Society was held at the little frontier church on July 20, 1884. In 1960 the General Conference of the United Methodist Church designated Rehoboth Church as one of ten Methodist Shrines in America.

The log building (hewn on the inside only) has a floor space 21 feet by 30 feet. There is only one door and two small windows. A gallery extends around three sides and the walnut and poplar pulpit is on a high platform. Backless truncheon benches of split logs with legs bored into the round bottoms show the smoothness of use. A large tin-roofed shed has been built over the church to protect it from further weathering.

The church is surrounded by a cemetery where pioneer worshippers of the eighteenth and nineteenth centuries are at rest in the shadow of their beloved Rehoboth.

Photo by Gerald S. Ratliff

DAIRY AND EGGS

Triple Sunflower

EGG CROQUETTES

9 hard boiled eggs
3 tablespoons butter,
     melted
4 tablespoons flour
1 cup milk
1 green onion, minced
½ teaspoon Worcestershire
     sauce

1 teaspoon finely chopped
     parsley
   Italian seasoned bread
     crumbs
2 eggs
2 tablespoons water

Grate the hard boiled eggs. Set aside. In a saucepan sauté onions in butter. Add flour, stirring to make a smooth paste. Gradually add milk, stirring to make a white sauce. Add Worcestershire sauce and parsley. Stir in grated eggs and chill 1 hour. Take a generous tablespoon of mixture and roll into bread crumbs, shaping into a croquette.* Combine eggs and water to make an egg bath. Dip each croquette in the egg bath, then dip in bread crumbs again. Chill 1 hour. Deep fry at 375° to 385° two at a time for 2 to 4 minutes. Serve plain or with Mushroom Sauce. Croquettes will keep for a few hours at room temperature. Reheat at 400° for a few minutes until hot.

*A croquette is a small ball or cone shape not larger than 1" x 1" x 2½".

MUSHROOM SAUCE

½ cup sliced mushrooms
2 tablespoons butter,
     melted
2 tablespoons flour

¾ cup chicken broth
½ cup cream
   Sherry to taste

Saute mushrooms in butter. Add flour, stirring until smooth. Gradually add chicken broth and cream, stirring constantly to make a medium white sauce. Add sherry. Serve with Egg Croquettes.

Mrs. Dorothy Reishman (Mrs. Vincent)

FANCY EGGS BENEDICT
A delightful change from traditional Eggs Benedict.

½ cup minced onion
1 tablespoon chopped green
   pepper
3 tablespoons butter
1 (10½ ounce) can cream
   of mushroom soup
⅔ cup evaporated milk
⅓ cup water
   Dash of cayenne pepper

¼ teaspoon dry mustard
1 teaspoon parsley
   Dash of pepper
4 English muffins, split
   and toasted
8 slices tomato
8 green pepper rings
8 slices Canadian bacon
8 poached eggs

Sauté onion and green pepper in butter. In a medium saucepan add sautéed mixture to soup, milk, water and seasonings. Heat to boiling, stirring well. Reduce heat and keep warm. Top each muffin with bacon, tomato and egg. Spoon sauce over. Garnish with pepper rings. Serves 4.

Deborah L. Sutton (Mrs. James)

CRAB MEAT OMELET

FILLING FOR TWO OMELETS

1 tablespoon butter
1 tablespoon flour
½ cup white wine
2 tablespoons cream
⅛ teaspoon tarragon

⅛ teaspoon basil
⅛ teaspoon lemon juice
1 cup crab meat, cleaned
   Fresh dill for garnish

Melt butter in a medium saucepan. Stir in flour, cooking 2 to 3 minutes until smooth and bubbly. Stir in wine, cream and seasonings. Fold in crab meat. Heat thoroughly. Set aside. Prepare basic omelet (double recipe). Place ½ the crab meat mixture in one omelet and fold over. Serve with fresh dill sprinkled on top.

BASIC OMELET
Makes one omelet

2 eggs
2 tablespoons water

Dash of salt and white
   pepper
1 tablespoon butter

Whisk eggs, water and seasonings together in a bowl. Heat

butter in an omelet pan until very hot. Pour egg into pan. Allow to set a few seconds. Using a spatula, gently pull egg mixture from outer edge toward center, allowing uncooked mixture to set. When set but still moist add the filling and fold over. Serve on a warm plate.

Margaret L. Workman

BAKED ASPARAGUS CHEESE SOUFFLÉ

6 (¾" thick) slices firm
   bread
6 slices Swiss cheese
4 eggs
2 cups milk
½ teaspoon salt
⅛ teaspoon pepper

¼ teaspoon nutmeg
1 tablespoon finely chopped
   onion
18 cooked asparagus spears
½ to 1 cup grated Cheddar
   cheese

Trim crusts from bread. Arrange in a buttered 9" x 13" baking dish. Top each slice with a slice of Swiss cheese. Beat eggs, milk, onion and seasonings together. Pour over bread. Bake at 325° for 25 minutes. Remove from oven. Top each bread slice with 3 cooked asparagus spears. Sprinkle with Cheddar cheese. Bake 10 to 15 minutes until custard sets and top is golden. Let stand 5 minutes. Serves 6.

Elizabeth M. Hamrick (Mrs. C. Page, III)

BRUNCH CASSEROLE

12 slices bread, crusts
   removed
½ pound shaved ham
1 cup grated Cheddar
   cheese
½ pound sliced mushrooms

6 eggs
3 cups milk
½ teaspoon salt
½ teaspoon dry mustard
1 cup seasoned croutons
2 tablespoons butter

Place 6 bread slices in a buttered 9" x 13" baking dish. Layer ham, cheese and mushrooms on bread slices. Cover with remaining slices of bread. Combine eggs, milk and seasonings, beating well. Pour over bread. Refrigerate covered overnight. Top with croutons and dot with butter. Bake uncovered at 350° for 1¼ hours. Let stand 10 minutes before cutting. Serves 12.

Joyce Bliss

SUNDAY BRUNCH CASSEROLE

4 cups day old bread, cubed
2 cups grated Cheddar
    cheese
10 eggs, lightly beaten
4 cups milk
1 teaspoon dry mustard
1 teaspoon salt

¼ teaspoon onion powder
    Dash of pepper
8 to 10 slices cooked bacon,
    crumbled
½ cup sliced mushrooms
½ cup peeled and chopped
    tomatoes

Place bread in bottom of a buttered 2 quart casserole. Sprinkle with cheese. Beat next 6 ingredients together. Pour over cheese and bread. Sprinkle with bacon, mushrooms and tomato. Refrigerate covered up to 24 hours. Bake uncovered at 325° for 1 hour or until set. Serves 8.

Carolanne Griffith

24 HOUR WINE AND CHEESE OMELET

1 large loaf day old French
    bread, broken into
    small pieces
6 tablespoons unsalted
    butter, melted
¾ pound Swiss cheese,
    grated
½ pound Monterey Jack
    cheese, grated
9 thin slices Genoa Salami
    or ham

16 eggs
3¼ cups milk
½ cup dry white wine
4 green onions, minced
1 tablespoon German
    mustard
¼ teaspoon pepper
⅛ teaspoon red pepper
1 cup sour cream
⅔ cup freshly grated
    Parmesan cheese

Butter two 9″ x 13″ baking dishes. Spread bread over bottom and drizzle with butter. Sprinkle evenly with cheeses and salami. Beat together next 7 ingredients. Pour over both casseroles, dividing evenly. Refrigerate covered with foil overnight or up to 24 hours. Remove from refrigerator 30 minutes before baking. Bake covered casseroles at 325° for 1 hour. Uncover, spread with sour cream and Parmesan cheese. Bake uncovered 10 minutes or until lightly browned. Serves 20.

Patricia S. Bibbee (Mrs. Charles C.)

SWISS CHEESE SCRAMBLE

2 cups soft bread cubes,
   crusts removed
1⅓ cups milk
8 eggs, beaten
¾ teaspoon salt
⅛ teaspoon pepper
4 tablespoons butter,
   divided

1 tablespoon finely chopped
   onion
¼ teaspoon seasoned salt
½ pound sliced Swiss cheese
¾ cup fine dry bread
   crumbs
8 slices cooked bacon,
   crumbled

Combine bread cubes and milk. After 5 minutes, drain, reserving milk. Combine drained milk with eggs, salt and pepper. In a skillet melt 2 tablespoons butter. Sauté onions until soft. Add egg mixture and scramble until soft, but not fully cooked. Add soaked bread cubes. Pour into a 9" square baking dish. Sprinkle with seasoned salt and Swiss cheese. Melt remaining butter and mix with bread crumbs. Sprinkle over cheese. Top with crumbled bacon. Bake at 400° for 10 to 15 minutes until cheese bubbles. Serve immediately. Serves 6 to 8.

Mary J. Payne (Mrs. Andrew, III)

CRAB QUICHE

3 eggs, beaten
¾ cup sour cream
½ cup milk
½ teaspoon salt
¼ teaspoon dry mustard
   Dash of cayenne pepper

1 cup grated Swiss cheese
1 (7½ ounce) can crab meat
2 tablespoons lemon juice
1 tablespoon chopped
   chives
1 unbaked 9" pie shell

Combine first 6 ingredients, blending well. Stir in remaining ingredients. Pour into pie shell. Bake at 375° for 30 to 40 minutes until set. Can be frozen. Serves 6 to 8.

Betsy G. Wyant (Mrs. David)

CHILI EGG PUFF

10 eggs
½ cup flour
1 teaspoon baking powder
½ teaspoon salt
1 (16 ounce) carton small
   curd cottage cheese

1 pound grated Monterey
   Jack cheese
½ cup margarine, melted
2 (4 ounces each) cans
   chopped green chilies

Beat eggs until light. Add remaining ingredients, blending until smooth. Pour into a buttered 9" x 13" baking dish. Bake at 350° for 40 minutes. Serves 8 to 10.

Jean W. Hutton (Mrs. John P.)

MUSHROOM ARTICHOKE PIE

1 unbaked double crust
   pie shell
2 garlic cloves, minced
1 tablespoon cooking oil
1 (14 ounce) can artichoke
   hearts, drained and
   halved
1 cup sliced mushrooms
4 eggs, beaten

1 cup grated Mozzarella
   cheese
1 cup grated Cheddar
   cheese
1 cup grated Gruyere
   cheese
¼ cup chopped ripe olives
⅛ teaspoon pepper

Preheat a baking sheet in a 350° oven. Sauté garlic, mushrooms and artichokes in hot oil. Spoon into bottom of pie shell. Combine remaining ingredients. Pour over vegetables. Fit other crust over pie, crimping edges. Cut slits in the top. Bake 40 to 45 minutes on warmed baking sheet. Let stand 5 minutes before serving. Serves 6 as a main course, 12 as an appetizer.

Sue Hancock Miller

SPINACH QUICHE

1 cup light cream
2 eggs
1 (3 ounce) package cream
   cheese, softened
½ cup dry bread crumbs
¼ cup Parmesan cheese
3 tablespoons butter,
   melted

1 onion, chopped
½ pound mushrooms, sliced
¾ teaspoon salt
1 teaspoon tarragon
1 (10 ounce) box frozen
   chopped spinach,
   thawed and drained
1 unbaked 9" pie shell

Blend together first 5 ingredients. Sauté onion and mushrooms in butter. Combine with spinach, tarragon and salt. Add to cream mixture. Pour into pie shell. Bake at 400° for 30 to 45 minutes. Serves 6.

Connie Morton McKee

SWISS PIE

1 cup finely crushed
  cracker crumbs
4 tablespoons butter,
  melted
6 slices bacon
1 cup chopped onion
1 (8 ounce) package grated
  Swiss cheese

2 eggs, beaten
¾ cup sour cream
½ teaspoon salt
  Dash of pepper
½ cup grated sharp
  processed American
  cheese

Combine cracker crumbs and melted butter. Press into an 8″ pie plate to form a crust. Cook bacon, drain and crumble. Reserve 2 tablespoons drippings. Sauté onion in drippings until tender. Combine remaining ingredients, except for American cheese. Pour into pie shell. Sprinkle with American cheese. Bake at 375° for 25 to 30 minutes until set. Let stand 5 to 10 minutes. To freeze: bake until done, freeze and reheat, covered, in 300° oven. Serves 6.

Bonnie G. O'Neal (Mrs. Richard)

TUNA QUICHE

CRUST

1 cup whole wheat flour
⅔ cup grated sharp
  Cheddar cheese
¼ cup chopped almonds

½ teaspoon salt
¼ teaspoon paprika
6 to 7 tablespoons oil

FILLING

3 eggs, beaten
1 cup yogurt
¼ cup mayonnaise
2 (6½ ounces each) cans
  tuna in oil

¾ cup shredded Cheddar
  cheese
1 tablespoon grated onion
¼ teaspoon dill weed

Combine crust ingredients, stirring in oil. Reserve ½ cup. Press remaining mixture into the bottom and sides of a 9″ pie plate. Bake at 400° for 10 minutes. Remove from oven and reduce temperature to 325°. Blend eggs, yogurt and mayonnaise in a bowl. Add remaining ingredients, including oil from tuna. Blend; mixture will be lumpy. Spoon into crust. Sprinkle with reserved crust mixture. Bake at 325° for 45 minutes or until firm. Crust and filling can be made ahead, then combined when ready to cook. Serves 6.

Lorena B. Surber (Mrs. Charles M., Jr.)

CHILI RELLENO CASSEROLE

1 (7 ounce) can green
   chilies
¾ pound Cheddar cheese,
   grated

¾ pound Monterey Jack
   cheese, grated
5 eggs, beaten
1 (13 ounce) can evaporated
   milk

Split chilies, spreading on bottom of a 8″ x 10″ baking dish. Sprinkle grated cheese over chilies. Blend eggs and milk together. Pour over cheese. Bake at 350° for 30 minutes, then at 425° for 5 to 10 minutes to brown top. Serves 6 to 8.

Sheri J. Wiles (Mrs. Edwin K.)

MADELEINE PARROTT'S EGG CASSEROLE

½ cup butter, divided
¼ cup flour
2 cups milk
½ teaspoon salt
¼ teaspoon thyme
¼ teaspoon marjoram
¼ teaspoon basil
¼ teaspoon chervil
   (optional)

½ pound sharp Cheddar
   cheese, grated
12 hard boiled eggs, chopped
1 pound cooked bacon,
   crumbled
¼ cup finely chopped
   parsley
1 cup fresh bread crumbs

Melt ¼ cup butter. Add flour and cook 2 to 3 minutes until smooth and bubbly. Slowly stir in milk, cooking until thickened. Add spices. Stir in cheese until melted and smooth. Set aside. Using half of the eggs, place a layer of eggs in a 9″ x 13″ casserole. Layer ½ the bacon and ½ the parsley. Cover with ½ the cheese sauce. Repeat layers. Melt remaining ¼ cup butter and toss with bread crumbs. Sprinkle bread crumbs over casserole. Bake uncovered at 350° for 30 minutes. Serves 10 to 12.

Claire Winterholler

MANSION HOUSE

The Mansion House was built in 1796 by Walter Newman as a tavern. The structure was the last in a series of buildings on the site beginning with Fort Blair (1774), Fort Randolph (1776 or 1777) and a third fort (1786-1795) garrisoned and commanded by Thomas Lewis. The tavern was said to be constructed of logs from the Ft. Blair stable or store. Daniel Boone had a farm and trading post at the point near Ft. Randolph during the period 1788-1794.

The beautiful point of land at the confluence of the Great Kanawha and Ohio rivers is best known as the site of the landmark engagement between the Virginia Militia men of Col. Andrew Lewis, and 800-1000 Indians led by the great Shawnee Chief Cornstalk. The Virginians had arrived at the scene after a grueling journey from their mustering point at Camp Union (Lewisburg). The battle, fought on October 10, 1774, was bitterly contested, consisting mainly of hand-to-hand attacks and counterattacks.

The Indians retreated to their towns across the Ohio and sought peace from Lord Dunmore. Only strong intervention by Dunmore kept Colonel Lewis from attacking the Shawnee towns. Lewis and his army had pursued the Indians across the Ohio. This important battle thus resulted in a temporary time of peace which permitted Virginians to recross the mountains to aid Revolutionary forces. In 1908 the U.S. Senate recognized the Battle of Point Pleasant as the first engagement of the Revolutionary War.

The point is now marked by Tu-Endie-Wei Park, a beautiful green space which includes the Mansion House, the Point Pleasant Battle Monument, the graves of Cornstalk and "Mad" Ann Bailey, and the bones and artifacts of countless occupants of the land dating back to Paleolithic times, about 15,000 years ago. The Indian words Tu-Endie-Wei mean, "the point between two waters."

Artifacts, heirlooms and pioneer relics are displayed in the hewn-log Mansion House which has stood at the point virtually unchanged since its construction in 1796. It was repaired in 1901 and the porches and eastern protective overhang were added in 1911.

Photo by Governor's Office of E.C.D.

SEAFOOD

Churn Dash

CRAB CAKES

1 pound crab meat
1 egg
2 tablespoons mayonnaise
½ cup cracker meal or
    seasoned bread crumbs

1 tablespoon mustard
Salt and pepper to taste
Chopped green onion to
    taste

Pick over crab meat, discarding shell and cartilage. Combine with remaining ingredients. Form into 6 to 8 patties. Fry over medium heat in lightly greased skillet until brown on each side, or deep fry at 350° until brown. Serves 4 to 6.

Mary T. Karr (Mrs. George W.)

CRAB SOUFFLÉ

16 slices bread, buttered
8 slices Swiss cheese
1 large can crab meat or
    1 (7 ounce) box frozen,
    drained

5 eggs
3 cups milk
1 teaspoon salt
Parmesan cheese

Remove crust from bread. Place 8 slices of bread in bottom of buttered 9″ x 13″ dish. Place Swiss cheese on bread. Remove cartilage from the crab; sprinkle on top of cheese. Place remaining 8 slices of bread on top. Beat eggs, milk and salt together; pour over all. Top with Parmesan cheese. Refrigerate overnight or at least 8 hours. Bake at 325° for 1 hour. Serves 8.

Judith H. McJunkin (Mrs. Brittain)

CRAB AND CORN SALAD

1 (8¼ ounce) can kernel
   corn, drained
1 (6½ ounce) can crab meat,
   drained
½ cup sour cream
¼ cup mayonnaise
½ cup chopped celery

½ cup chopped green
   pepper
½ small onion, chopped
Salt and pepper to taste
Pinch of dill weed
Lemon wedges

Mix all ingredients. Refrigerate 4 hours or longer. Serve on bed of lettuce with lemon wedge. Serves 2 to 3.

Kathryn S. Foster (Mrs. Daniel S.)

CRAB MEAT MORNAY

1 pound crab meat
3 egg yolks
½ cup light cream
1 (4½ ounce) can whole
   mushrooms, drained
2 cups hot Bechamel
   sauce, divided

2 tablespoon butter, melted
Salt to taste
2 tablespoons whipping
   cream
2 tablespoons grated
   Parmesan cheese

Pick over crab meat, discarding any bits of shell and cartilage. Mix egg yolks with light cream and add mushrooms. Add Bechamel sauce (reserving 2 tablespoons for topping), butter, salt and crab meat. Turn mixture into greased 1 to 1½ quart casserole. Combine remaining sauce with whipping cream and spread over top. Sprinkle with Parmesan cheese. Bake at 400° for 20 minutes until lightly browned and heated through. May also be served in a chafing dish with crackers as an appetizer. Serves 4 to 5.

BECHAMEL SAUCE

4 tablespoons butter
1 small onion, chopped
4 tablespoons flour
¼ teaspoon salt

2 cups hot milk or 1 cup hot
   milk and 1 cup hot
   chicken stock

Heat butter and onion together, but do not brown. Stir in flour; remove from heat. Add salt and hot milk; continue to stir until sauce is smooth. Return to heat, stirring constantly until sauce comes to a boil. Makes 2¼ cups.

Pamela B. Brown (Mrs. Ricklin)

SHERRIED CRAB MEAT

¼ cup butter, divided
3 tablespoons flour
½ teaspoon salt
  Dash of red pepper
¾ cup bottled clam juice
½ cup heavy cream
1½ tablespoons dry sherry
1 hard cooked egg, chopped
2 (6½ ounces each) cans
  crab meat, drained

1 tablespoon chopped onion
½ cup sliced mushrooms
1 tablespoon chopped
  parsley
1 tablespoon chopped
  chives
¼ cup bread crumbs
4 prepared patty shells

Melt 3 tablespoons butter in medium saucepan. Remove from heat. Stir in flour, salt and cayenne until smooth. Gradually stir in clam juice and cream. Bring mixture to boil, stirring constantly, until thickened and smooth. Stir in sherry, egg and crab meat. Keep warm. Heat remaining butter in small skillet. Sauté vegetables 5 minutes or until tender. Stir in bread crumbs. Fill shells with crab meat mixture. Top each with bread crumb mixture. Sauce may be prepared in advance, heated and sherry, egg and crab meat added when ready to serve. Bread crumb mixture may also be prepared in advance and heated to garnish. Does not freeze. Serves 4.

Deborah L. Sutton (Mrs. James)

CATFISH

4 whole catfish
1 cup chopped leeks
2 cloves garlic, minced
¼ cup unsalted butter,
  melted

Juice of 1 lemon
White pepper
Paprika
½ cup white wine

In small saucepan sauté leeks and garlic in butter until soft. Place fish in medium size baking dish. Squeeze lemon juice over top. Sprinkle with white pepper and paprika to taste. Put sautéed leek and garlic over top. Pour wine over. Bake at 350° for 15 to 20 minutes. Do not turn. May use chicken broth or other clear liquid in place of wine. Serves 4.

To cook on grill: Make a basting sauce by using all ingredients and adding an extra ½ cup melted butter. May also add fresh parsley and savory for additional flavoring. Place catfish in foil on grill over medium coals, baste several times. Cook 15 to 20 minutes until done. This sauce may also be used for basting under the broiler.

Vivian Ghiz (Mrs. Robert)

BAKED FISH IN A BAG

4 fish fillets
⅓ cup celery leaves
2 sprigs fresh parsley
   Juice of ½ lemon
2 tablespoons salt free
     margarine

1 small onion, minced
   Salt to taste
   Freshly ground pepper
     to taste
1 tomato, cut up

On a double sheet of aluminum foil place ingredients in order given. Fold foil tightly. Bake at 350° for 20 minutes or over charcoal grill. Serves 4.

Susan Kamer-Shinaberry

CARIBBEAN FISH

4 pounds snapper or bass,
     cleaned
   Juice of 2 limes
½ teaspoon white pepper
3 cups canned tomatoes
2 onions, thinly sliced
½ cup green olives

3 cloves garlic, crushed
2 tablespoons capers with
     liquid
2 bay leaves, crushed
½ cup olive oil
½ cup water

Make several shallow slashes on each side of fish. Place in large buttered baking dish. Mix remaining ingredients. Spread over fish. Bake at 500° for 15 minutes. Reduce heat to 400°. Bake until fish flakes easily with tip of knife, 20 to 30 minutes. Serves 4 to 6.

Paula S. McKenney (Mrs. Ronald A.)

FISH WITH SHRIMP

2 pounds fresh fillet of sole
1 (7 ounce) can shrimp,
     drained
   Juice of 1 lime
   Salt and pepper to taste

1½ cups sour cream
1 (10 ounce) can cream of
     shrimp soup
   Chopped chives and lime
     slices

Spread 1 tablespoon shrimp on each fillet. Roll fillet around shrimp, securing with a toothpick. Sprinkle with ½ of lime juice, salt and pepper. Bake at 350° for 15 minutes, or until fish flakes. Mix soup, sour cream, remaining lime juice and any remaining shrimp. Pour over fish. Bake at 450° for 5 to 10 minutes, or until top is bubbly. Garnish with chives and lime. Serves 6.

Marilou Morton (Mrs. Gordon)

SOLE FILLETS WITH SHRIMP

1 pound fillets of sole	1 teaspoon cornstarch
1 tablespoon lemon juice	1 cup half and half
Salt and pepper	1 cup cooked canned
¼ cup chopped parsley	shrimp, drained and
¾ cup small, whole	chopped
mushrooms	2 tablespoons bread crumbs
2 tablespoons butter	2 tablespoons Parmesan
divided	cheese
1 tablespoon Dijon mustard	

Brush each fillet with lemon juice and season with salt and pepper. Cut each fillet in half lengthwise and sprinkle with parsley. Roll each piece so that parsley is inside the roll; secure with a wooden pick. Stand rolls up in a baking dish. Bake covered at 425° for 10 minutes. Drain off juices and remove picks. Briefly sauté mushrooms in 1 tablespooon of melted butter. Place a whole mushroom inside each roll. Blend mustard into cornstarch. Stir in cream. Heat mixture until bubbly and slightly thickened. Add shrimp and pour over fish. Mix bread crumbs and cheese with remaining melted butter. Sprinkle over fish. Bake uncovered at 425° for 10 minutes. Serves 4.

Patricia M. Moyers (Mrs. Charles G., Jr.)

BAKED TROUT IN FOIL

Fresh native or rainbow	Onions, thinly sliced
trout	Butter slices
Foil pieces to wrap fish	Salt and pepper
Lemons, thinly sliced	Vermouth (optional)

Allow a 10 to 12 ounce fish for each trout lover. Rinse trout in cold water; pat dry on paper towels. If possible, leave trout head intact. If necessary, cut head directly behind gills. Tail may also be bobbed. Allow one large piece of foil per fish. Lay lemon, onion and butter slices on each piece of foil. Place fish on top. Lay lemon, onion and butter plus 1 tablespoon Vermouth inside belly of fish; salt and pepper. Vermouth is not necessary but will provide subtle taste and moisture. Close fish. Place lemon, onion and butter slices on top of fish. Salt and pepper. Fold fish in foil tightly; place on greased baking pan. Cook at 400° for 20 to 30 minutes. Fish should be flaky but not fall apart to the touch of a fork. If trout is fresh your dish will be a success regardless of how you add these seasonings.

Ray Muehlman, Sr.

PANFRIED NATIVE TROUT (CAMPFIRE STYLE)

4 fresh trout, cleaned and
  scaled
  Salt and pepper to taste
8 slices bacon
⅔ to 1 cup yellow corn meal

4 tablespoons cooking oil or
  bacon grease
1 small onion, thinly sliced
  (optional)

Season fish inside and out with salt and pepper. Secure end of a slice of bacon in gill of fish and wrap around fish. Start second slice of bacon where first slice ends and continue wrapping, ending at tail of fish. Secure with toothpick in tail. Repeat with each fish. Roll fish in corn meal, coating fully. Heat oil in large skillet over fire until very hot. Add trout. Panfry 4 minutes on each side until firm to touch and golden brown. Remove. Sauté onion slices in pan and spoon over fish if desired. Serves 4.

OYSTERS ON TOAST

1 tablespoon butter
1 pint oysters
  Large dash of Tabasco
  sauce
  Pinch of celery salt

1 tablespoon Worcester-
  shire sauce
  Toast slices
8 to 10 slices cooked bacon,
  crumbled
  Grated or sliced cheese

Brown butter. Pour in oysters and liquid. Add next three ingredients. Cook as you would for stew (until gills are well open). Drain. Place oysters on toast in shallow pan. Sprinkle with bacon and cover with cheese. Place under broiler until cheese melts. Serves 4.

Frank Henderson

HANGTOWN FRY

8 to 12 slices bacon
12 oysters
½ cup diced green pepper
½ cup chopped green onion
8 eggs
½ cup milk

1 tablespoon chopped
  parsley
¼ teaspoon salt
¾ teaspoon pepper
¼ cup butter, melted
  Pimento strips

Cook bacon, reserving 3 tablespoons grease. Sauté next 3 ingredients for 5 minutes in grease. Combine next 5 ingredients; scramble in butter. Place eggs on serving platter. Spoon oyster mixture on top. Decorate with bacon and pimento strips.

Mary Beth Erickson (Mrs. E. Dixon)

SALMON AU GRATIN

1 (16 ounce) can salmon
3 slices bread
4 tablespoons butter, divided
2 tablespoons flour
1½ cups milk

1 cup grated Cheddar cheese
1 teaspoon onion flakes
Salt and pepper to taste
Grated Cheddar cheese for top

Remove skin and bones from salmon. Finely crumble bread and brown in 2 tablespoons butter in frying pan. Melt remaining 2 tablespoons butter in saucepan. Stir in flour, cooking 2 minutes until smooth and bubbly. Slowly stir in milk, cooking until thickened to make a white sauce. Combine salmon, bread crumbs, white sauce, cheese and seasonings. Place in 3 or 4 individual au gratin dishes. Sprinkle top with additional cheese. Bake at 350° for 30 minutes, until bubbly. Cool a few minutes before serving. Serves 3 to 4.

Lucia Ann Weiden

HERBED GRAVLAX
Salmon marinated in dill

2 to 3 pounds salmon fillet with skin
1 teaspoon dill weed
2 teaspoons dill seed

3 tablespoons salt
5 teaspoons sugar
¼ teaspoon pepper
¼ cup vinegar

Rub dill weed into both sides and end of fillet. Place salmon, skin side down, in a tightfitting non-metallic dish. Mix remaining seasonings; pour over fillet. Pour on vinegar. Cover with plastic wrap and a styrofoam meat tray cut to fit dish. Weight tray with a 2 pound weight. After one day remove weight. Spoon juice over several times for two more days, turning fillet once a day. Scrape off dill to serve. Pat dry. Slice on diagonal, thinly, cutting away from the skin. Serve open face on a bagel spread with cream cheese or on buttered dark bread. For a main course serve on toast with lemon wedges and Hot Mustard Sauce and Cucumber Salad.

Mrs. Rain Purre

SALMON ROLL

SOUFFLÉ

5 tablespoons butter,
  melted
5 tablespoons flour
1¼ cups milk
½ cup grated Cheddar
  cheese

¼ cup grated Parmesan
  cheese
6 eggs, separated
¼ teaspoon cream of tartar
  Grated Parmesan cheese

Combine butter and flour in a saucepan over medium heat. Slowly stir in milk cooking until smooth. Add cheeses, stirring until smooth. Beat in egg yolks. Beat egg whites with cream of tartar until stiff. Combine mixtures; pour into oiled jelly roll pan lined with wax paper. Bake at 375° for 10 to 12 minutes until set. Do not overbake as it will break when rolled. Turn out on a towel liberally sprinkled with Parmesan cheese. Remove paper carefully. Roll up loosely. Cool. Unroll, fill and roll up. Reheat at 350° for 20 minutes until hot. Cover with Lemon Sauce. Serves 8.

FILLING

1 (15 ounce) can salmon
¼ cup chopped onion
¼ cup chopped celery
½ cup chopped mushrooms

1 tablespoon butter
¼ teaspoon pepper
¼ cup sour cream or
  mayonnaise

Drain and flake salmon, reserving liquid. Sauté vegetables in butter. Combine all ingredients. Spread over soufflé.

LEMON SAUCE

1 tablespoon butter, melted
1 tablespoon flour
1 cup salmon liquid and
  fish or chicken stock

1 egg yolk
1 tablespoon lemon juice
3 tablespoons chopped
  parsley

Combine butter and flour in saucepan over medium heat. Slowly stir in liquid, cooking until smooth. Beat in egg yolk, juice and parsley. Pour over roll. If soufflé breaks up too much, layer in dish with the filling. Heat and top with sauce. Not as pretty, but just as good. Serves 8.

Paula S. McKenney (Mrs. Ronald A.)

SALMON SOUFFLÉ

2 tablespoons butter, melted
2 tablespoons flour
1 cup milk
2 eggs, separated

1 (15½ ounce) can salmon, flaked
¼ teaspoon nutmeg
½ teaspoon salt
Dash of pepper

Combine flour and butter in saucepan. Cook 2 minutes, stirring until smooth and bubbly. Slowly stir in milk, cooking until thickened to make a white sauce. Slowly add small amount of sauce to beaten egg yolks, then stir into remaining sauce. Add next four ingredients. Beat egg whites until stiff and fold into salmon mixture. Bake in 1½ quart greased casserole at 325° for 45 minutes. Serve at once. Good served with mashed potatoes. Serves 4.

Kathy S. Chaney (Mrs. Malcolm)

BAKED SCALLOPS

1 pound scallops, cut in half
1 ounce sherry (optional)

6 tablespoons butter, melted and divided
½ cup dry bread crumbs

Arrange scallops in shallow buttered casserole. Sprinkle with sherry. Pour half the butter over scallops. Cover with bread crumbs. Pour rest of butter over bread crumbs. Bake at 375° for 15 minutes.

Kathy S. Chaney (Mrs. Malcolm)

SHRIMP CASSEROLE

2½ pounds cooked shrimp, peeled
1 tablespoon lemon juice
3 tablespoons cooking oil
2 tablespoons butter
¼ cup chopped green pepper
¼ cup chopped green onion
1 cup cooked rice
¾ cup blanched almonds

1 teaspoon salt
⅛ teaspoon pepper
1 (8 ounce) can sliced mushrooms, drained
1 (14 ounce) can artichokes, drained and chopped
1 (10 ounce) can tomato soup
1 cup heavy cream
½ cup sherry

Sprinkle shrimp with lemon juice and salad oil. Set aside. Sauté pepper and onion in butter. Combine all ingredients. Place in 2 quart casserole. Bake uncovered at 350° for 1 hour. Serves 6 to 8 as a luncheon dish.

Nancy S. Dodson (Mrs. Raymond G.)

SHRIMP AND ARTICHOKE CASSEROLE

1 (20 ounce) can artichoke
   hearts, drained
¾ cup cooked shrimp
¼ pound fresh mushrooms,
   sliced
4 tablespoons butter,
   divided
2 tablespoons flour

1½ cups milk
1 tablespoon Worcester-
   shire sauce
¼ cup dry sherry
   Salt and pepper to taste
¼ cup Parmesan cheese
   Paprika

Arrange artichokes in buttered 1½ quart baking dish. Spread shrimp over artichokes. Sauté mushrooms in 2 tablespoons butter for 6 minutes. Add to baking dish. Melt remaining 2 tablespoons butter in saucepan. Add flour, cooking 2 to 3 minutes until smooth and bubbly. Slowly stir in milk and cook until thickened. Add Worcestershire sauce, sherry, salt and pepper. Pour over mushrooms. Sprinkle top with cheese and paprika. Bake at 375° for 30 to 40 minutes. Serves 4.

Sandra W. Mantz (Mrs. Eric P.)

SHRIMP WITH LEMON RICE

1 cup uncooked rice
2 teaspoons ground
   turmeric
1 teaspoon mustard seeds
½ cup butter
2½ pounds raw shrimp,
   peeled and deveined

1 (7 ounce) jar pimentos,
   drained and diced
1 teaspoon salt
1 cup dry white wine
2 tablespoons lemon juice

Cook rice, following package directions. In large skillet heat turmeric and mustard seeds in butter for 2 to 3 minutes. Stir in shrimp; sauté 5 minutes. Reserving drippings, remove shrimp with a slotted spoon. Place in 10 cup baking dish. Stir rice into drippings in pan; heat slowly, stirring constantly until golden brown. Stir in pimentos and salt; spoon into baking dish. Mix wine and lemon juice in a cup; stir into rice mixture. Cover and bake at 350° for 1¼ hours. Just before serving, fluff with a fork. Serves 8.

Mrs. Graham Painter

SHRIMP SCAMPI

2 pounds raw shrimp
2 tablespoons butter
2 tablespoons olive oil

4 cloves garlic, minced
1 tablespoon chopped
   parsley

Wash and peel shrimp. Put butter and olive oil in skillet; heat over medium high heat. Add garlic and shrimp; sauté 4 to 5 minutes until shrimp are pink. Add parsley and mix lightly. Serve, pouring sauce over top. Good served on bed of rice. Serves 4.

Sara Z. Hoblitzell (Mrs. John R.)

SHRIMP SEVICHE

2 pounds medium shrimp, halved
1 cup lime juice
2 medium tomatoes, peeled, seeded and chopped
2 canned Jalapeno chili peppers, rinsed, seeded and chopped
2 pimentos, chopped
1 medium onion, chopped
2 tablespoons fresh coriander (cilantro), chopped
6 tablespoons cooking oil
Salt
Freshly ground pepper

Place shrimp in a bowl with the lime juice. Refrigerate 3 hours, or until shrimp are opaque, turning once or twice. Drain the shrimp, reserving lime juice. Place shrimp in a bowl with next five ingredients. Beat oil and 2 tablespoons of juice with salt and pepper to taste. Pour over the shrimp mixture. Toss lightly to mix. Serve on a bed of fresh lettuce leaves. Serves 4 to 6 as a salad, or 8 to 10 as an appetizer.

Paula W. Flaherty (Mrs. Thomas V.)

FETTUCCINI AND SHRIMP

1 pound cooked shrimp, medium size
½ pound fettuccini egg noodles (medium width)
1 cup sweet butter
½ pint whipping cream
Freshly ground pepper
Freshly grated nutmeg
Equal parts of Parmesan cheese and Romano cheese, grated

Cook noodles in salted water until just tender. Drain thoroughly and refresh with cold water. Melt butter in a deep saucepan. Slowly add cream. Add pepper to taste. Add 4 to 5 grates of nutmeg. When mixture is thoroughly heated, add noodles and shrimp and immediately begin adding cheese. Gently toss noodles and shrimp mixture with wooden implements. Add cheese until sauce thickens. Serve immediately. Serves 4.

Norman Fagan

SEAFOOD CASSEROLE

4 slices white bread
1 cup water
½ cup grated sharp Cheddar
  cheese
½ cup chopped green
  pepper
1 medium onion, chopped
½ cup chopped celery
¼ cup butter, melted

1 egg
1 cup shrimp
1 cup crab meat
½ cup mayonnaise
  Few drops Tabasco sauce
1 teaspoon salt
½ teaspoon pepper
  Bread crumbs (optional)

In a medium bowl mix together bread, water and cheese. Sauté green pepper, onion and celery in butter. Add to bread mixture. Add next 7 ingredients, stirring well. Place in small greased casserole. Bake at 350° for 30 minutes. May sprinkle with buttered bread crumbs prior to baking. Serves 4.

Elizabeth A. Thurston (Mrs. Clark W.)

HOT CROSSED TUNA CASSEROLE

2 (6½ ounces each) cans
  tuna, drained
1 (10 ounce) package frozen
  peas, thawed
1 cup grated sharp Cheddar
  cheese
1 cup chopped celery
½ cup bread crumbs
¼ cup chopped onion

¼ teaspoon salt
⅛ teaspoon pepper
1 cup mayonnaise
1 (8 ounce) can crescent
  rolls
2 tablespoons margarine,
  melted
  Sesame seeds

Combine first 9 ingredients. Spoon into 10" x 6" baking dish. Separate rolls into 2 rectangles; press perforations to seal. Cut dough into four long and eight short strips; place strips over casserole to form lattice design. Brush lightly with melted margarine and sprinkle with sesame seeds. Bake at 350° for 35 to 40 minutes, until crust is golden brown. Serve with Cool Cucumber Sauce. Serves 6 to 8.

COOL CUCUMBER SAUCE

½ cup mayonnaise
½ cup sour cream
½ cup chopped cucumbers
1 tablespoon chopped chives

1 teaspoon chopped parsley
¼ teaspoon salt
¼ teaspoon dill weed

Mix all ingredients well. Chill.

Paula W. Flaherty (Mrs. Thomas V.)

TUNA BURGERS

1 (7 ounce) can tuna,
   drained
½ cup chopped celery
½ cup bread crumbs

2 tablespoons minced onion
⅓ cup mayonnaise
1 teaspoon lemon juice
2 tablespoons chili sauce

Combine first four ingredients. Blend next three ingredients; stir into tuna mixture. Form into three patties. Fry in lightly greased skillet over medium heat for 4 minutes on each side. Serve on hamburger buns. Serves 3.

Julie Coburn

SEA CHICKEN CASSEROLE

¼ cup butter, melted
¼ cup flour
½ teaspoon salt
2 cups milk
1 (8 ounce) package noodles,
   cooked and drained
1 (16 ounce) can asparagus
   spears, drained
1 (7 ounce) can tuna, drained

1 (3 ounce) can sliced
   mushrooms, drained
¼ cup pimentos, drained
   and chopped
2 tablespoons chopped
   parsley
¾ cup grated Parmesan
   cheese, divided

Combine butter, salt and flour in medium saucepan. Slowly stir in milk, cooking until smooth and thickened. Set aside. In a greased 8" square baking dish layer noodles. Place asparagus over noodles. Combine next 4 ingredients and ½ cup cheese. Spoon over asparagus. Cover with white sauce. Sprinkle with remaining cheese. Bake at 350° for 15 minutes. Serves 6.

Connie Morton McKee

TUNA FRITTATA

2 (6½ ounces each) cans
   tuna
½ cup chopped onion
¼ cup chopped green
   pepper
1 clove garlic, minced
1 large eggplant, pared
   and cubed
1 (16 ounce) can tomatoes
1 (15 ounce) can tomato
   sauce

1 bay leaf
1 teaspoon basil
1 teaspoon sugar
½ teaspoon oregano
1 teaspoon lemon juice
   Salt to taste
1 (8 ounce) package
   macaroni, cooked
   Grated Parmesan cheese

Drain 2 tablespoons oil from tuna and heat in large skillet. Add onion, green pepper and garlic. Cook over medium heat until tender. Add next 9 ingredients. Simmer covered for 30 minutes. Stir in tuna and macaroni. Pour into 2 quart casserole. Bake uncovered at 375° for 30 minutes. Serve sprinkled with Parmesan cheese. Serves 6.

Mary Beth Ericson (Mrs. E. Dixon)

TUNA MOUSSE

2 envelopes unflavored
   gelatin
½ cup cold water
1 cup mayonnaise
1 (13 ounce) can chunk
   light tuna
½ cup diced celery
¼ cup green olives, chopped

1 tablespoon minced onion
2 tablespoons lemon juice
1½ teaspoons horseradish
¼ teaspoon salt
¼ teaspoon paprika
1 cup heavy cream,
   whipped

Soften gelatin in cold water. Dissolve over boiling water in top of a double boiler. Remove from heat. Stir in mayonnaise. Add all other ingredients except cream. Gently fold in whipped cream. Spoon into a 10" x 6" x 1½" casserole. Chill until firm, at least 4 hours. Serves 8 to 10.

Ann Hlusko (Mrs. G. Paul)

84

OLD STONE CHURCH

The Lewisburg Presbyterian Church was organized in 1783 and its first building was constructed of logs. It stood about a mile northeast of the present church location. The log building was later destroyed by fire.

The present building was erected in 1796, built of gray native limestone, with masonry work being done by Christopher Foglesong and John Brown. The Reverend Benjamin Grigsby was pastor of the Lewisburg congregation during the construction of "the Cathedral of Greenbrier". The building was erected on land donated by Colonel John Stuart who, along with his wife, gave most of the funds required to build the church.

Over the entrance of the church Colonel Stuart had an inscription chiseled into one of the stones which reads:

THIS BUILDING WAS ERECTED IN THE YEAR 1796 AT THE EXPENCE OF A FEW INHABITANTS OF THIS LAND TO COMMEMORATE THEIR AFFECTION & ESTEEM FOR THE HOLY GOSPEL OF JESUS CHRIST. READER IF YOU ARE INCLINED TO APPLAUD THEIR VIRTUES GIVE GOD THE GLORY.

The church is a fine example of Colonial vernacular architecture, rectangular, two-stories tall. The hipped roof, which no doubt was originally covered with riven wood shingles, is capped with an elegant open cupola belfry. Originally the building was about 44 feet square but in 1830 was extended to a rectangular shape 75 x 44 feet. The entrance was moved from the east to the west and some windows removed. A balcony around three sides was constructed to accommodate slaves of the worshippers. The churchyard cemetery was the first burial ground west of the mountains.

The building has been in continuous use now for almost two hundred years, the oldest church building in West Virginia in continuous use. Known for over a century as the Lewisburg Presbyterian Church, tradition is that the church was first called "Old Stone Church" in a descriptive phrase by the donors of a communion service in 1901.

Photo by Governor's Office of E.C.D.

MEATS AND MARINADES

Delectable Mountains

STUFFED TENDERLOIN

3 to 3½ pounds whole beef
    tenderloin
½ cup chopped onion
¼ pound fresh mushrooms,
    sliced

¼ cup margarine
1½ cups soft bread crumbs
½ cup diced celery
    Dash of salt and pepper
2 or 3 bacon slices

Split and flatten beef. Lightly sauté onion and mushrooms in margarine 3 to 4 minutes. Add bread crumbs, celery, and enough hot water to moisten. Season with salt and pepper. Spread stuffing over one-half of meat. Bring other side over and seam with toothpicks. Place bacon strips on top. Bake at 350° for 1 hour. Serves 6.

Karen W. Gage (Mrs. Charles Q.)

CHARCOAL GRILLED TENDERLOIN

3 to 4 pound whole beef
    tenderloin

2 cloves garlic, minced
    Cooking oil

Rub tenderloin with oil and garlic. Cook on prepared charcoal grill until desired doneness. Turn 2 to 3 times during cooking. Will take 30 to 45 minutes. Do not cook on a too hot grill. Slice and serve immediately. Serve with Bernaise sauce, if desired. May also be sliced very thin and served at a cocktail party on bread with hot mustard or horseradish sauce. Serves 8.

Sara Z. Hoblitzell (Mrs. John R.)

INDIVIDUAL BEEF WELLINGTONS

DUXELLES

4 tablespoons butter
1 pound mushrooms,
  minced
4 shallots, minced

1 (4¾ ounce) can liver paste
3 tablespoons fresh parsley,
  minced

Melt butter in medium-hot skillet. Add mushrooms and shallots. Cook, stirring frequently, until moisture evaporates and mixture is soft and well cooked. Remove from heat. Cool. Stir in fresh parsley. Stir in 1 tablespoon liver paste. (Paste may be used according to taste.) Set aside. Duxelles may be prepared the day before and refrigerated.

PASTRY AND FILETS

1 (17¼ ounce) package
  Pepperidge Farm
  frozen puff pastry
  (2 prerolled sheets)
1 egg yolk

8 (6 ounce) filets or one 3 to
  4 pound whole tender-
  loin, sliced into 8
  individual filets

Thaw pastry following package directions. Roll each piece lightly. Cut each sheet into four 6″ to 8″ squares. Sauté filets in skillet on medium heat on both sides until lightly browned and still rare on inside. Set aside.

ASSEMBLY

Divide duxelle mixture evenly into 8 portions. Spread each portion on one of 8 pastry pieces. Center filet on top of duxelles. Fold up corners of pastry. Pinch seams together, encasing duxelles and filet in pastry. Use a little water if necessary to "glue" seams together. Place on ungreased cookie sheet. Brush with egg yolk. Bake at 400° for 20 minutes for medium rare meat. Serve immediately. Serve with a red wine sauce if desired. May be assembled earlier in day and refrigerated until shortly before ready to bake. Bring to room temperature before baking. Serves 8.

Sara Z. Hoblitzell (Mrs. John R.)

FOOLPROOF ROAST BEEF

1 beef eye of round

Salt and freshly ground
  pepper

Preheat oven to 500°. Salt and pepper roast. Place on rack in shallow pan. Bake 4 to 5 minutes per pound. Turn off heat, but do not open oven door. Leave roast in oven for 1½ hours for a 4 pound roast or under. Leave in 2 hours for a larger roast. This will be medium rare. Can be reheated at 450° until hot. Other cuts of beef may be prepared using this cooking method. Serves 4 or more.

Mary Ann C. Hardison (Mrs. Richard E.)

ROAST BEEF

3 to 5 pound chuck roast
   (or sirloin tip)
2 cloves garlic, minced

Pepper
Water

Season meat with garlic and pepper. Do not use any salt. Place on rack in small pan. Pour water below rack. Roast in 350° oven for 30 minutes. Lower heat to 150° and roast 8 to 10 hours. Will be rare on inside and well done toward ends. If using a small roast, start with frozen roast or cook only 6 to 8 hours. Serves 6 to 8.

Nancy S. Dodson (Mrs. Raymond G.)

BRACIOLA

2 pounds boneless round
   steak, ¼″ thick
½ cup bread crumbs
½ cup Parmesan cheese
1 clove garlic, minced

1 egg, beaten
¼ teaspoon pepper
2 hard boiled eggs, sieved
2 cups meatless spaghetti
   sauce

Mix together bread crumbs, cheese, garlic, egg, pepper and sieved eggs. Spread over steak. Roll up meat and tie at 1″ intervals. Spread 1 cup spaghetti sauce in bottom of baking pan slightly larger than meat roll. Place meat on sauce and cover with remaining sauce. Cover and bake at 350° for 2 to 3 hours, or until fork tender. Serve on top of spaghetti. Serves 6.

Don Piper

MARINATED FLANK STEAK

½ cup soy sauce
1 garlic clove, minced
2 tablespoons brown sugar
½ teaspoon ginger

2 tablespoons Worcester-
   shire sauce
1 tablespoon lemon juice
1½ to 2 pound flank steak

Combine first 6 ingredients. Mix well. Pour mixture over steak. Refrigerate 6 to 24 hours, turning occasionally. Grill 5 minutes on each side or broil in oven 3 minutes on one side and 5 minutes on the other side. Slice thinly on diagonal across the grain. Serves 4 to 6.

Ann Dudley U. Belknap (Mrs. John)

ORIENTAL FLANK STEAK

1½ to 2 pound flank steak
½ to 1 teaspoon ground
   ginger
1 (12 ounce) can unsweet-
   ened pineapple juice

2 tablespoons Worcester-
   shire sauce
¼ teaspoon garlic powder
¼ cup soy sauce
1 (4 ounce) can mushroom
   pieces

Puncture flank steak on both sides with fork. Sprinkle both sides generously with ginger, rubbing into meat. Combine next 4 ingredients for marinade. Pour over steak. Marinate 8 to 24 hours in refrigerator. Turn occasionally. Charcoal or broil in oven 4 to 5 minutes on each side. Slice in thin strips diagonally across the grain. Add mushrooms to marinade. Heat. Serve as sauce with steak and wild rice. Serves 4.

Mary Ann C. Hardison (Mrs. Richard E.)

MAMA LOU'S BEEF ROAST SAUERBRATEN

4 pound piece top sirloin
   of beef, boned and
   rolled
2 teaspoons salt
¼ teaspoon pepper
2 cups water
2 cups vinegar
2 large onions, sliced
3 bay leaves

6 celery tops
12 peppercorns
1 large carrot, sliced
¼ teaspoon thyme
4 cloves
   Flour
2 tablespoons cooking oil
⅓ cup seedless raisins
5 gingersnaps, crushed

Rub beef with salt and pepper. Place in a large bowl with next 9 ingredients. Cover with plastic wrap. Marinate in refrigerator for 3 days. Turn about twice a day. When ready to cook, dust meat with seasoned flour, made by adding a little salt and pepper to the flour. Sear quickly in cooking oil. Add marinade and vegetables. Cover and simmer slowly for 3 hours until tender. Add more water while cooking if needed. Remove to hot platter and keep warm in a 200° oven. Strain the stock. Add raisins that have been plumped in boiling water and gingersnaps. Stir constantly until the stock is smooth and thickened. Season to taste. Pour part of the gravy over the meat. Serve the remaining gravy separately. Serves 8.

Elizabeth M. Hamrick (Mrs. C. Page, III)

GERMAN POT ROAST

3 pound pot or rump roast
Salt and pepper to taste
¼ cup flour
1 teaspoon celery salt
1 teaspoon thyme
1 tablespoon parsley
2 tablespoons cooking oil

2 cups sliced onion
1 clove garlic, minced
2 cups hot beef broth
3 tablespoons tomato paste
2 tablespoons sugar
2 tablespoons red wine
   vinegar

Combine seasonings and flour. Rub roast with this mixture. Heat oil in ovenproof casserole. Brown beef. Add onions and garlic, stirring until soft. Add remaining ingredients. Bake covered at 325° until tender, about 3 hours or on top of the stove on low heat. Good served with Sweet and Sour Cabbage (in *Mountain Measures*) or sauerkraut, mashed potatoes and pumpernickel bread.

Barbara H. Slack (Mrs. John M., III)

BAR'B'QUED BEEF

5 pound beef brisket
2 tablespoons liquid smoke
½ to 1 teaspoon seasoned
   salt
½ teaspoon celery powder
½ teaspoon garlic powder
1 small onion, chopped

2 tablespoons Worcester-
   shire sauce
1½ tablespoons brown sugar
½ teaspoon dry mustard
1 cup ketchup
1 cup beef broth
1 teaspoon celery seed
3 tablespoons butter

Rub brisket with liquid smoke. Sprinkle with seasoned salt, celery powder, garlic powder and chopped onion. Wrap tightly in foil and place in glass baking dish. Refrigerate overnight. Bake wrapped brisket at 250° for 5 hours. Combine remaining ingredients in saucepan over medium heat and simmer 10 minutes to make a sauce. Open foil, coat brisket with sauce and bake uncovered at 325° for 1 hour. Cool and slice to serve. May also be sliced very thin and served on hard rolls. Serves 10 to 12.

Ellen M. Fredrickson (Mrs. Robert A.)

DAUBE ROAST

3 pound chuck roast
   Pepper to taste
½ cup soy sauce
1 cup vinegar

1 cup water
10 to 12 cloves
2 onions, quartered
6 cloves garlic, halved

Pepper roast and brown on high in electric skillet. Combine remaining ingredients. Add to roast. Cover and simmer for 1½ hours. Serves 6.

Katherine S. Cooper (Mrs. James T.)

MAMA LOU'S ROULADEN

6 slices ⅛" thick round
   steak, 6" to 8" square
   in size
   Brown mustard
1 medium kosher dill
   pickle, chopped
2 medium onions, chopped

¼ teaspoon salt
¼ teaspoon pepper
6 slices bacon
3 tablespoons cooking oil
1 cup water
2 teaspoons flour
   Dash of garlic powder

Thickly spread each slice of steak with mustard. Sprinkle onions and pickle on top of mustard. Season with salt and pepper. Place 1 strip of bacon on top of each piece of meat and roll meat up jelly roll fashion. Secure with string. Brown rolls in oil in a large skillet over medium heat. Add ½ cup water, reduce heat to low, cover and simmer 1 hour or until meat is tender. Remove meat to warm platter and remove string. Make a thin paste with 2 teaspoons flour and remaining ½ cup water. Stir into pan juices, cooking until thickened. Add garlic powder. Serve over meat. Serve with mashed potatoes or spaetzel. Serves 6.

Elizabeth M. Hamrick (Mrs. C. Page, III)

BEEF, SNOW PEAS AND BEAN SPROUT SALAD

2 pound flank steak
¼ cup lemon juice
3 tablespoons soy sauce
2 tablespoons cooking oil
1 tablespoon sesame oil

2 slices fresh ginger root
½ teaspoon salt
½ pound snow peas
½ pound mung bean sprouts

Lightly score flank steak diagonally across the grain on both sides. Broil steak 2" from heat for 3 to 4 minutes on each side for rare meat. Transfer to a cutting board. Let rest for 10 minutes. Slice meat across the grain in ¼" slices. In a large bowl, combine next 4 ingredients. Add 2 slices ginger root, each the size of a quarter, peeled and shredded fine. Add salt and meat and mix well. Trim and remove strings from snow peas. Blanch in boiling, salted water for 30 seconds. Drain. Refresh the peas under cold water. Pat dry. Rinse bean sprouts under cold, running water. Drain well. Add snow peas and sprouts to meat. Toss until well coated. Serve the salad at room temperature. Serves 6.

Patricia S. Bibbee (Mrs. Charles C.)

FIERY CHINESE BEEF

1 pound round steak	6 ounces sliced mushrooms
⅓ cup soy sauce	1 cup pea pods
3 tablespoons sherry	¼ cup slivered almonds or
1 garlic clove, chopped	water chestnuts
3 tablespoons cooking oil	½ teaspoon ground ginger
1 bunch scallions, chopped	½ to 1 teaspoon hot pepper
2 cups thinly sliced carrots	flakes
1½ cups thinly sliced celery	

Slice beef into long, paper thin strips. This is easier to do when the beef is partially frozen. Mix next 3 ingredients in a bowl. Add beef. Marinate at least 1 hour at room temperature. In a wok or large skillet, heat oil until it sizzles. Add beef and stir fry until brown, about 3 to 4 minutes. Add marinade from beef and all remaining ingredients. Stir fry until vegetables are crisp tender, about 5 to 6 minutes. Add pepper flakes a little at a time as they are very hot. Serves 4.

Marta D. MacCallum (Mrs. Daniel)

KOREAN BULGOGI

1 tablespoon sugar	½ teaspoon pepper
2 teaspoons sesame oil	2 cloves garlic, crushed
2 green onions, chopped	1½ pounds lean, tender beef,
5 tablespoons soy sauce	thinly sliced

Combine first 6 ingredients, mixing well. Add beef, stirring well. Let stand 1 hour or longer. Broil to taste. Charcoal if possible. Serve hot with rice. Serves 4 to 6.

Judy M. Kim (Mrs. C. William)

BARBECUE FOR AN ARMY

5 pounds rump roast   5 pounds pork roast

Cook roasts for about 6 hours at 325° until done. May need to cover beef roast with aluminum foil to keep outside from becoming crisp. Drain fat from roasts and shred meat.

SAUCE

½ cup margarine, melted   4 teaspoons salt
4 medium onions, chopped   8 cups boiling water
8 cloves garlic   4 cups ketchup
1 cup Worcestershire sauce   4 teaspoons dry mustard
1 cup vinegar   8 teaspoons chili powder
4 dashes red pepper

In a large kettle, sauté onion and garlic in margarine until translucent. Add remaining ingredients. Bring to a boil. Add shredded meat. Reduce heat and cook to desired consistency. Serve on buns or rice. Makes approximately 35 servings on buns, or 16 to 18 on rice. Can freeze.

Mary Lee W. Lilly (Mrs. J.K., III)

MARINATED SHORT RIBS

5 pounds beef short ribs   ½ teaspoon dried basil
1½ cups red wine   2 tablespoons prepared
2 tablespoons browning   mustard
   sauce   2 cloves garlic, crushed
2 teaspoons salt   2 bay leaves

Place ribs in a shallow container. Mix remaining ingredients. Pour over ribs. Cover. Refrigerate 2 hours. Broil or grill over moderate heat for 1 hour, turning and brushing with marinade occasionally. Serves 4 to 6.

Elizabeth Y. Revercomb (Mrs. Paul H.)

CARNE CON CHILES

1 large round steak, cut in   1 (1 pound, 12 ounce) can
   1″ cubes   French style green
½ small onion, chopped   beans
1 to 2 (4 ounces each) cans   1 (16 ounce) can tomato
   chopped jalapeno   sauce
   peppers   Pepper to taste
1 (32 ounce) can tomatoes,   Garlic salt to taste
   peeled and diced

MEATS AND MARINADES 93

Trim round steak. Brown trimmed fat in a skillet until crisp. Remove and discard. Add meat. Brown until all juices are gone. Stir in onion and jalapeno peppers. Add remaining ingredients. Simmer for 1 hour, stirring occasionally. Serve with flour tortillas and refried beans. Serves 4 to 6.

Mary Lee W. Lilly (Mrs. J.K., III)

CARBONNADE A LA FLAMANDE
(Flemish Beef in Beer)

2½ pounds boneless chuck
    roast
3 to 4 tablespoons flour
½ teaspoon each: salt and
    pepper
½ pound lean bacon, cut in
    ½" pieces
5 tablespoons butter,
    divided
4 onions, thinly sliced

2 tablespoons bacon fat
2 garlic cloves, minced
2 (12 ounces each) bottles
    dark beer
4 teaspoons Dijon mustard
1 teaspoon dark brown
    sugar
1 tablespoon cider vinegar
2 bay leaves, crumbled
¼ teaspoon thyme

Cut meat across grain in ¼" thick slices. Cut slices into 3" by 1" strips. Dredge beef in flour seasoned with salt and pepper. In large, heavy skillet, cook bacon over medium heat, until cooked but not crisp. Transfer bacon with slotted spoon to paper towel to drain. Leave ¼ cup bacon fat in skillet. Reserve remaining fat. Add 2 tablespoons butter and onions to skillet. Cook, stirring, until onions are golden. Transfer onions to a bowl, using slotted spoon. Add remaining 3 tablespoons butter and 2 tablespoons bacon fat. Increase heat to high. Sear beef in batches, about 30 seconds on each side. When browned, transfer beef to bowl using tongs. Reduce heat to medium. Add garlic. Cook, stirring for 1 minute. Add remaining ingredients. Bring to a boil, stirring. Arrange ⅓ beef in 4 quart casserole. Cover with ½ the onion and ½ the bacon. Add ½ the remaining beef. Cover with remaining onions and bacon. Top with remaining beef. Pour sauce over top. Bake covered at 350° for 2 hours. Season with salt and pepper to taste. Serve with boiled potatoes. Serves 6.

Susan C. Harpold (Mrs. Robert R., Jr.)

VERSATILE BEEF STROGANOFF

2 pounds round steak
1 teaspoon salt
Dash of pepper
2 tablespoons cooking oil
1 onion, chopped
1 cup sour cream
1 cup grated American
  cheese

½ cup dry red wine
1 clove garlic, minced
½ teaspoon each: thyme,
  basil and marjoram
1 (10½ ounce) can cream of
  mushroom soup
1 (4 ounce) can mushrooms
  (optional)

Cut the beef into 1" cubes. Season with salt and pepper. In large skillet, brown meat in oil. Add onions and cook 2 to 3 minutes. Transfer the meat and onions to a large casserole. Add next 5 ingredients. Cover. Bake at 325° for 2 hours or until the meat is tender. Add soup and mushrooms. Mix and bake 20 minutes longer. Delicious used as a crepe filling or served over noodles.

Constance L. Hillenbrand (Mrs. Edward F., III)

BEEF BURGUNDY

¼ pound salt pork, diced
2 pounds lean beef, cut in
  2" cubes
1 teaspoon salt
  Freshly ground pepper
2 tablespoons flour
1½ cups dry red wine
1½ cups water

½ teaspoon thyme
1 bay leaf
1 garlic clove, crushed
½ pound mushrooms, thinly
  sliced
1 pound small onions
3 carrots, thinly sliced

Fry salt pork until crisp. Remove from pan and reserve drippings. In 2 tablespoons of drippings, brown beef slowly, 20 to 40 minutes. Remove beef. Sprinkle with salt, pepper and flour and place in a 2½ quart ovenproof casserole. Add salt pork. To the frying pan add wine, water, thyme, bay leaf and garlic. Bring to a boil. Pour over meat. Cover and cook at 350° for 2 hours. Skim off fat. Sauté onions and mushrooms in 2 tablespoons salt pork fat. Add to beef. Cook for 30 minutes. Add fresh carrots. Cook 10 minutes or until carrots are tender. Serve over rice. Serves 4 to 6.

Marta D. MacCallum (Mrs. Daniel)

BEEF RAGOUT

⅔ cup flour
1 teaspoon salt
½ teaspoon pepper
3 pounds round steak or boneless chuck, cut in 1" cubes
⅓ cup cooking oil
1 cup chopped onion
1 cup chopped green pepper
½ cup chopped celery
2 cloves garlic, crushed
1 (14½ ounce) can beef bouillon
1 (12 ounce) can beer
1 (6 ounce) can tomato paste
1 (14½ ounce) can tomatoes
2 teaspoons paprika
2 teaspoons Worcestershire sauce
1 tablespoon chopped parsley

Place flour, salt, pepper and beef cubes in bag. Shake to coat beef. Reserve excess flour. Brown meat in oil in large skillet. Remove meat and sauté onion, peppers and celery in drippings. Remove vegetables. Stir remaining flour into drippings. Slowly add bouillon, cooking until blended. Place all ingredients in large, ovenproof casserole. Bake covered at 325° for 2 hours. Serve with rice or noodles. Serves 6 to 8.

Donna L. Dean (Mrs. Rodney D.)

CHUCKWAGON STEW

2 pounds beef chuck, cut in 1½" cubes
2 tablespoons flour
2 tablespoons cooking oil
1½ teaspoons salt
1 teaspoon chili powder
½ teaspoon pepper
¼ teaspoon thyme
1 bay leaf
2 tomatoes, quartered
1 green pepper, chopped
1 (10½ ounce) can consommé
1 cup water
6 small potatoes, peeled and halved
6 carrots, halved
6 small whole onions
3 large celery stalks, chopped
2 cloves garlic, crushed
1 (8 ounce) can tomato sauce

Dust beef with flour. Brown in oil in Dutch oven. Add next nine ingredients. Cover and simmer over low heat 2 hours. Add potatoes, carrots, onions, celery and garlic. Cook 45 minutes. Add tomato sauce. Cook an additional 15 minutes. Serves 6 to 8.

Caroline D. Dlugosz (Mrs. James)

EASY ALL DAY STEW

2 pounds boneless chuck, cut in 1" cubes	2 cups tomato juice
4 stalks celery, cut in 1½" pieces	2 onions, quartered
	1 teaspoon salt
6 potatoes, peeled and halved	Pepper to taste
	1 bay leaf
6 carrots, halved	4 teaspoons tapioca (minute)

Place all ingredients in Dutch oven or large casserole dish. Bake covered at 250° for 5 hours. Add more juice if necessary the last hour of baking. Serves 4 to 6.

Kay A. Smith (Mrs. William W.)

DILL SAUCED MEAT LOAF

1½ pounds ground beef	1 cup ketchup
½ cup chopped onion	½ cup water
½ cup soft bread crumbs	4 tablespoons sugar
½ cup dill pickle juice	2 teaspoons Worcestershire sauce
1 egg	
1 teaspoon salt	1 cup chopped dill pickle
½ teaspoon pepper	

Combine first 7 ingredients. Shape into a loaf and place in a shallow baking dish. Combine remaining ingredients and pour over meat. Bake at 350° for 1¼ to 1½ hours, basting twice. Serves 6.

Diane S. Doty (Mrs. Steven)

CHEESE MEAT ROLL

1½ pounds ground beef	½ cup chopped onion
¾ cup cracker crumbs	2 (8 ounces each) cans tomato sauce
1 teaspoon salt	
⅛ teaspoon pepper	2 cups shredded cheese (Cheddar or Mozzarella)
1 teaspoon oregano	
1 egg	

Combine the first 7 ingredients and ⅓ cup tomato sauce. Mix well. Shape into a flat 10" x 12" rectangle on waxed paper. Sprinkle cheese evenly over meat mixture. Roll up and seal ends. Bake in a shallow pan at 350° for 1 hour. Drain excess fat. Pour remaining sauce over roll. Bake 15 minutes. Serves 8.

Mary T. Karr (Mrs. George)

BEEF 'N' BEANS

½ pound cooked bacon,
    crumbled
1 pound ground beef
1 (15½ ounce) can butter
    beans, rinsed
1 (15½ ounce) can kidney
    beans, rinsed

1 (15½ ounce) can baked
    beans
1 large onion, diced
1 cup brown sugar
4 tablespoons vinegar
1 cup ketchup

Brown beef in skillet, remove from heat and drain off fat. Combine all ingredients in a large, ovenproof casserole. Bake at 350° for 45 minutes to 1 hour, until bubbly. Serves 10 to 12.

Barbara W. Pressman (Mrs. Marty)

DESPERATION DELIGHT DINNER

1 pound lean ground beef
1 medium onion, chopped
1 clove garlic, chopped fine
2 tablespoons cooking oil
1 (10 ounce) package frozen
    chopped spinach
1 (16 ounce) jar spaghetti
    sauce with mushrooms
1 (8 ounce) can tomato
    sauce

1 (6 ounce) can tomato
    paste
½ teaspoon salt
1 (7 ounce) package shell
    macaroni, cooked
1 cup shredded sharp
    American cheese
½ cup soft bread crumbs
2 eggs, beaten
¼ cup cooking oil

Brown first 3 ingredients in 2 tablespoons oil. Set aside. Cook spinach according to package. Drain, reserving liquid. Add enough water to spinach liquid to make 1 cup. Combine liquid with next four ingredients. Stir into meat mixture. Combine spinach, macaroni and last 4 ingredients. Spread spinach mixture in a 9″ x 13″ casserole. Top with meat mixture. Bake at 350° for 30 minutes or until very hot. Let stand 5 to 10 minutes before serving. Can be prepared ahead. Refrigerate until ready to bake. Serves 6.

Susanne F. Berger (Mrs. Bruce W.)

EGGPLANT PARMESAN

1 medium eggplant	2 cups homemade or 1 (16
1 teaspoon salt	ounce) jar spaghetti
½ cup flour	sauce
½ cup margarine	8 ounces grated Mozzarella
1 pound ground chuck	cheese
	¼ cup Parmesan cheese

Peel and thinly slice eggplant. Place salt and flour in a plastic bag. Add eggplant and shake well to coat. Melt margarine in a large skillet. Brown eggplant on both sides. Remove from pan. Add ground chuck and brown. Drain. Place eggplant in a 9" x 13" pan. Layer with meat, spaghetti sauce, Mozzarella and Parmesan. Bake at 350° uncovered for 30 minutes. Serves 6.

Elizabeth A. Thurston (Mrs. Clark W.)

ENCHILADA CASSEROLE

1½ pounds ground beef	2 (10 ounces each) packages
1 medium onion, chopped	frozen chopped spinach,
¾ cup water	thawed
1 (1.4 ounce) package taco	3 cups shredded cheese
mix	1 cup diced ham
½ cup taco sauce	1 cup sour cream
10 corn tortillas	

Brown meat and onion. Add water and taco mix. Simmer 10 minutes. Set aside. Put ¼ cup taco sauce in a 9" x 13" casserole dish. Dip tortillas in remaining sauce. Overlap five in bottom of dish. Stir half of spinach into half of beef mixture. Place over tortillas. Sprinkle half of cheese over meat. Layer remainder of tortillas, rest of beef mix, rest of sauce, ham, sour cream and spinach. Top with remaining cheese. Bake at 350° for 50 minutes; 25 minutes covered, then 25 minutes uncovered. Can be prepared and frozen for several weeks. Serves 5 to 6.

Anne P. Wainstein

POTATO PATCH CASSEROLE

MEAT BALLS

1 pound ground beef	1 teaspoon salt
½ cup chopped onion	¼ teaspoon pepper
1 egg, beaten	¼ teaspoon celery salt
¼ cup bread crumbs	3 tablespoons cooking oil

Combine all ingredients except oil. Mix well. Shape into 10 large or 24 small meat balls. Brown in oil. Arrange meat balls in greased, shallow 3 quart casserole.

POTATOES AND CHEESE SAUCE

5 cups sliced potatoes	Dash of pepper
1 (10 ounce) package frozen peas and carrots, thawed	1½ cups milk
	1 package white sauce mix
1 teaspoon salt	½ pound processed cheese, cubed

Combine first 4 ingredients and place over meat balls. Gradually add milk to white sauce mix in a medium saucepan. Bring to a boil, stirring constantly. Stir in cheese and heat until melted. Pour over meat balls and potatoes. Bake at 375° for 45 minutes or until potatoes are done. Serves 6.

Kay J. Morgan (Mrs. Frederick M.)

CAVATINI

1½ pounds ground chuck	2 to 2½ cups water
½ pound hot sausage	3 (6 ounces each) cans tomato paste
1 medium onion, chopped	
2 cloves garlic, minced	8 to 12 ounces spiral noodles
½ pound mushrooms, sliced	8 ounces Mozzarella cheese
1 whole pepperoni stick, sliced	

Brown meat and sausage in large skillet. Pour off fat. Add onion and garlic. Cook for 2 to 3 minutes. Add mushrooms and pepperoni. Add tomato paste and water to make a thick sauce. Cook 20 minutes on low heat. Cook noodles according to package directions. Drain. Place noodles in a large serving bowl. Just before serving, tear cheese into pieces and push down into sauce until melted. Pour over noodles. Serve at once. Serves 6.

Suzanne H. Sims (Mrs. James)

LASAGNA

1½ pounds ground chuck
1 pound hot bulk sausage
1 large onion, finely
   chopped
3 cloves garlic, finely
   chopped
2 (12 ounces each) cans
   tomato paste

4 cups water
1 pound Lasagna noodles
1 (16 ounce) carton small
   curd cottage cheese
1 pound Mozzarella cheese
   Parmesan cheese

Brown beef and sausage together in large skillet. Pour off fat. Add onion and garlic and cook 3 to 5 minutes. Add tomato paste and water. Stir until well blended. Reduce heat and simmer 30 minutes. Cool slightly. Grease a 15½" x 10½" x 2½" pan. Cook lasagna according to package. Layer in order: drained noodles, meat sauce, cottage cheese, and Mozzarella cheese. Repeat layers ending with Mozzarella cheese. Sprinkle top with Parmesan cheese. Can be frozen at this point. Bake at 350° for 20 to 25 minutes. If frozen, remove from freezer, thaw and then cook. Serves 8.

Suzanne H. Sims (Mrs. James)

UPSIDE DOWN PIZZA

2 pounds ground chuck
1 onion, chopped
1 green pepper, chopped
1 (15 ounce) can tomato
   sauce
½ cup water
½ teaspoon oregano
½ teaspoon garlic powder

¼ teaspoon pepper
¼ teaspoon salt
1 (1½ ounce) package
   spaghetti sauce mix
2 packages pepperoni,
   sliced
1 (8 ounce) package sliced
   Mozzarella cheese

Sauté ground chuck, onion, and pepper until done. Add tomato sauce, water, spices and spaghetti sauce mix. Simmer for 10 minutes. Pour into 9" x 13" pan. Place pepperoni on top. Place cheese slices on top of pepperoni.

CRUST

2 eggs
1 cup milk
1 tablespoon cooking oil

1 cup flour
1 cup Parmesan cheese

Beat eggs, milk, and oil for 2 minutes. Add flour. Beat 1 more minute. Pour on top of cheese slices. Cover with Parmesan cheese. Bake at 400° for 20 minutes. Serves 8 to 10.

Rise C. Boggs (Mrs. Charles A., III)

SPAGHETTI SAUCE

2 cloves garlic, chopped
2 onions, chopped
1 to 2 green peppers,
    chopped
1 tablespoon cooking oil
2 pounds ground beef
3 to 4 chopped canned
    tomatoes, plus some
    juice
1 (6 ounce) can tomato paste

1 (32 ounce) can tomato
    juice
1 teaspoon sugar
⅓ cup ketchup
1 teaspoon oregano
1 teaspoon thyme
1 teaspoon salt
1 teaspoon pepper
3 tablespoons chili powder

Sauté garlic, onion, and green pepper in oil. Remove from pan. Set aside. Brown ground beef. Drain. Combine all ingredients in large saucepan. Simmer 2½ to 3 hours. Serves 6.

Nina S. Hall (Mrs. Grant P., Jr.)

TACO SALAD

2 pounds ground beef
1 (1.25 ounce) package taco
    seasoning mix, divided
1 medium onion, chopped
4 to 5 tomatoes, coarsely
    chopped
1 (8 ounce) package grated
    Cheddar cheese

1 to 2 heads lettuce, torn
    into pieces
1 (16 ounce) bag Doritos,
    crushed
1 cup Thousand Island
    dressing
¾ cup mayonnaise
¼ cup ketchup
    Hot taco sauce, optional

Brown ground beef. Drain. Add ½ package taco seasoning mix. Set aside to cool. Combine next 5 ingredients in a large bowl. Gently mix in meat. Combine Thousand Island dressing, mayonnaise, ketchup and remaining taco seasoning in a bowl to make a dressing. Pour over salad and toss. Serve with taco sauce spooned over top if desired. Serves 10 to 12.

F.J. Wehrle

HOT DOG CHILI

1 medium onion, chopped
3 tablespoons cooking oil
1½ pounds ground chuck
1 teaspoon salt
½ teaspoon black pepper
1 (6 ounce) can tomato paste

1 (15 ounce) can tomato
  purée
1 cup water
2 teaspoons chili powder
Garlic powder to taste

Sauté onion in oil 2 to 3 minutes. Add ground chuck and brown. Drain fat from meat. Add remaining ingredients. Simmer for 30 minutes. Serve chili sauce on top of hot dogs. Top with creamy slaw.

Patricia W. Berry (Mrs. Bruce)

SALAMI

2 pounds extra lean ground
  beef
½ teaspoon salt
¼ teaspoon freshly ground
  black pepper
¼ teaspoon onion salt

1 tablespoon liquid smoke
2 tablespoons tender quick
  salt (found in feed and
  seed store)
2 tablespoons mustard seed

Mix all ingredients by hand. Divide into 3 balls. Shape each ball into 6″ roll, width of Ritz crackers. Wrap each in plastic wrap. Refrigerate for 24 hours. Unwrap. Bake at 300° for 1 hour. Cool completely. Serve on crackers. May be frozen and defrosted at later date. Serves 20.

Mary C. Foster (Mrs. Ward E.)

KEITH'S DELUXE CREAMED CHIPPED BEEF

¼ cup butter
1 (4 ounce) jar chipped beef
2 tablespoons finely minced
  onion
3 tablespoons flour
1 cup milk
1 cup sour cream

1 (4 ounce) can mushroom
  pieces
Pepper to taste
2 cups shredded American
  cheese
2 tablespoons finely minced
  parsley

Melt butter in heavy saucepan. Cut beef into strips. Add beef and onions to butter and sauté until onion is transparent. Blend in flour. Add milk, stirring constantly. Cook until sauce is smooth and thickened. Stir in remaining ingredients and heat through. Serve over toast points. Serves 4 to 6.

Nina A. Ratrie (Mrs. Turner R., Jr.)

REUBEN CASSEROLE

1 (27 ounce) can sauer-
    kraut, drained
4 tablespoons Thousand
    Island dressing
2 tablespoons butter,
    divided
¼ teaspoon caraway seeds

3 (3 ounces each) packages
    sliced corned beef,
    shredded
2 cups shredded Swiss
    cheese
2 cups Rye bread crumbs

Spread sauerkraut in a 9″ x 13″ baking dish. Spread with salad dressing. Dot with 1 tablespoon butter and caraway seeds. Top with corned beef and cheese. Spread crumbs on top. Dot with remaining butter. Bake at 425° for 30 minutes. Serves 4 to 6.

Melea H. Brotherton (Mrs. William T., III)

CHARCOAL BUTTERFLIED LEG OF LAMB

5 to 6 pound leg of lamb
1 cup olive oil
⅓ cup white wine
1 onion, sliced
    Pepper to taste

2 teaspoons lemon juice
1 tablespoon dried
    rosemary
1 teaspoon salt
2 garlic cloves, minced

BASTING MIXTURE

6 tablespoons butter,
    melted
    Salt and pepper to taste

1 teaspoon crushed dried
    rosemary

Have butcher bone, butterfly and flatten leg of lamb. Place lamb in a shallow glass dish. Combine next 8 ingredients. Pour over lamb. Marinate at least 2 hours turning once or twice. Drain meat and dry with paper towels. Combine basting mixture ingredients. Grill lamb over hot coals turning and basting often with basting mixture for 1 hour or until desired doneness. Serves 6 generously.

Kitty I. Morgan (Mrs. John W.)

CARAWAY MUSTARD LEG OF LAMB

6 to 8 pound leg of lamb
5 to 6 garlic cloves

3 tablespoons Dijon mustard
1 tablespoon caraway seeds

Make tiny slits all over the surface of the lamb and insert garlic. Cover lamb with mustard and sprinkle with caraway seeds. Place in shallow roasting pan. Roast at 325° for 18 to 20 minutes per pound for medium doneness. Serves 8 to 10.

Mary J. Payne (Mrs. Andrew A., III)

ROAST LEG OF LAMB

5 to 6 pound leg of lamb
1½ cups yogurt
1 teaspoon ginger
1 teaspoon chili powder
5 cloves garlic, minced

1 teaspoon salt
1 teaspoon saffron
½ cup ground almonds
¾ cup butter

Remove most of fat from the leg of lamb and prick the entire area with a fork. Combine rest of ingredients except the butter, and rub the mixture into the meat. Cover loosely and let stand overnight at room temperature. Place lamb in a roasting pan, and dot with butter. Roast uncovered at 350° for 15 minutes, reduce heat to 300° and roast for 4 hours or until tender. Baste frequently during the roasting period. Delicious when cooked on a rotating spit. Serves 8.

Diane C. Merrifield (Mrs. John V.)

BRAISED LAMB SHANKS

4 lamb shanks or shoulder roast
2 tablespoons cooking oil
1 cup chopped celery
1 cup chopped carrots
4 medium onions, peeled and halved
1 clove garlic, minced

4 teaspoons fresh rosemary or 1½ teaspoons dried
2 (10 ounces each) cans chicken broth
Salt and pepper to taste
4 potatoes, pared and quartered
¼ cup flour
½ cup water

Brown lamb shanks or shoulder roast in oil in a Dutch oven. Remove and set aside. Sauté carrots, celery, and onion. Remove and set aside. Brown garlic, stir in rosemary, chicken broth, salt and pepper. Add lamb shanks. Cover, lower heat and simmer 30 minutes. Add sautéed vegetables and potatoes. Cover and simmer an additional 30 minutes until vegetables are tender. Combine flour and water in a separate bowl until smooth. Stir into broth, cooking over medium heat until mixture thickens. Serves 4.

Helen Z. Chilton (Mrs. Robert M.)

CURRIED LAMB

3 shoulder lamb chops (1½ pounds)
1 apple, sliced
2 tablespoons butter
3 tablespoons chopped onion

1½ teaspoons curry powder
4 mushrooms, sliced
1 clove garlic, minced
1 tablespoon flour
⅓ cup plain yogurt
½ cup beef broth

Cut meat from chops into bite size pieces. In skillet sauté apples in butter until crisp tender. Remove apples and set aside. In drippings, brown lamb. Add onion, garlic, curry powder and mushrooms. Cook until onion is tender. Cover and simmer 15 minutes. Remove meat, onion and mushrooms from skillet. Combine flour and yogurt. Stir into drippings. Stir in beef broth and cook until thickened. Return apples and meat mixture to pan and heat through. Serve with raisin rice. May garnish with parsley. Serves 2.

RAISIN RICE

1 cup water
½ cup raisins
1 teaspoon butter

¼ teaspoon salt
1 cup quick cooking rice

Combine water, raisins, butter and salt. Bring to boil. Stir in rice. Cover and remove from heat. Let stand 5 minutes. Serve lamb over rice.

Martha J. Nunley (Mrs. David M.)

MOUSSAKA

1 to 1½ pounds eggplant
Flour
6 tablespoons margarine
½ cup chopped onion
1 pound lean lamb
  shoulder, ground
1 (8 ounce) can tomato
  sauce
½ cup dry white wine
¼ cup chopped parsley

¼ teaspoon pepper
½ teaspoon salt
½ teaspoon paprika
1 medium tomato, sliced
1 tablespoon flour
2 eggs, beaten
½ teaspoon salt
½ cup plain yogurt
2 tablespoons grated
  Parmesan cheese

Peel and slice eggplant into ¼" to ½" thick slices. Lightly coat slices with flour. Melt margarine, brown eggplant slices on both sides a few at a time. Drain on a paper towel. Sauté onion, add lamb and cook 5 minutes, until lamb loses color. Add tomato sauce and wine to lamb. Blend in parsley and seasonings. Simmer for several minutes. Put ⅓ of the eggplant slices on the bottom of a 2 quart casserole. Pour ½ of the lamb mixture over the eggplant. Cover with ½ of the remaining eggplant, then the rest of the lamb mixture. On top, alternate the rest of the eggplant with the tomato slices, overlapping them in a circle. If desired, moussaka can be made to this point early in the day, then refrigerated. When ready to bake, beat 1 tablespoon flour into the eggs until smooth. Blend in ½ teaspoon salt and yogurt. Spoon over top of casserole and sprinkle with cheese. Bake at 350° for approximately 45 minutes. Serves 4.

Jackie Blankenship (Mrs. Frank)

QUICK CURRIED LAMB

2 cups cooked lamb, cubed
3 tablespoons cooking oil
1 cup boiling water
½ teaspoon salt
¼ teaspoon cracked pepper
⅔ teaspoon curry powder

¼ cup chopped onion
¼ cup chopped celery
2 tablespoons chopped
   parsley
1 to 2 tablespoons flour

Brown lamb in oil. Add all other ingredients except flour. Simmer, covered, 20 minutes, stirring frequently. Thicken with flour. Cook and stir for 2 minutes. Serve over rice. Serves 4.

Lynn H. Goldsmith (Mrs. Robert F.)

CHILI LAMBURGERS

1 pound ground lamb
1 teaspoon salt
½ cup chili sauce

1 tablespoon vinegar
1 teaspoon soy sauce
8 onion rings

Combine lamb and salt. Shape into 4 round patties. Combine chili sauce, vinegar, and soy sauce. Brush patties with chili sauce mixture. Broil about 5 minutes 3 to 4 inches from coals. Turn. Brush with additional chili sauce. Top with onion rings. Cook 3 to 5 minutes longer or until lamb is done. Serves 4.

Marion S. Jones (Mrs. George W., III)

ONE DISH LAMB LOAF DINNER

4 large potatoes, peeled
   and sliced
6 carrots, sliced
3 onions, sliced
1 (10½ ounce) can cream of
   celery soup
2 pounds ground lamb
1 cup dry bread crumbs
¼ cup finely chopped onion

¼ cup finely chopped
   parsley
1 clove garlic, finely
   chopped
¼ teaspoon salt
1 teaspoon dry mustard
2 eggs, beaten
¼ teaspoon garlic powder
3 strips bacon

Place potatoes, carrots and onions on bottom of large casserole. Cover with soup. Mix to coat. Combine all other ingredients except bacon to make a loaf. Place on top of vegetables. Top loaf with bacon strips. Can be refrigerated until ready to bake. Bake, covered, at 350° for 1 hour. Uncover and bake 15 minutes longer. Serves 4 to 6.

Lynn H. Goldsmith (Mrs. Robert F.)

PHIL'S FAVORITE CROWN PORK DINNER

1 crown pork roast
   (allow 2 ribs per
   person)

Salt, pepper and garlic
   powder to taste
Seedless large bing
   cherries

Have butcher form 2 ribs per person into crown roast. Season with salt, pepper and garlic powder. Place in a shallow roasting pan. Cover tips of rib bones with foil and bake at 325° for 30 to 35 minutes per pound. Fill with dressing and roast an additional hour. Place cherries on rib tips to serve. Cut between ribs to serve and spoon out dressing.

DRESSING

½ cup butter
½ cup chopped celery
¼ cup chopped onion
½ cup chopped prunes

3 cups dried bread crumbs
1 cup peeled, diced apples
   Water and pork juices

Sauté celery, onion and prunes in butter in skillet. Add bread crumbs, apples and enough liquid to make stuffing semi-soft. Place stuffing in roast.

Carol C. Gaujot (Mrs. Philip D.)

ROAST PORK

3 to 5 pound pork roast
3 bay leaves, crumbled
3 cloves garlic, minced
½ teaspoon thyme
1¾ tablespoons chopped
   parsley

2 tablespoons paprika
½ teaspoon salt
3½ tablespoons minced onion
   Juice of 1 lemon
⅓ cup white wine

Score fat on pork roast. Place in roasting pan. Combine next 7 ingredients. Mix and rub over skin of pork. Roast meat in 350° oven for ½ hour. Remove fat from bottom of pan. Combine lemon juice and wine. Continue to roast for 1½ hours basting with wine mixture. Add additional liquid to pan if needed. Serves 6.

Katherine S. Cooper (Mrs. James T.)

GREASELESS PORK CHOPS

8 pork chops, ½" thick	3 tablespoons basil
Salt and pepper to taste	¼ cup lemon juice
¼ cup honey	⅔ cup red wine

Trim chops and place in single layer in baking dish. Salt and pepper top of chops. Cover with ½ the honey and ½ the basil. Turn chops. Salt and pepper other side. Cover with remaining honey and basil. Combine lemon juice and wine. Pour over chops. Bake uncovered at 350° for 1 hour, turning once. Serves 4 to 6.

Catherine Bradford

SWEET AND SOUR PORK CHOPS

4 pork chops, 1" thick	2 tablespoons molasses
2 tablespoons flour	2 tablespoons soy sauce
1 tablespoon oil	2 tablespoons vinegar
1 (3 ounce) can sliced	1 medium onion, sliced
mushrooms	1 green pepper, cut in strips
½ teaspoon salt	

Dredge chops in flour and brown in oil in large skillet. Drain mushrooms, reserving juice, adding water to equal 1 cup. Combine juice, molasses, salt, soy sauce and vinegar. Pour over chops. Add onion, green peppers and mushrooms to chops. Cover and simmer 45 to 60 minutes. Serve with rice. Serves 4.

Chris Smith (Mrs. E.H.)

PORK CHOPS WITH APPLES

2 (20 ounces each) cans	1 (8 ounce) bag seasoned
apple pie filling	stuffing mix
6 to 8 thick pork chops	1 cup water
	½ cup margarine, melted

Spread apple pie filling in bottom of a large, shallow greased casserole. Place pork chops on top of apples in a single layer. Make stuffing following package directions using water and margarine. Place a mound of stuffing on top of each chop. Cover casserole with foil. Bake at 350° for 1 hour, reduce heat to 325° and bake an additional hour. Uncover and bake ½ hour longer. Serves 6 to 8.

Jean G. Campe (Mrs. Robert H., Jr.)

BARBECUED SPARERIBS

4 pounds pork spareribs
1 lemon, thinly sliced
1 large onion, thinly sliced
1 cup ketchup
3 tablespoons Teriyaki
 sauce

1 teaspoon chili powder
1 tablespoon lemon juice
2 dashes Tabasco sauce
1 cup water
¼ teaspoon garlic powder

Place ribs, meaty side up, in shallow baking dish. Place onion and lemon slices over meat. Roast uncovered at 450° for 30 minutes. Combine remaining ingredients and pour over ribs. Reduce oven to 350° and bake 1½ hours. Baste meat several times during cooking.

Beth H. Lovett (Mrs. L. Loring)

PRESSURE COOKER BARBECUED SPARERIBS

3 to 4 pounds spareribs
2 tablespoons cooking oil
½ onion, chopped
2 tablespoons vinegar
2 tablespoons Worcester-
 shire sauce

4 tablespoons brown sugar
1 teaspoon paprika
½ teaspoon pepper
1 cup ketchup
½ cup water
½ teaspoon salt

Brown ribs in oil in a skillet. Remove. Add onions and sauté 2 to 3 minutes. Combine with remaining ingredients and place in pressure cooker. Cook under pressure 20 minutes. Remove ribs and brown under broiler if desired.

Victoria G. Hardy (Mrs. Waller C., III)

JESSIE'S CITY CHICKEN

2 pounds lean pork
2 pounds veal
3 to 4 tablespoons water
1 egg

½ to 1 cup flour
½ to 1 cup bread crumbs
 Salt and pepper to taste
4 tablespoons shortening

Cut pork and veal in 1″ cubes. Alternate on 4″ or 5″ wooden skewers (available from meat department). Beat egg and water together. Roll each skewer in flour, then in egg mixture and then in bread crumbs. Season with salt and pepper. Brown in shortening in large skillet. Remove and place in 9″ x 13″ baking dish. Bake at 350° for 1 to 1½ hours. Serves 8 to 10.

Connie H. Toma (Mrs. George E.)

SNOWSHOE APRÉS SKI STEW

3 pounds boneless pork, cubed
½ to 1 cup flour
2 tablespoons oil
1 onion, sliced
1 garlic clove, chopped
2 carrots, chopped
4 stalks celery, chopped
1 green pepper, chopped
4 cups chicken stock

1 teaspoon dry mustard
3 tablespoons Hungarian paprika
Salt and pepper to taste
1 pound fresh mushrooms, quartered
3 potatoes, peeled and diced
3 tomatoes, peeled and chopped
1⅓ cups sour cream

Dredge pork in flour. Brown pork, in several batches, in hot oil in Dutch oven. Remove pork. Sauté onion and garlic 2 to 3 minutes. Add pork, carrots, celery, green peppers, chicken stock and seasonings. Add additional water to cover if needed. Cook 1½ hours at medium heat, uncovered. Add mushrooms, potatoes and tomatoes. Cook 1 hour. Serve with one tablespoon sour cream spooned on top of each helping. Serves 8.

Carol C. Gaujot (Mrs. Philip D.)

HUNGARIAN PORK WITH ONIONS

2 (1 pound each) pork tenderloins, cut in julienne strips
6 medium onions, chopped
½ cup cooking oil, divided
1 teaspoon salt
1 teaspoon paprika

¾ teaspoon pepper
¼ teaspoon crushed red chilies
1 or 2 sweet red peppers, cut into long strips
Feta cheese, optional

Sauté onions in ¼ cup oil in skillet 2 to 3 minutes. Stir in spices. Place on low heat to keep warm. In separate skillet brown pork in remaining ¼ cup oil. Cook over medium heat 15 to 20 minutes. Top with pepper pieces. Cover and simmer 5 minutes. Stir onion mixture into meat. Garnish with 1″ cubes of Feta cheese if desired. Serves 8.

Susan C. Harpold (Mrs. Robert R., Jr.)

PANCIT

1 pound lean pork
¾ pound raw shrimp
2 cloves garlic
2 tablespoons cooking oil
1 cup chopped onions
1 cup sliced green beans
2 cups shredded cabbage
1 cup carrot strips
½ cup bell pepper strips
1 to 2 packages dry fungus, optional

2 tablespoons soy sauce
1 package dry onion soup mix
Salt to taste
1 package Bizon rice noodles
5 green onions, chopped
2 hard boiled eggs, sliced
1 lemon, sliced

Cut pork and shrimp into strips. Sauté garlic in oil in large skillet. Add pork and brown. Add shrimp and sauté 3 to 4 minutes. Add vegetables and stir fry 2 to 3 minutes. Stir in soy sauce, soup mix and salt. Prepare noodles by pouring boiling water over them just before serving. Combine vegetables and meat mixture with noodles. Top with green onions and egg and lemon slices. Serves 6.

Sidney Rothstein

ALL PURPOSE FORMULA CHINESE DINNER

½ pound lean pork (may use veal, beef, fish or chicken)
2 tablespoons soy sauce
1 tablespoon sherry
1 teaspoon cornstarch
2 tablespoons minced onion
3 tablespoons peanut oil, divided

2 cups chopped vegetables (use any green vegetable, as well as carrots, squash, cauliflower)
½ cup something crunchy (bamboo shoots, water chestnuts, bean sprouts, almonds or celery)
¼ cup liquid, optional

Cut meat in strips or cubes. Marinate for 10 minutes in mixture of soy sauce, sherry and cornstarch. Heat 2 tablespoons peanut oil in wok until very hot. Add onion and stir fry 2 minutes. Add vegetables and stir fry 2 minutes. If more cooking is needed, add ¼ cup liquid or stock and simmer until liquid evaporates. Add crunchy ingredients, stir fry 1 minute. Remove vegetables to heated platter. Add remaining 1 tablespoon oil to wok. Add meat and stir fry 3 to 5 minutes or until done. (Chicken and fish are done when they turn white.) Do not overcook. Add marinade and cooked vegetables and toss until heated through. Serves 4.

Gina H. Rugeley (Mrs. Edward W., Jr.)

SHANGRI-LA PORK

2 (1 pound each) pork
   tenderloins
4 tablespoons cooking oil,
   divided
2 cloves garlic, minced
2 tablespoons cornstarch
1¼ cups water

⅓ cup soy sauce
⅓ cup light corn syrup
1 cup broccoli flowerets
2 onions, cut in wedges
1 carrot, cut in 1" strips
½ pound mushrooms, sliced
1 cup pea pods, halved

Heat 2 tablespoons oil in wok or large skillet. Slice pork into strips. Stir fry pork and garlic 8 minutes. In separate bowl blend cornstarch and water. Stir in soy sauce and corn syrup. With slotted spoon, remove pork from wok and add cornstarch mixture. Heat remaining 2 tablespoons oil in wok. Add vegetables. Stir fry 5 minutes or until tender. Add pork and sauce. Bring to boil. Serve pork over rice. Serves 4 to 6.

Lynn H. Goldsmith (Mrs. Robert F.)

EASY COOKOUT DINNER

2 to 3 bottles of beer
2 (1 pound each) packages
   kielbasa, precooked
½ pound fresh mushrooms
2 zucchini, sliced 1" thick
2 medium onions, chopped
3 green peppers, sliced 1" thick

2 yellow squash, sliced 1"
   thick
3 potatoes, parboiled
3 to 4 carrots, parboiled
1 package cherry tomatoes
   Salt and pepper to taste

Heat charcoal grill and allow coals to come to medium-hot stage. Place a large shallow pan on grill and heat. Pour in one bottle of beer. Place meat and all vegetables except tomatoes in pan. Cook 5 to 10 minutes and turn. Continue cooking for 20 to 30 minutes, stirring frequently. Since you are using precooked sausage it is not necessary to cook longer. Do not allow vegetables to become soft. Add tomatoes for the last 10 minutes. Add more beer as necessary to keep ½" depth in tray at all times. Quick and easy meal for a crowd as you can increase amounts and add any vegetables desired. Good served with Dilly Bread from *Mountain Measures*. Serves 8.

Larrie O. Bartrug (Mrs. Edwin M., Jr.)

PAM'S KIELBASA

1 pound kielbasa
4 cups thinly sliced
    cabbage
1 medium onion, sliced
¾ cup sour cream

2 tablespoons prepared
    brown mustard
¼ teaspoon salt
⅛ teaspoon pepper

Cut kielbasa into ½" pieces. In a large skillet combine cabbage, onion and kielbasa. Cover and cook over medium heat 15 to 20 minutes until cabbage and onion are soft and translucent. Stir in sour cream, mustard, salt and pepper. Cook until heated through. Serves 4.

Pam B. Brown (Mrs. Ricklin)

SAUSAGE AND PEPPERS

1 package hot sausage
1 package kielbasa
1 pound steak, cubed
6 or 7 green peppers,
    chopped
4 large onions, chopped

1 (15 ounce) can tomato
    sauce
¼ cup water
1 cup Italian spaghetti
    sauce
1 (4 ounce) can mushrooms

Slice and brown meats. Drain. Add remaining ingredients. Place in a 2 quart casserole. Bake covered at 350° for 1 hour, stirring occasionally. Serve over buns or spaghetti. Serves 8 to 10.

Nancy N. Cipoletti (Mrs. John C.)

SAUSAGE ZUCCHINI CASSEROLE

2 tablespoons butter
2 tablespoons flour
1 cup milk
½ teaspoon salt
1 cup shredded Mozzarella
    cheese, divided

½ pound mild Italian
    sausage
1 cup zucchini, sliced
¼ cup chopped onion
2 cups cooked noodles
½ cup chopped tomatoes

Melt butter in medium saucepan. Add flour and cook, stirring constantly, 2 to 3 minutes until bubbly and smooth. Slowly stir in milk and cook to medium thickness. Add salt and ½ cup cheese, stirring until cheese is melted. In separate skillet brown sausage. Add onion and zucchini and cook until tender. Drain. Stir in cheese sauce, noodles and tomatoes. Pour into 1½ quart casserole. Sprinkle with remaining ½ cup cheese. Bake at 350° for 20 minutes. Serves 4.

Janet C. Simpson (Mrs. Robert R., Jr.)

SUPER SAUERKRAUT WITH KNOCKWURST

6 slices bacon, diced
½ cup chopped onion
1 (27 ounce) can sauer-
   kraut, drained
2 medium carrots, sliced
1 tablespoon sugar
6 whole peppercorns
2 whole cloves
1 bay leaf

¾ cup chicken broth
½ cup dry white wine
4 potatoes, peeled and
   quartered
4 knockwurst, diagonally
   scored
4 smoked pork chops,
   optional

Cook bacon and onion in a 12″ skillet. Pour off fat. Add kraut, carrots and sugar to skillet. Tie peppercorns, cloves and bay leaf in a cheesecloth bag and bury in center of kraut. Add chicken broth and wine and bring to a boil. Reduce heat and simmer 10 minutes. Add potatoes, pushing them down into kraut. Cover and simmer 15 minutes. Top with knockwurst. Cover and simmer an additional 20 minutes. Remove cheesecloth bag and serve. May add smoked pork chops. Serves 6 to 8.

Diane C. Merrifield (Mrs. John V.)

PASTA WITH SAUSAGE

1 pound Italian sausage
1 clove garlic, minced
½ pound fresh mushrooms,
   sliced
1 medium onion, chopped

4 tablespoons margarine
1 pound pasta (any shape)
1 cup chopped parsley
1 cup Parmesan cheese
1 cup heavy cream

Remove casing from sausage, cut into small pieces and cook in a skillet. Drain. Sauté garlic, mushrooms and onion in butter. Mix sausage with mushroom mixture, set aside and keep warm. Cook pasta according to package directions and drain. Mix together pasta, sausage-mushroom mixture, parsley, cheese and cream. Heat through and serve immediately. Serves 4 to 6.

Frederic George

SAUSAGE RICE BAKE

2 pounds pork sausage
4 cups cooked rice
½ cup chopped onion
⅓ cup chopped green
   pepper
1 (10½ ounce) can cream of
   mushroom soup
¾ cup milk

½ cup shredded American
   cheese
1 (3 ounce) can sliced
   mushrooms
1 (2 ounce) jar pimentos,
   sliced
Salt and pepper to taste
Green pepper rings,
   optional

Brown sausage and drain. Combine cooked rice and sausage. Add onion and green pepper. Combine soup, milk, cheese, pimentos and mushrooms with juice. Add to sausage mixture and place in a baking dish. Bake at 350° for 45 minutes, until hot and bubbling. Garnish with green pepper rings if desired.

Jane H. Shuman (Mrs. James W.)

MAPLED SAUSAGE LINKS

1 (13½ ounce) can pineapple
   chunks
2 (8 ounces each) packages
   brown & serve sausage
   links
4 teaspoons cornstarch
½ teaspoon salt

½ cup maple syrup
⅓ cup water
⅓ cup vinegar
1 medium green pepper,
   diced
½ cup maraschino cherries,
   drained

Drain pineapple, reserving ½ cup juice. Cut each sausage into 3 pieces. Brown sausage in skillet. Combine in saucepan cornstarch, salt, pineapple juice, syrup, water and vinegar. Cook, stirring constantly, until mixture reaches boiling point. Add pineapple, sausage, green pepper and cherries. Heat through. Place in chafing dish over hot water and serve as a brunch dish or appetizer.

Charlotte D. Stallard (Mrs. Troy F.)

GRILLED HAM STEAKS

4 ham slices, cut ¾″ thick
½ cup apricot preserves
½ cup orange juice

1 tablespoon lemon juice
1 teaspoon ground ginger

Combine preserves, orange juice, lemon juice and ginger for basting sauce. Grill ham slices over hot fire for 10 minutes, basting frequently. Cut ham slices in half and serve. Serves 8.

Elaine R. Kroner (Mrs. Robert J.)

MARINATED GRILLED HAM STEAK

1 ham steak, 1½" thick	1 (8¼ ounce) can crushed
4 tablespoons prepared	pineapple
mustard	1 to 1½ cups red wine

Spread mustard over both sides of ham. Place in flat dish. Spread pineapple over top of ham. Pour wine over. Cover and refrigerate overnight. Cook on charcoal grill over medium coals 20 to 30 minutes, basting with marinade. Turn steak after 10 to 15 minutes. Serves 4 to 6.

Betsie M. Dobbs (Mrs. William F., Jr.)

LAYERED HAM CASSEROLE

3 large potatoes	½ cup whipping cream
3 cups cubed, cooked ham	1 cup grated sharp Cheddar
1½ teaspoons prepared	cheese
horseradish	Pepper to taste

Peel and cook potatoes just until tender. Grate or rice potatoes. Place in well buttered 9" x 13" dish. Sprinkle with salt and pepper. Place ham over potatoes. Whip cream and combine with horseradish and cheese. Spread over ham. Bake at 350° for 30 minutes until bubbly.

Rise C. Boggs (Mrs. Charles A., III)

TWICE BAKED HAM AND CHEESE POTATOES

6 medium potatoes	½ teaspoon onion salt
1 cup grated Cheddar	¼ teaspoon pepper
cheese	¼ cup butter
1½ cups milk	Paprika or parsley flakes
1 cup chopped ham	for garnish
½ pint sour cream	

Bake potatoes at 350° for 1 hour until soft. Slice potatoes lengthwise in half. Scoop out insides, leaving a firm shell. Place potato pulp and remaining ingredients in a mixing bowl. Beat at high speed until smooth. Fill potato shells with mixture. Bake at 350° for 20 to 30 minutes. Garnish with paprika or parsley flakes.

Julia S. Johnson (Mrs. David W.)

PAUPIETTES DE VEAU

2 pounds veal, pounded
   thin (about 16 slices)
16 thin slices boiled ham

½ cup flour
3 tablespoons cooking oil

FILLING

6 dried mushrooms
⅓ cup hot water
4 tablespoons butter,
   melted
½ cup chopped onion
1 teaspoon minced garlic

⅓ cup chopped celery
⅓ cup chopped parsley
3 tablespoons grated
   Parmesan cheese
⅓ cup Pignolia nuts

SAUCE

3 tablespoons butter
2 teaspoons minced garlic
½ cup chopped onion
½ cup chopped celery
½ cup chopped carrots

2 tablespoons flour
1 cup chicken broth
½ cup dry white wine
¼ cup chili sauce
½ pound fresh mushrooms,
   sliced

Prior to preparation of filling, soak dried mushrooms in water for 30 minutes. Drain and chop mushrooms. Set aside. Make filling: Sauté onion, garlic and celery in butter until soft. Add parsley, nuts, cheese and mushrooms. Season with salt and pepper.

Place veal slices on wax paper. Top each veal slice with a slice of ham. Place a heaping tablespoon of filling on top of ham and spread evenly. Roll, tucking in ends to hold stuffing. Secure with a toothpick. Dredge in flour just before browning. Heat oil in a large skillet and brown rolls quickly on all sides. Remove toothpicks. Place rolls close together, seam sides down, in a shallow casserole.

Prepare sauce: heat butter and garlic. Sauté vegetables until tender. Sprinkle flour over vegetables and stir to blend. Combine broth, wine and chili sauce. Gradually pour over vegetables. Stir and heat until thickened. Add sliced mushrooms. Simmer 5 minutes. Spoon over veal. Bake, covered, at 375° for 45 minutes. Serves 8.

May be frozen. Cool thoroughly after spooning sauce over veal. Cover, wrap securely and freeze. To serve, bake in a covered casserole at 375° for 1½ hours.

Deborah L. Sutton (Mrs. James)

WIENERSCHNITZEL
As prepared in Austria

8 (4″ x 2″) slices of veal, as
      cut for scallopini
4 tablespoons flour
2 eggs, beaten with 1
      tablespoon water

Bread crumbs
Cooking oil for frying
Salt to taste
1 lemon, sliced

On wooden board beat cutlets lightly on each side. Dip each cutlet in flour, then in beaten egg. Dip in bread crumbs. Fry in hot oil until golden brown on both sides. Salt to taste. Top each schnitzel with lemon slice. Serves 4.

BREAD CRUMBS

Cover cookie sheet with one layer of bread slices. Place in a 350° oven. Turn heat off after 3 minutes. Leave bread in oven overnight. Crush bread with rolling pin as needed for crumbs.

Fish fillets and breast of chicken or turkey slices may be prepared in the same manner as described above with excellent results. The original wienerschnitzel, however, is always made with veal cuts as for scallopini. They are traditionally served with rice, peas and Cucumber Salad.

Louise Wiseman

GRILLADES

1 veal round steak, ½″ thick
3 tablespoons flour
2 tablespoons bacon
      drippings
⅓ cup onion, chopped
1 (10 ounce) can tomatoes
1 teaspoon tomato sauce
⅓ cup green pepper, chopped

1 clove garlic, minced
⅛ teaspoon sugar
⅛ teaspoon marjoram
⅛ teaspoon thyme
⅛ teaspoon oregano
⅛ teaspoon basil
Salt and pepper to taste

Cut steak into bite size pieces. Dredge in flour and brown in drippings in a skillet. Remove meat, add any remaining flour and brown. Add onion and saute. Stir in tomatoes, sauce, vegetables, seasonings and meat. Simmer 1 hour. Serve with grits. Serves 6.

Elizabeth F. Trammell (Mrs. S. Willis)

VEAL PYRAMIDS

8 slices bacon, diced
2 carrots, diced
2 stalks celery, diced
2 small zucchini, diced
1 small onion, chopped
6 mushrooms, diced
½ cup peas
   Salt and pepper to taste

4 (4 ounces each) veal
   scallops
¼ cup butter
8 tablespoons dry vermouth
4 thin slices Prosciutto
   (or ham)
4 slices Mozzarella cheese

In a small skillet, sauté bacon until crisp. Transfer bacon to paper towel to drain. In bacon drippings, sauté carrots, celery, zucchini, onion and mushrooms until crisp tender. Stir in peas, bacon, salt and pepper. Set aside. Sprinkle veal scallops with salt and pepper. Brown in butter in skillet for 2 minutes on each side. Transfer to a baking dish. Pour 2 tablespoons vermouth over each scallop and top with Prosciutto. Divide vegetable mixture among scallops, mounding it slightly. Top each serving with a slice of Mozzarella cheese. Bake, tightly covered, at 350° for 15 minutes or until cheese is melted and vegetables are heated through. Serves 4.

Deborah L. Sutton (Mrs. James)

VEAL ITALIAN

1½ pounds veal, cut in slices
    and pounded very thin
2   tablespoons salt free, low
    fat margarine
    Salt substitute, to taste
    Freshly ground pepper to
    taste
2   cups thinly sliced onion
2   cups thinly sliced fresh
    mushrooms

½ teaspoon basil
3 garlic cloves, minced
1 teaspoon fresh parsley
   (Italian if possible)
1 cup salt free chicken
   bouillon
½ cup white wine
4 fresh tomatoes, cut up
½ teaspoon oregano

In heavy pan sauté veal in margarine with garlic and onions until translucent. Add other ingredients to pan. Cover and cook until tender, approximately 1 hour. Remove lid. If needed let sauce cook down. Serve over white rice. Serves 4 to 5.

Susan Kamer-Shinaberry

VEAL CREOLE

1½ pounds veal shoulder or breast, cut into 1" pieces	¾ cup chopped green pepper
3 tablespoons flour	½ bunch young carrots, cut into 1" strips
3 tablespoons cooking oil or margarine	½ cup ketchup
½ cup chopped onion	1 cup warm water
	Salt and pepper to taste

Dredge meat in flour. Sauté in hot oil in a heavy kettle until brown. Add onions and green pepper and continue to cook until onions are lightly browned. Add carrots, ketchup and water. Cook slowly, covered, for 1 hour or until meat is tender. Add more liquid if needed. Serve over rice. Serves 4.

Mary P. Ziebold (Mrs. William T.)

VEAL AND EGGPLANT PARMIGIANA

2 medium eggplants	1½ cups dry, unflavored bread crumbs
Salt and pepper to taste	
8 veal cutlets	3 cups tomato sauce
Cooking oil for frying	1½ cups freshly grated Parmesan cheese
2 eggs	

Peel eggplants. Cut lengthwise into ⅜" slices. Sprinkle lightly with salt and place in a large dish. Set another large dish on top of slices and let stand 30 minutes. Pat dry with paper towels. Place cutlets between 2 pieces of wax paper and pound thin. Heat oil in skillet. Cook eggplant over medium heat until golden brown on both sides. Remove from skillet and set aside. Beat eggs with salt and pepper. Dip cutlets in eggs, then in bread crumbs. Let stand 10 to 15 minutes. Heat more oil in skillet, add cutlets and cook until meat has a golden brown crust, 1 to 2 minutes on each side. Drain on paper towels. Butter a 9" x 13" baking dish. Line bottom of dish with ½ of eggplant. Arrange a layer of 4 veal cutlets over eggplant. Top with ½ of tomato sauce. Sprinkle with ½ of Parmesan cheese. Repeat, ending with the tomato sauce and Parmesan cheese. Bake at 350° for 15 to 20 minutes until cheese is melted and golden. Serves 8.

Judy Grigoraci (Mrs. Victor)

VEAL AND ARTICHOKE MOUSSAKA

¼ cup butter
1 large onion, chopped
2 pounds lean ground veal
½ cup red wine
2 large tomatoes, seeded
    and chopped
⅓ cup chopped parsley
1 teaspoon garlic powder
1 teaspoon salt

¼ teaspoon cinnamon
¼ teaspoon nutmeg
¼ teaspoon pepper
4 (9 ounces each) packages
    frozen artichokes
½ cup dry seasoned bread
    crumbs
½ cup grated Parmesan
    cheese

SAUCE

¼ cup butter
¼ cup flour
3 cups scalded milk
1 teaspoon salt
¼ teaspoon pepper

3 eggs, beaten
½ cup dry seasoned bread
    crumbs
½ cup grated Parmesan
    cheese

In a large skillet, heat butter and sauté onion until translucent. Add veal and cook until lightly browned. In a saucepan heat together wine and tomatoes. Blend into meat mixture. Add parsley, garlic, salt, cinnamon, nutmeg and pepper. Simmer, uncovered, for 30 minutes or until most of the liquid has been absorbed. Cook frozen artichokes according to package directions. Drain and set aside.

Prepare sauce: In large saucepan melt butter over low heat and blend in flour. Gradually stir in scalded milk, salt and pepper. Cook the sauce, stirring constantly, until thick and smooth. Stir 3 tablespoons of the sauce into the meat mixture. With a whisk, combine remaining sauce with beaten eggs and whisk until thick.

Butter a 3 quart shallow baking dish and sprinkle bread crumbs evenly over the bottom. Arrange half the cooked artichokes over bread crumbs. Cover with half the meat mixture. Sprinkle with half the grated cheese. Repeat the mixture with the remaining ingredients. Pour remaining sauce over entire casserole. Bake, uncovered, for 30 minutes at 300°. Serves 8.

Deborah L. Sutton (Mrs. James)

LAMB SAUCE

1 cup apple jelly
1 cup ketchup

1 teaspoon ground cloves

Mix and simmer for two hours, stirring occasionally. Delicious as a complement to lamb.

Alice Veazey

BARBECUE SAUCE

½ cup ketchup
½ cup water
1 (6 ounce) can tomato
   paste
1 tablespoon vinegar
¼ cup molasses

1 tablespoon prepared
   mustard
1 tablespoon Worcester-
   shire sauce
1 small onion, diced
2 tablespoons butter
   Dash of pepper

Combine all ingredients. Simmer 5 to 10 minutes. Add cooked meat which has been cut into cubes, or use to baste chops or chicken.

Mary M. Lobert

BAR-B-Q SAUCE

1 cup chili sauce
2 sliced onions
¾ cup water
3 tablespoons vinegar

2 tablespoons Worcester-
   shire sauce
1 teaspoon salt
¼ teaspoon pepper

Combine and heat 5 minutes. Makes 2 cups.

Charlotte C. MacCorkle (Mrs. Samuel)

BEEF FONDUE SAUCES

HORSERADISH SAUCE

1 cup sour cream
¼ cup horseradish
2 tablespoons chopped
   green onions

½ teaspoon salt
3 drops hot pepper
   seasoning

Mix and refrigerate 1 hour. Makes approximately 1½ cups.

DIABLOS SAUCE

½ cup ketchup
2 tablespoons spicy mustard

4 drops hot pepper sauce
1 large clove garlic, crushed

Mix and refrigerate 1 hour. Makes approximately ½ cup. Allow 8 ounces beef per person. Filet is best. Serve with tossed salad and garlic bread.

Catherine Bradford

JULIA'S LAMB SAUCE

1 egg yolk
1 (8 ounce) jar currant jelly
1 teaspoon brown sugar
2 tablespoons cider vinegar

1 tablespoon tarragon
   vinegar
1 teaspoon prepared
   mustard
1 teaspoon celery seed

Combine egg yolk and currant jelly in the top of a double boiler. Add brown sugar, vinegars, mustard and celery seed. Cook until thick, stirring constantly. Delicious over lamb or ham.

Nina A. Ratrie (Mrs. Turner R., Jr.)

GRILLED MEAT MARINADE

3 cloves garlic, sliced
3 tablespoons soy sauce
2 tablespoons ketchup

½ teaspoon oregano
½ teaspoon vegetable oil
   Pepper to taste

Combine all ingredients. Pour over scored flank steak or a piece of meat of lesser quality that you may wish to "dress up". Chill in refrigerator several hours before grilling.

Kathleen M. Muehlman (Mrs. Raymond L.)

FRESH MUSHROOM SAUCE

½ pound fresh mushrooms,
   sliced
2 tablespoons butter,
   melted
¼ cup minced onion

1 to 2 tablespoons flour
½ cup cream
½ cup sour cream
½ teaspoon salt
¼ teaspoon pepper

Sauté mushrooms and onions in butter in a skillet. Cook, covered, for 10 minutes on low heat until tender but not brown. Push mushrooms and onions to one side of pan. Stir flour into butter. Add remaining ingredients. Heat slowly, stirring constantly, almost to boiling. Serve over roast beef, baked chicken or other cuts of meat. Makes 1½ cups.

Susan S. Sibley (Mrs. Richard H.)

MUSTARD SAUCE

½ cup sugar
4 teaspoons dry mustard
1 teaspoon salt
2 eggs, beaten

½ cup milk
½ cup vinegar
¼ cup butter

In top of double boiler, stir sugar, mustard and salt. Separately whisk eggs and milk. Whisk into dry mixture. Add vinegar and butter. Cook in double boiler for 15 minutes stirring frequently. Mixture will thicken some. Serve with ham or chicken.

Susan S. Sibley (Mrs. Richard H.)

ORANGE SAUCE

1 cup sugar
¼ teaspoon salt
2 tablespoons cornstarch
1 cup orange juice
¼ cup lemon juice
¾ cup boiling water

1 tablespoon butter
1 teaspoon grated orange rind
1 teaspoon grated lemon rind

Mix in saucepan sugar, salt and cornstarch. Stir in orange juice, lemon juice and boiling water. Boil 1 minute stirring constantly. Remove from heat and stir in butter, orange rind and lemon rind. Serve hot over ham. Makes 2 cups.

Linda P. Jernigan (Mrs. W.H., Jr.)

SWEET AND SOUR MARINADE
For chicken, roasts or steaks. Tenderizes and flavors.

¾ cup soy sauce
1 cup sherry
3½ cups unsweetened pineapple juice

½ cup red wine vinegar
¾ cup sugar
1 teaspoon garlic powder

Combine all ingredients in a saucepan. Bring to a boil. Set aside to cool. Place meat in a large container with a lid or cover. Pour marinade over. Refrigerate 36 to 48 hours, turning once. Grill or roast in oven. Caution: marinade may color beef a deep shade of brown so that it appears to be cooked more than it actually is. Time carefully to avoid being undercooked.

Judy N. Pugh (Mrs. William A., Jr.)

HOLLY GROVE

Daniel Ruffner, fifth son of the prosperous salt industrialist, Joseph Ruffner, built Holly Grove for his family in 1815, on the site of his parents' log homestead. The mansion was the center piece of a large plantation with barns, shops, granary and other outbuildings placed across an open expanse where now stand the West Virginia Capitol building and Governor's Mansion.

Daniel opened his house to travellers in 1826 when the James River and Kanawha Turnpike passed near his home opening the Kanawha Valley to Richmond and the eastern markets. The Ruffner place became a popular stage stop and family tradition states that visitors included Daniel Boone, Henry Clay, John J. Audubon and Andrew Jackson.

Daniel Ruffner became a prominent and responsible citizen of the area, at various times holding public office as justice of the peace and high sheriff of the county.

Holly Grove was originally a square two-story brick structure with a brick dining room wing extending back almost to the separate kitchen. The plan was a typical central hall plan with four high ceilinged rooms opening onto the hall. The rooms on the right were open to one another by means of wide folding doors.

The present grand scale of the building took shape in 1902 when a new owner raised the roof to create a third floor apartment, added the semi-circular columned portico and painted the brick gray. The changes were made without destroying the basic symmetry of the original house or significantly altering the interior.

The building still stands in graceful elegance amid the great holly trees and boxwoods of its generous grounds.

Photo courtesy of W. Va. Dept of Culture and History

POULTRY AND GAME

Lobster

PAM'S CHICKEN ADRIANNE

4 chicken breasts
¼ cup cooking oil
2 (10 ounces each) packages
   frozen broccoli spears,
   cooked

6 slices crisp cooked bacon
1 (4 ounce) can sliced
   mushrooms, drained

Place chicken in shallow casserole. Add oil. Bake covered at 350° for 40 minutes. Remove chicken from oven, pour off fat. Arrange broccoli around chicken, top with bacon strips. Add mushrooms. Pour sauce over. Sprinkle with paprika. Bake at 350° for 15 to 20 minutes. Serves 4.

CHEESE SAUCE

1½ cups chicken broth
1 tablespoon chopped
   parsley
2 tablespoons minced green
   onion
½ teaspoon tarragon

½ teaspoon rosemary
4 tablespoons flour
6 ounces mild cheese,
   shredded
2 dashes cayenne pepper

In a saucepan combine broth, parsley, onions, tarragon and rosemary. Bring to boil, reduce heat and simmer 5 to 10 minutes. In separate cup combine ¼ cup hot broth with flour to make a paste. Add to broth mixture, stirring constantly until thickened. Stir in cheese, until melted. Add cayenne.

Pam H. Gillinson (Mrs. Andrew S.)

CHICKEN AND APPLES

4 pounds chicken pieces
3 tablespoons cooking oil
1 onion, sliced
1 cup chopped celery
2 apples, peeled and sliced
2 tablespoons flour
1½ cups chicken broth

¼ teaspoon thyme
¼ teaspoon marjoram
2 tablespoons Parmesan
   cheese
2 tablespoons sherry
Salt and pepper to taste

Brown chicken in oil in large skillet. Remove. Add onion, celery and apples. Sauté until soft. Blend in flour. Slowly add chicken broth, stirring until smooth. Add chicken and seasonings. Cook, covered, over low heat for 45 to 60 minutes. Add cheese and sherry. Serve over rice. Serves 8.

Barbara H. Slack (Mrs. John M., III)

MARY'S BAKED CHICKEN

2 chicken fryers or 8
   boneless breasts
1 cup flour
½ teaspoon salt
¼ teaspoon pepper
1 tablespoon paprika
¾ cup butter, divided

1 (3½ ounce) can pitted ripe
   olives, chopped and
   drained
1 cup orange juice
1 tablespoon brown sugar
½ teaspoon thyme
1 medium onion, sliced
Salt and pepper to taste

Mix flour, salt, pepper and paprika. Coat chicken and brown in ½ cup butter. Combine remaining ingredients including remaining butter in separate pan and simmer 4 minutes. Arrange chicken in flat casserole. Pour sauce over chicken. Sprinkle with paprika. Bake at 350° for 1½ to 1¾ hours. Baste 4 times during cooking. Serves 6 to 8.

Ann C. Brotherton (Mrs. William T., Jr.)

BAKED CHICKEN WITH HONEY

3 pounds chicken pieces
Salt and pepper
2 tablespoons cooking oil

½ cup soy sauce
2 tablespoons ketchup
1 cup honey

Sprinkle chicken with salt and pepper. Place in a casserole dish. Mix remaining ingredients and pour over chicken. Bake, covered, at 375° for 1 hour until sauce becomes caramelized. Serves 6 to 8.

Ann P. Wainstein

DIANE'S CHICKEN BREASTS

4 to 6 chicken breasts,
   boned
1½ cups heavy cream
2 tablespoons butter
½ cup chicken broth
⅓ cup sliced sour pickles
1½ tablespoons Dijon mustard

1½ teaspoon fresh or ½
    teaspoon dried tarragon
1 tablespoon chopped
   parsley
1½ teaspoons chopped chives
   Salt and pepper to taste

Flatten chicken between 2 pieces of waxed paper. Boil cream in medium saucepan until reduced to ¼ cup. Heat butter in large skillet, add chicken and cook 3 to 4 minutes on each side. Remove to a warm platter. Add broth to skillet, boil and reduce to ¼ cup. Stir in pickles, cream and mustard. Do not let boil at this point. Add remaining ingredients, including chicken, coat with sauce and serve. Serves 4.

Diane Merrifield (Mrs. John V.)

CHEESE SAUCED CHICKEN

6 boneless chicken breasts,
   skinned
1 teaspoon salt

¼ teaspoon white pepper
2 tablespoons flour
3 tablespoons butter

Place chicken between 2 pieces of waxed paper and pound with smooth mallet until ¼" thick. Mix flour, salt and pepper and rub on chicken. Melt butter in skillet and brown chicken. Place in shallow casserole.

CHEESE SAUCE

2 tablespoons butter
2 tablespoons flour
¾ to 1 cup milk

4 tablespoons grated Swiss
   cheese
6 tablespoons grated
   Parmesan cheese

Melt butter. Whisk in flour. Slowly whisk in milk, stirring constantly until it reaches boiling point. Cook 5 minutes over low heat, stirring constantly. Whisk in cheese until melted and smooth. Pour over chicken. May be made ahead and refrigerated at this point. Bake at 375° for 10 to 15 minutes (20 to 30 if made ahead) until browned. Serves 6.

Variations: Place a layer of slightly cooked broccoli, asparagus or artichoke hearts under chicken. May also add thinly sliced ham. Increase sauce recipe by ½ if using additions.

Susan S. Sibley (Mrs. Richard H.)

CHINESE CHICKEN

4 to 6 boneless chicken
   breasts
1 small head cabbage, sliced
1 onion, chopped

1 green pepper, chopped
1 pound mushrooms, sliced
2 tablespoons cooking oil
1 tablespoon soy sauce

Cut chicken breasts into bite size pieces. Stir fry in hot oil for 10 minutes. Remove. Stir fry vegetables until just tender. Add soy sauce and chicken, stirring until hot. Serve with additional soy sauce. Serves 4 to 6.

Leigh F. Norrid (Mrs. Tim)

CHICKEN CURRY

1 frying chicken, skinned
   and cut into pieces
4 tablespoons margarine
1⅓ cups chopped onion
1 clove garlic, minced
1½ teaspoons ginger
1 cup diced tomato
1 teaspoon salt

1 cinnamon stick (2″ length)
   Seeds from 1 small
    cardamon pod
   Dash of turmeric
   Dash of ground cumin
   Dash of paprika
   Dash of pepper
⅓ cup plain yogurt

Sauté chicken in margarine in large covered skillet for 10 to 15 minutes until evenly browned. Remove. Add onion, garlic and ginger. Sauté 10 minutes. Add tomato and spices. Cook over low heat for 3 minutes. Stir in yogurt. Add chicken, cover and simmer 30 to 40 minutes, turning occasionally. Serves 4.

Deborah L. Dent (Mrs. Robert E.)

OVEN CURRIED CHICKEN
Low Calorie

1 chicken fryer, cut into
   pieces
1 teaspoon granulated
   chicken broth
½ cup hot water
½ teaspoon dry mustard

1 garlic clove, minced
2 teaspoons curry powder
1 teaspoon oregano
½ teaspoon paprika
2 teaspoons Worcestershire
   sauce

Skin chicken pieces and place in ovenproof casserole. Mix remaining ingredients and pour over chicken. Bake at 350° for 1 hour. Serves 4.

Helen Z. Chilton (Mrs. Robert M.)

CHICKEN DIABLE

6 boneless chicken breasts,
   skinned
4 tablespoons butter
½ cup honey
¼ cup prepared mustard

1 teaspoon curry powder
1 to 2 teaspoons salt
½ to 1 cup white wine
   (optional)

Melt butter in shallow baking pan. Stir in remaining ingredients. Roll chicken in mixture to coat both sides. Arrange in a single layer in same pan. Bake at 375° for 1 hour, basting once. Serves 4 to 6.

Barbara S. Wilkerson (Mrs. Thomas S.)

CHICKEN DIJON

8 boneless chicken breasts,
   skinned
3 tablespoons butter
2 tablespoons flour
1 cup chicken broth

½ cup light cream
2 tablespoons Dijon
   mustard
1 (4 ounce) can sliced
   mushrooms, drained

Lightly brown chicken breasts in butter in a large skillet for 20 minutes. Remove to warm platter. Whisk flour into skillet drippings; add broth and cream. Cook and stir until thick. Stir in mustard. Add chicken and mushrooms. Heat, covered, for 10 minutes. May be made ahead, refrigerated and reheated at 300° for 30 minutes. Serves 6 to 8.

Nancy S. Cerutti (Mrs. John H.)

CHICKEN WITH HERBS AND WINE

4 chicken breasts, boned
   and cut into strips
2 tablespoons cooking oil
½ cup flour
½ teaspoon salt
4 tablespoons butter,
   melted

⅓ cup white wine
⅓ cup chicken broth
2 tablespoons minced onion
   Dash of pepper
2 pinches each: thyme,
   marjoram, oregano and
   rosemary

Dredge chicken in flour and salt. Brown in oil in skillet. Place in small casserole. Combine remaining ingredients in a saucepan. Bring to boil. Pour over chicken. Bake, covered, at 350° for 1 hour. Turn once during baking. Serves 3 to 4.

Marta D. MacCallum (Mrs. Daniel)

IMPERIAL CHICKEN
1980 National Chicken Cooking Contest Winner

1 chicken fryer, cut in
   pieces
6 tablespoons margarine,
   divided
2 cups dry bread crumbs
¾ cup grated Parmesan
   cheese

2 teaspoons salt
¼ cup chopped parsley
⅛ teaspoon pepper
⅛ teaspoon paprika
⅛ teaspoon marjoram
1 clove garlic, crushed

Melt 4 tablespoons margarine. In shallow dish, combine crumbs, cheese and seasonings. Dip chicken in butter, then roll in crumb mixture. Place in single layer in shallow roasting pan. Dot with remaining 2 tablespoons butter. Bake, uncovered, at 350° for 1 hour. Serves 4.

Freda Naylor

LIME BROILED CHICKEN (SMOKED)

1 frying chicken, cut into
   pieces
Salt and pepper
½ cup cooking oil
½ cup lime juice

2 tablespoons chopped
   onion
½ teaspoon ginger
¼ teaspoon garlic powder
½ teaspoon salt
½ teaspoon onion salt

Sprinkle chicken with salt and pepper. Place in single layer in baking dish. Combine remaining ingredients in blender, blending until smooth. Pour over chicken. Marinate 3 hours, turning occasionally. Grill 5 inches from heat, skin side up. Close hood for 10 minutes. Baste, close hood for 20 minutes. Turn, baste and cook 10 minutes more. Serves 6.

Joellen A. Kerr (Mrs. Roger W.)

CHICKEN WITH ORANGE SAUCE
Low Calorie

1 chicken fryer, cut into
   pieces
1½ cups unsweetened orange
   juice
3 tablespoons sherry
1 teaspoon grated orange
   rind

1 tablespoon flour
2 teaspoons dried parsley
2 tablespoons diced green
   pepper
Optional: chopped mush-
   rooms and onions as
   desired

Skin chicken pieces. Place in casserole. Bake uncovered at 350°
for 30 minutes. Meanwhile, in saucepan over medium heat, make
paste with flour and 3 to 4 tablespoons orange juice. Gradually add
remaining orange juice, stirring until thickened. Add remaining
ingredients. Set aside. When chicken is done, remove from dish and
pour off fat. Replace chicken. Pour sauce over top. Bake at 350° for
30 minutes. Serves 4.

Helen Z. Chilton (Mrs. Robert M.)

CHICKEN PAPRIKA
Low Calorie

2 whole chicken breasts, split and skinned	2 teaspoons Hungarian paprika
1 large onion, minced	2 tablespoons lemon juice
½ green pepper, sliced	2 tablespoons flour
1 cup fresh sliced mushrooms	Salt substitute to taste
3 tablespoons salt-free, low fat margarine	Freshly ground black pepper
	1 cup natural flavor yogurt

Sauté onion, green pepper, mushrooms and chicken in margarine until lightly browned. Add paprika and lemon juice. Add a
small amount of water. Cook covered over low heat until chicken is
tender. Remove chicken to warm platter. Add flour, salt and
pepper. Blend in yogurt, stirring constantly until smooth and thick.
Pour sauce over chicken. Serve with fluffy rice or spaghetti. Serves
3 to 4.

Susan Kamer-Shinaberry

PETTI DI PALLO

8 boneless chicken breasts, skinned	2 teaspoons salt
2 cups sherry	4 drops of onion juice
Juice of 2 lemons	1 teaspoon white pepper
4 eggs	½ to 1 cup bread crumbs
8 tablespoons cream	4 tablespoons margarine

Soak chicken in sherry and lemon juice for 2 hours (overnight is
best). Wipe dry. Flatten with mallet to ½" thick. Beat eggs with
cream. Add salt, onion juice and pepper. Dip chicken in this mixture. Roll in bread crumbs. Sauté in margarine until golden brown.
Bake, covered, in 9" x 13" baking dish at 325° for 1 hour. Serve with
lemon slices. Serves 8.

Sarah M. Foster (Mrs. Michael D.)

1/23/87 good spicy

PINEAPPLE CHICKEN CASSEROLE

4 to 6 boneless chicken breasts	1 (14 ounce) can pineapple chunks, with juice
¼ cup butter	2 tablespoons vinegar
½ cup chopped onion	¼ cup packed brown sugar
½ cup chopped green pepper	2 tablespoons soy sauce
½ cup chopped carrots	¼ teaspoon pepper
¾ cup ketchup	1 teaspoon ginger

Arrange chicken in shallow casserole. Melt butter in skillet; add onion, green pepper and carrots. Sauté 5 minutes. Add remaining ingredients, reserving pineapple chunks but using juice. Cook until mixture boils. Add pineapple chunks. Pour sauce over chicken. Bake, covered, at 400° for 1 hour. Serves 4 to 6.

Barbara H. Diznoff (Mrs. Lee)

EASY CHICKEN AND POTATO DINNER

3 to 4 potatoes	Corn flake crumbs
Low cal, non-stick vegetable spray	Hidden Valley Ranch dressing mix (original flavor)
Pepper to taste	
4 large chicken breasts, skinned	

Wash and slice potatoes into ½" slices. Spray casserole dish liberally with non-stick vegetable spray. Layer potatoes on bottom of dish. Pepper to taste. Spray lightly with vegetable spray. Coat chicken breasts by rolling in corn flake crumbs and pepper mixture. Arrange on top of potatoes, flesh side up. Sprinkle with salad dressing mix. Spray again with vegetable spray. Cook, covered, for 1 hour at 400°. Serves 4.

Roberta G. Heath (Mrs. Richard)

CHICKEN STROGANOFF

6 boneless chicken breasts	½ teaspoon thyme
¼ cup butter	1 tablespoon cornstarch
1 teaspoon salt	2 tablespoons cold water
1 medium onion, chopped	1 cup sour cream
1 pound mushrooms, whole or halved	1½ tablespoons paprika
¼ cup sherry	Sautéed sliced almonds (optional)

Cut chicken in strips. Melt butter in large skillet. Add chicken. Sprinkle with salt. Cook, stirring, for 3 minutes (until white). Add onions and mushrooms. Cook 2 minutes. Add sherry and thyme. Reduce heat to medium. Cook, covered, 4 minutes. Blend cornstarch and water. Add to chicken mixture. Cook and stir rapidly. Stir in sour cream and paprika. Do not boil. Serves 4 to 6.

Paula W. Flaherty (Mrs. Thomas)

STUFFED BREAST OF CHICKEN

4 boneless chicken breasts
1 (4½ ounce) can chopped mushrooms, drained
1 tablespoon finely chopped parsley
¼ cup finely chopped celery
4 tablespoons cooking oil, divided

½ cup flour
1 teaspoon salt
⅛ teaspoon pepper
1 cup thinly sliced onion
¼ teaspoon basil
¼ cup honey
½ cup water

Slit thick side of each chicken breast to form a pocket. In a large skillet sauté mushrooms, celery and parsley in 1 tablespoon of oil until tender. Spoon mixture into pockets. Pinch edges to seal. Coat chicken with flour, seasoned with salt and pepper. Brown chicken in remaining oil. Remove and arrange in baking dish. Sauté onion until lightly browned. Top chicken breasts with onion. Sprinkle with basil. Drizzle honey over chicken. Add water to skillet, scrape and pour over chicken. Bake, uncovered, at 350° for 30 to 40 minutes, basting twice with liquid in baking dish. Serves 4.

Mary Kouri Kousaie

STUFFED CHICKEN BREASTS O'BRIEN

½ pound fresh spinach, chopped fine
½ pound Ricotta cheese
4 ounces Mozzarella cheese, grated
½ teaspoon salt
Pinch of pepper

½ teaspoon garlic powder
¼ teaspoon thyme
½ teaspoon tarragon
4 whole chicken breasts, boned, but with skin intact
Softened butter

Combine spinach, cheeses and seasonings. Divide into 4 portions. Place one portion of filling under skin of each breast. Smooth skin over filling, tucking ends under. Rub each breast with butter and place in buttered baking dish. Bake, covered, at 350° for 45 minutes to 1 hour. Serve sliced, hot or cold. Serves 4.

Connie O. Skahan (Mrs. James)

SWEET AND SOUR ORANGE CHICKEN

4 to 6 chicken breasts
½ cup flour
¼ teaspoon garlic powder
3 tablespoons cooking oil
¾ cup orange juice
2 medium onions, thinly sliced
⅓ cup soy sauce

⅓ cup cider vinegar
2 tablespoons honey
2 tablespoons water
1 large green pepper, sliced
1 cup sliced mushrooms
1 (8 ounce) can sliced water chestnuts, drained

Mix flour and garlic powder. Dredge chicken. Heat oil in large frying pan. Brown chicken over medium low heat. Add orange juice and onions. Simmer covered for 20 minutes. Mix soy sauce, vinegar, honey and water. Pour over chicken. Add remaining ingredients. Bake, covered, at 350° for 30 minutes. Serves 4 to 6.

Karen Potesta

CHICKEN LEGS PARMESAN

12 chicken legs
¼ cup butter, melted
1 cup herb seasoned stuffing

⅔ cup Parmesan cheese
½ teaspoon parsley

Skin chicken. Dip in butter. Combine remaining ingredients, rolling chicken pieces in this mixture. Bake at 350° for 1 hour. Serves 4.

Louise B. Cleek (Mrs. David)

"BLACK" CHICKEN

8 to 12 chicken wings
¼ cup cooking oil
¼ cup soy sauce

¼ cup dark brown sugar
1 clove garlic, crushed
¼ teaspoon ground ginger

Discard wing tips. In blender, combine remaining ingredients, mixing well. Dip each wing into sauce, covering completely. Place skin side up in a shallow baking pan. Do not overlap. Bake at 325° for 1 to 1¼ hours until deep brown and "sticky". Turn twice while baking. Recipe may easily be doubled or tripled. May also be used as an appetizer: cut each wing into two sections before dipping in sauce. Serves 2 to 3.

Diane S. Doty (Mrs. Steven)

BARBARA'S CHICKEN LIVER CASSEROLE

½ pound bacon
1 pound chicken livers
⅓ to ½ cup flour
½ teaspoon salt

¼ teaspoon pepper
3 medium onions, sliced
¾ cup water

Cook bacon until crisp. Drain and crumble, reserving drippings. Roll livers in flour seasoned with salt and pepper. Sauté livers until browned, add onions and cook until soft. Drain. Layer ½ of the liver, onions and bacon in a 1½ quart casserole. Repeat layers. Add water, cover and bake at 375° for 30 to 45 minutes. Serves 4.

Lynn H. Goldsmith (Mrs. Robert F.)

CHICKEN LIVERS IN SOUR CREAM

2 tablespoons butter
½ pound chicken livers, halved
1 medium onion, finely chopped
1 medium green pepper, finely chopped

½ teaspoon salt
⅛ teaspoon pepper
½ bay leaf
¼ cup water
1 cup sour cream

Melt butter in large skillet. Add livers, onion, and green pepper. Sauté over medium heat, stirring until lightly browned. Add seasonings and water. Bring to boil. Simmer, covered, 20 minutes. Stir in sour cream. Heat thoroughly. Serve with rice or mashed potatoes. Serves 2.

Mary Lee W. Lilly (Mrs. J.K., III)

CHICKEN LIVERS IN WINE

2 tablespoons butter
1 medium onion
1 (4 ounce) can mushrooms, drained
1 pound chicken livers
½ cup flour

1 teaspoon salt
¼ teaspoon pepper
⅛ teaspoon paprika
⅛ teaspoon garlic powder
3 tablespoons cooking oil
¾ cup red wine

Slice onion into rings. Melt butter in saucepan. Sauté onions and mushrooms over low heat until onion is clear and tender. Remove from heat; set aside. Combine flour and seasonings. Heat oil in skillet. Coat livers with flour mixture and fry in oil until lightly browned and crisp. Reduce heat. Add onions, mushrooms and wine. Simmer, covered, 20 to 30 minutes. Serves 3 to 4.

Susan S. Hereford (Mrs. Philip B.)

CHICKEN AND ARTICHOKES

3 whole chicken breasts
¼ cup cooking oil
4 carrots, sliced
1 (6 ounce) can mushrooms, drained
1 (14 ounce) can artichoke hearts, drained and halved

½ cup chopped green onion
1 (8 ounce) can sliced water chestnuts, drained
⅛ teaspoon thyme
Salt and pepper
1½ cups chicken broth
¾ cup white wine
2 tablespoons cornstarch

Simmer chicken in water until tender. Reserve 1½ cups broth. Skin, bone, and cut chicken into bite size pieces. Brown in oil in a large skillet. Add carrots. Simmer covered 5 minutes. Add mushrooms, artichokes, onion, water chestnuts and seasonings. Cover and simmer 10 minutes. Combine broth, wine and cornstarch in small pan, stirring well. Cook over medium heat, stirring until thick. Place chicken and vegetables in greased 9" x 13" baking dish. Pour sauce over mixture. Bake at 375° for 45 minutes, basting occasionally. Serve over noodles or rice. Serves 4 to 6.

Susan Beattie

CHICKEN ASPARAGUS CASSEROLE

2 (8 ounces each) packages cream cheese
1 teaspoon salt
2 cups milk
¾ cup grated Cheddar cheese

3 whole chicken breasts, cooked, boned and cubed
1 (14½ ounce) can asparagus spears

In top of double boiler, heat milk, salt and cream cheese. Stir until thick and smooth. Add Cheddar cheese. Mix well. Place chicken and asparagus in 9" x 13" baking dish. Cover with sauce. Bake at 350° for 30 minutes. Serves 4 to 6.

Sandra M. Haden (Mrs. David S.)

CHICKEN ASPARAGUS CASSEROLE OLÉ

6 whole chicken breasts, cooked
1 medium onion, chopped
½ cup butter
1 (8 ounce) can mushrooms
1 (10 ounce) can cream of mushroom soup
1 (10 ounce) can cream of chicken soup
1 (15 ounce) can evaporated milk

½ pound sharp Cheddar cheese, grated
¼ teaspoon Tabasco sauce
2 teaspoons soy sauce
½ teaspoon salt
½ teaspoon pepper
2 tablespoons pimento
2 (14½ ounces each) can asparagus spears
½ cup slivered almonds

Bone chicken and cut into bite sized pieces. Set aside. Sauté onion in butter in large saucepan. Add remaining ingredients, except asparagus and almonds. Simmer sauce until cheese melts. To assemble: place a layer of chicken in a large casserole, a layer of asparagus and a layer of sauce. Repeat layers, ending with sauce. Top with almonds. Bake at 350° for 30 minutes, until bubbly. Do not add liquid, even if it looks dry. Freezes well. Serves 8 to 10.

Marie F. Nesius (Mrs. John)

CHICKEN ENCHILADAS

4 cups finely chopped, cooked chicken
1 (8 ounce) package cream cheese, softened
12 flour tortillas
1 (16 ounce) can peeled tomatoes

1 (4 ounce) can green chilies
1 cup sour cream
1 cup grated Monterey Jack cheese

Mix chicken with cream cheese. Fill tortillas with chicken mixture and fold. Place in 9" x 13" baking dish. Combine tomatoes, chilies and sour cream in blender, blending until smooth. Pour sauce over enchiladas. Top with grated cheese. Bake, covered, at 350° for 30 minutes. Freezes well. Serves 6.

Jean W. Hutton (Mrs. John P.)

CHICKEN AND MELON

1 (4 to 5 pound) chicken, cooked	2 teaspoons minced ginger root
5 tablespoons soy sauce	1 teaspoon crushed red peppercorns
2½ tablespoons honey	
1 clove garlic, crushed	1 head lettuce
3 tablespoons peanut oil	Honeydew melon and
3 green onions, chopped	cantaloupe slices

Skin, bone and cut chicken into bite size pieces. Refrigerate. Combine soy sauce, honey and garlic in bowl. In saucepan heat oil, onions, ginger and peppercorns. Simmer 3 minutes. Add soy sauce mixture. Cool. To serve, place lettuce on platter. Arrange chicken and melon slices alternately. Pour sauce over chicken pieces just before serving. Serves 8.

Elizabeth F. Trammell (Mrs. S. Willis)

CHICKEN AVOCADO SALAD

1 ripe avocado, peeled and chopped	½ cup mayonnaise Bibb lettuce leaves
2 tablespoons lemon juice	½ cup chopped green onions
½ pound cooked bacon, crumbled	½ cup chopped fresh parsley
2½ cups chopped, cooked chicken	12 pitted black olives, chopped

Toss avocado in lemon juice. Combine avocado, bacon and chicken. Toss lightly with mayonnaise. Arrange lettuce on platter. Mound chicken in center. Garnish with green onions, parsley and olives. Note: tomato and hard boiled egg wedges may also be used as garnish. Serves 4 to 6.

Sara Z. Hoblitzell (Mrs. John R.)

BLACKMAIL CHICKEN SALAD

2 pounds chicken, cooked, boned and chopped	1 cup shredded coconut
1 cup finely chopped celery	1½ cups mayonnaise
1 cup raisins	Slices of avocado and banana
1 cup salted peanuts	Lemon juice
1 cup mango chutney, chopped	Chow mein noodles (optional)

Combine first 7 ingredients. Toss. Garnish with banana and avocado slices that have been dipped in lemon juice. Surround with chow mein noodles to serve. Hint: bake chicken to retain texture and flavor. Serves 12.

Mary Lee W. Lilly (Mrs. J.K., III)

LAYERED CHICKEN OR TUNA SALAD

1 tablespoon gelatin
¼ cup cold water
1 cup mayonnaise
½ cup chopped celery
1 tablespoon grated onion
½ cup chopped pimento
2 cups cooked, chopped
   chicken or tuna, drained

1 (3 ounce) package strawberry gelatin
1 cup boiling water
¾ jar (14 ounce) cranberry-
   orange relish
1 (9 ounce) can crushed
   pineapple, drained

Soak gelatin in cold water and dissolve <u>over</u> boiling water. Fold in mayonnaise, celery, onion, pimento and chicken. Spread in 9" x 13" pan. Dissolve strawberry gelatin in boiling water. Stir in relish and pineapple. Pour over meat layer. Chill until set. Serves 6.

Lucy Payne Paynter (Mrs. George W.)

BARBEQUE SAUCE

2 (14 ounces each) bottles
   ketchup
1 (12 ounce) bottle chili
   sauce
1 tablespoon dry mustard
⅓ cup prepared mustard
2 tablespoons fresh ground
   pepper
1½ cups wine vinegar
1 cup fresh lemon juice

1½ cups brown sugar
½ cup bottled steak sauce
   Dash of Tabasco sauce
¼ cup Worcestershire sauce
1 tablespoon soy sauce
2 tablespoons cooking oil
1 (12 ounce) can beer
   Minced or crushed garlic
   (optional)

Combine all ingredients. Stores for several weeks in refrigerator. May be frozen. Good with chicken or any meat. Excellent as marinade. Makes 6 pints.

Francis R. Slack (Mrs. John M., Jr.)

CHICKEN BARBEQUE SAUCE

1½ cups cooking oil
2½ cups vinegar
2 tablespoons salt
1¼ teaspoons black pepper
2½ teaspoons poultry seasoning

1 teaspoon red pepper
1 teaspoon chili powder
⅓ cup Worcestershire sauce
   Juice from 1½ lemons

Mix all ingredients. Use to baste charcoaled chicken. Makes sauce for 6 chickens (12 halves). Store in refrigerator.

Elaine R. Kroner (Mrs. Robert J.)

MARINADE FOR CHICKEN

1½ cups cooking oil
¾ cup soy sauce
¼ cup Worcestershire sauce
2 tablespoons dry mustard
1 teaspoon salt
½ cup wine vinegar

1½ teaspoons chopped
    parsley
2 garlic cloves, minced
⅓ cup lemon juice
1 tablespoon pepper

Combine all ingredients. Marinate chicken up to 24 hours.

Francis R. Slack (Mrs. John M., Jr.)

ROAST CORNISH HENS WITH CURRANT JELLY

4 Cornish game hens
  Salt and pepper
4 tablespoons margarine
8 ounces red currant jelly

2 tablespoons vinegar
2 teaspoons prepared
    mustard
2 tablespoons sherry or
    Port wine

Wash hens inside and out. Dry cavity and salt and pepper lightly. Rub outside of hens with margarine and season. Place breast side up in roasting pan. Bake at 425° for 15 minutes. Prepare sauce by combining remaining ingredients in saucepan over medium heat, cooking until smooth. Baste hens with sauce for additional 15 to 20 minutes until nicely browned and glazed. Serves 4.

Sara Z. Hoblitzell (Mrs. John R.)

DOVE Á LA KING

2 cups cooked, diced dove
2 tablespoons butter
1 green pepper, chopped
1 cup sliced mushrooms
1½ to 2 cups chicken or dove
    stock

2 tablespoons cornstarch
2 egg yolks, beaten
1 tablespoon diced pimento
4 teaspoons sherry
½ cup sour cream

Melt butter in large saucepan. Sauté green peppers and mushrooms until tender. Add stock and dove meat, heating thoroughly. In a cup stir cornstarch and enough hot stock together to make a thin paste. Slowly stir back into saucepan and cook until thickened. Remove from heat. Slowly stir in egg yolks, sherry and pimento. Just before serving add sour cream and heat: do not boil. This can be served in a chafing dish and spooned over patty shells.

Mrs. Lee Weisnicht

CREAMED DOVE BREASTS

12 dove breasts
1 medium onion, chopped
2 tablespoons margarine, melted
2 stalks celery, chopped
1 (10½ ounce) can cream of mushroom soup
⅔ cup white wine or chicken broth
1 teaspoon fines herbes
1 teaspoon Worcestershire sauce
1 cup sour cream

Sauté onion and celery in margarine 2 to 3 minutes. Add soup, wine and seasonings. Place dove breasts in 9" x 13" baking dish. Pour sauce over breasts. Bake, covered, at 350° for 1 hour. Stir sour cream into sauce, uncover and bake 10 to 15 minutes until heated. Serve over wild rice or parsleyed noodles. Serves 6.

Harriet D. Bradford (Mrs. Bert, Jr.)

MANDARIN DUCK

4 to 5 pound duck
1 (6 ounce) can frozen orange juice
3 to 4 tablespoons soy sauce
Dash of Tabasco sauce
2 teaspoons prepared mustard
¼ cup brown sugar
Salt and pepper to taste

Cut duck into pieces. Bake at 400° for 45 to 60 minutes. Broil the last 5 minutes to brown on top if necessary. Drain grease from duck. Combine remaining ingredients, blending well. Pour over duck. Brown in oven until sauce is gooey and duck is crispy.

Mrs. Rex E. Moule

SMITH MOUNTAIN LAKE BARBECUED DUCK

2 to 4 wild ducks
½ cup margarine
¾ cup ketchup
1½ tablespoons sugar
1½ teaspoons lemon juice
1 teaspoon seasoned salt
1 tablespoon Worcestershire sauce
1 teaspoon salt
½ teaspoon Tabasco sauce
1 large onion, chopped
Pepper to taste

Soak ducks in vinegar water to cover for several hours. Rinse thoroughly and dry completely. In medium saucepan combine rest of ingredients and simmer 15 to 20 minutes to make barbeque sauce. Split ducks in half with a cleaver. Place ducks in roasting pan. Cover and bake at 350°, basting every 20 minutes with sauce. Cook 2 to 3 hours until tender and done.

Mrs. Lee Weisnicht

MAXINE WALTER'S CREAMED DUCK

(MY WAY)

2 wild ducks	½ pound fresh mushrooms
3 stalks celery	4 tablespoons butter
1 green onion	1 jar pearl onions
Salt and pepper to taste	½ pound slab bacon

SAUCE

6 tablespoons flour	Nutmeg
6 tablespoons butter	Salt and pepper
1¼ cups half and half	Tabasco sauce
1¼ cups milk	

PASTRY

1 cup flour	⅓ cup shortening
1 teaspoon sugar	3 tablespoons cold water
1 teaspoon salt	

Simmer duck in enough water to cover with celery, salt, pepper and green onion until tender, about 1½ hours. This may be done night before or early in day. When tender, remove meat from bones and cut into bite size pieces. Sprinkle with salt and pepper. Cover and set aside.

Pastry: Combine dry ingredients in bowl. Cut in shortening with fork, blending until crumbly. Add cold water. Blend, form ball and chill 20 minutes or longer.

Sauce: Combine flour and butter in saucepan over medium heat. Cook, stirring constantly, 3 to 5 minutes until light brown. Gradually add liquids, stirring until smooth and thickened. Season with salt, pepper, 2 dashes of nutmeg and Tabasco.

Combine sauce and duck pieces. Place in buttered 1½ quart casserole. Clean mushrooms and sauté in saucepan in butter. Place on top of duck. Drain pearl onions. Place on top of mushrooms. Cut slab bacon into 1" cubes and fry. Drain. Add to casserole. Roll out chilled pastry on floured surface. Place over top of casserole. Trim edges and press to seal edges. Pierce top of pastry in several places to allow steam to escape. Decorate top with pastry scraps cut into duck shapes. Bake at 325° for 30 minutes. May add peas, chopped carrots, parsley or chives to casserole if desired.

Mrs. Glenville A. Jewell

ROAST PHEASANT

1 (2 to 3 pound) pheasant
  for every two guests
Salt
Freshly ground pepper

1 lemon slice per pheasant
Soft butter
Thin sliced bacon
Tarragon vinegar

Salt and pepper pheasant inside and out. Place lemon slice in breast cavity. Rub bird with butter. Cover breast and legs with several slices of bacon. Place in shallow roasting pan. Cook at 350° for 30 minutes per pound. Baste bird with additional melted butter and vinegar. Remove bacon as it browns. Place birds on warm platter and serve with sauce.

SAUCE

2 tablespoons butter
  Pheasant liver

1 cup chicken stock
3 tablespoons Burgundy
  wine

Finely chop pheasant liver and sauté in butter. Add wine and chicken stock. Simmer 5 to 10 minutes.

Carolyn G. Henshaw (Mrs. Harry P., III)

PHEASANT TARRAGON

1 pheasant
½ teaspoon seasoned salt
½ teaspoon pepper
¼ teaspoon paprika
½ cup margarine
1 stalk celery, chopped
1 medium onion, chopped

½ pound mushrooms,
  chopped
1 teaspoon tarragon
1 teaspoon fresh parsley,
  chopped
½ cup white wine, water or
  chicken stock

Cut pheasant into pieces. Season with salt, pepper and paprika. Melt margarine in a large skillet over medium heat. Add pheasant and brown. Remove pheasant. Add celery, onion and mushrooms. Cook 2 to 3 minutes until tender. Add pheasant, tarragon, parsley and wine. Cover, reduce heat and simmer 45 to 60 minutes until tender. Serves 4.

Harriet D. Bradford (Mrs. Bert, Jr.)

QUAIL IN RED WINE

6 quail, cleaned*	1 cup consommé
Brandy	1 cup dry red wine
6 tablespoons flour	1 stalk celery, quartered
6 tablespoons margarine	Salt and pepper to taste
2 cups sliced mushrooms	Juice of 2 oranges,
¼ cup margarine, melted	strained

Rub quail with cloth soaked in brandy. Dust with flour. Melt 6 tablespoons margarine in large, heavy skillet. Add quail and sauté 10 minutes. In separate pan, sauté mushrooms in ¼ cup margarine. Pour over quail. Add consommé, wine, celery, salt and pepper. Cover and simmer 20 to 30 minutes, until quail is tender. Remove celery. Stir in orange juice. Heat thoroughly. Serve with wild rice. Serves 3 to 4 allowing 1½ to 2 quail per person.

*May use grouse.

Beverly S. McElroy (Mrs. William B.)

VENISON SAUTÉ WITH VEGETABLES

2 pounds venison steaks	½ teaspoon salt
or cutlets	Pepper to taste
2 tablespoons cooking oil	1 bay leaf
1 clove garlic, minced	3 tablespoons margarine
1 cup diced celery	3 tablespoons flour
½ cup chopped onion	1 cup sour cream
1 cup diced carrots	Fresh parsley
1½ cups water	

Brown venison in oil on both sides in heavy skillet. Remove to shallow 3 quart casserole. Add onion, garlic, celery and carrots to skillet and sauté 2 minutes. Add water, salt, pepper and bay leaf and pour over venison. Bake at 350° for 30 minutes. Remove from oven. Drain off broth and reserve. In saucepan melt margarine. Add flour and cook 2 minutes, stirring until smooth and bubbly. Slowly add broth and cook, stirring until thickened. Stir in sour cream. Pour over venison and vegetables. Garnish with parsley. Serves 6.

Helen Z. Chilton (Mrs. Robert M.)

RACK OF VENISON

6 to 8 pound rack or loin of venison	1 teaspoon pepper
Salt pork or bacon strips	2 tablespoons chopped parsley
2 medium carrots, chopped	Juice of 2 lemons
4 medium onions, chopped	Rind of 2 lemons, halved
2 cloves garlic, minced	1 cup olive oil
½ teaspoon thyme	2½ cups red wine: Burgundy
½ teaspoon oregano	or Cabernet, divided
½ teaspoon basil	4 tablespoons flour
1½ teaspoons salt	1 cup consommé

Make an incision every 2″ in venison and insert thin strips of salt pork or bacon. Cover top of venison with 2 to 4 additional thin strips of salt pork. Combine next 12 ingredients, mixing well. Place marinade and venison in a large oven roasting bag. Refrigerate 24 to 48 hours, turning frequently to ensure that all surfaces of the meat are kept moistened. Remove venison and place in a large roasting pan. Pour marinade over meat, first removing lemon rind from marinade. Bake, uncovered, at 325° allowing 20 minutes per pound for rare, 22 minutes for medium rare meat. Baste frequently. Add 2 cups red wine after 30 minutes cooking time. When done, remove meat to a heated platter. On top of stove over medium heat add flour to roasting pan. Stir flour with drippings until very smooth and browned. Gradually add remaining ½ cup wine and consommé. Stir, scraping the sides of the pan to include bits of meat on side of roaster. Correct seasonings if desired. Strain if a smooth gravy is desired. Serve meat sliced to medium thickness with sauce poured over. Potato Dumplings are a good accompaniment.

Mary Dills (Mrs. Napier)

VENISON SUPREME

2 pounds venison round steak	½ pound mushrooms, sliced
	1 cup sour cream
1 (10½ ounce) can cream of mushroom soup	½ cup sherry
	Salt and pepper to taste

Cut venison in cubes and brown in Dutch oven. Add rest of ingredients. Simmer several hours until tender. Serve over parsleyed noodles. Serves 4.

Mrs. Lee Weisnicht

CHUCK'S CHILI

2 pounds venison, moose,
   caribou or round steak
3 tablespoons cooking oil
3 medium onions, chopped
2 green peppers, thinly
   sliced
3 cloves garlic, chopped
2 (28 ounces each) cans
   whole tomatoes
1 (29 ounce) can tomato
   sauce

2 teaspoons paprika
6 tablespoons chili powder
2 teaspoons ground red
   pepper (or to taste)
1 teaspoon ground cumin
2 (15 ounces each) cans
   dark red kidney beans
4 teaspoons masa harina
   (may substitute flour or
   2 teaspoons cornstarch)
Grated Cheddar cheese

Dice meat into 1" cubes. In large skillet sauté meat in oil until grayish in color with onion, peppers and garlic. Drain and place in Dutch oven. Add tomatoes, tomato sauce and spices. Simmer, covered, for 1½ hours. Stir in kidney beans. Add small amount of hot liquid to masa flour in a separate cup, stirring to make a thin paste. Stir into chili. Cook an additional 15 minutes before serving. Top with Cheddar cheese to serve. Serves 8 to 10.

Diana H. Pettry (Mrs. Charles E., Jr.)

VENISON MEAT LOAF

2 pounds ground venison
¼ pound uncooked bacon,
   chopped
1 onion, chopped
1 cup bread crumbs

1 package dry onion soup
   mix
Several tablespoons of
   milk
¼ to ½ cup chili sauce
Parsley flakes

Mix first 6 ingredients, adding enough milk to bind together. Place in greased meat loaf pan. Spread chili sauce on top to cover and garnish with parsley. Bake, uncovered, at 375° for 1 hour. Remove bacon grease as meat loaf bakes. Serves 4.

Mrs. Lee Weisnicht

150

OLD STONE HOUSE — TYREE TAVERN

Of the thirty stage stands along the James River and Kanawha
Turnpike between Lewisburg and Charleston, probably the most
famous and popular was the Tyree Tavern at the western foot of
Big Sewell Mountain in Fayette County. The stone building was
built by Sam Tyree in 1824 and remained in the Tyree family until
1884 when it was sold to the Longdale Iron Company along with
many other tracts in the immediate area.

The Tavern was popular because of its location, about halfway
between Lewisburg and Charleston. Many prominent historic fig-
ures visited the Tavern including Henry Clay, Andrew Jackson,
Thomas H. Benton, Daniel Webster and John C. Breckenridge. The
Tavern was, at different times during the Civil War, the headquar-
ters of General Lee and General Rosecrans.

The original house, with 22 inch-thick stone walls, was about
forty feet long and thirty feet deep, and two-stories high plus attic.
Heat was provided by fireplaces on each floor which vented into
wide chimneys on each end of the house. There are two doors and
one window on the first floor of the front elevation, and three
windows on the second floor. Small windows flank the chimneys
on each end of the house at the attic level. Over the years the house
has changed somewhat architecturally with two additions to the
east end, a small porch and stoop at the rear and a deep, one-story
porch across the entire front.

A stone spring house outbuilding remains but the log outbuildings necessary to the operation of a stage stand have disappeared.
There is evidence that an outside kitchen once stood near the rear
of the east side of the house. The old stone wall and loading block
used by passengers alighting from stages stand near the road. The
road in front of the house is a remnant of the original James River
and Kanawha Turnpike.

The Old Stone Tavern still stands just off U.S. Route 60 about
two miles east of Clifftop.

Photo courtesy of Education Foundation

SALADS AND DRESSINGS

Flying Geese

ARTICHOKE RICE SALAD

1 (8 ounce) package chicken
   flavored rice
1 (6¼ ounce) package fried
   rice mix with almonds
½ cup chopped green
   pepper
½ cup chopped green onion

1 teaspoon curry
½ cup chopped pimento
   stuffed olives
2 (6 ounces each) jars marinated artichoke hearts,
   drained and sliced
½ cup mayonnaise

Prepare both packages of rice as directed, omitting margarine. Cool for 10 minutes. Combine with remaining ingredients. Toss and chill. Serves 8 to 10.

Caroline C. Nelson

AVOCADOS VINAIGRETTE

2 avocados
2 small red onions
2 cucumbers
¼ cup vinegar

¾ cup salad oil
2 teaspoon salt
2 teaspoons dry mustard
Pepper to taste

Slice cucumbers crosswise into 3 to 4 sections, then slice sections lengthwise. Slice onions into thin rounds. Slice avocados lengthwise, 12 slices per avocado. Mix together next five ingredients. Add vegetables and chill at least 2 to 3 hours. Serve vegetables on a salad plate with a tablespoon of marinade. Serves 4 to 6.

Mary Virginia Gray

BROCCOLI SUMMER SALAD

1 large bunch broccoli
1 medium cucumber
1 large tomato
1 medium red onion

1 cup grated sharp Cheddar
    cheese
¼ cup salad oil
¼ cup red wine vinegar
    Salt and pepper

Cut broccoli flowerettes into bite size pieces. Cook in boiling water 2 to 3 minutes. Drain. Peel and slice cucumber. Slice tomato and onion. Mix together and add cheese. Mix oil, vinegar, salt and pepper. Pour over broccoli mixture. Chill. (Your own choice of dressing may be substituted for the oil and vinegar.) Serves 4 to 6.

Judy Grigoraci (Mrs. Victor)

FROSTED CANTALOUPE SALAD

1 (8 ounce) package cream
    cheese
2 tablespoons milk
1 large cantaloupe

6 cups fresh fruit of your
    choice
    Grated coconut

Soften cream cheese and beat with milk until fluffy. Set aside. Peel cantaloupe. Cut a slice off the bottom, chop and add to the fresh fruit. Scoop out the seeds and fill with one cup of fruit. Place melon, cut side down, on plate. Frost with cream cheese mixture. Press coconut lightly on cheese. Place remaining fruit around cantaloupe. Refrigerate until serving. Cut cantaloupe into 6 servings.

Vicki M. Cunningham (Mrs. Jan)

MARINATED CARROTS

2 pounds carrots, sliced
1 medium green pepper
1 medium onion
1 (10 ounce) can tomato
    soup
½ cup salad oil
¾ cup sugar

¼ cup vinegar
¼ teaspoon mustard
1 teaspoon Worcestershire
    sauce
1 teaspoon salt
½ teaspoon pepper

Cook carrots 5 minutes. Drain. Cut pepper and onion into rings. Combine remaining ingredients. Pour over vegetables. Chill overnight. Serve cold. Keeps 2 to 3 weeks in refrigerator, covered.
May substitute 2 (16 ounces each) cans carrots for fresh carrots.

Melinda W. Crislip (Mrs. Stephen R.)

CUCUMBER SALAD

2 large cucumbers
½ cup sour cream
½ cup mayonnaise
2 teaspoons salt

½ teaspoon fresh ground
  pepper
¼ cup fresh dill, chopped or
  1 tablespoon dried dill

Peel cucumbers. Cut in half lengthwise, remove seeds and slice thinly into a bowl. Sprinkle with salt and let stand 10 minutes. Press out water with hands. Combine remaining ingredients. Pour over cucumbers. Serves 4.

Louise Wiseman (Mrs. Marrs)

CURRIED FRUIT AND NUT SALAD

SALAD

1 head red leaf or Romaine
  lettuce
1 cup fresh spinach
1 (11 ounce) can mandarin
  oranges, chilled and
  drained

1 cup grapes, halved and
  seeded
½ cup toasted and slivered
  almonds

DRESSING

½ cup salad oil
⅓ cup white wine vinegar
1 clove garlic, minced
2 tablespoons brown sugar

2 tablespoons minced
  chives
2 teaspoons curry powder
1 teaspoon soy sauce
1 avocado, sliced (optional)

Mix together salad ingredients. Combine dressing ingredients, blending well. Pour over salad just before serving. Garnish with avocado slices if desired. Serves 8.

Jane S. McEldowney (Mrs. Robert)

GRAPEFRUIT AND AVOCADO SALAD

SALAD

2 avocados   Lettuce leaves
2 grapefruits

POPPY SEED DRESSING

½ cup sugar   ¾ cup salad oil
1 teaspoon salt   1 tablespoon poppy seeds
1 teaspoon dry mustard   ⅓ cup fresh lemon juice
½ teaspoon grated lemon peel

Combine all ingredients for dressing except poppy seeds in electric blender or covered jar. Blend thoroughly. Stir in poppy seeds. Chill 2 to 3 hours before serving. Slice avocados into 12 slices. Section grapefruits. Arrange on bed of lettuce allowing 4 avocado slices and 5 grapefruit sections per serving. Top with dressing and serve. Serves 6.
Variations: 1. Add melon balls, orange sections or green grapes.
2. Add finely chopped pecans as garnish.

Mary Virginia Gray

KIDNEY BEAN SALAD

2 (16 ounces each) cans   ¼ cup chopped celery
   kidney beans, drained   ⅛ teaspoon pepper
3 sweet or dill pickles,   ¼ cup mayonnaise or sour
   chopped   cream
1 small onion, minced   4 hard boiled eggs, chopped
½ teaspoon salt   1 head lettuce

Combine all ingredients except eggs and lettuce. Chill several hours. Serve on bed of lettuce, garnished with eggs. Serves 10 to 12.

Mary Lee W. Lilly (Mrs. J.K., III)

MACARONI PICNIC BOWL

1 (8 ounce) package
   macaroni
1 (10 ounce) package frozen
   peas and carrots,
   thawed
1 cup diced Cheddar cheese
⅓ cup sliced celery
⅓ cup vinegar

⅓ cup salad oil
⅓ cup water
2 teaspoons sugar
1 teaspoon salt
½ teaspoon marjoram
½ teaspoon chervil
   Cherry tomatoes
   (optional)

Cook macaroni according to package directions. Rinse and drain. Combine peas and carrots with macaroni. Add cheese and celery. Cover and chill. Thoroughly blend remaining ingredients. Pour over macaroni mixture, tossing well. Chill several hours. Decorate with cherry tomatoes, if desired. Serves 12.

Kay J. Morgan (Mrs. Frederick M.)

MANDARIN SALAD

SALAD

¼ cup sliced almonds
1 tablespoon + 1 teaspoon
   sugar
¼ head lettuce
¼ head Romaine lettuce

2 green onions with tops,
   sliced thinly
1 (11 ounce) can mandarin
   oranges, drained

DRESSING

½ teaspoon salt
   Dash of pepper
2 tablespoons sugar
2 tablespoons vinegar

¼ cup salad oil
   Dash of red pepper sauce
1 tablespoon snipped
   parsley

Mix dressing in tightly covered jar. Chill. Cook almonds and sugar over low heat, stirring constantly until almonds are coated. Cool almonds and break apart. Tear lettuce and place in plastic bag. Add onion, fasten securely and refrigerate. Five minutes before serving, pour dressiong into bag. Shake. Add oranges. Shake. Add almonds. Shake and serve. Serves 4.

Ann W. Stowers (Mrs. Gerald R.)

GEORGIA'S CRUNCH SALAD

1 bunch broccoli
1 cup green or black olives
4 hard boiled eggs

1 tablespoon chopped onion
½ cup mayonnaise

Cut broccoli into bite size pieces, using flowerettes and part of stalk. Slice olives and eggs. Add to broccoli with onion. Mix well with mayonnaise. Serves 4 to 6.
Variation: Add one package frozen peas, thawed; add ⅓ cup of Parmesan cheese.

Georgia Menear

MARINATED SALAD

1 (14 ounce) can hearts of palm, drained and sliced
1 (14 ounce) can artichoke hearts, drained and quartered
6 ounces fresh mushrooms, sliced
1 or 2 red onions, sliced thinly

2 green peppers, cut in strips
1 bottle Good Seasons Italian dressing, made with red wine vinegar
½ cup white vinegar
Salad greens
Cherry tomatoes

Combine all ingredients except greens and tomatoes. Marinate overnight in refrigerator. To serve, toss with greens and tomatoes. Serves 12.

Mary J. Payne (Mrs. Andrew A., III)

HERBED PEA SALAD

2 (10 ounces each) package frozen peas, thawed
½ cup chopped celery
¼ cup chopped green onion
¼ cup chopped pimento (optional)
1 (.4 ounce) envelope buttermilk style herb dressing mix

1 cup mayonnaise
½ cup buttermilk
2 cups cubed cheese, any flavor
2 hard boiled eggs, chopped
1 cup herb flavored croutons

In large bowl, combine first four ingredients. In small bowl, mix together the next three ingredients, beating until smooth. Combine the two mixtures. Refrigerate covered 3 hours or overnight. Just before serving, fold in cheese, eggs and croutons. Serves 8 to 10.

Judy Grigoraci (Mrs. Victor)

CREAMY NEW POTATO SALAD

SALAD

6 cups new potatoes
5 hard boiled eggs, sliced
¼ cup grated onion, with
  juice

¼ cup chopped parsley
½ teaspoon salt
½ teaspoon pepper
Paprika

DRESSING

½ cup sugar
1 teaspoon dry mustard
¾ cup water
2 eggs, beaten

1 tablespoon cornstarch
½ teaspoon salt
¼ cup vinegar
1 cup mayonnaise

In saucepan over medium heat, combine dressing ingredients reserving mayonnaise. Cook, stirring until thick and bubbly. Remove from heat, cover and cool. Stir mayonnaise into cooled dressing. Cook potatoes in boiling water until fork tender. Cool and peel. Cut into ½" cubes. Combine potatoes, 4 eggs, onion, parsley, salt and pepper. Add dressing and toss gently. Garnish with reserved egg and paprika. Refrigerate, covered, until served. May be prepared the day ahead. Serves 8 to 10.

Judy M. Kim (Mrs. C. William)

POTATO SALAD VARIATION

4 hard boiled eggs
7 cups cooked chopped
  potatoes
10 slices cooked bacon,
  crumbled
⅓ cup sliced green onions

⅓ cup Italian dressing
¾ cup sour cream
⅔ cup mayonnaise
1½ teaspoons mustard
1 teaspoon salt
½ teaspoon celery seed

Cut eggs in half. Remove yolks and reserve. Chop whites, combining with potatoes, bacon and dressing. Add remaining ingredients, including yolks, mixing gently. Chill several hours or overnight. Serves 8.

Sandra W. Mantz (Mrs. Eric P.)

LAYERED POTATO SALAD

12 medium potatoes	1 teaspoon celery salt
2 cups mayonnaise	2 tablespoons chopped
½ cup sour cream	chives
2 tablespoons horseradish	1 cup chopped fresh parsley
½ teaspoon dill weed	

Cook whole potatoes in boiling water until fork tender. Remove skins and slice crosswise in thin slices. Mix next 6 ingredients. Layer ⅓ potato slices in serving bowl. Spread with ⅓ mayonnaise mixture. Sprinkle with ⅓ cup chopped parsley. Repeat layers twice. Cover and refrigerate overnight. Must be made ahead. Serves 8.

Sara Z. Hoblitzell (Mrs. John R.)

MAIN DISH POTATO SALAD

6 medium potatoes	1 stalk celery, chopped
1 medium onion, chopped	1½ cups sliced fresh
3 hard boiled eggs, chopped	mushrooms
2 teaspoons salt	8 slices cooked bacon,
1 teaspoon pepper	crumbled
⅓ cup mayonnaise	3 tablespoons hulled sun-
1 teaspoon mustard	flower seeds

Peel potatoes and boil until fork tender, about 25 minutes. Drain and cool. Cut into 1" cubes and place in a large bowl. Add remaining ingredients except sunflower seeds. Toss well. Spoon into serving dish and sprinkle with sunflower seeds. Serve warm or chilled. Serves 6.

Judy M. Kim (Mrs. C. William)

SALAD

⅓ cup red wine vinegar	1 small red onion, thinly
½ cup salad oil	sliced
1 (14 ounce) can artichoke	1 (2 ounce) jar pimento
hearts, drained	½ cup Parmesan cheese
1 (14 ounce) can hearts of	1½ heads iceberg lettuce
palm, drained	1½ heads red leaf lettuce

Mix oil and vinegar in a small bowl. Set aside. Mash artichokes and hearts of palm in bottom of a salad bowl. Tear lettuce in pieces and combine with onion, pimento and cheese in bowl. Pour oil and vinegar dressing over salad, tossing well. Refrigerate salad for at least 1 hour before serving. Serves 8 to 10.

Linda S. Faerber (Mrs. Kenneth)

SPINACH SALAD

1 pound fresh spinach
Salt and pepper to taste
½ to 1 teaspoon sugar
1 pound cooked bacon, crumbled
6 hard boiled eggs, chopped
1 (10 ounce) package frozen peas, thawed

1 medium onion, minced
2 stalks celery, chopped
½ cup mayonnaise
½ cup Miracle Whip
½ cup shredded Cheddar or Swiss cheese

Wash and dry spinach. Break into small pieces. Put in a large bowl. Sprinkle with salt, pepper, sugar, bacon and eggs. Next, layer peas, onion and celery. Mix mayonnaise and Miracle Whip together. Spread mixture on top of salad, sealing edges. Sprinkle with cheese, cover tightly, and chill overnight. Serves 10 to 12.

Sandra C. Tate (Mrs. Donald L.)

SALLY'S SPINACH SALAD

SALAD

1 pound fresh spinach
1 (16 ounce) can bean sprouts, drained, or equivalent fresh
½ cup water chestnuts, sliced

1 medium red onion, sliced
3 hard boiled eggs, diced
½ pound cooked bacon, crumbled

Wash and drain spinach. Remove tough stalks and tear into bite size pieces. Mix together with rest of ingredients. Toss with dressing. Serves 6 to 8.

DRESSING

½ cup salad oil
1 small onion, chopped
¼ cup ketchup

¼ cup sugar
¼ cup wine vinegar
4 dashes Worcestershire sauce

Mix ingredients in blender.

Carol C. Gaugot (Mrs. Philip D.)

STRAWBERRY SALAD

Lettuce
Fresh strawberries, sliced
½ cup sugar
2 tablespoons sesame seeds
1 tablespoon poppy seeds
1½ teaspoons minced onion
¼ teaspoon Worcestershire
   sauce
¼ teaspoon paprika

Place strawberries on lettuce leaves. Mix next six ingredients and sprinkle over berries. Serves 4.

Linda A. Faerber (Mrs. Kenneth)

TABOULEH

1 cup bulgar, cracked
   wheat
1 tablespoon crushed dried
   mint or 1 cup fresh
   mint, cut up
4 large tomatoes, chopped
1 bunch green onions,
   chopped
2 bunches parsley, chopped
Salt and pepper
¼ cup salad oil
Juice of 3 lemons

Soak bulgar wheat in cold water for 30 minutes. Squeeze water from bulgar wheat and mix with next 4 ingredients. Salt and pepper to taste. Add oil and lemon juice, tossing well. Refrigerate covered 6 to 8 hours. Will keep several days. Serve on lettuce, cabbage leaves or in pita bread. Serves 8.
Variation: Substitute ½ pound fresh spinach for 1 bunch parsley and add black olives for garnish.

Carolyn S. Rickey (Mrs. Jon H.)

TOMATO SALAD

1 clove garlic, mashed
½ teaspoon salt
¼ teaspoon pepper
¼ cup lemon juice
2 cucumbers
3 tomatoes
1 small onion, chopped
1 teaspoon parsley, chopped
¼ cup pimento stuffed
   olives, sliced (optional)
¼ cup salad oil
½ cup chopped green
   pepper (optional)

Combine garlic, salt, pepper and lemon juice. Cut cucumbers and tomatoes into bite size pieces. Add to lemon juice mixture along with rest of ingredients, tossing gently. Chill 2 hours before serving. Serves 4 to 6.

Elizabeth Jane Bowles (Mrs. Paul N., Jr.)

KRAUT SALAD

½ cup white vinegar
½ cup sugar
1 pint shredded kraut
2 tablespoons chopped
   pimento

1 cup thinly sliced onion
1 cup sliced green pepper
½ cup salad oil

Heat vinegar and sugar in saucepan to dissolve sugar. Cool. Rinse kraut with cold water and drain. Combine with next three ingredients in large bowl. Pour cooled vinegar and sugar over kraut mixture. Add oil and stir. Will keep, covered, in refrigerator 2 to 3 weeks. Serves 8.

Jonnie C. Shepler (Mrs. David C.)

MARINATED TOMATOES
Best made with garden fresh tomatoes

6 large garden tomatoes
1 (8 ounce) jar Italian style
   dressing
4 green onions, chopped

Fresh basil, parsley and
   chives (may use what-
   ever fresh herbs are
   available)

Slice tomatoes in 3 or 4 thick slices. Place in 9″ glass dish, or similar serving piece. Sprinkle with chopped onions and herbs. Pour dressing over, using just enough to cover bottom of dish. Cover and chill until ready to serve. Best prepared several hours ahead. Serves 8.

Sara Z. Hoblitzell (Mrs. John R.)

CRUNCHY VEGETABLE SALAD

1 head cauliflower
1 bunch broccoli
3 carrots, sliced
3 green onions, chopped
   (including tops)

½ cup chopped celery
1 cup sour cream
1 cup mayonnaise
1 package Good Seasons
   Cheese Garlic dressing

Cut broccoli and cauliflower flowerettes into bite size pieces. Combine with carrots, onions and celery. Blend last 3 ingredients and pour over vegetables. Toss until well coated. Refrigerate for several hours before serving. Serves 10 to 12.

Janice H. Flannery (Mrs. David M.)

MARINATED VEGETABLES

3 stalks celery
4 large carrots
3 small onions, thinly sliced

½ pound fresh mushrooms
10 radishes
2 cucumbers

Cut all vegetables into bite size pieces. Toss with dressing. Serves 8 to 10.

FRENCH DRESSING

¼ cup tomato sauce
⅓ cup red wine vinegar
1 cup salad oil
1 teaspoon salt
1 teaspoon basil
1 tablespoon sugar

1 teaspoon Worcestershire sauce
¼ teaspoon dry mustard
⅛ teaspoon hot pepper sauce
¼ teaspoon pepper
1 clove garlic, minced

Blend until smooth. Pour over vegetables and toss gently. Cover and refrigerate several hours.
Variations: Can add most any favorite vegetables.

Janet C. Simpson (Mrs. Robert R., Jr.)

"WHITE" MARINATED VEGETABLE SALAD

1 (10 ounce) package each, frozen: broccoli spears, asparagus spears, French green beans
2 (14 ounces each) cans artichoke hearts, drained and halved
¾ cup chopped fresh parsley

1 cup peeled, thinly sliced cucumber
1 green pepper, chopped
2 tablespoons fresh lemon juice
2 tablespoons garlic vinegar
1 cup mayonnaise
½ cup half & half
¼ cup chopped onion

Cook frozen vegetables until crisp tender. Drain and cool. Combine with artichokes, parsley, cucumber and pepper. Mix remaining ingredients, blending well. Pour over vegetables. Refrigerate in a sealed container for 24 hours, stirring occasionally. Serves 8.

Susan S. Sibley (Mrs. Richard H.)

"CLASSIC" WALDORF SALAD

2 cups diced apple	1 tablespoon sugar
1 cup diced celery	½ teaspoon lemon juice
½ cup broken walnuts	Salt to taste
½ cup raisins	1 cup whipped cream or
¼ cup mayonnaise	whipped topping

Combine apple, celery, walnuts and raisins. In a separate bowl blend together mayonnaise, sugar, lemon juice and salt. Stir dressing into fruits. Fold in whipped cream. Chill 2 to 3 hours. Serves 4.

Mary Beth Hansen (Mrs. Randall)

ASPARAGUS MOLD

1 teaspoon unflavored gelatin	½ cup Green Goddess dressing
½ cup cold water	½ cup diced celery
1 (3 ounce) package lemon gelatin	1 (14½ ounce) can cut asparagus, drained
2 cubes chicken bouillon	2 tablespoons finely chopped green pepper
1 cup boiling water	
1 tablespoon lemon juice	

Soften unflavored gelatin in cold water. Dissolve lemon gelatin and bouillon in boiling water. Add unflavored gelatin and stir until dissolved. Add dressing and lemon juice. Stir with wire whisk until smooth. Chill until slightly thickened. Stir in vegetables. Pour into oiled 1 quart mold and chill until firm. Serves 6.

Mrs. William A. Rice, Sr.

AVOCADO SALAD

1 (3 ounce) package lemon gelatin	3 tablespoons lemon juice
1 cup boiling water	1 cup mayonnaise
Green food coloring	1 cup mashed avocados
	½ teaspoon salt

Dissolve gelatin in boiling water. Add a drop or two of green food coloring. Cool. Add rest of ingredients. Place in a small mold. Chill until firm.

Tommie Sue Roncaglione

MOLDED APRICOT SALAD

2 (8 ounces each) cans or 4
   cups apricot halves
2 (3 ounces each) boxes
   orange gelatin
Dash of salt

1 (6 ounce) can frozen
   orange juice
2 tablespoons lemon juice
1 (7 ounce) bottle lemon-
   lime soda (not diet)

Drain apricots, saving 1½ cups juice. Purée apricots in blender. Combine reserved juice, salt and gelatin. Heat to boiling, stirring constantly. Remove from heat and add purée, orange juice concentrate and lemon juice. Slowly pour lemon-lime soda down side of pan. Mix gently with up and down motion. Pour into 6½ cup mold. Chill. Unmold to serve and garnish with fresh fruit or additional apricots. Serve with a mayonnaise and whipped cream dressing. Serves 6 to 8.

Susan B. Halonen (Mrs. Robert)

APRICOT GELATIN SALAD

1 (6 ounce) package apricot
   gelatin
1 cup crushed pineapple
2 bananas, mashed
1 cup miniature
   marshmallows
½ cup pineapple juice
2 tablespoons butter

¾ cup sugar
1 tablespoon flour
1 egg, beaten
1 (8 ounce) package cream
   cheese
1 package whipped topping
   mix

Mix gelatin according to package directions, chilling until slightly thickened. Add fruit and marshmallows. Chill until firm. Combine juice, butter, sugar, flour and egg in saucepan. Cook, stirring, until thickened. Add cream cheese and beat until smooth. Cool mixture. Mix topping according to package directions. Add to cooled mixture. Spread mixture over gelatin and refrigerate. Serves 8 to 10.

Kathy S. Chaney (Mrs. Malcolm)

BUTTERMILK GELATIN SALAD

2 (3 ounces each) boxes
   gelatin, any flavor;
   apricot or orange
   recommended
1 (20 ounce) can crushed
   pineapple in its own juice

2 cups buttermilk
1 (8 ounce) carton frozen
   whipped topping,
   thawed

Mix gelatin and pineapple in a saucepan. Bring to a boil, but do not allow to stick to the pan. Remove from heat. While still hot, add buttermilk and topping. Mix well by hand. Pour into mold or bundt pan. Chill.

Kay Y. Miller (Mrs. Joe)

CRANBERRY HOLIDAY SOUFFLE

1 (3 ounce) package lemon
   gelatin
1 cup hot water
1 (16 ounce) can whole
   cranberry sauce
½ cup mayonnaise

1½ ounces cream cheese
1 tablespoon lemon juice
¼ teaspoon salt
2 oranges, peeled and diced
¼ cup chopped pecans
½ cup chopped celery

Dissolve gelatin in hot water. Heat cranberry sauce until melted. Strain off ½ cup juice and add it to gelatin. Blend mayonnaise and cream cheese. Add to gelatin with lemon juice and salt. Blend thoroughly. Turn into freezer tray and chill until firm 1" from edge but soft in the center (20 minutes). Pour into a bowl and whip until fluffy. Fold in remaining ingredients. Pour into 3½ cup mold and chill until firm. Unmold and garnish with salad greens.

Rebecca B. Goldman (Mrs. J. Crawford)

CRANBERRY SALAD

1 (16 ounce) can pineapple
   chunks
1 (16 ounce) can pitted Bing
   cherries
2 (6 ounces each) packages
   strawberry gelatin

2 (16 ounces each) cans
   whole cranberry sauce
1 (16 ounce) package frozen
   whole strawberries
1 cup chopped nuts,
   optional

Drain juice from canned fruits and reserve. Measure juice and add water to make 2 cups. Combine gelatin and juice in saucepan over medium heat. Bring to a boil, stirring until gelatin is dissolved. Add cranberry sauce, cherries and pineapple. Slice partially thawed strawberries and add to cooled mixture. Add nuts if desired. Pour into oiled 3 quart mold and chill until firm. Serves 12.

Barbara H. Slack (Mrs. John M., III)

CRANBERRY ORANGE SALAD

1 pound fresh cranberries
2 oranges, peeled, seeded
    and membranes
    removed
1 (16 ounce) can crushed
    pineapple, drained
1 orange peel, grated

1 large apple, peeled
1½ cups sugar
2 (3 ounces each) packages
    lemon gelatin
3 cups hot water
1½ cups chopped nuts
    (optional)

Grind first 5 ingredients together using a food grinder or processor. Add sugar. Let stand 1 hour. Combine gelatin and water, stirring until gelatin dissolves. Let stand until gelatin starts to thicken. Add ground fruit and nuts. Place in a large mold. Refrigerate several hours until firm.

Jane R. McCabe (Mrs. Dyer B.)

GRAPEFRUIT SALAD

⅓ cup water
⅓ cup sugar
1 tablespoon unflavored
    gelatin
2 tablespoons cold water

¾ cup grapefruit juice
1 tablespoon lemon juice
    Dash of salt
1 to 2 cups grapefruit
    sections

Boil sugar and water 3 minutes. Soften gelatin in cold water. Add to sugar water along with juices and salt. Stir well to dissolve gelatin. Strain into cold, wet mold in which grapefruit sections have been placed. Chill. Serve on bed of lettuce with orange or avocado slices. Serves 4.

Catherine I. Morgan (Mrs. John W.)

ORANGE SALAD

1 (11 ounce) can mandarin
    oranges
1 (8 ounce) can crushed
    pineapple
1 (3 ounce) package orange
    gelatin

1 (12 ounce) carton small
    curd cottage cheese
1 (8 ounce) carton frozen
    whipped topping,
    thawed

Drain fruit. Combine with gelatin, cottage cheese and whipped topping, stirring gently. Place in small mold. chill several hours. Serves 8.

Anne C. Kepple (Mrs. William)

ORANGE GELATIN

1 (6 ounce) box orange
   gelatin
2 cups hot water
2 cups orange sherbet,
   softened

½ cup mandarin oranges,
   drained
½ cup crushed pineapple,
   drained
½ cup sliced bananas

Dissolve gelatin in hot water. Add remaining ingredients, mixing well. Chill until set. A favorite with children. Serves 8 to 10.

Mary T. Karr (Mrs. George W.)

PINEAPPLE CHEESE MOLD

1 envelope unflavored
   gelatin
1 cup cold water
1 (8 ounce) can crushed
   pineapple
¾ cup sugar

Juice of 1 lemon
1 cup grated Cheddar
   cheese
½ pint whipping cream,
   whipped

Dissolve gelatin in water. Boil pineapple, sugar and lemon juice until sugar dissolves. Add gelatin, stirring until dissolved. Cool until partially set. Add cheese and whipped cream. Pour into oiled mold and chill until set. Serves 4 to 6.

Mrs. John J. Herlihy

RED RASPBERRY RING

1 (10 ounce) package frozen
   red raspberries
1 (6 ounce) package red
   raspberry gelatin

2 cups boiling water
1 pint vanilla ice cream
1 (6 ounce) can frozen
   lemonade
¼ cup chopped pecans

Drain raspberries and set aside. Dissolve gelatin in boiling water. Add ice cream by spoonfuls, stirring until melted. Stir in lemonade and chill until partially set. Add raspberries and pecans. Chill. Serves 8.

Judy Ellen Hanlen

FROZEN FRUIT MELANGE

1 cup sugar
3 cups water
1 (12 ounce) can frozen
    orange juice plus 1 can
    water
6 bananas, chopped
1 (16 ounce) can frozen
    strawberries with syrup
1 (20 ounce) can crushed
    pineapple with juice

Place sugar and water in a medium saucepan. Bring to a boil and cook until sugar is dissolved. Combine with remaining ingredients in a large bowl. Cover and place in freezer, stirring occasionally as the mixture freezes. Freeze overnight. Set out 1 hour before serving. Break up slightly for ease in serving. Delicious served with brunch, as a dessert or spooned over pound cake.

Joan W. Carey (Mrs. Mark)

TOMATO ASPIC

2 cups V-8 juice
1 (3 ounce) package lemon
    gelatin
2 teaspoons vinegar
4 to 6 dashes Worcester-
    shire sauce
3 dashes Tabasco sauce
¼ cup chopped onion
¼ cup sliced green olives
⅓ cup sliced radishes
½ teaspoon celery seed

Heat V-8 juice to boiling. Remove from heat and add gelatin, vinegar, Tabasco and Worcestershire sauce. Stir well to dissolve gelatin. Allow to cool. Add other ingredients. Pour into a 1½ quart mold or 6 individual molds. Chill until firm. Serves 6.

Patricia S. Bibbee (Mrs. Charles C.)

BLUE CHEESE DRESSING

1 cup plain yogurt
1 cup mayonnaise
½ teaspoon garlic powder
Pinch of salt
4 ounces Blue cheese

Blend first 4 ingredients until smooth. Add Blue cheese and chill. Yield: 2 cups.

Lorena B. Surber (Mrs. Charles M., Jr.)

CELERY SEED DRESSING

½ cup sugar
1 teaspoon dry mustard
¼ small onion, grated

⅓ cup vinegar
1 cup salad oil
1 tablespoon celery seed

Mix first four ingredients. Slowly add oil. Add celery seed. Chill. Delicious on fruit salad. Yield: 1½ cups.

Frances Hancock (Mrs. Glenn)

FRENCH DRESSING

2 teaspoons grated onion
2 teaspoons salt
1 teaspoon paprika
2 garlic cloves, halved
1 teaspoon Worcestershire
  sauce

1 cup tomato soup
½ cup sugar
1 teaspoon dry mustard
2 to 3 drops of Tabasco
¾ cup salad oil
¾ cup vinegar

Combine first 9 ingredients. Add vinegar and oil, mixing thoroughly. Chill. Stores well. Yield: 2½ cups.

Jane C. Quenon (Mrs. Andrew R.)

FRESH FRUIT DRESSING

2 eggs, beaten
¼ cup sugar
¼ cup fresh lemon juice
¼ cup orange-pineapple
  juice

½ teaspoon grated lemon
  rind
⅛ teaspoon salt
½ cup cream, whipped
½ pint vanilla ice cream

Combine first six ingredients in double boiler and cook until thick. Cool. Stir in cream and ice cream. Serve with fruit sections. Especially good over pineapple, strawberries, citrus sections and avocado.

Rebecca K. Palmer (Mrs. John C., III)

PINEAPPLE DRESSING FOR FRESH FRUIT SALADS

Juice of 1 lemon
1 cup pineapple juice
2 tablespoons butter,
   melted
1 tablespoon flour

¾ cup sugar
2 eggs, separated
½ cup whipped cream
   (or more)

Heat pineapple juice and lemon juice until warm in top of double boiler. Blend flour and butter together; add beaten egg yolks and sugar. Fold in stiffly beaten egg whites. Add to warm juices. Cook until thick. Cool. Add whipped cream, the more the better. Use on fresh fruit salads with English walnuts added.

Mrs. Kirk Dolin

THOUSAND ISLAND DRESSING

1 cup mayonnaise
4 tablespoons chili sauce
1 tablespoon chopped
   chives
3 tablespoons ketchup
1 tablespoon tarragon vinegar

1 tablespoon chopped green
   pepper
1 tablespoon chopped red
   pepper
1 teaspoon paprika

Mix together and chill. Yield: 1½ cups.

Elizabeth Beury

TWIN FALLS HOMESTEAD

The restored farm buildings located at Twin Falls State Park in Wyoming County, West Virginia are typical of pioneer architecture in most of the state.

Families who ventured from settled regions of the east to cross the mountains in search of new homes would not carry great quantities of goods and household articles with them. A few simple tools, however, would be essential to the clearing and grubbing of homesites and the construction of the new home.

Probably the most important tool was the axe; the mattock was used for grubbing the house site and fields; cultivating was done with the hoe; plow points were necessary for breaking the ground; a tool called a frow was used to split logs or trunks of trees into clapboards (roof shingles) by striking its top edge with a mallet; and an auger was brought for boring holes for pins to fasten parts of the house together.

After the trees were cleared from the homestead, they were cut into correct lengths, collected at the proper place, notched, hewn in a squared-off shape and fitted together. The first large "sill" logs were placed firmly on stone foundations. The roof was formed by making rib poles and placing clapboards on them as a protective cover. Spaces between logs were blocked up with slabs or short pieces of rails and the spaces sealed by daubing all crevices with clay mortar. A huge fireplace occupied one end of the cabin.

Settlements usually consisted of several neighboring farmsteads remote enough from one another to assure plenty of space for working the land and the privacy and freedom they sought when moving into the new territory, yet close enough to provide mutual security and to help one another at planting and harvest times.

The Wyoming Homestead is preserved as a testimony to the rugged pioneer farmers who helped settle this land west of the mountains.

Photo by Gerald S. Ratliff

VEGETABLES AND SIDE DISHES

Turkey Tracks

ACORN SQUASH WITH CRANBERRY FILLING
Microwave

2 acorn squash
Salt to taste
¼ teaspoon ground cloves
½ teaspoon ground nutmeg

4 tablespoons butter
4 tablespoons honey
1 (8 ounce) can whole berry
cranberry sauce

Wash and dry squash. Place in microwave oven. Heat on high uncovered for 8 to 10 minutes until soft to touch. Let stand 5 minutes. Cut squash in half and remove seeds. Place cut side up in a shallow non metallic baking dish. Sprinkle with salt, cloves and nutmeg. Place 1 tablespoon butter and 1 tablespoon honey in each half. Heat on high uncovered for 2 to 4 minutes or until butter has melted. Spread honey-butter mixture over cut surfaces of squash. Place 1 spoonful cranberry sauce in each squash half. Return squash to microwave. Heat on high 2 to 4 minutes until cranberry sauce is hot. Serves 4.

Shawn B. Gross

ASPARAGUS SOUFFLÉ

4 eggs
1 (15½ ounce) can asparagus spears
1 cup shredded cheese

1 cup mayonnaise
½ teaspoon salt
1 (10½ ounce) can cream of
mushroom soup

Beat eggs in blender. Add remaining ingredients one at a time. Pour into a greased 1½ quart casserole. Place dish in a larger pan of hot water. Bake at 350° for 55 to 60 minutes. Serves 6 to 8.

Mary J. Payne (Mrs. Andrew, III)

ARTICHOKE MUSHROOM BAKE

3 cups fresh mushrooms,
  halved
½ cup sliced green onion
  with tops
5 tablespoons butter,
  melted and divided
2 tablespoons flour
⅛ teaspoon salt
  Dash of pepper
¾ cup water

¼ cup milk
1 teaspoon granulated
  chicken bouillon
1 teaspoon lemon juice
⅛ teaspoon nutmeg
1 (10 ounce) package frozen
  artichoke hearts,
  cooked and drained
1 to 2 slices bread,
  crumbled

Cook mushrooms and onion in 4 tablespoons butter until tender. Remove and set aside. Blend flour, salt and pepper into pan drippings. Add water, milk, granulated chicken broth, lemon juice and nutmeg. Cook and stir until bubbly. Add mushrooms, onions and artichokes. Place in a 1 quart casserole. Combine bread crumbs and remaining butter. Sprinkle around edges of casserole. Bake at 350° for 20 minutes. Serves 6 to 8.

Sheri J. Wiles (Mrs. Edwin K.)

GREEN BEANS DIJON

4 slices bacon, diced
¼ cup chopped green onion
2 cloves garlic, minced
2 tablespoons Dijon
  mustard

¼ cup chicken broth
1 pound green beans,
  cooked until tender
  Salt and pepper to taste

Sauté bacon in skillet until crisp. Add onion and garlic; sauté until tender. Stir in mustard. Reduce heat. Gradually add broth. Pour over green beans. Mix well and season to taste. Serves 4.

Diane S. Doty (Mrs. Steven)

MOM'S FRESH GREEN BEANS

5 pounds green beans
1 small onion, diced
1 beef bouillon cube
1 tablespoon salt

1 teaspoon sugar
2 tablespoons butter
1 teaspoon bacon grease

String, snap and wash beans. Place in a deep, heavy pan. Do not add water; water clinging to beans should be enough. Add 2 tablespoons water only if necessary. Add remaining ingredients. Cover, bring to a boil, reduce heat and simmer 10 minutes. Stir beans several times, moving top beans to bottom to ensure even cooking. Beans should be crunchy when ready. Serves 12.

Tommi Sue Roncaglione

SPANISH GREEN BEANS

1 tablespoon cornstarch	2 cups or 1 pound cooked
2 tablespoons water	green beans
1 (10 ounce) can stewed	Club cracker crumbs
tomatoes	1 to 2 tablespoons butter
Pinch of salt	¼ to ½ cup grated Cheddar
Pinch of sugar	cheese

Dissolve cornstarch in water in a saucepan. Add tomatoes, salt and sugar. Heat, stirring until thickened. Place green beans in a small, greased casserole. Add tomatoes. Sprinkle with cracker crumbs and cheese. Dot with butter. Bake at 400° for 20 minutes. Serves 4.

Ester L. Heath (Mrs. George R.)

LIMA BEAN AND MUSHROOM CASSEROLE

½ onion, chopped	1 (8 ounce) can mushrooms
3 tablespoons butter,	½ tablespoon water
divided	1½ tablespoons flour
1 (10 ounce) package frozen	1½ cups half and half
lima beans	⅛ cup sherry
½ teaspoon sugar	1 egg yolk, beaten
¼ teaspoon salt	¼ cup shredded American
⅛ teaspoon pepper	cheese

Sauté onion in 2 tablespoons butter in a saucepan until tender. Add beans, cover and cook 5 minutes, separating beans with a fork. Add sugar, salt, pepper, mushrooms and water. Cook covered until tender. Melt remaining 1 tablespoon butter in a separate pan. Whisk in flour. Gradually whisk in cream, cooking until thickened. Remove from heat. Add sherry and egg yolk. Add beans and mushrooms. Pour into a greased 1½ quart casserole. Sprinkle with cheese. Bake at 350° for 35 minutes. Serves 4 to 6.

Marion S. Jones (Mrs. George W., III)

HARVARD BEETS

⅓ cup sugar
½ teaspoon salt
1 tablespoon cornstarch
½ cup vinegar

2 tablespoons butter
1 teaspoon minced onion
3 cups beets, cooked and
diced

Blend sugar, salt and cornstarch in top of double boiler. Add vinegar, stirring and cooking over boiling water until thickened. Add butter, onion and beets. Heat for 20 minutes. Serves 6 to 8.

Phyllis H. Highland (Mrs. William D.)

PICKLED BEETS AND EGGS

12 eggs
1 quart canned beets,
water packed

1 cup sugar
1 cup vinegar
1 tablespoon pickling spices

Place eggs in cold water in a covered saucepan. Bring to a boil over medium heat. Remove from heat. Let stand for 10 minutes. Place in cold water to cool. Peel and place in a deep bowl. Meanwhile, put sugar, vinegar and spices in kettle. Bring to a boil. Boil for 5 minutes. Add beets and juice. Heat to boiling. Cool slightly and pour over eggs. Refrigerate overnight.

Mrs. Karney Tinney

BROCCOLI CASSEROLE

2 (10 ounces each) packages
frozen broccoli spears
1 (10½ ounce) can cream of
shrimp soup

1 (3 ounce) package cream
cheese
¼ cup butter
½ cup grated Amercan
cheese

Cook broccoli according to package instructions. Mix remaining ingredients in a saucepan, heating until cheese melts. Place broccoli in an oblong casserole. Cover with sauce. Bake at 350° for 30 minutes. Serves 6.

Louise C. Christensen (Mrs. David)

BROCCOLI CORN BAKE

1½ tablespoons margarine
1½ tablespoons flour
1 cup milk
1 head fresh broccoli or 2
   (10 ounces each)
   packages frozen spears

1 (10 ounce) package frozen
   corn
1 cup grated Monterey Jack
   cheese
1 (2.8 ounce) can onion
   rings

Combine margarine and flour in saucepan over medium heat, cooking 2 minutes until smooth and bubbly. Slowly stir in milk, cooking until thickened. Set aside. Cut and separate broccoli into spears. Steam 8 to 10 minutes until crisp tender. Place broccoli in shallow baking dish. Pour corn over. Top with white sauce, cheese and onion rings. Bake at 350° for 30 minutes. Serves 4 to 6.

Donna L. Dean (Mrs. Rodney D.)

ITALIAN BROCCOLI CASSEROLE

2 (10 ounces each) packages
   frozen cut broccoli
2 eggs, beaten
1 (10½ ounce) can Cheddar
   cheese soup

½ teaspoon dried oregano,
   crushed
1 (8 ounce) can stewed
   tomatoes, chopped
3 tablespoons Parmesan
   cheese

Cook broccoli in boiling water 5 to 7 minutes until tender. Drain. Combine eggs, soup and oregano. Stir in tomatoes and broccoli. Place in a 10" x 6" x 2" baking dish. Sprinkle with cheese. Bake uncovered at 350° for 30 minutes until heated completely through. Serves 6 to 8.

Sheri J. Wiles (Mrs. Edwin K.)

BRUSSELS SPROUTS WITH BLUE CHEESE

3 pints fresh Brussels
   sprouts or 2 (10 ounces
   each) packages frozen

2 tablespoons Blue cheese
¼ cup margarine, softened

Cook Brussels sprouts in water until just tender. Drain. Press cheese through sieve. Blend with butter. Add to hot sprouts. Serves 4 to 6.

Carolyn G. Henshaw (Mrs. Harry P., III)

CARROTS WITH WATER CHESTNUTS

1 pound peeled carrots, cut
   diagonally ½" thick
3 tablespoons butter,
   melted
1 (8 ounce) can water chestnuts, drained and sliced

¾ teaspoon thyme
½ teaspoon sugar
¼ cup dry white wine
1 tablespoon chopped
   parsley

Cook carrots in a small amount of salted water until crisp tender, 10 to 15 minutes. Drain. Cook chestnuts, thyme and sugar in butter for 2 to 3 minutes in a saucepan. Add wine, parsley and carrots. Cook, stirring until hot. Serves 6.

Patricia M. Moyers (Mrs. Charles G.)

FANCY COOKED CARROTS

4 cups carrots, cut in
   julienne slices
¼ cup minced onion
¼ cup butter
3 tablespoons powdered
   sugar

2 tablespoons minced fresh
   parsley
¼ teaspoon salt
⅛ teaspoon peeled and
   grated ginger root

Boil carrots in salted water 10 minutes. Drain. Combine remaining ingredients in a bowl, mixing well. Place in a buttered baking dish. Bake at 350° for 20 to 30 minutes. Serves 6 to 8.

Sherry S. Sims (Mrs. H. Herchiel, Jr.)

CURRIED BAKED CAULIFLOWER

1 head cauliflower
½ teaspoon salt
1 (10½ ounce) can cream of
   chicken soup
⅓ cup mayonnaise

1 cup grated Cheddar
   cheese
1 teaspoon curry powder
¼ cup dried bread crumbs
2 tablespoons butter,
   melted

Break cauliflower into flowerets. Boil covered in 1" salted water for 10 minutes. Drain well. Combine soup, mayonnaise, cheese and curry in a 2 quart casserole. Stir in cauliflower. Toss crumbs in butter. Sprinkle over casserole. Bake at 350° for 30 minutes. Serves 8.

Louise C. Christensen (Mrs. David)

BUBBA'S FRIED CORN

8 to 10 ears tender white corn
3 tablespoons bacon grease
1½ cups milk
2 tablespoons butter
Salt and pepper to taste

Shuck corn, rubbing off silks. Take a sharp knife and run down the center of the grains. Scrape all the soft pulp off the cob. Sauté corn in bacon grease over low heat for 10 to 15 minutes until tender. If corn sticks to pan, add a little water. Add milk, butter, salt and pepper. Bring to a boil. Serve immediately. Serves 6 to 8.

Linda P. Jernigan (Mrs. W. Henry, Jr.)

CORN FRITTERS

3 eggs, separated
1⅔ cups corn kernels
½ teaspoon salt
⅛ teaspoon pepper
¼ cup flour
6 tablespoons cooking oil

Beat egg yolks until light. Add corn, seasonings and flour. Fold in stiffly beaten egg whites. Drop by spoonfuls into hot oil in a skillet. Cook on both sides until brown. Serve with butter, syrup or jam. Serves 6.

Phyllis H. Highland (Mrs. William D.)

TAMALE CORN

2 eggs, beaten
2 (16 ounces each) cans cream style corn
¾ cup corn meal
¾ teaspoon garlic salt
½ teaspoon baking powder
¼ cup cooking oil
2 (4 ounces each) cans chopped green chilies
½ pound sharp cheese, grated

Mix all ingredients. Pour into a greased baking dish. Bake at 350° for 45 to 60 minutes. Can be cooked ahead and reheated. Serves 6 to 8.

Kathy S. Foster (Mrs. Daniel S.)

SCALLOPED EGGPLANT

1 large eggplant, peeled and diced	¼ cup chopped onion
⅓ cup milk	1¼ cups herb stuffing mix, divided
1 (10½ ounce) can cream of mushroom soup	2 tablespoons butter, melted
1 egg, beaten	1 cup grated Cheddar cheese

Cook eggplant in salted water 6 to 7 minutes until tender. Drain. Combine milk, soup and egg in a bowl. Add eggplant, onion and ¾ cup stuffing. Toss lightly. Pour into a 2 quart casserole. Finely crush remaining ½ cup herb stuffing. Mix with butter. Sprinkle over casserole. Top with cheese. Bake at 350° for 20 minutes.

Mary T. Karr (Mrs. George W.)

GREEN PEPPER CLOUDS

2 large green peppers, halved and seeded	½ cup grated Cheddar cheese, divided
¼ cup mayonnaise	2 tablespoons grated onion
	2 egg whites

Cook peppers in boiling water 3 to 5 minutes. Drain. Mix ¼ cup cheese, mayonnaise and onion. Beat egg whites until stiff. Fold into cheese mixture. Fill pepper halves. Sprinkle with remaining cheese. Broil on middle rack for 3 to 5 minutes until golden. Serves 4.

Barbara H. Slack (Mrs. John M., III)

PEPPERS AND SQUASH

4 medium green peppers	½ teaspoon leaf oregano
2 medium yellow summer squash or zucchini	½ teaspoon sweet basil
4 medium tomatoes	½ teaspoon salt
½ cup cooking oil	Dash of pepper
1 to 2 small onions, chopped (optional)	6 tablespoons capers (optional)
1 teaspoon sugar	2 teaspoons wine vinegar

Cut peppers into 1″ cubes. Dice squash and tomatoes in 1″ to 2″ pieces. Sauté green peppers, onion and squash in hot oil in a large skillet 5 minutes until tender. Add remaining ingredients. Simmer covered for 5 minutes. Serve at once. Serves 8 to 12.

Mary V. Gray

OLD FASHIONED KALE

1 pound fresh kale
1 tablespoon sugar

1 teaspoon salt
Bacon grease to taste

Soak kale in cold water 30 minutes. Combine all ingredients. **Cook** covered over medium heat in just enough water to cover kale **for 35** to 40 minutes. May be garnished with crumbled bacon, chopped eggs or vinegar.

Patricia H. Frazier (Mrs. Jerry L.)

CURRIED MUSHROOMS

½ pound mushrooms
4 tablespoons butter
¾ cup minced onion
1 clove garlic, crushed

1 teaspoon curry powder
⅓ cup beef broth
¼ teaspoon salt

Rinse, pat dry and slice mushrooms. Heat butter in a medium saucepan. Add mushrooms and onion. Sauté 5 minutes until lightly browned. Add garlic and curry powder. Cook 2 minutes longer until curry powder is darkened. Add beef broth and salt. Reduce heat; simmer 8 to 10 minutes. Serve over cooked rice or noodles, if desired. Serves 4.

Susan Kamer-Shinaberry

SHERRIED MUSHROOMS

1 pound mushrooms
6 tablespoons butter, divided
¼ cup finely sliced green onions
⅛ teaspoon salt
⅛ teaspoon white pepper

1 tablespoon flour
1 cup light cream or half and half
1 tablespoon sherry
⅛ teaspoon garlic powder
Paprika

Rinse, pat dry and slice mushrooms. Heat 4 tablespoons butter in a medium saucepan. Sauté mushrooms and onions until mushrooms are lightly browned, stirring occasionally. Stir in salt and pepper. Set aside and keep warm. Melt remaining 2 tablespoons butter in a small saucepan. Add flour and cook, stirring, over low heat until lightly browned. Gradually add cream, stirring constantly. Add sherry and garlic powder. Cook, stirring over low heat, until mixture thickens. Add sautéed mushrooms and onions. Serve over toast or patty shells. Garnish with paprika. Serves 4.

Susan Kamer-Shinaberry

BATTER FRIED MUSHROOMS

40 large mushrooms
2 cups flour
2 to 3 teaspoons salt
1 to 1½ teaspoons garlic
   powder

1 teaspoon baking powder
1½ cups beer
½ to 1 cup cooking oil

Wash and dry mushrooms. Set aside. Combine next 4 ingredients. Add beer, blending until smooth. Refrigerate covered for 30 minutes. Blend again. Refrigerate until ready to use. Heat oil to 375°. Dip mushrooms in batter. Fry until golden brown. Drain on paper towels. Serves 6 to 8.

Janet C. Simpson (Mrs. Robert R., Jr.)

IRISH MUSHROOM PIE

1 pound fresh mushrooms,
   sliced
½ medium onion, chopped
2 tablespoons butter
   Salt and pepper to taste
½ cup water

1 beef bouillon cube
½ teaspoon lemon juice
½ cup dry white sherry
3 tablespoons flour
1 unbaked 9″ pie shell

Sauté mushrooms and onion in butter in a skillet. Add salt and pepper to taste. Stir in water, bouillon cube, lemon juice, sherry and flour. Cook 2 minutes over low heat. Pour into pie shell. Bake at 450° for 8 minutes. Reduce heat to 350°. Bake an additional 20 to 25 minutes. Serves 6 to 8.

Susan Hartman

SOUTHERN FRIED OKRA

5 cups okra, sliced ½″ thick
½ cup flour
½ cup corn meal

1 tablespoon bacon grease
   Dash of garlic salt
   Dash of pepper

Combine flour and corn meal in a bag. Add okra. Shake, coating well. Fry slowly in bacon grease over low heat for 30 to 45 minutes until golden brown. Season with garlic salt and pepper.

Patty W. Bowers

TARTE A L'OIGNON
(Onion Pie)

PASTRY

1 cup sifted flour
¼ teaspoon salt
¼ cup butter, cut into
    small pieces

1 egg
2 tablespoons cold water

Measure flour into a bowl. Add salt. Combine butter with the flour, using fingertips. Add egg and water. Stir with a fork and form into a ball. Wrap in wax paper. Chill for 1 hour. Roll out pastry and fit into an 8″ pie plate.

FILLING

3 tablespoons butter
2 medium yellow onions,
    cut into thin rings
¼ teaspoon salt

Freshly ground black
    pepper
Dash of nutmeg
3 egg yolks
⅔ cup heavy cream

Sauté onions in butter over moderate heat. Simmer covered for 30 minutes, stirring occasionally. Season with salt, pepper and nutmeg. Combine egg yolks and cream. Add onion. Pour into pastry shell. Bake at 400° for 30 minutes. Serves 6 to 8.

Barbara S. Moore (Mrs. James D., Jr.)

ONION RINGS

3 or 4 large Bermuda
    onions
3 cups buttermilk
1 egg, beaten
1 teaspoon salt
1½ teaspoons baking powder

⅔ cup water
1 cup flour
1 tablespoon cooking oil
1 teaspoon lemon juice
Additional cooking oil
    for frying

Peel and slice onions into ⅜″ thick slices. Separate into rings. Soak in buttermilk for 30 minutes. Combine remaining ingredients, except oil for frying. Heat oil in a large skillet. Remove rings from buttermilk one at a time. Dip into batter, coating heavily. Fry in oil until golden brown, turning once. Drain. Serves 6 to 8.

Mary J. Payne (Mrs. Andrew, III)

SOUBISE

1 cup long grain rice	½ teaspoon salt
½ tablespoon salt	¼ to ½ teaspoon cracked
3 to 4 quarts water	pepper
6 tablespoons butter,	¼ cup whipping cream
divided	½ cup grated Swiss cheese
2 pounds onions, thinly	½ teaspoon parsley
sliced	

Cook rice in boiling, salted water for 5 minutes. Drain and rinse. Heat 4 tablespoons butter in a 3 quart casserole until foamy. Stir in onions, rice, ½ teaspoon salt and pepper. Bake covered at 300° for 1 hour, stirring occasionally. Just before serving fold in cream, cheese and remaining 2 tablespoons butter. Garnish with fresh parsley. Serves 6 to 8.

Beth W. Hall (Mrs. Carl B., Jr.)

PARSNIPS

2 pounds parsnips	¼ cup brown sugar
½ teaspoon salt	2 tablespoons margarine

Peel and cut parsnips into quarters. Cook in a small amount of water until barely tender. Place in a small greased casserole. Sprinkle with salt and brown sugar. Dot with margarine. Bake at 400° for 15 to 20 minutes. Serves 4.

Elaine R. Kroner (Mrs. Robert J.)

GESTUMPZEL

8 large potatoes, peeled and	¾ cup butter
chopped	1 to 2 cups milk, warmed
1 (10 ounce) package frozen	Salt to taste
chopped spinach,	White pepper to taste
cooked and drained	1 egg, beaten

Cook potatoes in boiling water until tender. Drain. Combine with butter in a large mixing bowl. Mash, stirring in enough warm milk to make a creamy texture. Salt and pepper to taste. Beat in egg. Add cooked, drained spinach. Mix well, but gently. Serves 8 to 10.

Mary Lee W. Lilly (Mrs. J.K., III)

POTATO CASSEROLE

½ cup margarine
2 pounds frozen hash
   brown potatoes
1 (8 ounce) carton sour
   cream
½ cup chopped onion

1 (10½ ounce) can cream of
   chicken or mushroom
   soup
2 cups grated Cheddar
   cheese
½ to ¾ cup bread crumbs

Melt margarine in a 9″ x 13″ baking dish. Spread frozen hash browns over margarine. Combine the next four ingredients. Spread over potatoes. Sprinkle with bread crumbs to cover. Bake at 375° for 1 hour. Serves 8.

Mary Esther Vredeveld (Mrs. D.R.)

POTATOES AU GRATIN

3 medium onions, peeled
   and thinly sliced
6 tablespoons butter,
   divided
8 medium potatoes, peeled
   and thinly sliced

1½ cups grated Swiss cheese
1 cup chicken stock
   Salt to taste
   Freshly ground pepper
   to taste

Sauté onions in 3 tablespoons butter. Place ½ the potatoes in a greased 9″ x 13″ baking dish. Layer with ½ the onions and ¾ cup of the cheese. Dot with 1½ tablespoons butter. Repeat layers. Pour stock over top of casserole. Season with salt and pepper. Bake uncovered at 425° for 35 minutes until potatoes are tender and liquid is absorbed. Serves 6.

Patricia M. Moyers (Mrs. Charles G., Jr.)

BAKED PARMESAN POTATO WEDGES

4 large potatoes
½ cup flour
½ cup Parmesan cheese

Salt and pepper to taste
¼ teaspoon paprika
½ cup margarine, melted

Wash potatoes. Do not peel. Slice lengthwise in half. Slice each half lengthwise again into three pieces. Combine next four ingredients in a bag. Add potato wedges and shake well to coat potatoes. Place margarine in a 9″ x 13″ baking dish. Add potato wedges, skin side down. Bake at 375° for 20 to 30 minutes until golden brown and slightly soft. Baste with butter 2 or 3 times during cooking. Serve immediately. Serves 4.

Sara Z. Hoblitzell (Mrs. John R.)

POTATO GNOCCI WITH MARINARA SAUCE

4 large potatoes, peeled	1½ teaspoons salt
1 cup Parmesan cheese, divided	½ cup butter, divided
1 cup flour	2 cups tomato sauce (optional)
2 egg yolks	

Cook potatoes in boiling water until tender. Drain and mash. Add ½ cup Parmesan cheese, flour, egg yolks, salt and 1 tablespoon butter, mixing well. Using 1 cup potato mixture at a time, roll into finger shapes (small ropes) and cut into 1″ lengths. Cook in a large quantity of simmering water for 3 to 5 minutes until potato shapes rise to the surface. Drain well and place in a baking dish. Melt remaining butter and combine with remaining cheese. Pour over casserole. Bake at 350° for 15 to 20 minutes. Serves 6.

Potato Gnocci may be served with or without sauce. If desired heat tomato sauce (canned or homemade) and pour over top of casserole before baking. Serve with additional sauce.

Judi Grigoraci (Mrs. Victor)

BAKED POTATOES FLORENTINE

MORNAY SAUCE

2 tablespoons butter, melted	Dash of nutmeg
2 tablespoons flour	1 cup milk
¼ teaspoon salt	2 egg yolks
Dash of pepper	½ cup grated Swiss cheese

Combine butter, flour, salt, pepper and nutmeg in a saucepan. Cook, stirring, over medium heat 2 to 3 minutes until well blended and smooth. Gradually add milk, stirring constantly. Bring to a boil, reduce heat and simmer 1 minute. Beat egg yolks in a small bowl. Stir in half of the hot sauce, mixing well. Stir egg mixture back into saucepan. Add cheese and cook, stirring, over low heat until thickened. Do not boil. Remove from heat, cover and set aside.

POTATOES

6 medium potatoes, baked and slightly cooled	6 tablespoons butter, divided
½ (10 ounce) package frozen chopped spinach, cooked and drained	½ teaspoon salt
	Dash of pepper
1 cup cottage cheese	4 tablespoons grated Swiss cheese
	⅓ cup dried bread crumbs

Remove a thin slice from the top of each potato. Scoop out potato pulp. Mash in a large bowl, adding 4 tablespoons butter, cottage cheese, spinach, Mornay Sauce, salt and pepper. Mix well. Fill potato shells. Top with Swiss cheese. Melt remaining 2 tablespoons butter, combine with bread crumbs and sprinkle over cheese. Broil until golden brown. Serves 6.

Patty W. Bowers

COTTAGE POTATOES

5 large potatoes, cooked, peeled and diced
½ pound Cheddar cheese, chopped
1 medium onion, chopped
½ cup chopped parsley
½ cup chopped pimentos
½ green pepper, diced
Salt and pepper to taste
½ slice bread, diced
½ cup butter, melted
½ cup hot milk
½ cup corn flake crumbs

Combine first 8 ingredients; mixing well. Place in a lightly greased 9" x 13" baking dish. Pour butter and milk over top. Sprinkle with corn flake crumbs. Bake at 400° for 30 minutes. Serves 6 to 8.

Karen R. Huffman (Mrs. William)

TWICE BAKED POTATOES
Microwave

4 medium potatoes
6 slices bacon
¼ cup chopped green onion
¼ cup grated Cheddar cheese
1 (8 ounce) carton sour cream
1 teaspoon salt
¼ teaspoon pepper
Paprika

Scrub potatoes, dry and prick with a fork. Microwave on high for 12 to 14 minutes, turning and rearranging potatoes once. Let cool. Cut skin from top of each potato and remove pulp, being careful not to break shell. Mash pulp. Microwave bacon on a bacon rack on high for 7 minutes or until crisp. Drain, reserving 3 tablespoons drippings. Crumble bacon and set aside. Microwave onion in reserved drippings on high for 3 minutes. Combine potato pulp, bacon, onion, cheese, sour cream, salt and pepper. Refill shells. Sprinkle with paprika. Microwave on high for 6 minutes, turning after 3 minutes. Potatoes may be prepared several hours ahead, refrigerated until serving time and reheated on high for 6 minutes. Serves 4.

Bonnie H. Brothers (Mrs. Riley C.)

MASHED POTATOES WITH CABBAGE

6 large potatoes, peeled
    and cubed
4 cups sliced cabbage
4 tablespoons butter
1 cup lukewarm milk

1 teaspoon salt
½ teaspoon pepper
6 green onions, sliced
    lengthwise

Cook potatoes in boiling water until tender. Drain. Cook cabbage in boiling water until tender. Drain and sauté in butter for 3 to 5 minutes. Mash potatoes with milk, salt and pepper. Stir cabbage and onions into potatoes and serve. Serves 6 to 8.

Emily M. Roles (Mrs. Forrest H.)

SAL'S SWEET POTATOES

1 (16 ounce) can whole
    sweet potatoes (not
    yams)

1 cup mincemeat
3 tablespoons maple syrup

Drain potatoes. Cut lengthwise, hollowing out a small portion in the center of each half. Fill with mincemeat. Place in a greased 9" square baking dish. Drizzle with syrup. Bake at 350° for 30 minutes. Serves 6.

Mrs. Nicholas F. Cody

SWEET POTATOES

4 medium white sweet
    potatoes
1 cup sugar
    Dash of salt
1 teaspoon cinnamon

Dash of nutmeg
6 tablespoons butter
2 slices lemon
1 tablespoon flour
¼ cup water

Peel and cut potatoes into serving size pieces. Place in a 9" square baking dish. Sprinkle with next 4 ingredients. Dot with butter slices and lemon. Sift flour over top. Add just enough water to cover bottom of pan—do not cover potatoes. Bake at 400° for 1 hour, basting frequently. Serves 4.

Ann W. Stowers (Mrs. Gerald R.)

SWEET POTATO CASSEROLE

¾ cup margarine, melted
   and divided
1 (24 ounce) can sweet
   potatoes, drained
¼ cup milk
2 eggs
1 teaspoon vanilla extract
1 cup sugar

¼ cup flour
½ cup brown sugar
1 egg
1 (8 ounce) can crushed
   pineapple, partially
   drained
1 cup chopped pecans
   (optional)

Combine ¼ cup margarine with next 5 ingredients, mashing well. Place in a 9″ square casserole. Combine rest of ingredients, including remaining ½ cup margarine. Pour over sweet potato mixture. Top with pecans. Bake at 350° for 30 to 35 minutes. Serves 6 to 8.

Elizabeth Beury

SCALLOPED RAMPS AND POTATOES

4 medium potatoes, peeled
   and thinly sliced
Salt and pepper to taste
3 cups coarsely chopped
   ramps, including green
   tops

1 cup milk
1 (4 ounce) package grated
   Cheddar cheese
½ cup fresh bread crumbs
Paprika

Place a layer of sliced potatoes in a greased 1½ quart baking dish. Sprinkle with salt and pepper. Place a layer of ramps on top of potatoes. Continue alternating layers, ending with potatoes as top layer. Pour milk over top. Sprinkle with cheese, bread crumbs and paprika. Bake covered at 425° for 20 minutes. Uncover and bake an additional 15 minutes or until potatoes are tender. Serves 6.

Peg Thompson (Mrs. Gordon)

RHUBARB

1½ pounds rhubarb, stems only	¼ cup water
	1 cup sugar

Clean and wash rhubarb. Cut in 1" to 2" pieces. Combine water and rhubarb in a large stainless steel pan. Cook covered over low heat for 5 minutes. Stir well, cover and continue cooking. When rhubarb starts to break down, increase heat and stir (should look like applesauce). Add sugar. Cook, stirring, for 5 minutes. Add more sugar to taste. Serves 4 to 6.

Rebecca B. Goldman (Mrs. J. Crawford)

MUSHROOMS AND SPINACH

1 pound fresh mushrooms	1 teaspoon salt
¼ cup finely chopped onion	1 cup grated Cheddar cheese
¼ cup butter, melted and divided	⅛ teaspoon garlic salt
2 (10 ounces each) packages frozen chopped spinach, cooked and drained	

Wash and dry mushrooms. Remove stems and discard. Sauté caps and onion in 2 tablespoons butter. Set aside. Combine spinach, salt and remaining butter. Spread ½ spinach in a 10" casserole. Layer with ½ mushroom mixture and ½ cup cheese. Repeat layers. Season each layer with garlic salt. Bake at 350° for 20 minutes. Serves 6.

Mary Lee W. Lilly (Mrs. J.K., III)

MOTHER'S NO FAIL SPINACH CASSEROLE

2 (10 ounces each) packages frozen chopped spinach	1 cup grated sharp cheese
1 (10½ ounce) can cream of mushroom soup	1 small onion
	2 to 4 tablespoons butter
1 cup mayonnaise	½ cup dried bread crumbs or herb seasoned stuffing mix
2 eggs, beaten	

Cook spinach 5 minutes. Drain. Combine soup, mayonnaise, eggs, cheese and onion. Add to spinach, mixing well. Pour into a casserole. Dot with butter. Top with bread crumbs. Bake at 350° for 45 minutes. Serves 6 to 8.

Suzy M. Barton

SPINACH GNOCCHI

1 (10 ounce) package frozen chopped spinach
¼ cup plus 2 tablespoons Parmesan cheese
2 eggs, beaten
1½ cups Ricotta cheese
2 tablespoons minced green onion

½ teaspoon minced garlic
½ teaspoon pepper
Salt to taste
1 cup dry bread crumbs
1 (16 ounce) can tomato sauce or 2 cups favorite homemade recipe
2 tablespoons butter, melted

Thaw and squeeze dry spinach. Combine with ¼ cup Parmesan cheese. Add next 6 ingredients. Stir in bread crumbs. Mixture will stiffen. Roll a teaspoonful of the mixture at a time into small balls. Bring 1½ to 2 quarts salted water to a boil. Add several gnocchi. Cook 4 to 5 minutes until gnocchi are puffed and firm. Remove with a slotted spoon. Set aside. Repeat with remaining gnocchi. Place tomato sauce in bottom of an 8″ square baking dish. Arrange gnocchi on top of sauce in a single layer. Brush lightly with butter. Sprinkle with remaining Parmesan cheese. Bake at 350° for 10 minutes until hot. Serves 6 to 8.

Karen Potesta

RATATOUILLE

3 to 4 medium zucchini or yellow squash, cubed (or combination of both)
1 large green pepper, cubed
2 medium onions, sliced

2 cloves garlic, minced
1 teaspoon sweet basil
2 or 3 ripe tomatoes, peeled and sliced
Salt and pepper to taste
Parmesan cheese

Combine first 5 ingredients. Place on the bottom of a 9″ square casserole. Layer tomatoes on top. Bake, covered, at 350° for 20 to 30 minutes until squash is tender. Stir twice during baking. Uncover, top with cheese and bake until cheese melts. May be frozen, but do not add cheese until ready to bake. Serves 6 to 8.

Ann Wilcher

YELLOW SQUASH CASSEROLE

4 medium yellow squash, sliced
⅓ cup chopped onion
⅓ cup butter, melted

2 hard boiled eggs, chopped
1 cup grated Cheddar cheese
1 cup crushed corn chips

Cook squash in boiling water for 5 minutes until tender. Drain. Sauté onions in butter in a separate pan. Add squash, mixing well. Pour into a greased 1 quart casserole. Top with eggs, cheese and corn chips. Bake at 350° for 15 minutes. Serves 4.

Julie Coburn

SQUASH CASSEROLE

2 pounds yellow squash, sliced
½ cup butter, melted
1 (8 ounce) package herb seasoned stuffing mix
1 (5 ounce) can sliced water chestnuts

1 cup sour cream
1 (10½ ounce) can cream of chicken soup
1 small onion, chopped
Salt and pepper to taste
1 cup grated carrots (optional)

Cook squash in boiling water for 5 minutes until just tender. Drain. Combine butter and stuffing mix. Spread ½ stuffing mixture in bottom of a 9″ x 13″ baking dish. Combine squash with remaining ingredients. Place on top of stuffing. Sprinkle with remaining stuffing mix. Bake at 350° for 30 minutes. Serves 6 to 8.

Elizabeth S. Pugh (Mrs. H. Reid, II)

PECAN SQUASH CASSEROLE

1 pound summer squash, sliced in ½″ slices
1 tablespoon sugar
1 egg
½ cup mayonnaise

½ cup grated Cheddar cheese
Salt and pepper to taste
¼ cup butter, melted
½ cup chopped pecans
⅓ cup dry bread crumbs

Cook squash in boiling water for 5 minutes until just tender. Drain. Combine with next 5 ingredients. Place in a small casserole. Combine butter, pecans and bread crumbs. Sprinkle over squash. Bake at 400° for 20 minutes. Serves 4.

Marta D. MacCallum (Mrs. Daniel)

CHEESY SQUASH CASSEROLE

2 large summer squash	3 tablespoons milk
1 onion, chopped	2 eggs, beaten
1½ cups grated Cheddar cheese	2 teaspoons baking powder
	1½ tablespoons flour
2 tablespoons butter	Salt and pepper to taste

Cook squash in boiling water for 5 minutes. Drain and mash. Combine with remaining ingredients. Place in a medium size greased casserole. Bake at 350° for 35 to 40 minutes. Serves 6 to 8.

Beth W. Hall (Mrs. Carl B., Jr.)

STUFFED BAKED TOMATOES

8 medium tomatoes	⅓ cup fresh parsley, chopped
¼ cup olive oil	
6 green onions, chopped	½ teaspoon basil
1 (10 ounce) package frozen chopped spinach, thawed and squeezed dry	½ teaspoon thyme
	6 tablespoons Feta cheese, crumbled and divided

Slice tops off tomatoes. Scoop out pulp and reserve. Lightly salt inside of tomatoes, invert on paper towels to dry. Sauté onions and chopped tomato pulp in hot oil in a medium skillet. Add spinach, parsley, basil and thyme. Cook over medium high heat until liquid is dissolved, stirring frequently. Stir in 3 tablespoons Feta cheese. Stuff tomato shells with spinach mixture. Place in a greased baking dish. Sprinkle remaining cheese over top. May be refrigerated at this point until ready to heat. Cook at 375° for 10 to 15 minutes. Do not let skins split. Serves 6 to 8.

Sara Z. Hoblitzell (Mrs. John R.)

FRIED GREEN TOMATOES WITH CURRY SAUCE

3 medium, partly ripe
  green tomatoes

¼ cup flour
2 tablespoons butter

CURRY SAUCE

2 tablespoons butter,
  melted
1½ teaspoons flour

½ teaspoon curry powder
1 cup milk

Sauce: Combine butter and flour in a saucepan. Cook, stirring, over medium heat 2 to 3 minutes until smooth and bubbly. Add curry powder. Slowly stir in milk, cooking until thickened. Set aside, keeping warm.

Tomatoes: Slice tomatoes ¾" thick. Dip in flour. Sauté in butter on medium heat in a large skillet until golden brown, turning once. Place on a hot platter and serve with curry sauce spooned on top. Good served for breakfast with crisp bacon and hot biscuits. Serves 4.

Mary P. Ziebold (Mrs. William T.)

ZUCCHINI CASSEROLE

¼ cup margarine, melted
3 tablespoons flour
1 teaspoon salt
2 medium zucchini, thinly
  sliced
2 medium onions, thinly
  sliced
1 large stalk celery,
  chopped

1 large green pepper,
  cut in strips
2 tablespoons brown sugar
1 (8 ounce) can tomato
  sauce
6 to 8 slices American
  cheese
½ to 1 cup croutons

Melt margarine in a large skillet, adding flour and salt. Add next 4 ingredients. Sauté for 10 minutes, stirring to coat vegetables with flour. Add sugar and tomato sauce. Pour into a 2 quart casserole. Bake at 350° until bubbly. Cover with cheese and croutons. Bake for 30 to 40 minutes until zucchini is tender. Serves 6 to 8.

Mrs. Jane Snyder

SPINACH STUFFED ZUCCHINI

3 medium zucchini
Salt
2 tablespoons flour
½ cup milk
1 (10 ounce) package frozen
   chopped spinach,
   cooked and squeezed dry

½ cup grated Cheddar
   cheese
4 slices cooked bacon,
   crumbled
Chopped pimento

Wash zucchini and cut off stem ends. Place zucchini in a small amount of boiling, salted water. Cover, lower heat and cook 8 to 10 minutes. Drain and cool. Cut zucchini in halves lengthwise. Remove pulp, leaving shells firm. Sprinkle shells with salt and set aside. Chop pulp. Combine flour and milk. Add zucchini and spinach and cook over low heat, stirring constantly until thickened. Spoon mixture into shells. Sprinkle with cheese and bacon. Place in a shallow baking dish. Bake at 350° for 15 to 20 minutes. Garnish with pimento. Serves 6.

Dana W. Sharp

ZUCCHINI IN DILL CREAM SAUCE

2¼ pounds zucchini, cut
   in strips
¼ cup chopped onion
½ cup water
1 teaspoon salt
1 teaspoon granulated
   chicken bouillon

½ teaspoon dill weed or 1
   teaspoon fresh dill
2 tablespoons butter
2 teaspoons sugar
2 teaspoons lemon juice
2 tablespoons flour
½ cup sour cream

Combine first 6 ingredients in a saucepan. Cook over medium heat until tender. Do not drain. Add butter, sugar and lemon juice. Combine sour cream and flour. Add to zucchini mixture. Heat and serve. Serves 6.

Mary Lou Ivey

SUZY'S ZUCCHINI NIBBLERS, ATLANTA STYLE

2 pounds zucchini, cut in
   ½" thick slices
Butter

Parmesan cheese
Pepper

Place zucchini slices on a cookie sheet. Dot each slice with butter. Sprinkle each slice heavily with cheese and a dash of pepper. Bake at 350° for 20 minutes. Serves 3 to 4.

Suzy M. Barton

ZUCCHINI

4 medium zucchini, cut
   in 3″ strips
3 tablespoons cooking oil

1 medium onion, sliced
2 tablespoons sesame seeds
2 tablespoons soy sauce

Heat oil on medium heat in a large skillet. Add zucchini and onion. Stir fry for 5 minutes. Add sesame seeds and soy sauce. Cook 3 to 5 minutes. Serves 4.

Deborah L. Sutton (Mrs. James)

ZUCCHINI CASSEROLE

4 to 6 medium zucchini,
   sliced
2 eggs, separated
1 cup sour cream
2 tablespoons flour

1½ cups grated Cheddar
   cheese
½ pound cooked bacon,
   crumbled

Cook zucchini in boiling water for 5 minutes. Drain and cool. Beat egg yolks until thick. Add sour cream and flour. Beat egg whites until stiff and fold into yolk mixture. Layer in a 1½ quart casserole ½ the zucchini, ½ the egg mixture and ½ the cheese. Add all the bacon. Repeat layers. Bake at 350° for 20 to 25 minutes. Serves 8.

Barbara H. Slack (Mrs. John M., III)

GARDEN JAMBALAYA

2 cups thinly sliced,
   unpeeled cucumber
1 cup diced celery
1 cup thin strips green
   pepper
⅓ cup thinly sliced onion
3 tablespoons butter

1 tomato, peeled and cut in
   wedges
1¼ teaspoons salt
⅛ teaspoon pepper
½ tablespoon lemon juice
1⅓ cups Minute Rice
1½ cups beef bouillon

Sauté first 4 ingredients in butter in a large skillet until vegetables are just tender. Add tomatoes, salt, pepper and lemon juice. Stir in rice and bouillon. Bring to a boil. Simmer, covered, 5 minutes until rice is tender. Fluff rice with a fork and serve. Serves 6 to 8.

Rebecca B. Goldman (Mrs. J. Crawford)

FRESH VEGETABLE CASSEROLE

2 medium carrots, sliced
  thin
2 small potatoes, cubed
4 medium tomatoes,
  quartered
1 red onion, sliced
1 small head cauliflower,
  separated in small
  pieces
1 cup fresh green beans
3 small zucchini, sliced
1 (8 ounce) can artichoke hearts

1 small bunch fresh
  broccoli, separated into
  small pieces
1 cup beef bouillon
1 cup olive oil
1 clove garlic, minced
2 teaspoons salt
1 bay leaf
½ teaspoon savory
¼ teaspoon tarragon
½ cup wine vinegar

Place vegetables in an ungreased 9″ x 13″ baking dish. Heat remaining ingredients to boiling. Pour over vegetables. Cover with foil. Bake at 350° for 1 hour. Serves 10 to 12.

Beverly S. McElroy (Mrs. William B.)

VEGETABLE CASSEROLE

1 (10 ounce) package frozen
  chopped broccoli
1 (10 ounce) package frozen
  baby lima beans
1 (8 ounce) can water
  chestnuts
1 (10½ ounce) can cream of
  mushroom soup

1 cup sour cream
1 envelope dry onion soup
  mix
2 tablespoons chopped
  pimento
3 cups rice krispies
½ cup margarine, melted

Cook broccoli and lima beans in boiling water for 5 minutes. Drain. Combine with remaining ingredients, except margarine and rice krispies. Place in a greased casserole. Brown rice krispies in margarine in a skillet. Spread on top of casserole. Bake at 350° for 30 minutes. Serves 8 to 10.

Joellen A. Kerr (Mrs. Roger W.)

MIXED VEGETABLE CASSEROLE

1 (10 ounce) package frozen
    lima beans
1 (10 ounce) package frozen
    corn
1 (10 ounce) package frozen
    French style green
    beans
¼ cup sliced and drained
    pimento

½ teaspoon salt
⅛ teaspoon pepper
1 cup whipping cream,
    whipped
¾ cup grated Cheddar
    cheese
1 cup mayonnaise
¼ cup Parmesan cheese

Thaw and drain frozen vegetables. Layer in a buttered 2 quart baking dish. Sprinkle with pimento, salt and pepper. Combine whipped cream, Cheddar cheese and mayonnaise in a separate bowl. Spread over vegetables. Sprinkle with Parmesan cheese. Bake uncovered at 325° for 50 to 60 minutes. Serves 6.

Beth H. Lovett (Mrs. L. Loring)

VEGETABLE CASSEROLE

1 (10 ounce) package frozen
    mixed vegetables,
    thawed
1 small onion, diced
1 cup grated sharp Cheddar
    cheese

½ cup mayonnaise
1 (8 ounce) can sliced water
    chestnuts
¾ cup Ritz cracker crumbs
2 tablespoons butter,
    melted

Combine all ingredients except cracker crumbs and butter. Place in a buttered 1½ quart casserole. Sprinkle cracker crumbs on top. Pour butter over crumbs. Bake at 350° for 30 minutes. Serves 4 to 6.

Elizabeth H. Thomas (Mrs. Jeffrey E.)

GARDEN STEW

1 cup chopped onion
¼ cup butter, melted
2 pounds fresh tomatoes, peeled and cut in wedges
1½ teaspoons salt
1 teaspoon sugar

⅛ teaspoon pepper
2 cups peeled and cubed potatoes
1½ cups fresh corn or green beans
1 cup sliced carrots

Cook onions in butter in a large saucepan until tender. Add tomatoes, salt, sugar and pepper. Cover and simmer 20 minutes. Add potatoes, corn or beans and carrots. Cook, covered, for 20 minutes until tender. Serves 6.

Sarah T. Shepherd (Mrs. Walton S., III)

KATE'S FRIED APPLES

6 to 8 apples, Yellow Delicious or Winesap
4 tablespoons butter

¼ to ½ cup brown sugar
2 tablespoons water
Cinnamon

Peel and slice apples. Melt butter in an iron skillet. Add apple slices. Sprinkle with brown sugar and cinnamon. Add water. Sauté, covered, 15 to 20 minutes, turning gently several times.

Jo Silman

NANA'S APPLESAUCE

15 to 17 apples, McIntosh or Winesap
2 cups water
½ teaspoon salt

⅔ cup sugar
⅔ teaspoon nutmeg
Juice of ¼ lemon

Core, peel and quarter apples. Combine with water and salt in a large kettle. Bring to a boil, reduce heat and simmer 20 minutes, stirring occasionally. Add remaining ingredients. Simmer 10 minutes. Makes 2½ quarts.

Victoria Hardy (Mrs. Waller C., III)

BAKED BANANAS

1 banana
2 tablespoons butter,
    melted
  Juice of ½ lemon or 1
    lime

2 tablespoons brown sugar
  Paprika for garnish
1 pinch each: red pepper
    and turmeric (optional)

Peel and halve banana. Combine butter and lemon juice. Roll banana in butter mixture, then in brown sugar. Place in a pie plate. Sprinkle lightly with paprika and other spices. Bake at 350° for 15 minutes. Serves 2.
May multiply for a crowd.

Frankie S. McCain (Mrs. James H.)

BAKED FRUIT

1 (16 ounce) can apricot
    halves, drained
1 (16 ounce) can purple
    plums, pitted and
    drained
1 (28 ounce) can peach
    halves, drained

1 orange, thinly sliced
½ cup orange juice
¼ cup light brown sugar
2 tablespoons butter
⅓ cup grated coconut

Arrange fruit alternately in a greased round, flat baking dish (such as a large quiche dish). Place the orange slices between the peach halves. Combine the orange juice and brown sugar. Pour over fruit. Dot with butter. Sprinkle with coconut. Bake at 350° for 15 to 20 minutes until bubbly. Serves 4 to 6.

Elaine R. Kroner (Mrs. Robert J.)

FRUITABLE

1 (16 ounce) can crushed
    pineapple
2 tablespoons cornstarch
¼ cup brown sugar

3 bananas
2 apples
4 peaches or equivalent
    frozen or canned free-
    stone peaches

Combine pineapple, cornstarch and brown sugar in a saucepan. Simmer 10 minutes until slightly thickened, stirring often. Remove from heat. Cool. Slice and combine other fruit. Add to pineapple. To make more, but not double, add an additional fruit, such as grapes, kiwi or strawberries. Serve hot in the winter, chilled in the summer. Serves 6 to 8.

Frankie S. McCain (Mrs. James H.)

FRUIT COMPOTE

1 (16 ounce) can pears
1 (11 ounce) can mandarin
  oranges
1 (16 ounce) can apricots
1 (16 ounce) can pineapple
  chunks
1 (16 ounce) can sliced
  peaches
1 (16 ounce) can blueberries
  Maraschino cherries for
  color
  English walnut halves
⅓ to ½ cup brown sugar
4 tablespoons butter
¾ cup crushed coconut
  macaroons

Drain fruit on paper towels. Layer in a baking dish. Sprinkle each layer with brown sugar and nuts. Dot with butter. Top with macaroons. Bake at 300° for 30 minutes. Serves 8 to 10.

Deborah J. Spradling (Mrs. Marshall)

FRIED PEACHES

4 to 6 firm, ripe peaches
6 tablespoons margarine,
  divided
3 to 4 tablespoons brown
  sugar

Peel peaches, slice in half and remove pits. Melt 4 tablespoons margarine in skillet over medium heat. Place peaches, hollow side up in the skillet. Add small pieces of remaining margarine to the center of each peach. Add a small amount of brown sugar to the center of each peach. Cook until the bottom of each peach is lightly browned and slightly soft, about 5 minutes. Turn peaches over and cook an additional 5 to 10 minutes until slightly soft. Brown sugar will melt in margarine to make a sauce to spoon over when serving. Remove from heat. Good served with fried chicken or barbecued ribs. Serves 4.

Sara Z. Hoblitzell (Mrs. John R.)

VERSATILE SAUCE

¾ cup mayonnaise
1 teaspoon horseradish
3 to 4 teaspoons lemon juice
½ cup butter, melted
Salt or onion salt to taste

Mix mayonnaise, horseradish and lemon juice in a bowl. Slowly add butter, beating until smooth. Season to taste. Store, covered, in refrigerator. Bring to room temperature to serve over hot vegetables; serve cold over chilled vegetables.

Maury R. Reishman (Mrs. Robert S.)

MAITRE D'HOTEL BUTTER

½ cup butter
1 tablespoon lemon juice
10 drops onion juice

1 tablespoon chopped
   parsley
Salt and pepper to taste

Cream butter. Add lemon juice a little at a time, blending well. Stir in onion juice, parsley and seasonings. Form into a ball or a flat cake. Refrigerate several hours. Delicious on baked potatoes, vegetables and mild fish.

Kitty W. Atkins (Mrs. E. Garfield)

BLENDER HOLLANDAISE SAUCE

3 egg yolks
2 tablespoons lemon juice

Dash of salt
½ cup butter, melted

Place egg yolks, lemon juice and salt in blender. Turn blender to high. While blender is running, slowly add butter. Turn off as soon as blended. Serves 4.

Lynn H. Goldsmith (Mrs. Robert F.)

OGLEBAY MANSION

The architectural history of the Oglebay Institute Mansion Museum, as it is known today is generally divided into three distinct phases.

The original brick Greek Revival style house was erected about 1845 by Hanson W. Chapline. It was a rectangular, two-story building with five bays and a median pitch hipped roof. The brick is laid in Flemish bond and openings have smooth, cut stone lintels and sills. Exterior details of the original building which survive are windows with 6/6 sash arrangements and iron gratings on side and rear basement windows.

The interior has a center hall plan with four rooms on each floor and exterior doors at both ends of the main hall. The stairway has a landing at the back wall and returns to the second floor hall. All rooms but the dining room have the original painted pine woodwork.

In 1856 the second phase was implemented by George W. Smith who named the property "Waddington Farm". Changes were made in the original building and a large wing was built onto the right rear of the house. By 1879 a porch had been added to the front although exact date of the addition is not known.

The third phase was a complete renovation by Mr. E.W. Oglebay in 1901-1905. The building took on classical revival forms and another large addition was erected on the left side. It was during this period the building was painted yellow with white trim.

The building today houses an excellent collection of Wheeling historical and industrial development exhibits. The collection also includes important items relating to the political history and social life of Wheeling.

One of the owners, James W. Paxton (1872-1878) actively worked for the formation of the state of West Virginia and was elected one of the council of five to aid Governor Pierpont.

Oglebay Mansion has always been, and remains today, an important building in the life of Wheeling, whose owners have made outstanding contributions to Wheeling and West Virginia.

Photo by Gerald S. Ratliff

PASTA AND GRAINS

Dutch Mill

GRANDFATHER'S CHEESE GRITS

1 cup quick grits	½ cup butter
3 cups boiling water	2 eggs
1 teaspoon salt	Milk
1 (6 ounce) roll bacon cheese	½ (3 ounce) bottle bacon bits
	1 cup seasoned stuffing mix

Cook grits according to package directions using first three ingredients. Add butter and cheese. Stir until melted. Beat eggs adding enough milk to make 1 cup. Combine with grits, stuffing and bacon bits. Mix well. Pour into greased casserole. Bake at 350° for 40 minutes. Serves 10 to 12.

Mary J. Payne (Mrs. Andrew A., III)

HOT GRITS

1 cup grits	1 tablespoon Tabasco sauce
4 cups boiling water	2 cloves garlic, crushed
½ teaspoon salt	3 eggs, well beaten
½ pound sharp cheese, grated	1 to 2 (4 ounces each) cans chopped green chilies
½ cup butter	

Add grits to boiling, salted water. Cook 2½ to 5 minutes until thick. Add remaining ingredients to grits. Bake in a 1½ quart greased casserole at 350° for 45 minutes. Serves 8 to 10.

Kay M. Davis (Mrs. Sidney P., Jr.)

FETTUCCINI ALFREDO

1 (8 ounce) package fettuccini or medium egg
   noodles
2 tablespoons half and half
¼ teaspoon salt

¼ cup butter, melted
½ cup grated Parmesan
   cheese
⅛ teaspoon pepper

Cook noodles according to package directions. Drain and keep
hot. In warm serving dish, combine remaining ingredients. Toss
hot noodles with cheese mixture to coat well. Serve immediately.
May sprinkle with additional cheese as served. Serves 4 to 6.

Pamela B. Brown (Mrs. Ricklin)

FETTUCCINI

1 pound egg noodles
¾ cup unsalted butter
1 cup freshly grated
   Parmesan cheese

1 cup heavy cream
8 ounces Ricotta cheese
2 eggs, beaten
   Freshly ground pepper

Cook noodles until tender in salted water. Drain. Melt butter in
a heavy pan, add noodles and coat. Add remaining ingredients. Toss
until well mixed. Serve immediately. Serves 8 to 10.

Susan Kamer-Shinaberry

APPLE NOODLE CASSEROLE

1 (8 ounce) package wide
   egg noodles
1 (8 ounce) package fine
   egg noodles
7½ cups sour green apples

2 cups sugar, divided
1 cup butter, divided
½ cup chopped almonds
1 teaspoon cinnamon

Cook noodles separately according to package directions.
Drain. Add ½ cup sugar and ⅓ cup butter to each size noodle.
Spread wide noodle mixture in a 9" x 13" pan. Cut apples into
chunks. Mix with 1 cup sugar, nuts, and cinnamon. Spread over
wide noodles. Layer fine noodles on top of apples. Dot with remaining butter. Bake, covered, at 300° for 1½ hours. Serve with pork,
ham or poultry as a side dish. Freezes well. Serves 10 to 12.

Martha Hedrick

NOODLE PUDDING

1 (16 ounce) package wide
  egg noodles
1 (16 ounce) can sliced
  peaches, drained
1 (8 ounce) can crushed
  pineapple, drained
4 eggs, beaten

¾ cup sugar
½ cup butter, melted
1 teaspoon salt
3 cups cottage cheese
1 cup sour cream
1½ teaspoons vanilla extract

Cook noodles per package directions. Drain. Combine with fruit. Combine eggs, sugar and butter. Add to noodles. Stir in remaining ingredients. Place in a 9" x 13" baking dish. Bake at 350° for 1½ hours. Delicious with any meat.

Nancy S. Dodson (Mrs. Raymond G.)

BEA'S RICE SAVOY

2 tablespoons butter
2 tablespoons cooking oil
1 cup uncooked rice
1 clove garlic
1 small onion, minced

2 (10½ ounces each) cans
  beef consommé
1 tablespoon white wine
½ teaspoon parsley
1 teaspoon paprika
½ teaspoon savory

Melt butter and oil in heavy saucepan. Fry rice, onion and garlic until lightly browned, stirring constantly. Add remaining ingredients. Cover and simmer 1 hour. Serves 6.

Elizabeth Y. Revercomb (Mrs. Paul H.)

BOUILLON RICE

¼ cup butter
½ cup celery
¼ cup chopped onions
1 (4 ounce) can mushrooms
1½ cups uncooked, long grain
  rice

1 (10½ ounce) can beef
  bouillon
1 (10½ ounce) can
  consommé

Sauté celery and onions in butter. Stir in remaining ingredients. Place in a 1½ quart casserole. Bake, covered, at 350° for 1¼ hours. Stir once after 45 minutes. This can be held in a 250° oven after baking. Keep dish covered. Serves 6 to 8.

Bonnie W. Bartsch (Mrs. James D.)

CHINESE FRIED RICE

2 tablespoons peanut oil
2 cups chopped onions
2 cups cold cooked rice

2 eggs, slightly beaten
1 tablespoon soy sauce
½ teaspoon salt

Heat oil in wok or skillet. Add onions, stir fry until brown. Add cold rice and sauté. Add eggs seasoned with soy sauce and salt. Saute until heated through. For variety add one or more of the following: 2 cups chopped cooked meat (bacon, ham, shrimp, chicken, pork, or beef), chopped green pepper, peanuts or mushrooms. Serves 4 to 6.

June L. Marlowe (Mrs. L. Gilbert)

GREEN RICE

2 eggs
⅓ cup cooking oil
2 cups cooked rice
1 medium onion, finely
    chopped
1 cup evaporated milk

2 tablespoons dried parsley
½ teaspoon garlic salt
8 ounces Cheddar or Colby
    cheese, grated
Dash of Tabasco sauce

Beat eggs and oil. Add remaining ingredients. Place in a greased casserole dish. Bake at 275° for 30 minutes.

Diane Minsker (Mrs. Michael)

MUSHROOM ALMOND RICE

3 cups boiling water
5 chicken bouillon cubes
1½ cups uncooked rice
2 to 3 teaspoons diced onion
½ cup slivered almonds

½ pound fresh mushrooms,
    sliced
Salt and pepper to taste
2 tablespoons butter

Dissolve bouillon cubes in water. Combine with next 5 ingredients. Place in a 1½ quart casserole. Dot with butter. Bake at 350° for 1 hour. Serves 8.

Connie L. Hillenbrand (Mrs. Edward F., III)

VEGETABLE RICE MEDLEY

1 (10 ounce) package frozen
   green peas, thawed
1 (6 ounce) package long
   grain and wild rice
1 (4 ounce) can sliced
   mushrooms, drained

½ cup slivered almonds
2½ cups boiling water
1 tablespoon butter
1 beef bouillon cube

Combine peas, rice (reserve seasoning packet), mushrooms and almonds in a greased 2 quart shallow casserole. Combine boiling water, butter, bouillon cube and seasoning packet. Stir until butter is melted and bouillon cube is dissolved. Pour over mixture in casserole. Cover tightly and bake at 350° for 50 to 60 minutes or until rice is tender. Serves 6.

Note: To serve as a main dish, add 1 cup cooked, cubed chicken or beef. If using chicken, substitute chicken bouillon for beef bouillon.

Dr. James Peden, Jr.

PASTA WITH GARDEN MARINARA SAUCE

½ pound vermicelli
6 large ripe tomatoes
4 tablespoons olive oil
2 large garlic cloves,
   minced

1 cup fresh basil, chopped
   Freshly ground pepper to
   taste
4 tablespoons butter
   Parmesan cheese

Cook pasta. Drain and refresh with cold water. Peel tomatoes by dipping into boiling water for 1 minute and then pulling off skins. Core tomatoes. Squeeze and discard juice and seeds from each half. Place oil in deep saucepan. Add garlic. Heat but do not brown. Roughly chop tomato pulp and add to oil. Add basil and pepper to taste. Cook on medium heat until tomato pulp is tender and juice has nearly disappeared. Swirl in butter and toss ingredients with vermicelli. Serve with freshly grated Parmesan cheese. Serves 6 to 8.

Norman Fagan

PASTA PRIMAVERA

ROMANO SAUCE

6 tablespoons butter
1 cup half and half
¾ cup grated Romano cheese

¼ teaspoon salt
Dash of pepper

Heat butter and cream until butter melts. Remove from heat. Add cheese, salt and pepper. Mix well and set aside.

PASTA AND VEGETABLES

1 pound spaghetti or
  fettuccini
1 tablespoon butter
2 tablespoons cooking oil
1 clove garlic, split
1 zucchini, sliced ¼" thick
½ pound mushrooms, sliced

½ pound broccoli, cut into
  1½" flowerets
½ green or red pepper, cut
  into ¼" strips
½ pound whole fresh snow
  pea pods, ends trimmed
¼ cup Romano cheese

Cook spaghetti according to package directions. Drain. Heat butter and oil in a large skillet. Add garlic, zucchini, mushrooms, broccoli and pepper. Stir fry 5 minutes until vegetables are crisp tender. Add pea pods and stir fry 1 additional minute. Cook vegetables, covered, another 1 to 2 minutes, but do not overcook. Discard garlic. Toss pasta with Romano Sauce and place on a heated serving platter. Place vegetables on top of spaghetti and sprinkle with cheese. Toss at the table just before serving. Serves 6.
Variation: Add sautéed shrimp to vegetables.

Mrs. Catherine Bradford

BROCCOLI SPAGHETTI

1 (8 ounce) package
  spaghetti
1 bunch broccoli, separated
  into flowerets

½ cup butter, melted
1 cup whipping cream
3 ounces Parmesan cheese
  Garlic or onion salt

Cook pasta, rinse and drain. Cook broccoli 5 minutes in boiling water. Drain. Combine butter, spaghetti and broccoli. Add whipping cream and Parmesan cheese, tossing until coated. Heat through. Add garlic or onion salt to taste. Serves 4 to 6.

Linda S. Faerber (Mrs. Kenneth)

RIGATONI CON BROCCOLI

1 bunch broccoli
6 tablespoons olive or
   cooking oil
1 teaspoon pressed garlic
   Salt

1 pound Ricotta cheese
½ cup milk
1 pound rigatoni or similar
   type pasta
½ cup grated Parmesan
   cheese

Cut broccoli flowerets off stem and cut stem into bite size pieces. Cook broccoli in boiling water for 3 minutes. Drain. Run cold water over broccoli to chill quickly. (Broccoli should remain crisp.) Heat oil in skillet, add garlic and cook briefly without browning. Add broccoli, tossing to heat through. Salt lightly to taste. Remove garlic and set aside. Combine Ricotta cheese and milk in a bowl, mixing until smooth. Set aside. Cook pasta in boiling water; do not overcook. Rinse, drain and return to pot. Add Ricotta mixture, stirring well. Add the broccoli mixture and toss well. Simmer for 2 to 3 minutes over low flame in covered pot. Pour into heated bowl. Sprinkle with Parmesan cheese. Serve immediately. Serves 4 to 6.

Karen Potesta

MASLIN-GAMBLE HOUSE

Moorefield, Hardy County, West Virginia is the site of this fine two-story Greek Revival style antebellum house built by Thomas Maslin, a local land speculator, in 1847. The house is representative of the growth and prosperity in the South Branch Valley prior to the Civil War. The broad flat lands in the area invited large-scale farming and a plantation-style economy was the result.

During his lifetime, Thomas Maslin bought and transferred more than 7500 acres in Hardy County. Mr. Maslin was one of the leading spokesmen of the county from the 1840's through the 1870's. He was a justice of the Hardy County court from 1850 through May 15, 1865. Thomas Maslin, who leaned toward the South in the Civil War years (he represented Hardy County at the Virginia Secession Convention in 1861, but abstained from voting), was the Hardy County delegate to the West Virginia Constitutional Convention in 1872. He presented an eagle quill pen to the Convention which was used to sign the Constitution. Thus this southern gentleman was a leader in healing the former divisions.

In the late 1890's the Maslin property was sold to Mortimer Gamble II, a distinguished lawyer, who served in the West Virginia House of Delegates in 1893-1895, as a county justice and as prosecuting attorney in 1908-1912 and 1920-1924. The Gamble family still continues to be active in Moorefield affairs.

The house was built in the Greek Revival style with paired Ionic columns supporting the pedimented portico, dentiled cornice, hipped roof and a roof deck with turned-baluster rail. The brick was made on the site and wood cut from nearby forests. The entrance door has divided sidelights and a fanlight. Windows have a 6/6 sash arrangement and brick flat-arch heads.

Interior wood detailing includes splayed window reveals, applied paneling, carved corner blocks (acanthus leaves, stars, bulls-eyes), and a finely proportioned stair with curved rail.

The Maslin-Gamble house still reflects the prominence of its owners in local history and area development.

Photo by Douglas Bishoff

BREADS

Cornucopia

PARMESAN BREAD

1 package active dry yeast
¼ cup warm water
1 cup scalded milk
¼ cup margarine, softened

¼ cup sugar
2 eggs
4½ cups flour, divided

Dissolve yeast in warm water. Add margarine to milk to melt. Cool. Combine liquids, eggs, sugar and ½ of flour. Beat well. Add remaining flour. Cover. Refrigerate overnight. Roll out into a large rectangle. Add filling. Cut crosswise into 3 sections. Roll up lengthwise. Seal well. Roll against board to lengthen slightly. Place the 3 rolls crosswise on baking sheet. Let rise 1 hour. Make a slash the length of each roll halfway through. Let finish rising until double. Bake at 350° for 20 minutes. Yield: 3 loaves.

FILLING

½ cup margarine, softened
⅓ cup Parmesan cheese

1 teaspoon garlic salt

Combine all ingredients until smooth.

Paula S. McKenney (Mrs. Ronald A.)

FRENCH BREAD
Moist and light with a nice crispy crust

1 package active dry yeast
1 cup warm water
2 tablespoons sugar, divided
1 teaspoon salt

2 tablespoons cooking oil
3 cups flour, divided
2 egg whites, stiffly beaten
1 tablespoon corn meal

In small dish dissolve yeast in warm water with 1 tablespoon sugar. Set aside. In a large bowl combine salt, remaining sugar, oil, 2 cups flour and yeast mixture. Gently stir in 1 cup flour and egg whites. Dough will be sticky. Let rise in greased bowl 1 hour. Shape into large loaf. Place on greased baking sheet that has been sprinkled with corn meal. Bake at 400° for 10 minutes. Reduce to 350°. Bake 20 additional minutes. Rub loaf with butter.

Nancy Larrick

OLD FASHIONED SQUASH BREAD

2 packages active dry yeast
  Pinch of sugar
½ cup lukewarm water
5 to 6 cups flour
½ cup sugar

1 teaspoon salt
1 cup puréed acorn squash
1 cup lukewarm milk
½ cup + 1 tablespoon soft butter

Combine yeast, pinch of sugar and water. Proof for 10 minutes. Sift 5 cups flour, sugar and salt into large bowl. Make a well in center. Pour squash, milk, yeast mixture and butter into well. Mix until dough forms a ball. (May need to add more flour.) Knead until smooth and elastic. Place in greased bowl, cover with towel and let rise in a warm place for 2 hours. Punch down. Roll into a large rectangle 1″ thick. Cut with biscuit cutter. Arrange biscuits on edge in a ring in a well greased 10″ bundt pan. Brush with butter. Let rise 45 minutes. Bake at 375° for 35 to 40 minutes. For last 10 minutes, cover with foil to prevent browning. Turn bread onto platter and serve.

Libby Hamel (Mrs. William R.)

WHOLE WHEAT CUMIN BREAD

2 packages active dry yeast	1 egg, beaten
¼ cup lukewarm water	4 cups whole wheat flour
Pinch of sugar	2½ cups white flour
⅓ cup butter	1 cup flour, as required for
¼ cup brown sugar	kneading
¼ cup honey	1 tablespoon ground cumin
2 teaspoons salt	4 tablespoons butter
2 cups scalded milk	4 tablespoons honey
⅓ cup orange juice	

Dissolve yeast in lukewarm water and sugar for 5 minutes. Set aside. Combine butter, brown sugar, honey and salt. Add milk. Cool to lukewarm. Blend in orange juice, yeast mixture and egg. Stir in flour and cumin. Knead dough with additional cup of flour as necessary. Put dough in buttered bowl, turning to grease well on all sides. Cover and let rise for 1 hour or until doubled. Punch down and knead 1 minute. Place in buttered bowl. Let rise for 30 minutes. Punch down. Divide dough in half. Place in 2 greased 9" x 5" loaf pans. Cover and let rise until doubled. Bake at 425° for 10 minutes. Reduce heat to 350°. Bake an additional 25 to 30 minutes. Cool in pans 5 minutes. Remove and brush tops with honey-butter. Yield: 2 loaves.

Rebecca D. Ross (Mrs. Alexander)

TWO WAY ROLLS: CRESCENT AND CINNAMON ROLLS

1 cup milk, scalded	1 teaspoon salt
1 cup butter	4 egg yolks, beaten
2 packages active dry yeast	4½ cups flour
¼ cup sugar	Softened butter

Combine butter and milk. Cool. Stir in yeast, sugar and salt. Add egg yolks and flour. Mix well, but do not knead. Turn dough a few times on floured surface to be sure it is properly mixed. Let rise in warm place 1 hour until doubled. Divide dough into 4 parts. Roll each part into a circle. Spread with softened butter. Cut into 12 pie shaped wedges. Roll each wedge into a crescent, large end to small tip. Place on greased baking sheet. Let rise again 1 hour until doubled. Bake at 400° for 12 minutes. Makes 48 rolls.

For cinnamon rolls: Roll dough into circles as above. Spread with softened butter, cinnamon and sugar. May also add chopped nuts, chopped apples, raisins or dates. Roll up jellyroll fashion, tucking ends under. Cut into 1" slices. Place on greased baking sheet. Let rise 1 hour. Bake at 400° for 12 minutes.

Madeline Rowan (Mrs. Edward M.)

ALABAMA BISCUITS

2 tablespoons butter	1 package active dry yeast
1 cup milk	½ teaspoon sugar
1 teaspoon salt	3 cups flour
3 tablespoons sugar	¼ cup butter, melted
½ cup warm water	

Combine first 4 ingredients in saucepan. Heat until bubbly. Remove from heat and set pan in tepid water to cool. Mix water, yeast and sugar in bowl. Let stand 10 minutes. Add lukewarm milk mixture to yeast mixture. Place flour in a large bowl. Slowly add liquid to flour, mixing well. Cover bowl with cloth. Let rise 1 hour. Turn dough onto a lightly floured surface; knead gently. Pat to ¾" thickness. Cut with biscuit cutter. Dip each biscuit into melted butter. Place touching in a lightly greased 9" x 13" pan. Let rise another 40 to 60 minutes. Bake at 375° for 20 to 30 minutes. Yield: 2 dozen.

Jonnie C. Shepler (Mrs. David)

SWEET WATER BAGELS

5 cups flour, divided	1½ cups hot tap water
3 tablespoons sugar	1 egg white
1 package active dry yeast	1 tablespoon water

Combine 1½ cups flour, sugar and yeast. Add hot water. Beat with mixer on medium speed for 2 minutes. Add ½ cup flour and beat on high speed for 2 minutes. Gradually stir in remaining flour. Knead well. Cover. Let rise 20 minutes. Dough will not double. Divide dough into twelfths. Roll each into ball. Flatten. Force finger through center to pull out hole as bagel cooks. Cover. Let rise 20 minutes. Fill large skillet with 2 inches boiling water. Place 4 bagels in water. Lower heat and simmer for 7 minutes, turning each bagel over once. Repeat process for remaining bagels, remembering to start each batch with boiling water. Cool on cloth towel for 5 minutes. Place on greased baking sheet. Bake at 375° for 25 to 30 minutes. May be glazed with 1 egg white beaten with 1 tablespoon water. Yield: 1 dozen.

Paula S. McKenney (Mrs. Ronald A.)

GRANDMA'S POCKETBOOK ROLLS

1 package active dry yeast	½ cup cold water
¼ cup warm water	½ teaspoon salt
1 tablespoon sugar	1 egg, beaten
½ cup boiling water	3¾ cups flour
½ cup shortening	Butter
⅓ cup sugar	

Dissolve yeast and 1 tablespoon sugar in warm water. Set aside for 10 minutes. Pour boiling water over shortening and sugar. Stir until shortening melts. Add cold water, salt, egg and yeast mixture. Stir in flour. Refrigerate overnight. Roll out dough to rectangle ½" thick. Cut with biscuit cutter. Dent each circle of dough across middle with back of knife blade. Spread with touch of butter and fold over. Place on greased cookie sheet. Let rise for 1 hour. Bake at 350° for 10 to 12 minutes. Yield: 2½ dozen.

Janet T. Hovius (Mrs. Joseph C.)

HOT ROLLS

1 package active dry yeast	1 egg
1¼ cups very warm water, divided	1½ tablespoons cooking oil
¼ cup sugar	4 cups flour
1 teaspoon salt	2 tablespoons butter, melted

Combine ¼ cup water and yeast in a small bowl. Let stand 5 minutes until yeast is dissolved. Combine sugar, salt, egg and oil in a large bowl, mixing well. Stir in yeast mixture. Add remaining 1 cup *very warm* water. Mix in flour, 2 cups at a time. Roll out immediately on a floured surface, using more flour as needed to prevent sticking. Cut into 2" to 3" rounds. Fold rounds over. Place in a large greased pan for 2 to 3 hours. Brush with melted butter. Bake at 400° for 15 minutes.

Dough may be refrigerated overnight in a large bowl before cutting into rounds. Cover with wax paper.

Jo Ann R. Vanderford (Mrs. Thomas, IV)

ADA'S WHOLE WHEAT ROLLS

1 package active dry yeast	1 cup mashed potatoes
½ cup lukewarm water	1 cup scalded milk
1 teaspoon sugar	2 eggs, beaten
⅔ cup shortening	5 to 6 cups flour
1½ teaspoons salt	1 cup whole wheat flour
½ cup sugar	

Dissolve yeast in warm water with 1 teaspoon sugar. Set aside for 5 minutes. Cream together next 6 ingredients. Add yeast to potato mixture. Add flours gradually. Dough will be sticky. Knead lightly on floured surface. Let rise in warm place 1½ hours until doubled. Punch down. Rub with melted butter. Cover. Refrigerate until ready to use, up to 4 days. Pinch off dough to form rolls. Let rise 1½ hours. Bake at 425° for 10 to 15 minutes. Makes 2½ dozen rolls.

Donna L. Dean (Mrs. Rodney D.)

WHOLE WHEAT ROUNDS

½ cup milk	¼ to ½ cup sunflower seeds
3 tablespoons sugar	½ to 1 cup coconut
3 tablespoons butter	5½ to 6 cups flour
2 teaspoons salt	1 cup whole wheat flour
1 package active dry yeast	½ cup raisins, nuts or
1½ cups warm water	dates, optional

Scald milk. Add next 3 ingredients. Set aside to cool. Dissolve yeast in warm water. Add to milk mixture. Add coconut and seeds. Mix. Add flour and any optional ingredients. Knead 7 to 10 minutes. Place in greased bowl. Let rise for 1 hour. Punch down. Divide dough in half. Place each half in greased round cake pan. Let rise 1 hour. Bake at 400° for 20 to 25 minutes.

Marta D. MacCallum (Mrs. Daniel)

POPOVERS

3 eggs	1 tablespoon butter, melted
1 cup milk	1 teaspoon cinnamon,
1 cup sifted flour	optional
½ teaspoon salt	

Beat all ingredients until smooth. Pour batter into greased, unheated cups, filling ⅓ full. Bake at 400° for 35 minutes until popovers are crusty and brown. Makes 10 popovers. Serve with apple jelly.

Jane H. Shuman (Mrs. James W.)

BEST EVER CORN BREAD

1½ cups yellow cornmeal	6 tablespoons margarine,
1 cup flour	melted and cooled
⅓ cup sugar	6 tablespoons shortening,
½ to 1 teaspoon salt	melted and cooled
1 tablespoon baking powder	1½ cups milk
2 eggs	

Mix dry ingredients. Beat together remaining ingredients. Add to dry mixture. Stir until smooth. Pour into greased, hot 10″ skillet. Bake at 400° for 30 minutes. Serve hot. Serves 6 to 8.

Larrie O. Bartrug (Mrs. Edwin M., Jr.)

MEXICAN CORN BREAD

1 cup self-rising cornmeal
1 cup flour
¼ cup sugar
½ tablespoon salt
1 tablespoon crushed red
   pepper
1 egg

½ cup cooking oil
1 cup milk
½ cup cream style corn
½ cup chopped green pepper
¼ cup chopped onion
1 cup shredded Longhorn
   cheese

Mix all ingredients in bowl. Pour into greased 10 inch skillet or muffin pans. Bake at 425° for 30 to 35 minutes. Serves 6 to 8.

Deborah L. Dent (Mrs. Robert)

OLD FASHIONED MUFFINS

2 eggs
½ cup shortening
1 cup sugar
1½ cups flour
1½ teaspoons baking powder

½ teaspoon nutmeg or
   lemon extract
½ cup milk
½ teaspoon vanilla extract

Cream first 6 ingredients. Add milk and vanilla. Mix. Pour into greased muffin pans. Bake at 375° for 20 to 25 minutes. Makes 12 muffins.

Debbie J. Spradling (Mrs. Marshall)

PECAN MUFFINS

1 cup light brown sugar
⅓ cup flour
   Pinch of salt

1 cup coarsely chopped
   pecans
2 eggs
½ teaspoon vanilla extract

Combine first 4 ingredients. Mix well. Add eggs and vanilla, stirring well. Fill well greased muffin pans ½ full. Bake at 350° for 20 to 25 minutes. Remove from pans while warm. Makes 1 dozen.

Mary Ann Cody

WHEAT GERM MUFFINS

⅔ cup packaged biscuit mix	⅓ cup water
⅓ cup wheat germ	2 tablespoons peanut butter
¼ cup sugar	½ teaspoon vanilla extract
1 egg, slightly beaten	

Combine biscuit mix, wheat germ and sugar. Set aside. Beat remaining ingredients with mixer just until smooth. Add egg mixture to dry ingredients, stirring just until moistened. Spoon batter into greased or paper-lined muffin pans until ⅔ full. Bake at 375° for 20 to 25 minutes. Makes 6 muffins.

Shawn B. Gross

BRAN MUFFINS

1 cup boiling water	½ cup shortening
1 cup 100% Bran	1 cup sugar
2½ cups flour	2 eggs
2½ teaspoons soda	2 cups All Bran
1 teaspoon salt	2 cups buttermilk

Mix water and 100% Bran. Set aside. Sift together flour, soda and salt. Set aside. In a large bowl cream shortening and sugar. Add eggs to creamed mixture, beating well after each addition. Add All Bran and buttermilk to creamed mixture. Combine three mixes until moistened. Pour into greased muffin tins. Bake at 350° for 15 to 20 minutes. Batter may be refrigerated covered for 4 weeks. Makes 3 dozen.

Kathy M. Muehlman (Mrs. Raymond L.)

BISCUIT CINNAMON ROLLS

1 (10 count) can Hungry Jack biscuits	¼ cup butter, melted
	Cinnamon
¾ cup brown sugar	Raisins

Brush muffin pans with butter. Put ¼ teaspoon brown sugar in each cup. Press biscuits into rectangular shape on lightly floured board. Brush each biscuit with butter, spoon on 1 tablespoon brown sugar and sprinkle with cinnamon and raisins. Roll up lengthwise and fasten by pinching edges together. Cut each roll into three pieces and arrange cloverleaf fashion in muffin pan. Dot with butter. Let rise 10 minutes. Bake at 350° for 12 to 15 minutes. Invert on platter to serve. Makes 10 rolls.

Ester Heath (Mrs. George R.)

CREAM CHEESE LOAF

2¼ cups cake flour
1½ teaspoons baking powder
¼ teaspoon salt
4 eggs
¾ cup unsalted sweet
   butter, melted
1¼ cups sugar

1 (3 ounce) package cream
   cheese, room tempera-
   ture and cut into 1"
   cubes
½ cup small curd cottage
   cheese
1½ teaspoons vanilla extract
1 teaspoon lemon juice

Sift flour, baking powder and salt together. Set aside. Blend eggs and butter. Add remaining ingredients, stirring after each addition. Add flour mixture, one-half at a time. May need to blend last half with spoon. Pour into 9" x 5" loaf pan. Bake at 325° for 1 hour and 10 minutes until toothpick comes out clean. Cool 30 minutes. Remove from pan. Wrap in plastic overnight. Serve plain or as you would pound cake. May be refrigerated up to 1 week. Freezes well. Makes 1 loaf.

Kathryn S. Foster (Mrs. Daniel S.)

SPICED APPLESAUCE BREAD

1¼ cups applesauce
1 cup sugar
½ cup cooking oil
2 eggs
3 tablespoons milk
2 cups flour
1 teaspoon soda

½ teaspoon baking powder
½ teaspoon cinnamon
¼ teaspoon salt
¼ teaspoon nutmeg
¼ teaspoon allspice
½ cup pecans

Combine first 5 ingredients. Stir in dry ingredients, mix well. Fold in pecans. Pour into a greased 9" x 5" loaf pan. Sprinkle with topping. Bake at 350° for 1 hour. Makes 1 loaf.

TOPPING

¼ cup chopped pecans
¼ cup brown sugar

½ teaspoon cinnamon

Combine all ingredients.

Debbie E. Brown (Mrs. John H., Jr.)

BOSTON BROWN BREAD

2 tablespoons solid
   shortening
2 teaspoons soda
2 cups boiling water
1 (16 ounce) box raisins
2 eggs, beaten

2 cups sugar
4 cups flour
1 teaspoon salt
2 teaspoons cinnamon
6 (#202) cans or 10 (10
   ounce) soup cans

Mix shortening and soda in boiling water. Add raisins. Soak overnight. Combine remaining ingredients. Add raisin mixture. Grease and flour cans. Fill cans ½ full with batter. Place cans on cookie sheet. Bake at 350° for 1 hour or until toothpick comes out clean.

Kitty W. Atkins (Mrs. E. Garfield)

CREAM CHEESE BANANA BREAD

1 cup sugar
1 (8 ounce) package cream
   cheese, softened
1 cup mashed ripe bananas

2 eggs
2 cups Bisquick
½ cup chopped pecans

Cream sugar and cream cheese until fluffy. Beat in banana and eggs. Stir in Bisquick and nuts. Do not beat. Pour into a greased 9″ x 5″ loaf pan. Bake at 350° for 45 to 60 minutes or until done. Cover with tin foil the last 15 minutes. Freezes well. Yield: 1 loaf.

Mary Lu W. MacCorkle (Mrs. John)

POPPY SEED BREAD

3 cups flour
2 cups sugar
1 teaspoon salt
1 teaspoon soda
2 ounces poppy seed

4 eggs
1 cup milk
1½ cups cooking oil
1 teaspoon vanilla extract

Combine all ingredients in large bowl. Beat 5 minutes. Pour into two 5″ x 9″ loaf pans. Bake at 325° for 1 hour. Slice and serve with Sweetened Cheese Spread.

SWEETENED CHEESE SPREAD

1 (8 ounce) package cream
   cheese, softened

1 cup powdered sugar
1 teaspoon vanilla extract

Combine all ingredients. Stir until smooth.

Jonnie C. Shepler (Mrs. David)

LEMON NUT BREAD

½ cup black walnuts	Grated rind of 1 lemon
1½ cups flour	⅓ cup cooking oil
1 teaspoon baking powder	2 eggs
1 cup sugar	½ cup milk

Combine all ingredients, mixing by hand. Pour into a greased and floured 8″ x 4″ loaf pan. Bake at 350° for 45 to 60 minutes. Spoon topping over bread while still warm.

TOPPING

Juice of 1 lemon   ¼ cup granulated sugar

Stir together.

Connie Morton McKee

PINEAPPLE ZUCCHINI BREAD

3 cups flour	3 eggs, beaten
1 teaspoon soda	2 cups sugar
1 teaspoon salt	1 cup cooking oil
1 teaspoon baking powder	2 teaspoons vanilla extract
3 teaspoons cinnamon	2 cups grated zucchini
1 teaspoon allspice	1 (8 ounce) can crushed
1 teaspoon cloves	pineapple, drained
¾ cup nuts	Raisins (optional)

Combine first 8 ingredients. Add eggs to dry ingredients. Mix in oil, sugar and vanilla. Fold in zucchini, pineapple and raisins. Pour into 2 greased and floured 9″ x 5″ loaf pans. Bake at 325° for 1 hour. Cool 10 minutes. Remove from pans. Yield: 2 loaves.

Mary Lu MacCorkle (Mrs. John)

BEER BREAD

1 (12 ounce) can beer,
  room temperature
3¼ cups flour
¼ teaspoon salt

3 tablespoons sugar
3 teaspoons baking powder
2 tablespoons butter,
  melted

Mix all ingredients until a sticky dough is formed. Let rise in a greased covered bowl for 1 hour. Pour into greased loaf pan. Smooth top of dough. Bake at 350° for 1 hour. Brush with melted butter for last 10 minutes of baking. Makes 1 loaf.

Dana W. Sharp

PUMPKIN BREAD

⅔ cup shortening
2⅔ cups sugar
4 eggs
1 (16 ounce) can pumpkin
⅔ cup orange juice
3½ cups flour
2 teaspoons soda

1½ teaspoons salt
½ teaspoon baking powder
1 teaspoon cloves
2 teaspoons cinnamon
⅔ cup chopped nuts
⅔ cup chopped dates

Cream shortening and sugar. Beat eggs. Add to creamed mixture. Stir in pumpkin and juice. Sift all dry ingredients together. Add to pumpkin mixture. Fold in dates and nuts. Mix well. Pour in 2 greased 9″ x 5″ loaf pans. Bake at 350° for 50 minutes. Test for doneness. Yield: 2 loaves.

Brenda B. Jones (Mrs. Laurence G.)

RHUBARB NUT BREAD

⅓ cup sugar
1 tablespoon butter, melted
1½ cups firmly packed light
  brown sugar
⅔ cup cooking oil
1 egg
1 cup buttermilk

1 teaspoon soda
1 teaspoon salt
1 teaspoon vanilla extract
2½ cups flour
1½ cups diced raw rhubarb
½ cup nuts

In small bowl combine sugar and butter. Set aside. Combine brown sugar, oil and egg in large bowl. In third bowl mix buttermilk, soda, salt and vanilla. Add milk mixture alternately with flour to the brown sugar mixture, beating well with each addition. Fold in rhubarb and nuts. Pour into 2 buttered and floured 8″ x 4″ loaf pans. Sprinkle with reserved sugar and butter mixture. Bake at 350° for 1 hour. Yield: 2 small loaves.

Beverly Howard Poole

BREAKFAST TARTS

2 cups margarine
2 (8 ounces each) packages
   cream cheese
½ cup sugar
½ teaspoon vanilla extract
4 cups flour
½ teaspoon baking powder
1 jar jam or preserves

Cream margarine. Add cheese, mixing well. Add sugar and vanilla. Sift in flour and baking powder. Form into 2 or 3 balls and refrigerate overnight. The next day roll out a small amount of dough. Cut with a 3¼″ round cutter. Spoon a small amount of preserves in the center of each round. Fold over and pinch together. Repeat until all the dough is used. Bake at 350° for 20 minutes until browned. Yield: 6 dozen.

Sandra C. Tate (Mrs. Donald L.)

EASY YUMMY SWEET ROLLS

1 package active dry yeast
1 cup warm water
1 egg
1⅓ cups sugar, divided
¼ cup cooking oil
3 cups flour
¼ cup butter, melted
1½ tablespoons cinnamon
Nuts
Raisins

Dissolve yeast in water in large bowl. Add egg, ⅓ cup sugar and oil. Whip with fork or spoon. Add flour and whip again for 2 minutes until smooth. Cover with cloth and place in barely warm (but turned off) oven. Let rise for 20 to 30 minutes until doubled in size. Punch down. Stir slightly until smooth. Kneading is not necessary. Roll out on floured surface. Spread with butter, remaining sugar, cinnamon, nuts and raisins. Roll up in jellyroll fashion. Either slice 1½″ thick and place on greased glass pan with slices almost touching, or make an arc with the large roll and place seam side down on greased cookie sheet. If left intact clip around edge with scissors in 3 or 4 places to allow roll to rise properly. Let rise in warm (turned off) oven. Bake at 375° for 20 minutes for slices or 25 minutes for roll. May frost with glaze.

GLAZE

1 cup powdered sugar
2 teaspoons milk
¼ teaspoon vanilla extract

Combine all ingredients.

Larrie O. Bartrug (Mrs. Edwin M., Jr.)

APRICOT DANISH

2 packages active dry yeast
½ cup warm water
1 (8 ounce) package cream
  cheese
1 cup sugar
4 cups flour
¼ teaspoon salt

1½ cups butter
2 eggs, beaten
1 jar Baker's apricot cake
  filling
Pecans or almonds,
  chopped

Dissolve yeast in warm water. Set aside. Cream sugar and cream cheese. Set aside. Combine flour and salt. Using a pastry blender, add butter to flour mixture until it forms crumbs. Add eggs and yeast to flour mixture mixing until dough forms. Divide dough into 5 equal balls. Roll out each ball until ¼″ thick. Spread with cream cheese mixture. Top with cake filling. Sprinkle with nuts. Roll up lengthwise and place on cookie sheet. Using sharp knife slice halfway through dough along the top. Bake at 375° for 20 to 25 minutes. Makes five 12″ pastries. Can be frozen.

Marta D. MacCallum (Mrs. Daniel)

APPLE PEAR COFFEE CAKE

½ cup butter, softened
1 cup sugar
2 eggs
1 teaspoon vanilla extract
½ teaspoon salt
1 teaspoon baking soda

2 cups flour
1 teaspoon baking powder
1 cup sour cream
2 cups finely chopped
  apples and pears (2
  apples to 1 pear)

Cream butter and sugar. Mix in eggs and vanilla. Beat well. Combine dry ingredients and add alternately with sour cream. Fold in apples and pears. Spread batter into a greased 9″ x 13″ pan. Sprinkle topping evenly over batter. Bake at 350° for 45 to 55 minutes. Best served warm with whipped cream.

TOPPING

1 cup brown sugar, packed
½ cup chopped nuts

2 tablespoons butter,
  softened
1 teaspoon cinnamon

Combine all ingredients.

Susan C. Harpold (Mrs. Robert R., Jr.)

SOUR CREAM CHOCOLATE COFFEE CAKE

½ cup margarine, softened
1 cup sugar
2 cups flour
1 teaspoon soda

1 teaspoon baking powder
1 teaspoon vanilla extract
2 eggs
1½ cups sour cream

Combine margarine and sugar with fork. Mix in dry ingredients. Add vanilla, eggs and sour cream. Pour ½ batter into a greased 10" tube pan. Pour ⅔ of filling mixture over batter. Add remaining batter. Top with remaining filling. Bake at 375° for 50 to 60 minutes.

FILLING

¾ cup sugar
1 teaspoon cinnamon
1 cup chopped nuts

2 (1 ounce each) squares
   unsweetened chocolate,
   melted

Combine all ingredients in saucepan.

Barbara S. Moore (Mrs. James D., Jr.)

STREUSEL COFFEE CAKE

¼ cup butter, softened
1 cup sugar
1 egg
1 teaspoon salt

½ cup milk
1½ cups flour
2 teaspoons baking powder

Combine all ingredients. Pour into a greased and floured 7" x 11" pan. Add topping. Bake at 375° for 20 minutes.

TOPPING

½ cup brown sugar
2 tablespoons flour
½ cup chopped nuts

½ cup butter, melted
2 teaspoons cinnamon

Combine all ingredients.

Donna L. Dean (Mrs. Rodney D.)

BOURBON FRENCH TOAST

12 eggs
4 teaspoons sugar
1¼ cups bourbon, divided
1 cup milk

Cooking oil
1½ loaves French bread
Powdered sugar
2 cups pure maple syrup

Beat eggs and sugar. Stir in 1 cup bourbon and milk. Film griddle with oil. Cut bread in ½″ thick slices. Dip in batter. Fry until crisp and brown on both sides. Dust with powdered sugar. Serve with syrup to which ¼ cup bourbon has been added. Keep extra toast hot on cookie sheet in oven. Serves 10.

Paula S. McKenney (Mrs. Ronald A.)

PEACHES 'N CREAM FRENCH TOAST

3 eggs
½ cup peach preserves
¾ cup half and half
6 slices French bread, cut
    ½″ thick

½ cup butter, softened
    and divided
*2 fresh peaches, peeled
    and sliced
Powdered sugar
Toasted almonds

*Sliced, canned peaches may be used if fresh peaches are not available.

In small bowl beat eggs and 3 tablespoons peach preserves until blended. Beat in half and half. Place a single layer of bread slices in a 7″ x 11″ baking dish. Pour egg mixture over bread. Refrigerate covered several hours or overnight until most of liquid is absorbed. In a small bowl beat with electric mixer on high the remaining peach preserves and 4 tablespoons butter until fluffy. Set aside until ready to serve. At serving time melt 2 tablespoons butter in large skillet. Add 3 slices of bread and cook on medium-high until browned, turning once. Remove from skillet to warm platter. Repeat with remaining bread slices and butter. Serve toast topped with 1 tablespoon peach butter and peach slices. Sprinkle with toasted almonds and powdered sugar. Serves 4 to 6.

Judy Grigoraci (Mrs. Victor)

ORANGE PECAN TOAST

8 slices French or Italian
    bread, cut ½″ thick
2 tablespoons butter,
    softened
¼ cup finely chopped pecans

2 tablespoons light cream
⅓ cup packed light brown
    sugar
2 teaspoons grated orange
    rind

Place bread slices in a single layer in baking dish. Toast lightly in a 400° oven. Turn toast. Spread butter over each slice. Mix brown sugar, cream, rind and pecans. Spread over buttered side of toast. Bake 7 minutes, or until topping bubbles. Makes 8 pieces.

Dana W. Sharp

NO GUILT PANCAKES

6 to 8 medium peaches,
      peeled and sliced (or
      ¾ cup frozen peaches or
      other fruit)
¼ cup packed brown sugar
¼ cup butter
½ teaspoon cinnamon
6 eggs

1 cup cream style cottage
      cheese
½ cup flour
¼ cup milk
2 tablespoons oil
½ teaspoon salt
½ teaspoon vanilla extract
   Whipped cream or butter

In a large saucepan combine first 4 ingredients. Cook over low heat, stirring until butter melts. Keep warm. Blend remaining ingredients in blender container on high for 1 minute. For each pancake pour ¼ cup batter onto hot, lightly greased griddle. Cook on both sides until brown. Serve with fruit mixture. For company use fruit mixture inside a folded pancake, topped with whipped cream or butter. Makes 12 pancakes.

Elizabeth M. Hamrick (Mrs. C. Page, III)

FATHER'S DAY CREPES

2 eggs
1 cup milk
½ teaspoon salt
¾ cup flour

Fresh blackberries or
   black raspberries
Sour cream
Powdered sugar

Place eggs, milk, salt and flour in blender. Blend well. Refrigerate overnight. In morning stir batter and pour small amount of batter on greased, very hot skillet or crepe pan and tip skillet to coat. When one side is lightly browned, turn crepe over and brown other side. Remove and repeat until all batter is used. Place fresh blackberries in center of each crepe with a dollop of sour cream. Roll crepe around berries. Dust with powdered sugar. Serves 4 to 6.

We do this on Father's Day because that is when the berries are ready for picking in Upshur County.

Angela and Caroline Galyean

BREAKFAST GRANOLA

7 cups quick rolled oats
1 cup wheat germ
½ cup powdered nonfat dry
   milk
½ cup Spanish peanuts or
   sunflower seeds

1 cup raisins
1 cup coconut
½ cup cooking oil
1 cup honey
   Other dried fruits to taste

Combine all ingredients. Mix well. Spread on cookie sheets. Heat at 350° for 15 to 20 minutes. Stir once. Cool and store in tightly covered jars.

Mrs. Marilyn Zimmerman

HOMECOMING STUFFING

4 to 6 tablespoons butter
1 cup chopped onion
3 cups chopped celery
   Turkey liver, cut up and
   seasoned
1 pound fresh mushrooms,
   sliced

4 cups bread cubes
2 cups peeled, chopped
   apple
½ teaspoon sage
   Salt and pepper to taste

Sauté onion and celery in 4 tablespoons butter until lightly browned. Transfer to bowl. Brown liver and mushrooms in same skillet, adding more butter as needed. Add liver mixture to onion mixture. Toast bread cubes in same skillet. Add to bowl. Add apple and seasonings, mixing gently until combined. Use to stuff turkey or bake in a covered casserole at 325° for 1 hour. Uncover last 30 minutes to brown top. Baste with pan drippings. Can be used for 16 to 20 pound turkey.

Pat Fisher (Mrs. E. Stephen, Jr.)

ITALIAN BREAD CRUMB MIX

½ loaf stale French or
   Vienna bread
4 cups grated Romano
   cheese
½ small clove garlic,
   chopped (or ⅛ teaspoon
   garlic powder)

¼ teaspoon black pepper
2 teaspoons parsley,
   chopped
1 tablespoon fresh or dried
   celery leaves, chopped
1 teaspoon basil, chopped

Finely grate bread to make 4 cups. Add remaining ingredients. Mix well with hands. Will keep in refrigerator or may be frozen.

Lena Panzera (Mrs. Joe)

WOODBURN HALL

The academic center and geographic landmark of West Virginia University since its founding is Woodburn Circle, a distinct group of structures built on the original grounds granted the state after the Civil War.

The three buildings on the circle include Martin Hall, completed in 1870, Woodburn Hall, completed in 1876, and Chitwood Hall, completed in 1893.

Woodburn Hall was built on the site of an earlier structure, known as Woodburn Female Seminary, established by Rev. John R. Moore and his wife, Elizabeth, before the Civil War. The seminary and its main building survived the Civil War and the properties were donated to the state in 1867. By an act of the West Virginia Legislature, the Agricultural College of West Virginia was permanently established and, on December 4, 1868, the name was changed to West Virginia University. Tragically, the Woodburn Seminary building was destroyed by fire in February, 1873.

Woodburn Hall dominates the famous circle. It is eclectic Second Empire in architectural style. The building is symmetrical with a central block and two wings connected by recessed vestibules. The wings are topped with two dormers front and back and a small tower on the extreme ends. The dormers are crowned with pediments. Dormers in the vestibules have arched tops. First floor windows are arched while those on the second floor have lower bowed arches.

The large central tower is fitted with a large cupola and clock tower which contains a large Seth Thomas Clock. The clock was originally located in Martin Hall.

Woodburn Hall has been used for a variety of purposes, including commencements, music classes, and social classes. As time passes the Woodburn Circle cluster has always remained the center of the campus, the original focal point from which the school grew.

Photo by Harry W. Ernst
    Communications Services, West Virginia University

DESSERTS, CAKES AND PIES

Melon Patch

ANGEL CHARLOTTE RUSSE

1 pint whipping cream
1 teaspoon vanilla extract
1 envelope unflavored
   gelatin
¼ cup cold water
¼ cup <u>very</u> hot water

1 cup sugar
¼ cup chopped maraschino
   cherries
½ cup chopped blanched
   almonds
6 dry macaroons, cut up

Whip cream until stiff. Add vanilla. Soften gelatin in cold water, then add hot water and sugar. Stir gelatin and sugar until dissolved. Fold into whipping cream. Add remaining ingredients. Refrigerate at least one hour. To serve, spoon into dessert glasses. Serves 6.

Susan S. Hereford (Mrs. Philip B.)

ANGELS DELIGHT

3 eggs, separated
1 cup sugar
1 cup milk
1 teaspoon vanilla extract
1 envelope unflavored
   gelatin

¼ cup cold water
½ pint heavy cream
1 small angel food cake
   Coconut, chopped pecans
   and maraschino
   cherries

Combine egg yolks, sugar and milk in top of double boiler over hot water. Cook, stirring over medium heat until mixture thickens and coats a spoon. Remove from heat. Add vanilla. Soften gelatin in ¼ cup cold water and add to hot custard, stirring well to dissolve gelatin. Cool. Whip cream, reserve ⅔ cup and add rest to egg yolk mixture. Beat egg whites until stiff and fold in. Butter a 9″ x 13″ dish. Break cake into small pieces. Alternate layers of cake and custard beginning with cake and ending with custard. Top with reserved whipped cream, chopped pecans, cherries and coconut. Chill 12 hours. Serves 12 to 14.

Alice Veazey

APPLE STRUDEL

DOUGH

¾ cup margarine,
softened
3 egg yolks

1 cup milk
3½ cups flour

FILLING

4 cups apples or pears,
peeled and sliced thin
2 cups crushed Ritz
crackers
6 tablespoons margarine,
melted

Cinnamon
½ cup chopped pecans
1 cup coconut
½ cup raisins
Additional ¾ cup
margarine, melted

Cream margarine, milk and eggs. Add flour and work dough until smooth. Divide into three balls. Cover and refrigerate overnight. The next day, mix first six filling ingredients together. Divide into thirds. Roll out each ball of dough on foil, sprinkling foil with flour. Brush top of dough generously with melted butter, adding more flour and butter as you work to roll very thin. Spread filling on dough, sprinkle with cinnamon and roll jelly roll fashion. tucking in and sealing edges. Leaving strudel on foil and rolling foil edges to form rim, place foil and strudel on cookie sheets. Bake at 350° for one hour. May be frozen and reheated. Makes 3 strudels, each serving 8.

Ruby McClure

BAUMKUCHEN
Unique and well worth the extra effort

10 eggs, separated
¾ cup butter
1 cup sugar, divided
1 tablespoon lemon rind

1 teaspoon almond or
vanilla extract
1 cup flour
½ cup cornstarch

Beat egg yolks until very light and thick, 8-10 minutes. Set aside. In separate bowl beat butter and ¾ cup sugar until fluffy. Add lemon rind and vanilla. Beat in flour and cornstarch. Blend butter mixture into egg yolks. In separate bowl beat egg whites to soft peak stage, gradually adding remaining ¼ cup sugar. Fold egg whites into egg yolk mixture. Grease a 10″ springform pan. Spread ½ cup mixture on bottom of pan and broil at 400° five inches from heat until light brown. WATCH CAREFULLY. Repeat steps, spreading ½ cup mixture and broiling until light brown until all batter is used. Move oven rack down if necessary as cake builds higher to prevent burning. Be sure each layer is set before adding the next layer. Remove sides from springform pan to serve. Cut in very thin wedges, sprinkle with powdered sugar, brush with heated, melted jelly or top with strawberries. Good for wine and cheese parties. Serves 16.

Paula S. McKenney (Mrs. Ronald A.)

BLUEBERRY CRACKLE

4 cups blueberries	¾ cup quick oats
¼ cup sugar	½ cup flour
2 tablespoons tapioca	½ teaspoon cinnamon
2 tablespoons lemon juice	Dash of salt
⅔ cup brown sugar	6 tablespoons margarine
½ teaspoon grated lemon peel	Vanilla ice cream

Stir together first 6 ingredients. Place in 8" square baking dish. Combine dry ingredients. Cut in margarine. Sprinkle over blueberry mixture. Bake at 375° for 20 minutes. Serve hot with ice cream. Serves 6.

Lynn H. Goldsmith (Mrs. Robert F.)

CREME CARAMEL

1 cup sugar, divided	1 teaspoon vanilla extract
4 eggs	Pinch of salt
2 cups milk	6 lemon peel twists

In small saucepan over medium heat cook, stirring constantly, ½ cup sugar until sugar melts and is light caramel in color. Pour immediately into 6 buttered ovenproof custard cups. In large bowl beat eggs and remaining ½ cup sugar until well blended. Add milk, vanilla and salt. Mix well. Pour into custard cups. Place in larger pan filled with 1" hot water. Bake at 325° for 50 to 55 minutes or until a knife inserted into the middle of the custard comes out clean. Cover and chill. Unmold each custard onto plate, allowing caramel topping to drip onto custard. Garnish with lemon twists. Serves 6.

Diane Merrified (Mrs. John V.)

CHOCOLATE MINT DESSERT

1 cup butter	1 teaspoon peppermint
2 cups powdered sugar	flavoring
4 (1 ounce each) squares	24 vanilla wafers
unsweetened chocolate,	Whipped cream
melted	Chopped nuts
4 eggs	Maraschino cherries
2 teaspoons vanilla extract	24 cupcake liners

Cream butter and sugar. Blend in melted chocolate. Add eggs and beat well. Blend in vanilla and peppermint. Place one vanilla wafer in bottom of each cupcake liner and fill each one ¾ full. Top with whipped cream, nuts and cherry. Freeze 2 to 3 hours before serving. May be frozen in muffin tins and transferred to airtight container when frozen. Will store several weeks. Remove from freezer 20 minutes before serving. Yield: 2 dozen.

Teresa H. Bachman (Mrs. Stephen)

CHOCOLATE MOUSSE TORTE

8 (1 ounce each) squares	2½ teaspoons vanilla extract
semi-sweet chocolate	⅛ teaspoon salt
1 tablespoon instant coffee	Fine dry bread crumbs
¼ cup boiling water	1½ cups heavy whipping
8 eggs, separated	cream
⅔ cup sugar	¼ cup sifted powdered sugar

Place chocolate in top of double boiler over hot water. Dissolve coffee in ¼ cup boiling water and add to chocolate. Cover and let stand over very low heat, stirring occasionally. When chocolate is almost melted remove from heat and whisk until smooth. Meanwhile, beat egg yolks until thick. Slowly beat in sugar until mixture is thick and lemon-colored. Slowly beat chocolate and 1 teaspoon vanilla into yolk mixture. In separate bowl, beat egg whites and salt until stiff but not dry. Stir ¼ of the egg whites into chocolate mixture and then gently fold in remainder. Dust a well-buttered 9" pie plate with dry bread crumbs. Fill plate with ¾ of the chocolate mixture and refrigerate remaining mixture. Bake at 350° for 25 minutes. Turn oven off and leave in for 5 more minutes. Remove and cool—center will fall. When cool, spread torte with remaining chilled chocolate mixture, mounding in center. Chill until ready to serve. To serve, beat cream with sugar and remaining vanilla until stiff. Slice torte and top with whipped cream and chocolate shavings. Serve small slices as this is very rich. Serves 8 to 10.

Barbara S. Moore (Mrs. James D., Jr.)

QUICK CHOCOLATE MOUSSE

1 quart heavy whipping
  cream
1½ cups sugar
¾ to 1 cup sifted unsweetened cocoa

¼ teaspoon vanilla extract
  Semi-sweet chocolate
  (garnish)

Whip cream and sugar on low speed with mixer until sugar dissolves. Then whip on high until mixture peaks. Remove one cup to pipe rosettes. Fold sifted unsweetened cocoa powder into cream. Fold in vanilla extract. Pipe into serving glasses, pipe rosettes on top and grate semi-sweet chocolate over mixture. Serves 6.

Richard Welles, Lexington, Kentucky

BLENDER CHOCOLATE BAVARIAN

1 envelope unflavored
  gelatin
½ cup cold milk
1 (12 ounce) package semi-
  sweet chocolate chips
1 cup hot milk
1 cup heavy cream

2 eggs
⅓ cup sugar
2 tablespoons light rum
1 cup ice cubes
  Whipped cream for
  garnish

Sprinkle gelatin over cold milk in a 5 cup blender container. Let stand until gelatin softens. Add chocolate chips and hot milk. Cover and blend on low speed until chocolate melts, 1½ minutes. Stop blender. Add cream, eggs, sugar and rum. Blend at high speed until well mixed. With blender running, remove center cap of blender lid and add ice cubes one at a time until melted. Pour at once into individual dessert dishes and chill 3 hours or until set. Garnish with whipped cream. Serves 8 to 10.

Betsie M. Dobbs (Mrs. William F.)

FUDGE NUT DESSERT

4 eggs, beaten
2 cups sugar
1 cup butter, melted
½ cup flour

½ cup cocoa
½ cup chopped walnuts
1 teaspoon vanilla extract

Mix all ingredients. Pour into buttered 9″ square pan. Place pan in a larger pan containing 1″ hot water. Bake at 350° for one hour. Serve warm, topped with vanilla ice cream or whipped cream. Serves 4 to 6.

Patricia M. Moyers (Mrs. Charles G.)

CHOCOLATE SOUFFLÉ

3 tablespoons butter
3 tablespoons flour
1 cup milk
3 (1 ounce each) squares
  unsweetened chocolate
½ cup sugar

⅓ cup boiling water
3 egg yolks
6 egg whites
1 teaspoon vanilla extract
  Whipped cream

Melt butter in saucepan over medium heat. Stir in flour to make a smooth paste and cook 1 to 2 minutes until bubbly. Slowly add milk, stirring constantly until thick and smooth. Cook one minute. Beat egg yolks and stir. Set aside. Melt chocolate over hot water in double boiler or in microwave. Remove from heat and stir in sugar and water. Fold egg yolk mixture into chocolate. In separate bowl beat egg whites until stiff. Fold a small portion of egg whites into chocolate, then gently fold in remainder. Place in ungreased soufflé dish. Place dish in slightly larger pan of hot water 1″ deep. Bake at 325° for 45 minutes. Serve topped with a spoonful of whipped cream. Serves 6.

Maude G. Carr (Mrs. Robert)

OLD FASHIONED PEACH COBBLER

1 egg
1 cup sugar, divided
3 tablespoons butter,
  melted
⅓ cup milk
½ cup sifted flour

2 teaspoons baking powder
½ teaspoon salt
4 cups fresh peaches,
  peeled and sliced
¼ teaspoon nutmeg
¼ teaspoon cinnamon

Beat together egg, ½ cup sugar, butter and milk. Sift together flour, baking powder and salt. Beat into egg mixture. Combine peaches, remaining ½ cup sugar, nutmeg and cinnamon. Pour fruit into greased 8″ square baking dish. Spread batter smoothly over top. Bake at 375° for 30 minutes. Serve hot. May be topped with whipped cream or ice cream. Serves 6.

Kay J. Morgan (Mrs. Frederick)

GRANDMA'S COBBLER

½ cup butter	½ teaspoon salt
1 cup flour	1 cup milk
1 cup sugar	3 cups fresh fruit (blue-
2 teaspoons baking powder	berries, peaches, black-berries or apples)

Preheat oven to 350°. Melt butter in 9" square baking dish in oven. Mix together flour, sugar, baking powder, salt, and milk and pour over butter. Add fresh fruit on top. Do not mix. Bake 40 minutes. Serve warm. Serves 6.

Diana H. Pettry (Mrs. Charles E., Jr.)

COCONUT CREAM DESSERT

60 Ritz crackers	1 cup milk
½ cup margarine, melted	1 (13 ounce) carton frozen
½ gallon vanilla ice cream	whipped topping
2 (3¾ ounces each) boxes instant coconut pudding	1 (3 ounce) can coconut

Finely crush crackers. Mix well with melted margarine. Spread in 9" x 13" pan. Soften ice cream (do not allow to become runny). Mix ice cream, pudding mix and milk using chilled beaters and bowl. Pour over crumbs. Spread a layer of whipped topping over pudding mix and sprinkle with coconut. Freeze until serving time. Serves 10 to 12.

Karen R. Huffman (Mrs. William)

MICROWAVE CUSTARD

¼ cup sugar	2 cups milk
2 tablespoons cornstarch	1 teaspoon vanilla extract
2 egg yolks	

Mix sugar and cornstarch in a 4 cup glass measuring cup. Stir in egg yolks. Slowly add milk, mixing thoroughly. Microwave on high for 5 minutes, stirring after 3 minutes. Remove from microwave and stir. If not thick, return for 30 to 45 seconds. Stir and add vanilla. If mixture curdles, mix with an electric mixer. May be used as filling for pies, cream puffs or filling for a cake.

Variation: Add 2 tablespoons dry cocoa powder to sugar-cornstarch mixture for chocolate custard.

Rebecca D. Ross (Mrs. Alexander J.)

GRAND MARNIER SOUFFLÉ

2 envelopes unflavored
   gelatin
¾ cup sugar
½ cup cold water
5 eggs, separated

⅓ cup Grand Marnier
¼ teaspoon cream of tartar
   Pinch of salt
½ pint whipping cream

Mix sugar and gelatin in ½ cup cold water. Heat over low heat until dissolved to make a thin syrup. Beat egg yolks. Pour syrup in a thin stream into egg yolks, beating constantly. Add Grand Marnier. Beat egg whites until foamy in a separate bowl. Add cream of tartar and salt and continue beating until stiff. Whip cream and fold into egg yolk mixture. Fold in egg whites. Pour into a 6 cup soufflé dish that has a 2″ foil rim added around the top. Refrigerate 2 hours or overnight. Serve with Fruit Dessert Sauce, if desired. Serves 8 to 10.

Sandra W. Mantz (Mrs. Eric P.)

GRAPES RAPALLO
"One of my grandmother's favorites"

2 pounds large seedless
   white grapes, halved
2 tablespoons sugar

3 tablespoons brandy or
   cognac (peach brandy
   recommended)
2 cups whipping cream
   Dark brown sugar

Place grapes (peel if desired) in 8″ square baking dish. Sprinkle with sugar. Drizzle brandy over top. Whip cream and cover grapes. Refrigerate 2 to 3 hours. Sprinkle top with dark brown sugar. Run under broiler until sugar melts, watching carefully. Serves 6.

Connie Morton McKee

LEMON MERINGUES

4 eggs, separated
1½ cups sugar, divided
¼ teaspoon cream of tartar
½ teaspoon salt
3 tablespoons lemon juice

1 tablespoon lemon rind
½ pint frozen whipped
   topping
½ pint whipping cream

Meringues: Beat egg whites until stiff but not dry. Sift 1 cup sugar and cream of tartar. Add one tablespoon at a time to egg whites while continuing to beat. Using large serving spoon place approximately ⅓ to ½ cup on greased cookie sheet. Make hole or cavity in center for filling without going through to cookie sheet. Bake at 275° for one hour. Cool on cookie sheet.

Filling: Beat egg yolks. Add remaining ½ cup sugar, salt, lemon juice and rind. Cook in double boiler over hot water until thickened. Add ½ pint whipped topping and mix well. Put filling on top of cooled meringues and chill overnight. Top with whipped cream before serving. Serves 10 to 12.

Frances Hancock (Mrs. Glenn)

PEACHES CHABLIS

1½ cups pink Chablis wine
½ cup sugar
¼ teaspoon ground nutmeg
1 cinnamon stick
4 whole cloves
8 large ripe peaches

In a glass bowl combine Chablis, sugar and nutmeg. Stir until sugar dissolves. Add cinnamon stick and cloves. Peel peaches, slice and add to wine mixture. Cover with plastic wrap. Refrigerate 6 hours or overnight. Serve in glass dessert dishes or champagne glasses. Serves 6 to 8.

Kitty I. Morgan (Mrs. J.W.)

FRESH PEAR DESSERT

6 medium size pears
½ cup sugar
2 tablespoons lemon juice
2 tablespoons butter
1 cup water
1 (3 ounce) package cream cheese, softened
Strawberry preserves

In small saucepan combine sugar, lemon juice, butter and water. Bring to boil, reduce heat and simmer 5 minutes. Carefully peel pears and place in baking dish. Add syrup, cover (using a tent of aluminum foil) and bake at 350° for 45 minutes, until tender. Cool slightly, cut in half and remove core. Serve warm with dollop of cream cheese in cavity. Top with heated strawberry preserves.

For taste variety replace half of water with red or white wine or fruit flavored brandy. Serves 6.

Phyllis H. Highland (Mrs. William D.)

POTS DE CREME

1 (6 ounce) package semi-
sweet chocolate chips
3 eggs, separated
2 tablespoons light rum

¼ teaspoon almond extract
¼ teaspoon nutmeg
Whipped cream

Melt chocolate in microwave or in top of double boiler over medium heat. Beat egg yolks until thick. Gradually stir ¼ chocolate into yolks, then add remaining chocolate stirring constantly. Stir in rum, almond extract and nutmeg. Beat egg whites until stiff. Fold into chocolate mixture. Put into pots de creme or demitasse cups and chill. Top with whipped cream. Serves 4 to 6.

Beverly S. McElroy (Mrs. William B.)

BLENDER POTS DE CREME

¾ cup milk
1½ cups semi-sweet
chocolate chips
1 egg
3 tablespoons sugar

1 tablespoon orange liqueur
(optional)
Pinch of salt
Whipping cream
Freshly grated orange
peel

Place chocolate chips, egg, sugar, salt and orange liqueur in blender. Whirl briefly. Scald milk and add to blender. Blend on low 1 to 2 minutes. Pour into demitasse cups and chill. Whip cream and flavor with 1 teaspoon additional orange liqueur if desired. Top pots de creme with whipped cream and orange peel. Serves 6.

Beverly S. McElroy (Mrs. William B.)

HOLIDAY LEMON CHIFFON PUDDING
"Our traditional Christmas dinner dessert"

1 cup sugar
⅓ cup flour
3 tablespoons margarine,
softened
3 eggs, separated

Juice of 1 lemon
1 cup milk
Whipped cream, mara-
schino cherries and
nuts for garnish

Blend together sugar, flour and margarine. Add beaten egg yolks, lemon juice and milk. Mix well. Beat egg whites until stiff and fold into first mixture. Pour into 6 small well-buttered oven-proof custard cups or into a small, deep buttered casserole dish. Set in larger pan of ½" deep hot water. Bake individual dishes at 350° for 30 minutes or until tops of pudding are browned. Bake larger pudding 40 minutes at 325°, increase heat to 350° and bake 10 additional minutes. Serve warm or cold. Top each serving with whipped cream and garnish with cherry or nuts. Will be cake like on top with custard on bottom. Serves 6.

Mrs. Herbert Meckfessel

ENGLISH PLUM PUDDING

½ pound suet
1 cup currants
1 cup raisins
1 cup citron
2 lemon rinds, grated
½ cup flour
1 cup sugar

½ teaspoon each ground cloves, nutmeg, ginger
1 cup stale bread crumbs
1 tablespoon cinnamon
6 eggs
½ cup brandy

Finely chop suet. Chop raisins, currants and citron. Combine with suet. Add lemon rind, sugar, spices, flour and bread crumbs. Beat eggs and add. Add brandy and mix well to moisten. Turn into pudding mold or two (1 pound) coffee cans. Cover mold with tight lid or with foil held in place with rubber band. Place in large kettle on rack or trivet. Cover kettle and steam in simmering water. Water level should come halfway up mold. Steam 3 hours or longer, checking to see if done—may be steamed on low temperature for up to 8 hours. Serve with Genevieve's Hard Sauce and Honey-Orange Sauce. May be frozen for up to one year. Steam one hour prior to serving if stored for long period of time. Serves 8 to 10.

Kitty W. Atkins (Mrs. E. Garfield)

STRAWBERRIES CREME BRULEE

1 (8 ounce) package cream cheese
1½ cups sour cream
6 tablespoons sugar

2½ pints strawberries, hulled and sliced
1 cup brown sugar

Beat cream cheese until fluffy. Add sour cream and granulated sugar, blending thoroughly. Arrange berries in shallow ovenproof serving dish. Spoon cream cheese mixture over berries and sprinkle with brown sugar. Place on lowest broiler rack and broil until sugar bubbles and browns lightly. Serve immediately. Serves 8 to 10.

Connie H. Toma (Mrs. George E.)

STRAWBERRIES WITH SABAYON

6 egg yolks
1½ cups powdered sugar
½ cup Harvey's Bristol
    Cream Sherry

1½ cups whipping cream
1 quart fresh strawberries

Combine egg yolks and sugar in top of double boiler. Cook over medium heat, slowly stirring in sherry, until mixture coats a spoon, 15 to 20 minutes. Stir frequently to avoid lumping. Remove from heat, cover and refrigerate two hours. When custard is chilled, whip cream until stiff peaks form. Fold into custard mixture. Refrigerate until serving time. To serve: wash strawberries, place several in a dessert dish and spoon sauce over. Serves 8 to 10.

Patty W. Bowers

SHORT CAKES

½ teaspoon salt
2 cups sifted flour
¼ cup sugar
3 teaspoons baking powder
2 cups sifted flour
1 egg, beaten
⅓ cup milk

Fresh sliced seasonal
    fruit: peaches, straw-
    berries, blueberries, or
    blackberries
½ pint whipping cream,
    whipped

Sift together first 4 ingredients. Cut in shortening until mixture resembles coarse corn meal. Stir in egg until well combined. Stir in milk. Turn dough out onto lightly floured surface. Knead until smooth. Roll out to ½" thickness. Cut to desired size. Place on greased cookie sheet. Bake at 450° for 10 to 12 minutes. To serve, split cake into 2 layers. Place fresh fruit in middle and on top of cake. Top with whipped cream. Makes 8 to 10.

Marion J. Sinclair (Mrs. K. Richard)

LUCY'S STRAWBERRY TRIFLE

1 (6 ounce) package
  strawberry gelatin
1 cup boiling water
2 (16 ounces each) packages
  frozen strawberries
  with syrup
½ cup sherry (or to taste)

1 pound cake, angel food
  cake or 1 dozen lady-
  fingers, split
1 (4 ounce) box vanilla
  pudding prepared (not
  instant) or 2 cups
  cooled custard
½ pint whipping cream

Dissolve gelatin in boiling water. Thaw strawberries and drain, reserving juice. Add water to juice to make 1½ cups liquid. Add to gelatin. Chill until slightly thick and add sherry. Slice cake in strips. Arrange layer of cake in deep, straight-sided clear glass bowl. Place a layer of berries on top. Repeat layers ending with layer of berries. Pour gelatin over. Spoon custard over top of gelatin. Gently insert a spoon in the dish to let gelatin flow through cake. Chill overnight. Top with whipped cream. Serves 8 to 10.

Mrs. Michael Albert

TRIFLE

1 dozen ladyfingers
½ to 1 cup port, sherry,
  rum or Madeira
1 (12 ounce) jar raspberry
  or currant jam

1 (3½ ounce) box vanilla
  pudding
2 cups milk
½ pint whipping cream

Line deep, straight-sided clear bowl with half of ladyfingers split in half. Sprinkle ladyfingers with choice of wine or liquor to moisten. Spread half of the jam over ladyfingers. Prepare pudding mix with milk following package directions. Do not allow to set. Spread half of pudding over jam. Repeat layers again. Whip cream. Spread over top. Serves 8.

Maribeth H. Moore (Mrs. J. Thomas)

TOASTED SNOW

1 envelope unflavored gelatin	3 eggs, separated
4 tablespoons cold water	¼ teaspoon salt
1 cup boiling water	1 teaspoon vanilla extract
⅔ cup sugar	16 graham crackers, crushed

Sprinkle gelatin over cold water. Soak 5 minutes. Add boiling water. Stir until gelatin is dissolved. Add sugar and stir until sugar dissolves. Let cool slightly. Add egg whites (reserve yolks for sauce), salt and vanilla. Beat at high speed for 10 to 15 minutes until mixture is light and resembles thick cream. Gelatin will settle if this is not done for a long enough time. Turn into 9" x 13" pan. Chill several hours. Cut into 1" squares. Roll in graham cracker crumbs. Arrange several squares in dessert glasses. Top with Butter Sauce.

BUTTER SAUCE

3 egg yolks	1 tablespoon grated lemon rind
⅓ cup butter, melted	
2 tablespoons lemon juice	⅓ cup heavy cream
⅓ cup sugar	

Beat egg yolks several minutes until thick and lemon colored. Gradually add sugar while still beating. Blend in butter, lemon rind and lemon juice. Whip cream in separate bowl. Fold into lemon mixture. Chill. Serves 10.

Sally M. Rowe (Mrs. C. Tom)

FRENCH CHOCOLATE ICE CREAM

8 eggs	1 (12 ounce) package semi-sweet chocolate chips
1 cup sugar	
½ cup water	4 tablespoons strong black coffee
½ teaspoon cream of tartar	
	7 cups heavy cream

Beat eggs until thick. Combine sugar, water and cream of tartar. Heat to boiling and stir until sugar dissolves. Melt chocolate and coffee together in top of double boiler or in microwave. Add to eggs and blend in heavy cream. Freeze in ice cream freezer according to manufacturer's directions. Makes 3 quarts.

Harriet D. Bradford (Mrs. Bert, Jr.)

LIME SHERBET

1 cup sugar
1 cup water
¼ teaspoon salt
1 (12 ounce) can frozen
    limeade concentrate

1 teaspoon vanilla extract
4 drops green food coloring
1 (14 ounce) can condensed
    milk plus milk to equal
    4 cups

Boil sugar and water until it makes a slightly thickened syrup. Add salt and cool. Add remaining ingredients. Freeze in ice cream freezer following manufacturer's directions. Makes 3 quarts.

Lucy Payne Paynter (Mrs. George W.)

PEACH ICE CREAM

12 to 15 ripe peaches
2½ cups sugar
 ½ pint whipping cream
1 (13 ounce) can evaporated
    milk

½ pint half and half
½ teaspoon almond
    flavoring

Peel and slice peaches. Cover with sugar and let stand for several hours. Purée in blender. Mixture should be very sweet, add more sugar if necessary. Add cream, milk, half and half and almond flavoring. Freeze in ice cream freezer according to manufacturer's directions.

For strawberry ice cream substitute two quarts strawberries for peaches.

Tia C. McMillan (Mrs. Robert A.)

RASPBERRY KISSEL

3 (10 ounces each) packages
  frozen raspberries
1 cup water, divided

½ cup sugar
2½ tablespoons cornstarch
1 cup whipping cream
  (optional)

Simmer raspberries, ¾ cup water and sugar for 3 to 4 minutes in a saucepan over medium heat. Place in blender. Blend 10 to 15 seconds. Strain. Dissolve cornstarch in remaining ¼ cup water. Heat with raspberry purée. Cook stirring over medium heat 4 to 5 minutes until clear and slightly thickened. Pour into 8 individual glass dishes or a medium size serving bowl. Refrigerate several hours. Top with whipped cream if desired. Consistency of Kissel will be similar to whipped cream; will not be fully congealed. May also be frozen and served as a raspberry ice. Serves 8.

Betsie M. Dobbs (Mrs. William F., Jr.)

GENEVIEVE'S HARD SAUCE

1 cup butter
1 (1 pound) box powdered
  sugar

1 tablespoon vanilla extract
Rum to flavor

Cream butter. Add sugar gradually. Add vanilla and rum (1 or more tablespoons). Whip until mixture peaks. Refrigerate until hard—3 hours. Spoon over warm plum pudding, fruit cake, chocolate pound cake, gingerbread, etc. Will keep in refrigerator 1 to 2 weeks. Cover tightly.

Genevieve R. Smith

HONEY-ORANGE SAUCE

⅓ cup honey
1 tablespoon cornstarch
1 teaspoon grated orange
  rind

½ cup orange juice
¼ cup water
2 tablespoons butter

Combine honey, cornstarch and orange rind in medium saucepan. Whisk in orange juice and water. Bring to boil. Simmer one minute. Add butter. Cool slightly before serving. Sauce will thicken as it cools. Good over gingerbread, ice cream, French toast. Yield: 1 cup.

Donna L. Dean (Mrs. Rodney D.)

FRUIT DESSERT SAUCE

2 pints fresh berries:
    strawberries, rasp-
    berries, blackberries
2 tablespoons sugar

2 tablespoons Kirsch,
    Cointreau, or Grand
    Marnier

Purée berries in blender. Stir in sugar and liqueur. Cover and chill. Serve over Grand Marnier Soufflé, pound cake or ice cream.

Sara Z. Hoblitzell (Mrs. John R.)

STEVE'S SUPER HOT FUDGE SAUCE

1 (12 ounce) package
    chocolate chips
1 (14 ounce) can sweetened
    condensed milk

4 tablespoons butter
1 teaspoon vanilla extract

Place ingredients in microwave-safe bowl. Microwave 4 minutes at full power or until chips are melted. Remove and stir with whisk until ingredients are well blended. Serve warm. Can be refrigerated and reheated. Yield: 2 to 2½ cups. (If microwave not available, heat in saucepan over medium heat.)

Diane S. Doty (Mrs. Steven)

HOT FUDGE SAUCE

1 cup sugar
⅓ cup cocoa
2 tablespoons flour
¼ teaspoon salt

1 cup boiling water
1 tablespoon margarine
½ teaspoon vanilla extract

Mix dry ingredients together in saucepan. Add boiling water and margarine. Stir. Cook over medium heat until thick. Remove from heat. Stir in vanilla. Makes 1½ to 2 cups.

Catherine C. Rice (Mrs. Joseph V.)

APPLE KUCHEN

½ cup margarine, softened
1 box yellow cake mix
½ cup flaked coconut
1 (20 ounce) can sliced
    apples (not pie filling)

½ cup sugar
1 teaspoon cinnamon
1 cup sour cream
1 egg

Cut margarine into dry cake mix. Add coconut. Spread in 9″ x 13″ pan. Pat down lightly. Bake at 350° for 10 minutes. Remove from oven. Arrange apples on top. Combine sugar and cinnamon. Sprinkle over apple layer. Mix together sour cream and egg. Drizzle over apples. Bake at 350° for 25 to 35 minutes. Let stand for 15 minutes. Serve warm. May also be served for brunch. Serves 12.

Rebecca K. Palmer (Mrs. John C., IV)

DELICIOUS APPLE CAKE

1 cup cooking oil
2 eggs
2 cups sugar
2½ cups sifted flour
1 teaspoon soda
1 teaspoon salt
1 teaspoon cinnamon

1 teaspoon baking powder
3 cups peeled and diced
    cooking apples
1 cup chopped nuts
    (optional)
1 (6 ounce) package
    butterscotch chips

Combine oil, eggs and sugar. Mix well. In separate bowl, sift dry ingredients. Add to creamed mixture. Stir in nuts and apples. Spread in a greased 9″ x 13″ pan. Sprinkle chips on top of batter. Bake at 350° for 50 to 60 minutes or until cake tests done. For better flavor, bake one day before serving.

Rebecca M. Beattie (Mrs. P.J., Jr.)

JEWISH APPLE CAKE

3 cups flour
2 cups sugar
3 teaspoons baking powder
1 teaspoon salt
½ cup orange or pineapple
    juice

1 cup cooking oil
4 eggs
5 medium apples, peeled
    and sliced
5 tablespoons sugar
3 teaspoons cinnamon

Sift together flour, sugar, baking powder and salt. Beat juice, oil and eggs into flour mixture. Pour ½ batter into greased and floured tube pan. Mix remaining sugar and cinnamon. Place ½ apples on batter and cover with ½ sugar and cinnamon mixture. Pour the rest of the batter over apples. Arrange remaining apples on top and sprinkle with remaining sugar and cinnamon. Bake at 350° for 1 hour 20 minutes. Serves 10 to 12.

Mary Ann Cody

ROMAN APPLE CAKE

1½ cups flour	1 cup sugar
1 teaspoon soda	1 egg
¼ teaspoon baking powder	½ cup milk
½ teaspoon salt	2 cups peeled and chopped
½ cup shortening	apples

Sift together first four ingredients. Cream shortening and sugar. Add egg and milk, mixing well. Fold in apples. Pour into greased and floured 8″ square pan. Sprinkle with topping. Bake at 350° for 45 minutes. Serves 4 to 6.

TOPPING

½ cup brown sugar	1 tablespoon butter
1 teaspoon cinnamon	½ cup chopped nuts
2 teaspoons flour	

Mix together sugar, cinnamon, flour and nuts. Cut butter into mixture. Sprinkle over cake batter.

Patricia W. Berry (Mrs. Bruce)

SUE ANN'S APPLESAUCE CAKE

½ cup margarine	1 (16½ ounce) can apple-
2 cups sugar	sauce
1 egg	2½ cups flour
¼ teaspoon salt	½ cup water
2 teaspoons cinnamon	2 teaspoons soda
½ teaspoon cloves	½ cup raisins
½ teaspoon allspice	½ cup chopped nuts

Cream margarine and sugar. Add egg. Mix well. Add next six ingredients. Beat 5 minutes. Boil water. Add soda to water, stirring until dissolved. Add to cake mixture. Mix well. Stir in raisins and nuts. Pour into a greased and floured tube pan or two loaf pans. Bake at 350° for 50 to 60 minutes for tube pan; 40 to 50 minutes for loaf pans, or until a toothpick inserted in center comes out clean. Freezes well. Flavor improves if baked a day ahead.

Larrie O. Bartrug (Mrs. Edwin M., Jr.)

ONE EGG BANANA CAKE

2 cups cake flour
1¼ cups sugar
1 teaspoon baking powder
1 teaspoon soda
1 teaspoon salt
⅓ cup shortening

½ cup buttermilk
1 cup mashed ripe
  bananas (3)
1 teaspoon vanilla extract
1 egg

Grease and flour two 9″ square pans or two 8″ round pans. Blend together flour, sugar, baking powder, soda and salt. Add shortening, buttermilk, bananas and vanilla. Beat 2 minutes at medium speed with electric mixer. Add egg. Beat 2 minutes more. Pour into pans. Bake at 350° for 30 minutes (square pans require 5 additional minutes). Cool. Ice with Cream Cheese Icing.

CREAM CHEESE ICING

1 (8 ounce) package cream
  cheese
1 cup margarine

2 teaspoons vanilla extract
1 (16 ounce) box powdered
  sugar

Cream together cheese and margarine. Add vanilla. Gradually add sugar and continue beating until desired consistency.

Selina F. Cosby (Mrs. Lowell)

GRANDMA MATIC'S BLACKBERRY CAKE

2 cups sugar
1½ cups butter
6 eggs, separated
2 teaspoons baking powder
3 cups flour
2 teaspoons soda

2 teaspoons cinnamon
2 teaspoons nutmeg
1 teaspoon cloves
1 cup buttermilk
1 cup fresh blackberries

Cream butter and sugar. Add egg yolks, beating well after each addition. In separate bowl, combine next six ingredients. Stir in buttermilk and blackberries. Add to creamed mixture. Mix well. Beat egg whites until they form soft peaks. Fold into batter. Pour into three 9″ greased and floured cake pans. Bake at 350° for 35 to 40 minutes or until brown and springy to the touch. Cool and frost.

ICING

½ cup butter
1 cup brown sugar

2 tablespoons milk
1 (16 ounce) box powdered
  sugar

Bring butter, brown sugar and milk to a boil. Remove from heat. Stir in powdered sugar. Add more milk if necessary to make the correct consistency for icing. Ice cooled cake.

Carolyn S. Rickey (Mrs. Jon H.)

CARROT CAKE

2¾ cups flour
1 tablespoon soda
1 teaspoon salt
1 tablespoon cinnamon
1 teaspoon nutmeg
4 eggs
¾ cup cooking oil

1¾ cups sugar
1 teaspoon vanilla extract
1 (16 ounce) can applesauce
3 cups shredded carrots
1 cup chopped nuts
  (optional)
1 cup raisins (optional)

In large bowl, mix first five ingredients. Set aside. Beat eggs with a whisk. Stir in oil, sugar and vanilla. Add applesauce and carrots. Mix well. Add to flour mixture, stirring just to moisten. Fold in raisins and ½ cup nuts. Pour into greased and floured tube pan. Sprinkle with remaining ½ cup nuts. Bake at 350° for 1 hour. Cool for 10 minutes and remove from pan.

Sandra M. Haden (Mrs. David S.)

CHOCOLATE CHIP KAHLUÁ CAKE

1 yellow cake mix
1 cup cooking oil
4 eggs
1 cup milk
1 (3¾ ounce) package
  instant vanilla pudding

1 (6 ounce) package semi-
  sweet or milk chocolate
  chips
1 (8 ounce) package semi-
  sweet chocolate, grated
½ cup Kahluá
¼ cup powdered sugar,
  as garnish

Combine first five ingredients. Mix well. Stir in chocolate chips and all but ¼ cup grated chocolate. Pour into greased and floured bundt pan. Bake at 350° for 45 to 55 minutes. Poke holes in cake while cooling in pan. Drizzle the Kahluá into the holes. Remove cake from pan. Sprinkle with powdered sugar and reserved grated chocolate.

Mrs. Carol Gravely Shave

CHOCOLATE ZUCCHINI CAKE

3 cups sugar
1½ cups cooking oil
4 eggs
2 cups flour
1 cup self-rising flour
¾ teaspoon soda

½ cup cocoa
1 teaspoon salt
3 cups grated zucchini
2 teaspoons vanilla extract
1 cup chopped pecans

Combine sugar and oil. Add eggs, one at a time, mixing well. Sift together dry ingredients. Add ⅓ of dry ingredients to mixture. Beat well. Add zucchini. Gradually add remaining dry ingredients and vanilla. Mix thoroughly. Stir in nuts. Bake in greased and floured tube pan at 350° for 1 hour. Keep chilled. Serve with whipped topping or ice cream.

Nancy Beers Nix (Mrs. James H.)

SOUR CREAM CHOCOLATE CAKE

½ cup butter, softened
2 cups sugar
1 cup boiling water
4 (1 ounce each) squares
   unsweetened chocolate,
   melted

2 eggs, beaten
1 cup sour cream
2 cups flour
2 teaspoons soda
2 teaspoons baking powder

Cream butter and sugar. Add next four ingredients, beating well after each addition. Combine dry ingredients and add to mixture. Mix well. Bake in greased and floured 9" x 13" pan at 325° for 40 minutes.

Ann C. Kepple (Mrs. William T.)

CHEESECAKE

CRUST

¾ (16 ounce) box zwieback,
   finely ground

½ cup butter, melted
¼ cup sugar

Combine ingredients and press into the bottom of a 9" spring-form pan.

FILLING

15 ounces cream cheese,
   softened
4 eggs, separated
1 cup sugar

2 tablespoons flour
1 cup coffee cream
2 teaspoons vanilla extract
¼ teaspoon lemon juice

Beat cream cheese until fluffy. Add egg yolks, one at a time, mixing well after each addition. Sift together sugar and flour. Slowly add to cheese mixture. Add next three ingredients and mix well. In a separate bowl, beat egg whites to soft peaks. Fold into cheese mixture. Pour into pan. Bake at 300° for 70 minutes. Cool. Spread topping over cake. Refrigerate.

TOPPING

1 pint sour cream	3 tablespoons sugar
1 teaspoon vanilla extract	

Combine all ingredients, blending well. Pour over cooled cake. Best made at least 1 to 2 days ahead. Serves 12 to 16.

Sarah M. Foster (Mrs. Michael D.)

CLOUD NINE CAKE

1 box yellow or butter cake mix	1 (13 ounce) can pina colada mix
1 cup flaked coconut, divided	2 (1.4 ounces each) envelopes whipped topping

Mix cake according to package directions. Add ½ cup coconut to batter. Stir. Bake according to directions in a 9″ x 13″ pan. When cake is done and still hot, prick the entire top of the cake with a fork. Spoon pina colada mix over cake. Prepare topping according to package directions. Frost cooled cake with topping. Sprinkle remaining ½ cup coconut over frosting. Store in refrigerator.

Linda K. Meckfessel (Mrs. Richard R.)

BOGGS FAMILY COCONUT CAKE

1 cup butter, softened	1 cup milk
3 cups sugar	4 eggs, well beaten
4 cups flour	1 fresh coconut, grated
2 heaping teaspoons baking powder	

Cream butter and sugar until light. Sift flour with baking powder. Add to creamed mixture alternately with milk. Mix well. Add eggs and grated coconut. Pour into well greased and floured tube pan. Bake at 350° for 1 hour. For even better flavor, bake one day ahead. Freezes well if tightly wrapped.

Rise C. Boggs (Mrs. Charles A., III)

COCONUT CAKE

1 box yellow cake mix
2 cups sugar
2 (8 ounces each) cartons
    sour cream

2 (8 ounces each) packages
    frozen shredded
    coconut
1 (8 ounce) carton frozen
    whipped topping

Prepare cake mix according to package directions, baking in two 9" round pans. Cool. Split each layer in half to make four layers. Combine sugar, sour cream and coconut, reserving ¾ cup for frosting. Spread mixture between the layers. Combine reserved sour cream-coconut mixture and topping. Blend until smooth. Spread on top and sides of cake. Refrigerate, in airtight container, for 3 days before serving.

Sarah M. Foster (Mrs. Michael D.)

NETTIE TRUMBO'S EGGLESS JAM CAKE

4 cups flour
1 tablespoon cinnamon
1 teaspoon nutmeg
1 teaspoon cloves
2 teaspoons soda
2 cups buttermilk

½ cup shortening, softened
2 cups brown sugar
1 cup blackberry jam
1 cup raisins
1 cup chopped nuts

Sift together flour, cinnamon, nutmeg and cloves. In a separate bowl add soda to buttermilk. In a third bowl cream shortening and sugar. Add jam and mix well. Add milk and flour mixtures alternately to creamed mixture, blending well after each addition. Stir in raisins and nuts. Pour into a greased and floured tube pan. Bake at 350° for 1 to 1¼ hours or until cake tests done. May be served plain or with Brown Sugar Glaze. Can be frozen without glaze.

BROWN SUGAR GLAZE

½ cup butter
1 cup brown sugar

½ cup milk
½ cup powdered sugar

Boil butter and brown sugar for 2 minutes. Add milk. Stir, bringing to a boil. Cool to lukewarm. Add enough powdered sugar to thicken. Spread on cooled cake.

Bonnie H. Brothers (Mrs. Riley C.)

LIMA BEAN CAKE

½ cup butter or margarine	1 cup lima beans, cooked
1½ cups sugar	and mashed
3 eggs	2 cups flour
1 teaspoon cinnamon	1 teaspoon salt
1 teaspoon nutmeg	1 teaspoon soda
1 teaspoon allspice	1 teaspoon baking powder
	1 cup sour milk

Cream butter and sugar. Add eggs, spices and lima beans. Mix thoroughly. Combine flour, salt, soda and baking powder. Add dry ingredients alternately with the sour milk to the creamed mixture. Mix well after each addition. Pour into greased and floured 9" x 13" pan. Bake at 350° for 30 minutes. Spread topping over warm cake. Put cake under broiler until lightly browned.

TOPPING

¾ cup butter	2 cups coconut
1 cup milk	1 teaspoon vanilla extract
1½ cups brown sugar	½ cup pecans

Melt butter. Remove from heat and add remaining ingredients, mixing well. Spread over warm cake. Broil until lightly browned.

Patricia E. Bivens (Mrs. S. Lee, Jr.)

HOT MILK CAKE

4 eggs	1 cup milk, scalded
2 cups sugar	½ cup butter, melted
2 cups flour	1 teaspoon vanilla extract
2 teaspoons baking powder	

Beat eggs. Slowly add sugar. Mix well. Add flour and baking powder. Stir in milk, butter and vanilla. Pour into greased 9" x 13" pan. Bake at 350° for 1 hour. Serve warm with topping.

TOPPING

1 cup sugar	½ teaspoon soda
½ cup buttermilk	½ teaspoon vanilla extract
¼ cup butter	

Combine ingredients in a saucepan. Bring to a boil. Boil 4 minutes and stir. Serve warm as a sauce poured over hot cake.

Linda K. Meckfessel (Mrs. Richard R.)

DELICIOUS HEATH TOFFEE CAKE

1 angel food cake
1 pint whipping cream
4 tablespoons cocoa

1 cup powdered sugar
6 Heath bars (crush while
   frozen)

Fold cocoa and sugar into whipping cream. Refrigerate over-night. The next day, whip cream mixture and add crushed Heath bars. Cut cake into 3 layers. Spread whipped cream mixture on top of each layer and sides.

Gail Scott (Mrs. Ross)

MOUNTAIN FUDGE CAKE

1½ cups butter
1½ cups sugar
6 eggs
2 cups flour

2 cups chopped walnuts
1 package Double Dutch (or
   Fudge) frosting mix

Cream butter and sugar. Beat in eggs. Stirring by hand, add rest of ingredients. Put in angel food cake pan and bake at 350° for 60 minutes.

Jolie P. Carter (Mrs. Timothy E.)

OATMEAL CAKE

1 cup boiling water
1 cup rolled oats
½ cup raisins
½ cup butter, softened
1 cup honey
2 eggs

1½ cups whole wheat pastry
   flour
1 teaspoon soda
½ teaspoon salt
1 teaspoon cinnamon
1 teaspoon nutmeg
½ cup chopped nuts

Pour 1 cup boiling water over oats and raisins. Set aside to cool. Cream butter and honey, add eggs and beat well. Sift together the flour, soda, salt, cinnamon and nutmeg. Combine the cooled oats with the honey mix. Stir in dry ingredients—do not beat. Stir in chopped nuts. Bake in a greased 9″ square pan at 350° for 20 to 25 minutes, or until done. Recipe can be doubled to make a 9″ x 13″ cake or a two layer cake. Frost with a cream cheese frosting and sprinkle with nuts.

Lorena B. Surber (Mrs. Charles M., Jr.)

PEACH SPICE CAKE

2 cups sugar
1 cup cooking oil
2 eggs
4 cups flour
2 teaspoons soda
1 teaspoon salt
1 teaspoon cinnamon

1 teaspoon cloves
1 teaspoon nutmeg
1 teaspoon allspice
1 (1 pound 13 ounce) can
  peaches and juice,
  cut up
1 cup chopped pecans

Combine all ingredients except nuts in large mixing bowl. Using an electric mixer, blend thoroughly. Stir in nuts. Pour into greased tube pan. Bake at 375° for 1¼ hours. Cool in pan for 15 minutes. Slide knife around sides of pan to loosen cake. Invert. Cool. Serve with whipped topping, if desired.

Rise C. Boggs (Mrs. Charles A., III)

PINEAPPLE CARROT CAKE

3 eggs
¾ cup cooking oil
¾ cup buttermilk
2 cups sugar
2 teaspoons vanilla extract
2 cups flour
2 teaspoons soda
2 teaspoons cinnamon

¼ teaspoon salt
1 cup crushed pineapple,
  drained
2 cups grated carrots
1 (3½ ounce) can flaked
  coconut
1 cup chopped nuts

Beat eggs. Add oil, buttermilk, sugar, and vanilla. Combine dry ingredients and add gradually. Add remaining ingredients. Mix well. Pour into greased and floured 9" x 13" pan. Bake at 350° for 1 hour.

GLAZE

1 cup sugar
½ teaspoon soda
½ cup buttermilk
½ cup margarine

1 tablespoon light corn
  syrup
1 teaspoon vanilla extract

In saucepan, over medium heat, combine first five ingredients. Boil five minutes. Remove from heat. Add vanilla. Pour over hot cake. If cake is slow in absorbing the glaze, prick top with a fork.

Julie C. Coburn

PLUM CAKE

2 cups self-rising flour
2 cups sugar
1 cup cooking oil
3 eggs
1 cup finely chopped pecans

1 teaspoon cinnamon
1 teaspoon cloves
1 Jr. size jar plum baby
   food (with tapioca)

Combine all ingredients. Pour into greased and floured tube or bundt pan. Bake at 325° for 1 hour. Cool 15 minutes and remove from pan. Glaze with following recipe.

Mrs. David H. Cleland

GLAZE

½ cup powdered sugar

2 tablespoons lemon juice

In a small saucepan warm lemon juice and sugar just enough to dissolve sugar. Drizzle icing over cake.

Bonnie H. Brothers (Mrs. Riley C.)

BROWN SUGAR POUND CAKE

½ cup shortening
1 cup margarine
1 (16 ounce) box brown
   sugar
1 cup sugar
5 eggs

3 cups sifted flour
½ teaspoon baking powder
½ teaspoon salt
1 cup milk
1 teaspoon vanilla extract
1 cup chopped nuts

Cream shortening, butter and sugars. Add eggs, one at a time, beating after each addition. Sift dry ingredients together. Combine milk and vanilla, and add alternately with dry ingredients to creamed mixture, beginning and ending with dry ingredients. Beat well after each addition. Pour into greased and floured tube pan. Bake at 350° for 1½ hours.

Gwen Lovett (Mrs. John)

CHOCOLATE POUND CAKE

1½ cups butter
3 cups sugar
5 eggs
3 cups flour
½ cup cocoa

¼ teaspoon salt
1 teaspoon baking powder
1 teaspoon vanilla extract
1½ cups milk

Cream butter and sugar until light and fluffy. Add eggs, one at a time, beating well after each addition. Sift together flour, cocoa, salt and baking powder. Add vanilla to milk and add alternately with dry ingredients to creamed mixture, beating until smooth after each addition. Pour batter into well greased tube pan. Bake at 300° for 1½ hours or until it tests done. Cool 10 to 15 minutes and remove from pan.

Omit cocoa for plain pound cake.

Patricia E. Bivens (Mrs. S. Lee, Jr.)

GRANDMA HANSEN'S SOUR CREAM POUND CAKE

1 cup butter
3 cups sugar
6 eggs, separated
3 cups flour, sifted

¼ teaspoon soda
¼ teaspoon salt
½ pint sour cream

Cream butter and sugar. Add egg yolks, one at a time. Sift together flour, soda and salt. Add flour mixture alternately with sour cream to creamed mixture. Beat egg whites until stiff. Fold into cake mixture. Pour batter into greased and floured 10″ tube pan. Bake at 300° for 1½ hours. Cool in pan for 15 minutes before removing. Freezes well. Improves with age.

Mary Elizabeth B. Hansen (Mrs. Randall)

PEACH BRANDY POUND CAKE

3 cups sugar
1 cup butter, softened
6 eggs
3 cups flour
¼ teaspoon soda
Pinch of salt
1 cup sour cream

3 teaspoons rum
1 teaspoon orange extract
½ teaspoon almond extract
½ teaspoon lemon extract
1 teaspoon vanilla extract
½ cup peach brandy

Cream sugar and butter until light and fluffy. Add eggs, one at a time, mixing well after each addition. Combine dry ingredients. Add to creamed mixture alternately with sour cream. Beat well. Stir in remaining ingredients. Pour into greased and floured tube or Bundt pan. Bake at 325° for 1 hour 20 minutes or until cake tests done.

Beverly S. McElroy (Mrs. William B.)

PRUNE CAKE

2 cups self-rising flour
2 cups sugar
1 teaspoon cinnamon
1 teaspoon nutmeg
1 teaspoon allspice

3 eggs
1 cup cooking oil
2 small jars prune baby
    food
1 cup raisins or nuts

Sift dry ingredients together. Blend together eggs, oil and prunes. Add dry ingredients and mix. Stir in raisins or nuts. Pour into a greased and floured tube pan. Bake at 350° for 1 hour.

ICING

1 cup sugar
½ cup milk

1 teaspoon vanilla extract
½ cup butter

Mix all ingredients together and cook over low heat until it boils. Pour over the hot cake while cake is still in the pan. Cool 30 minutes before serving.

Tia C. McMillan (Mrs. Robert A.)

PUMPKIN CAKE

1 (16 ounce) can pumpkin
1 cup cooking oil
2 cups sugar
4 eggs, beaten
2 cups flour

2 teaspoons soda
2 teaspoons cinnamon
½ teaspoon salt
½ cup chopped nuts
    (optional)

Combine all ingredients and mix thoroughly. Bake in greased tube pan at 350° for 40 to 50 minutes. Frost with following Pumpkin Cake Icing.

PUMPKIN CAKE ICING

1 (8 ounce) package cream
   cheese
½ cup margarine

1 (16 ounce) box powdered
   sugar
1 teaspoon vanilla extract

Beat cream cheese and margarine until soft. Add sugar and vanilla and beat until fluffy. Spread on cooled cake.

Teresa H. Bachman (Mrs. Stephen)

SPICE CAKE

½ cup butter
1 cup sugar
1 egg, beaten
1 teaspoon soda
1 (10½ ounce) can tomato
   soup
1⅓ cups flour

⅛ teaspoon salt
1½ teaspoons cloves
1 teaspoon cinnamon
½ teaspoon nutmeg
1 cup chopped nuts
1 cup chopped dates
½ cup raisins

Cream butter and sugar. Stir in egg. Dissolve soda in soup. In separate bowl, sift together flour, salt, and spices. Add alternately with soup to creamed mixture. Add dates, nuts, and raisins. Bake at 325° for 1 to 1¼ hours in greased and floured 9″ x 5″ x 3″ loaf pan. Freezes well.

Catherine K. Bradford

STRAWBERRY CAKES

1 yellow cake mix
1½ cups sugar
4 tablespoons cornstarch
3 cups water
1 (6 ounce) box strawberry
   gelatin

3 (16 ounces each) packages
   sliced frozen straw-
   berries
1 (8 ounce) container frozen
   whipped topping
1 (8 ounce) package cream
   cheese
1 tablespoon cream or milk

Bake cake according to package directions in two 9″ x 13″ pans. Let cool. In a medium saucepan, combine and cook sugar, cornstarch and water until thick and clear (about 8 minutes). Stir in gelatin. Fold in strawberries. Pour over cooled cakes and refrigerate for 2 hours. Combine topping, cream cheese and milk. Beat until smooth. Spread over strawberry topping and refrigerate overnight. Makes two cakes. Serves 24.

Betsy C. Peterson

SOUTHERN SPICY GINGERBREAD

¾ cup brown sugar
¾ cup molasses
¾ cup butter or Crisco,
　melted
2 eggs
2 teaspoons soda
2 teaspoons ginger

2½ cups flour
1½ teaspoons cinnamon
½ teaspoon cloves
½ teaspoon nutmeg
½ teaspoon baking powder
1 cup hot coffee

Combine sugar, molasses and melted butter. Stir in eggs. Sift dry ingredients together. Add to first mixture. Add hot coffee. Mix well. Bake at 350° for 30 to 40 minutes or until cake tests done. Serve topped with whipped cream. Serves 6 to 8.

Judy E. Hanlen

JAN'S PUMPKIN ROLL

3 eggs
1 cup sugar
⅔ cup canned pumpkin
1 teaspoon lemon juice
¾ cup flour
1 teaspoon cinnamon

1 teaspoon ginger
½ teaspoon nutmeg
½ teaspoon salt
1 teaspoon baking powder
¾ cup chopped nuts

Beat eggs for 5 minutes at medium speed. Gradually add sugar. Stir in pumpkin and lemon juice. Mix together next six ingredients. Add to pumpkin mixture. Mix well. Pour into a greased and floured 15″ x 9″ x 1″ jelly roll pan. Sprinkle with chopped nuts. Bake at 350° for 15 minutes. Turn out onto a cloth towel which has been dusted with powdered sugar. Immediately roll up starting at the short end. Let cool. Unroll, spread with filling and roll up again. Chill 2 hours before serving. Serves 8 to 10.

FILLING

1 (8 ounce) package cream
　cheese
1 cup powdered sugar

4 tablespoons butter,
　softened

Combine ingredients. Mix well. Spread on cooled pumpkin roll.

Katherine S. Cooper (Mrs. James T.)

CHRISTMAS TORTE

1 cup butter
2 cups sugar
6 eggs
1 (12 ounce) box vanilla
    wafers
½ cup milk

1 (7 ounce) package flaked
    coconut (optional)
1 cup chopped pecans
Powdered sugar as
    garnish
Whipped cream (optional)

Cream butter and sugar. Add eggs one at a time while beating thoroughly. Crush vanilla wafers and add alternating with the milk. Stir in coconut and pecans. Pour into a greased and floured 9" springform pan. Bake at 325° for 1 hour 45 minutes or until done. (Do not overbake.) Cool. Remove from pan. Sprinkle top with powdered sugar. Garnish with holly in center. May be served with whipped cream. Serves 10 to 12.

Bonnie W. Bartsch (Mrs. James D.)

BLACK BOTTOM CUPS

CHEESE MIXTURE

1 (8 ounce) package cream
    cheese
1 egg
⅓ cup sugar

⅛ teaspoon salt
1 (12 ounce) package semi-
    sweet chocolate chips

Combine first four ingredients. Beat well. Stir in the chocolate chips. Set aside.

CHOCOLATE BATTER

1½ cups flour
1 cup sugar
¼ cup cocoa
1 teaspoon soda
½ teaspoon salt

1 cup water
½ cup cooking oil
1 tablespoon white vinegar
1 teaspoon vanilla extract

Sift first five ingredients together. Add remaining ingredients. Beat thoroughly. Fill greased, miniature muffin cups ⅓ full with chocolate batter. Top each with a heaping teaspoonful of cheese mixture. Bake at 350° for 20 to 25 minutes. Yield: 36 miniature cupcakes.

Barbara S. Moore (Mrs. James D., Jr.)

CHEESE GOODIES

20 vanilla wafers
2 (8 ounces each) packages
    cream cheese
1 teaspoon vanilla extract
    Dash of salt
¾ cup sugar

¾ teaspoon lemon extract
3 eggs, beaten
    Fruit topping of your
    choice
    Whipped cream

In each of 20 cupcake liners, place one wafer on bottom. Combine next 6 ingredients and beat thoroughly. Pour over wafers. Bake at 375° for 12 to 15 minutes. Cool and remove paper. Place whipped cream on top, then fruit of your choice. Yield: 20 cupcakes.

Sally M. Rowe (Mrs. C. Tom)

JEWELED CUPCAKES

3 (8 ounces each) packages
    cream cheese, softened
5 large eggs
1¼ cups sugar, divided

1¾ teaspoons vanilla
    extract, divided
1 pint sour cream

Have all ingredients at room temperature. Cream the cheese. Add eggs one at a time. Beat in 1 cup of the sugar and 1½ teaspoons of vanilla. Pour into paper lined cupcake pans, filling to ⅛" from top. Bake at 300° for 40 minutes. Cakes will appear cracked and browned on edges. Remove from oven and cool 5 minutes on wire racks. Mix sour cream, remaining ¼ teaspoon vanilla and remaining ¼ cup sugar. Pour 1 teaspoonful of mixture on top of each cake. Return to oven. Bake at 300° for 5 minutes. Cool. Refrigerate. When ready to serve, top with a spoonful of pineapple filling. (Prepared pie fillings may be substituted.) Yield: 20 to 24 cupcakes.

PINEAPPLE FILLING

1 (16 ounce) can crushed
    pineapple, in syrup
2 tablespoons cornstarch
½ cup sugar

¼ teaspoon salt
1 tablespoon butter
1 tablespoon lemon juice

Drain juice from pineapple into saucepan and stir in cornstarch. (May add 1 tablespoon cold water if not enough juice.) Add pineapple, sugar and salt. Cook over low heat until juice is clear. Remove from heat. Stir in butter. When melted, add lemon juice. Stir. Cool before using on cupcakes.

Filling may also be used as a pie filling or as a cake sauce or filling.

Frances B. Meyerhans (Mrs. Robert H.)

MADELINES

1¼ cups cake flour
½ teaspoon baking powder
3 eggs
1 teaspoon vanilla extract
⅔ cup sugar
2 teaspoons grated lemon
   rind

¾ cup <u>butter</u>,
   melted and cooled
Additional melted butter
   for molds
Powdered sugar, as
   garnish

Mix flour and baking powder. Set aside. Beat eggs until light. Add vanilla and sugar. Beat until quadrupled in size. Fold in lemon rind, flour and butter. Prepare madeline pans by brushing each mold with melted butter. Spoon batter into molds, filling no more than ½ to ¾ full (about 1 tablespoon). Bake at 350° for 10 to 12 minutes or until firm. Let sit briefly, invert and rap sharply on counter to unmold. Dust with powdered sugar. Perfect for tea (or with lemonade, as made famous by Proust). Makes 3 to 4 dozen.

Paula S. McKenney (Mrs. Ronald A.)

ICE CREAM ICING

2 cups powdered sugar
1 egg white
½ cup shortening
2 tablespoons flour

2 tablespoons milk
2 tablespoons margarine,
   melted
1 teaspoon vanilla extract

Combine ingredients. With mixer, beat until smooth and fluffy. Makes enough frosting for a 2 layer cake.

Catherine C. Rice (Mrs. Joseph V.)

FLUFFY NO FAIL FROSTING

¾ cup sugar
2 tablespoons water
2 egg whites
¼ teaspoon cream of tartar

⅓ cup light corn syrup
1 teaspoon vanilla extract
Pinch of salt

Cook all ingredients in top of double boiler, over hot water, beating with electric beaters until it will hold in stiff peaks. This will frost a 9″ two layer cake.

Note: For a beige icing, use ¾ cup firmly packed brown sugar instead of granulated sugar.

Jane S. McEldowney (Mrs. Robert E., III)

YUM-YUM FROSTING

1 (8 ounce) package cream
  cheese
1 (4 ounce) carton frozen
  whipped topping
1 (3½ ounce) box instant
  vanilla pudding

1 cup milk
1 (16 ounce) can crushed
  pineapple, drained
1 cup grated coconut
½ cup finely chopped
  walnuts

Combine cream cheese and topping in a bowl. In a separate bowl combine pudding and milk, stirring until smooth. Add to cream cheese mixture. Stir in pineapple. Use as a frosting or topping on yellow, white, angel food or pound cake. Sprinkle with coconut and walnuts.

Connie C. Muldoon (Mrs. Andrew)

APPLE CREAM PIE

5 to 6 apples, peeled
1 to 2 teaspoons cinnamon
½ teaspoon nutmeg
1 unbaked 9″ pie shell

2 tablespoons flour
Pinch of salt
¾ cup sugar
½ pint cream

Core and slice apples thinly. Sprinkle cinnamon and nutmeg over apples and toss well. Place in pie shell. Mix next four ingredients. Pour over apples. Bake at 450° for 10 to 15 minutes, then 1 hour at 350°. Serves 6 to 8.

Susan S. Sibley (Mrs. Richard H.)

APPLE CUSTARD PIE

2 cups thick stewed apples
4 eggs
1 cup sugar

3 cups milk
Nutmeg to taste
1 unbaked 9" pie shell

Strain apples through a colander. Beat eggs lightly and add to apples. Add sugar and milk. Flavor with nutmeg. Pour into pie crust and bake at 350° for 30 minutes.

Kitty Atkins (Mrs. E. Garfield)

APPLE TORTE

½ cup margarine
1 cup sugar, divided
¾ teaspoon vanilla extract, divided
1 cup flour
1 (8 ounce) package cream cheese, softened

1 egg
½ teaspoon cinnamon
4 cups apples, peeled and sliced
¼ cup sliced almonds

Cream margarine, ⅓ cup sugar and ¼ teaspoon vanilla. Blend in flour. Spread dough into bottom and sides of a 9" springform pan. Combine cream cheese and ⅓ cup sugar. Mix well. Add egg and remaining vanilla. Pour into pastry lined pan. Combine remaining sugar and cinnamon. Toss apples in sugar mixture. Spoon mixture over cream cheese layer. Sprinkle with almonds. Bake at 450° for 10 minutes. Reduce heat to 400° and bake 25 minutes. Cool before removing sides of pan. Serves 8 to 10.

Kay J. Morgan (Mrs. Frederick M.)

BANANA CREAM PIE

1 cup sugar	3 egg yolks (reserve whites
3 heaping tablespoons	for meringue)
cornstarch	1 tablespoon vanilla extract
3 cups milk	3 sliced bananas
	1 baked 9″ pie shell

Stir together sugar and cornstarch. Place in top of a double boiler over hot water. Combine milk with egg yolks and add to sugar. Cook mixture, stirring constantly until thick and smooth 15 to 20 minutes. Remove from heat. Add vanilla and bananas. Pour into baked, cooled pie shell. Top with meringue.

Variations: For **coconut cream,** omit bananas and substitute one handful of shredded coconut.

For **chocolate cream,** omit bananas and add 4 tablespoons cocoa to sugar mixture. Add 4 tablespoons margarine when removed from heat. Add vanilla. Stir until butter is melted.

MERINGUE

3 egg whites	½ teaspoon cream of tartar
¼ teaspoon salt	6 tablespoons sugar

Beat egg whites and salt until frothy. Add cream of tartar. Add sugar, 1 tablespoon at a time. Continue beating until stiff, but not dry. Spread on top of pie. Bake at 375° for 10 to 12 minutes until golden brown. Let stand until pie reaches room temperature. Refrigerate until serving time. Serves 6 to 8.

Mildred Ball

BRANDY ALEXANDER PIE

1 envelope unflavored	2 cups heavy cream,
gelatin	divided
½ cup cold water	9″ graham cracker pie shell
⅔ cup sugar, divided	2 to 3 tablespoons powdered
½ teaspoon salt	sugar
3 eggs, separated	Grated chocolate for
¼ cup cognac	garnish
½ cup créme de cacao	

Sprinkle gelatin on cold water in saucepan. Add ⅓ cup sugar, salt and egg yolks. Blend. Cook over low heat until just thickened. Do not boil. Remove from heat. Add cognac and créme de cacao. Chill until mixture starts to mound slightly. Beat egg whites until stiff, add remaining sugar and fold into thickened mixture. Whip 1 cup cream and fold in above. Pour into pie shell. Chill several hours or overnight. Whip remaining cream with powdered sugar. Use as garnish with grated chocolate.

GRAHAM CRACKER CRUST

1 cup graham cracker crumbs
4 tablespoons butter, melted

3 tablespoons powdered sugar
¼ teaspoon unflavored gelatin

Mix ingredients together and press into 9″ pie plate.

Sandra W. Mantz (Mrs. Eric P.)

CHOCOLATE FUDGE PIE

1 cup sugar
3 tablespoons cocoa
¼ cup flour
2 eggs, beaten
¼ cup milk

6 tablespoons butter, melted
1 teaspoon vanilla extract
½ cup chopped pecans
1 unbaked 9″ pie shell

Mix sugar, cocoa and flour. Stir in eggs, milk, butter and vanilla, blending well. Add chopped pecans. Pour into pie shell. Bake at 325° for 1½ hours.

Mary T. Karr (Mrs. George W.)

FROZEN CHOCOLATE PIE

1 (8 inch) crumb crust, graham or chocolate
4 milk chocolate candy bars with almonds
½ of 10 ounce package marshmallows

½ cup milk
1 cup whipping cream, whipped
Chopped nuts and additional whipped cream, optional

Melt candy, marshmallows and milk in top of double boiler over hot water. Stir mixture until smooth. Refrigerate 30 to 40 minutes until thickened. Fold whipped cream into mixture. Pile into crust and freeze until firm. Garnish with nuts or whipped cream. Serves 6 to 8.

Barbara H. Diznoff (Mrs. Lee)

CHOCOLATE PIE

FILLING

1 cup sugar
2 heaping tablespoons cocoa
4 tablespoons flour
2 cups milk

2 egg yolks (reserve
   whites for meringue)
1 tablespoon butter
1 teaspoon vanilla extract
1 baked 9″ pie shell

Combine sugar, cocoa and flour. Place in top of a double boiler over hot water. Combine milk and egg yolks. Stir into sugar mixture. Cook, stirring constantly until thickened, 15 to 20 minutes. Remove from heat. Stir in vanilla and butter. Top with meringue. Bake at 425° for 3 to 5 minutes. Serves 6 to 8.

MERINGUE

2 egg whites

2 tablespoons sugar

Beat egg whites until frothy. Add sugar and beat until stiff. Place over pie filling. This is a thin meringue.

Bobby Jean Bolling (Mrs. Stephen E.)

CHOCOLATE CHESS PIE

1 unbaked 9″ pie shell
½ cup butter, melted
1 cup brown sugar
½ cup sugar
1 tablespoon flour
2 eggs

½ egg shell of milk
1 teaspoon vanilla extract
1½ ounces unsweetened
   chocolate, melted
Whipped cream or ice
   cream

Bake pie crust at 475° for 3 minutes. Combine remaining ingredients. Place in pie shell. Bake at 325° for 40 minutes or until done. (Shake gently to be sure center is set.) Cool. Serve with whipped cream or ice cream. Serves 6 to 8.

Lucy Payne Paynter (Mrs. George)

CHOCOLATE SWIRL CHEESE PIE

2 eggs
4 (3 ounces each) packages
   cream cheese, softened
½ cup sugar
1½ teaspoons vanilla extract

½ cup semi-sweet chocolate
   chips
1 9″ unbaked graham
   cracker crust pie shell

Beat eggs, cream cheese, sugar and vanilla until smooth. Set aside. Melt chocolate chips over low heat, stirring constantly, for 2 minutes. Pour cheese mixture into pie shell. Drop chocolate by teaspoonfuls evenly over cheese mixture. Swirl chocolate through filling with a fork. Bake at 325° for 20 to 25 minutes or until center appears set. Cool, chill and serve.

Susanne F. Berger (Mrs. Bruce)

DEWBERRY CREAM PIE

1 cup sugar	Pinch of salt
2 eggs, beaten	1 quart dewberries
½ cup flour	1 unbaked 9″ pie shell
1 cup sour cream	

Cream sugar and eggs. Mix flour, salt and sour cream with sugar mixture. Pour over berries that have been put in pie shell. Allow mixture to settle to bottom. Add topping. Bake at 325° for 45 minutes.

TOPPING

8 tablespoons sugar	¼ cup margarine
8 tablespoons flour	

Mix until crumbly. Spread over top of the pie.

Note: Dewberries are a type of blackberry that grow along the ground. They ripen with the early dew before the first blackberries. Fresh peaches may be used instead of dewberries.

Ruby McClure

LAYERED LEMON PIE

25 Oreo cookies	1 (21 ounce) can lemon pie
½ cup pecans	filling
¼ cup butter, melted	Frozen whipped topping
1 pint vanilla ice cream, softened	

Crumble cookies and pecans. Mix with butter and pat into a pie pan. Bake at 350° for 8 minutes. Chill for 1½ hours. Place ½ of vanilla ice cream in pie shell. Freeze until set. Layer ½ of lemon filling over ice cream. Freeze until set. Layer remaining ice cream and freeze until set. Layer remaining pie filling. Freeze. Top with whipped topping and decorate with cookie crumbs, shaved chocolate or candied lemon wedges. Serves 8 to 10.

Diana L. Moore (Mrs. Blair)

RUBY'S OLD FASHIONED LEMON PIE

2 eggs, separated
1 cup sugar
1 tablespoon flour
1 tablespoon butter, melted
Juice of 1 large lemon

1 teaspoon grated lemon rind
1 cup milk
1 unbaked 8″ deep dish pie shell

Preheat oven to 400°. Cream egg yolks and sugar with an electric mixer. Whisk flour and butter together. Add to egg yolk mixture. Cream until smooth. Beat in lemon juice, rind and milk. Beat egg whites until stiff. Fold into lemon mixture. Pour into pie shell. Reduce oven to 350° and bake for 50 minutes. Serves 6.

Joan C. Steven (Mrs. John C.)

JAE SPEARS' MOUNTAINEER PIE

⅔ cup butter
⅔ cup sugar
2 eggs, beaten
⅔ cup white corn syrup

⅔ cup rolled oats
1 teaspoon vanilla extract
Dash of salt
1 unbaked 9″ pie shell

Cream butter and sugar. Add eggs. Mix in corn syrup and then oatmeal, vanilla and salt. Place in pie shell. Bake at 375° for 40 minutes until filling is set.

Senator Jae Spears

ORIENTAL PIE

½ cup margarine, melted
1½ cups sugar
4 eggs
1 tablespoon vinegar
1 tablespoon vanilla extract

1 teaspoon lemon juice
1 cup pecan pieces
1 cup flaked coconut
1 cup white raisins
1 unbaked 9″ pie shell

Beat together margarine, sugar and eggs. Stir in vinegar, vanilla and lemon juice. Add nuts, coconut and raisins. Pour into pie shell. Bake at 350° for 30 to 40 minutes. Serves 6 to 8.

Kay Miller

FRESH PEACHES AND CREAM PIE

Graham cracker pie shell*
10½ ounces miniature marshmallows

2 tablespoons orange juice
1 tablespoon lemon juice
½ pint whipping cream
2 cups fresh sliced peaches

Melt marshmallows in double boiler with juices. Remove from heat. Whip cream. Fold peaches and cream into marshmallow mixture. Pour into crust and chill well before serving. Serves 6 to 8.
*Plenty of filling for 10" crust.

Elizabeth A. Thurston (Mrs. Clark W.)

PEACH CUSTARD PIE

2 cups fresh peaches,
    peeled and sliced
3 eggs, beaten
1 cup sugar

Cinnamon
1 tablespoon butter
1 unbaked 9" pie shell

Fill pastry shell ¾ full with peaches. Beat eggs, add sugar, blend well and pour over peaches. Sprinkle with cinnamon and dot with butter. Bake at 400° for 10 minutes, reduce temperature to 350° and continue baking for approximately 35 minutes.

Marta D. MacCallum (Mrs. Daniel)

STRUESEL TOPPED PEACH PIE

CRUST

1½ cups flour
2 teaspoons sugar
1 teaspoon salt

½ cup cooking oil
2 tablespoons milk

Blend crust ingredients in large bowl to form a soft dough. Press evenly on bottom and sides of 9" pie pan.

FILLING

½ cup powdered sugar
⅓ cup flour

3 to 4 cups sliced peaches
    (fresh or canned)

Stir filling ingredients until blended. Spoon into unbaked crust.

TOPPING

¾ cup flour
½ cup firmly packed brown
    sugar

1 teaspoon cinnamon
⅓ cup margarine, softened

In medium bowl blend topping ingredients to form crumbs. Sprinkle over fruit. Bake at 375° for 40 to 45 minutes until topping is golden. Serves 6 to 8.

Sharon H. Hall (Mrs. William R.)

PEANUT BUTTER PIE

1 cup sugar	1 teaspoon vanilla extract
2 cups milk	3 tablespoons butter
2 egg yolks, beaten	½ cup peanut butter
3 tablespoons cornstarch	9″ graham cracker crust

Cook sugar, milk, eggs and cornstarch until thick. Stir in vanilla, butter and peanut butter. Pour into graham cracker crust. Top with Meringue. Bake at 425° for 10 minutes. Cool or chill before serving.

Edith Marsteller (Mrs. L.B.)

PEANUT BUTTER CREAM PIE

2 cups milk, divided	1 tablespoon margarine,
½ cup sugar	melted
¾ cup brown sugar	3 tablespoons peanut butter
¼ cup flour	Crushed peanuts, optional
½ teaspoon salt	1 baked 9″ pie shell
3 egg yolks (reserve whites for meringue	

Heat 1½ cups milk in the top of a double boiler over hot water. Combine next four ingredients. Add to milk. Combine egg yolks, margarine and remaining ½ cup milk. Stir into double boiler. Cook, stirring constantly until thickened, 15 to 20 minutes. Remove from heat. Stir in peanut butter. Pour into pie shell. Top with meringue. Sprinkle crushed peanuts on top. Bake at 375° for 10 to 12 minutes until golden brown on top.

MERINGUE

3 egg whites	¼ teaspoon cream of tartar
½ teaspoon vanilla extract	4 tablespoons sugar

Beat egg whites until frothy. Add vanilla and cream of tartar. Gradually add sugar, beating until stiff.

Sandra W. Mantz (Mrs. Eric P.)

PECAN CHOCOLATE CHIP PIE

1 cup sugar
½ cup flour
½ cup margarine, melted
2 eggs, slightly beaten

1 (6 ounce) package
   chocolate chips
1 cup pecans, chopped
1 teaspoon vanilla extract
1 unbaked 9″ pie shell

Mix together sugar and flour. Add margarine and blend well. Stir in eggs, chocolate chips, pecans and vanilla. Pour mixture into pie shell. Bake at 325° for 50 to 60 minutes until light golden brown. Edge of crust may be covered with foil to prevent excessive browning. Delicious topped with whipped cream or ice cream. Serves 6 to 8.

Bonnie O'Neal (Mrs. Richard)

PECAN NUT CUPS

CRUST

½ cup butter
1 (3 ounce) package cream
   cheese

1 cup flour

Cream butter and cheese that has come to room temperature. Blend in flour. Chill one hour. Shape into 24 balls. Press dough into tiny ungreased muffin tins.

FILLING

1 egg
¾ cup light brown sugar
1 tablespoon butter,
   softened

1 teaspoon vanilla extract
⅔ cup broken pecans

Beat together above ingredients until smooth. Fill each shell. Bake at 325° for 25 minutes or until filling is set. Cool and remove from pans. Yield: 24 nut cups.

Mary Ann Cody

PINEAPPLE CREAM CHEESE PIE

1 (8 ounce) package cream
  cheese
¼ cup sugar
1 cup heavy cream

1½ cups crushed pineapple,
   well drained
9" graham cracker crust

Soften cream cheese to room temperature. Whip together cream cheese and sugar. Whip cream and fold into cream cheese mixture. Fold in pineapple. Spoon into pie shell. Chill thoroughly until well set, approximately 2 hours. Serve chilled. Serves 6 to 8.

Mary Virginia Gray

PRALINE PUMPKIN PIE

CRUST

1 unbaked 9" pie shell
⅓ cup ground pecans

⅓ cup brown sugar
2 tablespoons butter,
  softened

Combine pecans, brown sugar and butter. Press into pie shell. Bake at 450° for 10 minutes. Add filling and bake at 325° for 40 to 45 minutes.

FILLING

3 eggs, beaten
1 cup pumpkin
⅔ cup firmly packed brown
  sugar
1 tablespoon flour

¼ teaspoon cloves
½ teaspoon salt
½ teaspoon ginger
½ teaspoon cinnamon
1 cup evaporated milk

Mix all above ingredients until creamy.

Dorothy Dean

GRANDMOTHER'S RAISIN RHUBARB PIE

1 cup seedless raisins	½ teaspoon salt
¾ cup water	1 egg
3 cups rhubarb, cut in 1″ pieces	Grated rind of 1 lemon
1 tablespoon butter	1 tablespoon lemon juice
1 cup sugar	1 unbaked 9″ pie shell
2 tablespoons cornstarch	1 cup sour cream
	1 tablespoon honey

Rinse and drain raisins. Add water and rhubarb and bring to boiling point. Stir in butter. Blend sugar, cornstarch and salt. Beat egg lightly and stir in lemon rind, juice and sugar mixture. Stir carefully into hot mixture. Cook and stir until thickened and glossy. Cool slightly. Pour into pie shell. Bake at 450° for 10 minutes, reduce heat to 350° and bake 25 to 30 minutes. Cool. Serve with sauce made by sweetening sour cream with honey or top with vanilla ice cream.

Connie Morton McKee

THE GREATEST SHOO-FLY PIE

1½ cups flour	½ teaspoon soda
1 cup packed brown sugar	½ cup butter
¼ teaspoon cinnamon	1 cup molasses
¼ teaspoon nutmeg	1 cup boiling water
¼ teaspoon ground cloves	1 egg, beaten
¼ teaspoon ginger	½ teaspoon soda
¼ teaspoon salt	1 unbaked 10″ pie shell

Combine first 8 ingredients in medium sized bowl. Cut butter in until like cornmeal. In separate bowl combine next 4 ingredients. Add 1 cup of crumb mixture to liquid. Put in pie crust. Sprinkle remaining crumb mixture over pie. Bake 50 to 60 minutes at 375°. Pie is done when center is firm when pie is shaken. Cool on rack. Serves 8.

Shoo-Fly Pie is a Pennsylvania Dutch treat. It is served for breakfast or dinner. It can be served plain or topped with ice cream or whipped cream.

Kathy S. Chaney (Mrs. Malcolm)

FRENCH STRAWBERRY PIE

1 baked and cooled 9″ pie
    shell
1 (3 ounce) package cream
    cheese
3 to 4 tablespoons sour cream

1 quart whole fresh
    strawberries
1 (8 ounce) jar red currant
    jelly

Cover pie shell with cream cheese which has been softened with sour cream. Fill with strawberries which have been washed, dried and hulled. Heat currant jelly until melted. Cool slightly and spoon over berries. Refrigerate 2 to 3 hours before serving.

Elizabeth E. Stultz (Mrs. Gardner M.)

STRAWBERRY ICEBOX PIE

½ pound marshmallows
    (about 32)
½ cup milk
2 cups whipped cream,
    divided

1 teaspoon vanilla extract
¼ teaspoon salt
1½ cups sliced strawberries
1 baked 9″ pie shell

Melt marshmlallows in top of double boiler. Cool thoroughly, but do not allow to jell. Beat out lumps. Fold in 1 cup whipped cream, milk, vanilla and salt. Arrange fruit and marshmallow mixture in layers in pie shell. Chill at least 1 hour before serving. Remove from refrigerator 20 minutes before serving. Top with remaining whipped cream.

Mrs. George R. Callender

STRAWBERRY PIE

2½ tablespoons cornstarch
1 cup sugar
1 cup water
1 (3 ounce) package straw-
    berry gelatin

1 quart strawberries
1 baked 9″ pie shell or 1
    Keebler cookie crust

Blend cornstarch and sugar in saucepan. Add water and cook 3 to 5 minutes. Add gelatin and mix until dissolved. Allow to cool. Pour mixture over cleaned and sliced berries. Blend together. Pour into crust. Chill 2 to 3 hours. Top with whipped cream. Serves 6 to 8.

Donna L. Dean (Mrs. Rodney D.)

HOT FUDGE SUNDAE PIE

HOT FUDGE SAUCE

1 cup sugar
½ cup cocoa
1 teaspoon instant coffee

1 cup heavy cream, divided
¼ cup margarine

Mix sugar, cocoa and coffee in saucepan. Add ½ cup cream. Blend until smooth. Add remaining cream, cooking over medium heat until sugar is dissolved, stirring constantly. Add butter and cook until thick and smooth, 5 to 8 minutes.

FILLING

1 quart French vanilla ice
cream, softened,
divided
1 quart your favorite chocolate ice cream (sugges-
tions: Jamoca almond
fudge, rocky road, mint
chocolate chip)

9" chocolate pie shell
1 can Redi Whip or real
whipped cream
Nuts and maraschino
cherries for garnish

Spread ½ quart vanilla ice cream over pie shell and freeze. Pour ½ of chocolate sauce over top. Let harden. Spread remaining ½ quart vanilla ice cream on top and freeze. When ready to serve arrange scoops of chocolate ice cream around outside and fill center with additional scoops. Decorate with whipped cream, cherries and nuts. Drizzle with remaining hot fudge sauce. Cut and serve immediately. Serves 8 to 10.

Sara Z. Hoblitzell (Mrs. John R.)

QUICK AND EASY PEANUT BUTTER-CHOCOLATE PIE

¼ cup creamy peanut butter
¼ cup margarine
1⅓ cups graham cracker
crumbs
1 quart vanilla ice cream,
softened

1 package fudge frosting
mix, prepared (or 1 can
fudge frosting or your
favorite recipe)
Chopped nuts, optional

Melt peanut butter and margarine together in top of double boiler. Add graham cracker crumbs and blend. Pat into bottom of 9" pie pan. Fill crumb shell with ice cream. Spread frosting over ice cream. Garnish with chopped nuts or leave plain. Freeze until ready to serve. Serves 8 to 10.

Alison Bernard

ENGLISH TOFFEE PIE

½ cup butter
2 cups powdered sugar
2 eggs, separated
2 tablespoons cocoa
1 cup chopped toasted pecans

Whipped cream
1 10" graham cracker or
   vanilla wafer cookie pie
   crust

Mix butter, sugar, egg yolks and cocoa. Beat 10 minutes. Beat egg whites until stiff. fold in toasted pecans. Fold egg white mixture into cocoa mixture. Put in pie crust and refrigerate. To serve, ice with whipped cream. Serves 8.

Lucy Payne Paynter (Mrs. George)

PIE PASTRY

4 cups flour
1 teaspoon sugar
2 teaspoons salt
1¾ cups Crisco

½ cup water
1 egg
1 teaspoon vinegar

Sift first 3 ingredients together. Cut in Crisco. Mix together water, egg and vinegar. Mix with flour mixture. Makes 2 double crust pies. May be frozen for an indefinite period of time. Divide into 4 balls and roll out on a floured surface before placing in pie pan.

Patricia W. Berry (Mrs. Bruce)

ST. JOHN'S EPISCOPAL CHURCH

St. John's Episcopal Church, a Gothic Revival Style building located on the southeast corner of Broad and Quarrier Streets in Downtown Charleston, was designed by Philadelphia architect Isaac Pursell in 1883. The selection of Gothic Revival as the architectural style is interesting since the style was more characteristic of non-litergical sects than of Episcopal churches of the period.

The cornerstone was laid in 1884, the first service was held in 1888 and the church building was consecrated on June 9, 1901. A major addition, consisting of the parish house and offices was designed by the Charleston architectural firm of Warne, Tucker, Silling and Hutchinson and constructed in 1928. The church is used for religious services while the parish house is used for parish-related activities and community work.

The plan of the original building is in the form of a truncated Latin cross with corner entrances located in a great bell tower which dominates the church exterior and has long served as a Charleston architectural landmark. The tower is extraordinarily tall relative to the scale of other architectural features. A stair turret extends from the tower corner.

Features of the building identified with the Gothic architectural style are the steep roofs, pointed arches over windows and doors, open-truss ceilings, and the tracery in the stained glass windows (in this case, wood tracery). All exterior walls, the tower, and sculptured details are fashioned from beautifully worked sandstone.

Historically the church has enjoyed strong lay and professional leadership. Among its early Rectors was Rev. James Craik, grandson of George Washington's physician and son of President Washington's secretary during his second term. Rev. Craik served St. John's in 1839-1844.

Photo courtesy of W. Va. Dept. of Culture and History

COOKIES AND CANDY

Flower Basket

NEW ENGLAND BLUEBERRY SQUARES

3 cups flour	1 teaspoon vanilla extract
1½ cups sugar	1 cup cold margarine
2 teaspoons baking powder	1 (21 ounce) can blueberry
2 eggs	pie filling

Mix first 6 ingredients with pastry blender until crumbly. Put half of the crumb mixture in 9" x 13" pan. Cover with pie filling. Top with remainder of crumb mixture. Bake at 375° for 30 to 35 minutes. Cut in squares. May be made with cherry pie filling instead. Also good served topped with ice cream or whipped cream. Makes 12 to 14 large squares.

Gina H. Rugeley (Mrs. Edward W., Jr.)

BROWNIES

1 cup butter	1 teaspoon baking powder
1 (12 ounce) package semi-sweet chocolate chips	1½ teaspoons vanilla extract
	Pinch of salt
1 cup sugar	1 (6 ounce) package milk
1 cup flour	chocolate chips
4 eggs	

Melt butter and semi-sweet chocolate chips together. Combine remaining ingredients, reserving milk chocolate chips. Mix well. Add to melted chocolate. Pour into greased 9" x 13" pan. Pour milk chocolate chips on top. Bake at 350° 20 to 25 minutes. Cool and cut into squares.

Sarah Hoblitzell Howell

RICH CHOCOLATE BROWNIES

1 cup margarine	8 eggs
8 (1 ounce each) squares unsweetened chocolate	4 teaspoons vanilla extract
	½ teaspoon salt
4 cups sugar	2 cups flour

Melt margarine and chocolate together in microwave or in top of double boiler over hot water. Beat together eggs and sugar in a large bowl. Add chocolate, vanilla and salt, blending well. Add flour. Mix. Mixture should be glossy and not too runny. Line a 9" x 13" and a 9" square pan with wax paper. Pour brownie mix in two pans. Bake at 300° for 45 to 50 minutes. Cool 10 minutes. Turn out of pan. Peel off wax paper. Best when slightly underbaked and very moist inside. Can be frozen. Makes 4 to 5 dozen.

Suzanne H. Sims (Mrs. James)

BROWNIE SCOTCHES

1 box yellow cake mix	1 (6 ounce) package butterscotch chips
1 egg	
¼ cup water	½ cup chopped nuts (optional)
¼ cup cooking oil	

Combine all ingredients. Mix well. Pour into greased and sugared 9" x 13" pan. Bake at 350° for 20 to 30 minutes. Do not overcook. Cool and cut into squares. May also be baked in 2 pie pans, topped with ice cream and served for dessert.

Susan S. Sibley (Mrs. Richard H.)

BUTTER GOOEY BARS

1 box yellow cake mix	1 (16 ounce) box powdered sugar
½ cup butter, softened	
4 eggs	½ teaspoon vanilla extract
1 (8 ounce) package cream cheese	

Combine cake mix and butter. Add 2 beaten eggs. Spread mixture on bottom of greased 9" x 13" pan. Cream together remaining 2 eggs, cream cheese, powdered sugar and vanilla. Pour on top of cake mixture. Bake at 350° for 35 to 40 minutes, until sides of cake have separated slightly from pan. Cool and cut into bars.

Kathleen M. Muehlman (Mrs. Raymond L., Jr.)

CHERRY SURPRISES

2 cups chopped pecans	1 cup cake flour
½ cup brown sugar	¼ teaspoon baking powder
¼ cup sugar	48 maraschino cherries,
½ cup butter	drained
2 eggs, separated	Powdered sugar
½ teaspoon vanilla extract	

Grease small muffin tins and sprinkle chopped pecans in bottom of tins. Cream together sugars and butter. Add egg yolks and vanilla. Blend. Sift together flour and baking powder. Add to mixture. Beat egg whites until stiff and fold in. Place 1 teaspoon batter on top of nuts and press whole cherry into center. Bake at 350° for 10 minutes. Remove while warm and roll in powdered sugar. Makes 4 dozen cookies.

Sandra C. Tate (Mrs. Donald L.)

CHOCOLATE CHIP-OATMEAL COOKIES

1 cup shortening	1 teaspoon soda
1 cup sugar	1 teaspoon vanilla extract
1 cup brown sugar	2 cups rolled oats
2 eggs	½ cup chopped walnuts
2 cups flour	1 (12 ounce) package semi-
½ teaspoon salt	sweet chocolate chips
½ teaspoon baking powder	

Cream shortening and sugars. Add eggs. Mix. Combine flour, salt, baking powder and soda. Add to creamed mixture, blending well. Stir in remaining ingredients. Shape cookies in walnut size balls and place on greased cookie sheet. Bake at 350° for 8 to 12 minutes for chewy cookie, 12 to 15 minutes for crisp cookie. Cool slightly before removing from sheet. Makes 4 dozen cookies.

Emily M. Roles (Mrs. Forrest H.)

PIZZELLES
Italian Waffle Cookies

12 eggs	3 cups sugar
1 cup butter, melted	6 ounces bourbon
1 cup cooking oil	4 cups flour

Add ingredients in order given in electric mixer. Mix until smooth. Drop one tablespoon batter on each section of pizzelle iron. Close lid. Cook until light brown, 30 seconds.

Susan Kamer-Shinaberry

THREE LAYER CHOCOLATE BARS

FIRST LAYER

½ cup margarine
¼ cup sugar
5 tablespoons cocoa
1 teaspoon vanilla extract
1 egg, beaten

2 cups graham cracker
  crumbs
½ cup chopped nuts
1 cup coconut (optional)

In top of double boiler over hot water combine margarine, sugar, cocoa, vanilla and egg. Cook, stirring, until margarine melts and mixture resembles custard. Add graham cracker crumbs, nuts and coconut. Mix. Press mixture in an ungreased 9″ square pan.

SECOND LAYER

¼ cup margarine
3 tablespoons milk
2 cups powdered sugar

3 tablespoons instant
  vanilla pudding powder

Cream margarine until fluffy. Add milk, sugar and pudding powder. Mix well. Spread evenly over first layer. Chill until firm; best done day ahead.

THIRD LAYER

4 (1 ounce each) squares
  semi-sweet chocolate

1 tablespoon margarine

Melt chocolate with margarine. Stir until smooth. Cool slightly and spread over second layer. Cool and cut into squares.

Linda K. Meckfessel (Mrs. Richard R.)

GERMAN CRISPS

1 cup butter	¼ teaspoon salt
2 cups brown sugar	1 teaspoon soda
2 eggs	1 teaspoon vanilla extract
3½ cups flour	1 cup chopped walnuts

Cream butter and sugar. Add eggs; beat thoroughly. Sift together flour, salt and soda. Add to creamed mixture. Stir in vanilla and nuts. Shape into log, wrap in waxed paper and refrigerate overnight. Slice into ¼" slices. Place on ungreased cookie sheet. Bake at 375° for 10 minutes, watching closely to prevent burning. Store in airtight container. Makes 6 to 8 dozen cookies, depending on size.

Eleanor K. Rashid (Mrs. Richard C.)

GOBS

2 cups sugar	½ teaspoon salt
½ cup shortening	½ cup cocoa
2 eggs	1 cup sour milk*
4 cups flour	½ cup boiling water
2 teaspoons soda	2 teaspoons vanilla extract
½ teaspoon baking powder	

*Sour milk: 1 cup milk plus 1 tablespoon vinegar or lemon juice—let stand 5 minutes.

Sift together flour, baking powder, soda, salt and cocoa. Mix in other ingredients. On lightly greased cookie sheets drop one rounded teaspoon dough, spacing 2" apart. Bake at 450° for 4 minutes. Remove from cookie sheets. Cool. When cool, place filling between 2 chocolate cookies, like a sandwich.

FILLING

4 tablespoons flour	½ cup shortening
1 cup milk	1 cup sugar
½ cup margarine	1 teaspoon vanilla extract

In saucepan over medium heat stir milk into flour. Bring to boil and cook until thick, stirring frequently. Remove from heat and cool. Cream shortening, margarine and sugar together until fluffy. Combine 2 mixtures, add vanilla and beat until fluffy. Turn mixer speed to low and beat 5 minutes. Makes 3 to 4 dozen cookies.

Victoria H. Duncan (Mrs. C. Ronald)

GRASSHOPPER BARS

1½ cups sifted flour
2 cups sugar
¾ cup plus 2 tablespoons Carnation instant hot cocoa mix
1½ teaspoons salt
1 teaspoon baking powder

1¾ cups butter, softened
4 eggs
2 teaspoons vanilla extract
2 tablespoons light corn syrup
2 cups chopped nuts

Sift together first 5 ingredients. Add butter, eggs, vanilla and corn syrup. Mix well. Stir in nuts. Spread into oiled 9" x 13" pan. Bake at 350° for 40 to 45 minutes or until soft in center and edges slightly firm. Do not overbake. Cool completely before frosting.

MINT FROSTING

2 cups sifted powdered sugar
4 tablespoons butter, softened
2 tablespoons milk

1 tablespoon Creme de Menthe (or peppermint extract)
Green food coloring (as desired)

Combine above ingredients. Mix well. Spread evenly over pastry. Cut into squares. Do not remove from pan. Freeze. When frozen cover with chocolate glaze.

CHOCOLATE GLAZE

2 (1 ounce each) squares unsweetened chocolate

2 tablespoons butter
Decorative sprinkles (optional)

Melt chocolate and butter in microwave or in top of double boiler over hot water. Stir until smooth. Cool. Brush or drizzle glaze over mint bars. Decorate with sprinkles. Refrigerate until glaze is hardened. Recut bars and remove. Store in airtight container or freeze until ready to use. Makes 40 bars.

Diane S. Doty (Mrs. Steven)

KOURABIEDES
Greek Wedding Cookies

1 cup unsalted butter
⅓ cup powdered sugar
2 cups flour
1 egg yolk

1 tablespoon cognac or bourbon
1 teaspoon vanilla extract
⅛ teaspoon salt

Cream butter and sugar. Add flour and mix. Blend in remaining ingredients. Wrap in wax paper; chill one hour. Shape into small balls and place on cookie sheet. Bake at 325° for 20 to 25 minutes. Cool and dust lightly with powdered sugar. Store in closed container. Makes 3 dozen cookies.

Monique Von Damme Jordan

GRANDMOTHER CLARA'S LEMON CRACKERS

1 ounce baking ammonia*	1 teaspoon salt
1 cup milk	2 eggs
2½ cups sugar	7 cups flour
1 cup shortening	1 teaspoon oil of lemon*

*Obtain baking ammonia from prescription counter at pharmacy. Also find oil of lemon at pharmacy.

Pulverize baking ammonia and combine with milk. Let stand until ammonia has dissolved. Strain to eliminate chunks that may be left. Cream sugar and shortening. Add salt and eggs, mixing well. Add ammonia-milk mixture and oil of lemon. Add flour, kneading well. (Use additional flour if needed to make a dough that can be handled easily. Kneading step is very important.) Roll to ½″ thickness. Cut with cookie cutter—square cutter is traditional. Prick top with fork. Bake on cookie sheet at 400° for 10 to 12 minutes, until light brown. Makes 3 to 4 dozen large or 6 to 8 dozen small cookies.

Deborah J. Spradling (Mrs. Marshall)

LEMON WHIPPERSNAPS

1 package lemon cake mix	1 egg
1 (4½ ounce) carton frozen whipped topping, thawed	½ cup sifted powdered sugar

Combine cake mix, whipped topping and egg in large bowl. Stir until well mixed. Drop by spoonfuls into powdered sugar. Roll to coat. Place 1½″ apart on greased cookie sheet. Bake at 350° for 10 to 15 minutes until light golden brown. Makes 4 dozen cookies.

Dana W. Sharp

MICHIGAN ROCKS

"Served by my grandmother at holidays - if not eaten within 2 days they turn hard as rocks and were dunked in coffee before eating."

1¼ cups sugar	1 teaspoon cream of tartar
1 cup butter	1 teaspoon baking soda
4 eggs	2 cups chopped nuts
1 teaspoon vanilla extract	2 (8 ounces each) boxes
3 cups flour	chopped dates
1 teaspoon cinnamon	

Cream butter and sugar. Beat in eggs and vanilla. Sift together next 4 ingredients and beat into creamed mixture. Stir in nuts and dates. Drop by teaspoonfuls onto greased cookie sheets. Bake at 350° for 8 to 10 minutes until golden brown.

Nancy B. Chaney (Mrs. Michael T.)

OLD FASHIONED MOLASSES COOKIES

¾ cup butter	½ teaspoon soda
¾ cup molasses	½ teaspoon salt
2 eggs, beaten	1½ teaspoons cinnamon
¼ cup milk	½ cup chopped nuts
2¼ cups flour	English walnut halves
2 teaspoons baking powder	

Cream butter. Add eggs and molasses. Mix. Sift together flour, baking powder, soda, salt and cinnamon. Add to first mixture alternately with milk. Stir in nuts. Drop by teaspoonfuls onto greased cookie sheet. Top each cookie with walnut half. Bake at 425° for 10 to 12 minutes. Makes 4 to 5 dozen cookies.

Connie Morton McKee

SOFT MOLASSES COOKIES
A gingerbread cookie

2 cups flour	½ cup brown sugar
1 teaspoon soda	1 egg
½ teaspoon salt	⅓ cup molasses
1½ teaspoons ginger	⅓ cup buttermilk
½ teaspoon cinnamon	½ cup margarine
½ teaspoon ground cloves	

Sift together first 6 ingredients. Add remaining ingredients and beat well. Drop by teaspoonfuls onto greased cookie sheet. Bake at 350° for 15 to 18 minutes. Makes 3 to 4 dozen cookies.

Janice H. Flannery (Mrs. David M.)

OATMEAL LACE COOKIES

1 cup butter	½ teaspoon soda
2 tablespoons water	1 teaspoon baking powder
2 tablespoons maple syrup*	2½ cups quick oats
1 cup flour	½ cup sugar for rolling
1 cup sugar	

*Note: do not use "Lite" syrup.

Melt butter with water. Add syrup. Sift together dry ingredients. Add oatmeal. Mix well. Add butter mixture to oatmeal. Chill one hour. Form into 1" balls, roll in sugar and place on ungreased cookie sheet. Flatten slightly. Bake at 350° for 12 to 15 minutes. Remove immediately. Cool on rack. Makes 4 dozen cookies.

Tia C. McMillan (Mrs. Robert A.)

OATMEAL MACAROONS

1 cup shortening	1 teaspoon soda
1 cup sugar	½ teaspoon salt
1 cup brown sugar	½ teaspoon cinnamon
1 teaspoon vanilla extract	½ cup chopped walnuts
2 eggs	3 cups quick oats
1¼ cups flour	

Mix together shortening, sugars, vanilla and eggs. Sift together flour, salt, soda, and cinnamon. Add to egg mixture, blending well. Stir in walnuts and oats. Drop by spoonfuls onto cookie sheet. Bake at 325° for 12 to 15 minutes. Makes 4 dozen cookies.

Ann W. Stowers (Mrs. Gerald R.)

ORANGE BALL COOKIES
No Bake

1 (12 ounce) box vanilla wafers	1 (16 ounce) box powdered sugar
1 (6 ounce) can frozen orange juice, thawed	½ cup margarine
	1 cup chopped nuts
	1 small package coconut

Crush vanilla wafers until fine. Mix all ingredients except coconut. Roll into walnut-size balls. Roll balls in coconut. Store in covered container in refrigerator. Will keep several weeks. Makes 5 dozen cookies.

Nancy C. Martin (Mrs. Kirby)

CHEWY PECAN BARS

1 cup butter	2 tablespoons butter
1 cup brown sugar	2 tablespoons flour
2 cups sifted flour	1 teaspoon vanilla extract
1 cup dark corn syrup	¼ teaspoon salt
4 eggs	1 cup chopped pecans
¾ cup sugar	

Make a crust by combining 1 cup butter, brown sugar and 2 cups flour with fork until crumbly. Press into 9″ x 13″ pan. Bake at 350° for 10 minutes. Beat together next 7 ingredients until well blended. Add pecans. Pour over hot crust. Bake at 300° for 50 minutes. Cut into squares.

Elizabeth A. Thurston (Mrs. Clark W.)

CRANBERRY BARS

½ cup margarine	1½ cups rolled oats
¼ cup butter	2 (14 ounce) jars cranberry-orange relish
1 cup brown sugar	
1¾ cups flour	2 tablespoons cornstarch
½ teaspoon soda	2 teaspoons ground ginger
¾ teaspoon salt	1 cup chopped nuts

Cream margarine, butter and sugar. Add flour, soda and salt. Mix well. Stir in oats. Press half of crumb mixture into greased and floured 9″ x 13″ pan. Mix relish, cornstarch and ginger in saucepan over medium heat. Stirring constantly, bring to boil and cook one minute. Remove from heat. Add nuts and cool. Spread relish mixture over crumb mixture. Cover with remaining crumb mixture, pressing lightly. Bake at 400° for 25 minutes or until light brown. Cool and cut into bars. Makes 30 bars.

Cherry C. Rice (Mrs. William A., Jr.)

EASY SUGAR COOKIES

½ cup butter
½ cup cooking oil
½ cup sugar
½ cup powdered sugar
1 egg
1 teaspoon vanilla extract

2 cups flour
½ teaspoon baking powder
½ teaspoon cream of tartar
½ teaspoon salt
Additional sugar

Cream butter, oil and sugars. Add egg and vanilla. Sift together dry ingredients. Add to creamed mixture; mix well. Drop by teaspoonfuls onto cookie sheet. (May also let dough chill one hour and roll into walnut size balls.) Flatten cookie with a glass bottom dipped in sugar. Bake at 350° for 8 to 10 minutes. Makes 4 dozen 2½" cookies.

Brenda B. Jones (Mrs. Laurence G.)

SUGAR COOKIES

½ cup butter, softened
1 cup sugar
1 egg
2 tablespoons cream or
    milk

½ teaspoon vanilla extract
½ teaspoon salt
2 teaspoons baking powder
1½ cups flour

Combine butter, sugar, egg, cream and vanilla, beating until smooth. Mix remaining ingredients and beat into butter mixture. Chill 1 to 2 hours. Roll out to ⅛" to ¼" thickness on a floured surface. Cut with a cookie cutter into desired shapes. Sprinkle with sugar. Bake at 375° for 8 minutes. Remove with a spatula. Cool on wire rack. Yield: 2 to 3 dozen cookies.

Good used during different holidays cut into your favorite shapes and sprinkled with colored sugars.

Sallie P. Jefferds

SKILLET COOKIES

½ cup margarine
2 eggs
¾ cup sugar
1 (8 ounce) package
    chopped dates

1 teaspoon vanilla extract
2 cups rice krispies
½ cup chopped pecans
1 cup coconut (optional)

Melt margarine in skillet over low heat. Beat eggs and sugar together. Add to margarine. Add dates. Cook for 15 minutes, stirring constantly. Remove from heat. Stir in vanilla, rice krispies and nuts. When cool to touch, shape into balls. Roll in coconut. Makes 5 dozen cookies.

Rebecca K. Palmer (Mrs. John C., IV)

ENGLISH TOFFEE COOKIES

1 cup butter	1 teaspoon vanilla extract
1 cup packed brown sugar	Pinch of salt
1 egg yolk	6 to 8 Hershey bars
2 cups cake flour	½ to 1 cup chopped nuts

Cream butter and sugar. Add egg yolk, flour, vanilla and salt. Pat down very thin on a large greased cookie sheet or jellyroll pan. Bake at 375° for 15 minutes or until light brown. Remove from oven. Place Hershey bars on top. When bars are soft, spread with knife to cover. Sprinkle with chopped nuts. Let stand 15 minutes. Cut into squares.

Betsy C. Peterson

TOM THUMBS

1½ cups brown sugar, divided	2 eggs
½ cup butter	½ teaspoon baking powder
1 cup plus 2 tablespoons flour	¼ teaspoon salt
	1½ cups coconut
1 teaspoon vanilla extract	½ cup chopped pecans

Cream together ½ cup brown sugar, butter and 1 cup flour. Spread in bottom of greased 8″ square pan. Bake at 325° for 15 minutes. Mix together remaining 1 cup brown sugar, 2 tablespoons flour, vanilla, eggs, baking powder, salt, coconut and pecans. Spread over baked layer. Bake at 325° for 25 minutes. Cool and cut in squares. May also be served warm topped with ice cream.

Deborah L. Dent (Mrs. Robert E.)

VANILLEKIPFERL

8 tablespoons powdered sugar	1 cup unsalted butter
2 cups unbleached flour	2 tablespoons vanilla extract
1½ cups (½ pound) ground hazelnuts (also called filberts)	

VANILLA SUGAR

1 vanilla bean	1 (16 ounce) box powdered sugar

Combine sugar, flour and nuts. Cut in butter with pastry blender. Sprinkle vanilla over mixture. Knead to make dough. Divide into 4 equal parts. Roll each into a 10" long roll. Cut into 1" pieces. Roll each piece into a 2½" long cylinder. Bend into crescent shape and place on ungreased baking sheet. Bake at 350° for 15 minutes. Cool. Roll in vanilla sugar made by immersing a cut-up vanilla bean in tightly covered jar of powdered sugar. This is a traditional Austrian Christmas cookie. May be frozen. Freeze before rolling in vanilla sugar. Roll after defrosted. Makes 40 cookies.

Louise Wiseman

SODA CRACKER BARS
Taste like Heath Bars

Soda crackers
1 (12 ounce) package chocolate chips

1 cup butter or margarine
1 cup brown sugar

Line a 9" x 13" pan with aluminum foil. Place layer of soda crackers on bottom. (Do not need to break up.) Melt butter in a saucepan over medium heat. Add brown sugar. Bring to boil and simmer 3 to 5 minutes. Pour over crackers. Bake at 400° for 5 to 7 minutes. Soda crackers will melt. Remove from oven. Let stand 1 minute. Scatter chocolate chips over top, spreading as they melt to form frosting. Chill in refrigerator until hard. Break or cut into pieces.

Julie Meyers Seibert

BUCKEYES

2 cups powdered sugar
1½ cups peanut butter
½ cup butter, softened

1 (12 ounce) package semi-sweet chocolate chips
¼ of a quarter-pound stick paraffin

Combine sugar, peanut butter and butter to form dough. Roll into small bite-sized balls. Set aside. In microwave or in top of double boiler over hot water melt chocolate chips and paraffin. Using a toothpick, dip balls into chocolate mixture. Place on wax paper to cool. Store in airtight container. Makes 4 to 5 dozen.

Anne C. Kepple (Mrs. William)

CARAMELS
This recipe won a state fair ribbon in its category.

1 (16 ounce) bottle white
   corn syrup
Dash of salt
2 cups sugar
½ cup unsalted butter

1 (13 ounce) can evaporated
   milk
1 teaspoon vanilla extract
½ cup nuts (optional)

In heavy saucepan bring corn syrup, sugar and salt to boil. Reduce heat to medium high and stir constantly to crack stage (about 10 minutes). Add butter, allowing to melt completely. Add milk gradually, stirring until mixture thickens. Test in cup of cold water: the consistency it holds in water will be the consistency when cool. Pour into greased 9" x 13" pan. Cool and cut into pieces. Roll in waxed paper.

Roxanne Cullen Nelson

CHRISTMAS CARAMELS
"Made by my father every Christmas for 60 years."

1 cup sugar
¾ cup dark brown corn
   syrup
½ cup butter
1 cup light cream, divided

1 teaspoon vanilla extract
½ cup chopped nutmeats
   (black walnuts or
   pecans)

Combine sugar, corn syrup, butter and ½ cup cream in heavy, deep saucepan. Bring to boil over medium heat, stirring constantly. Add rest of cream. Cook slowly until candy reaches 244° (between soft ball and hard ball stage) for soft caramel. For brickle-like candy bring to hard ball stage. Remove from heat. Stir in vanilla and nutmeats. Pour into well buttered 9" square pan. When partially cool mark into squares. When cool cut into squares. Wrap each caramel in wax paper. May be dipped in chocolate before wrapping for variation.

Jo Silman

CARAMEL POPCORN

1 cup margarine
½ cup white corn syrup
2 cups brown sugar
1 teaspoon salt
¼ teaspoon cream of tartar

1 teaspoon soda
1½ cups Spanish peanuts
   (optional)
6 to 7 quarts popped
   popcorn

Combine butter, syrup and sugar in medium saucepan. Bring to boil over medium heat and cook for 6 minutes. Add cream of tartar, salt and soda. (Mixture will froth up.) Pour over popcorn in large bowl and mix well. Spread mixture on 2 lightly greased baking sheets. Bake at 200° for 40 minutes. Rotate cookie sheets on oven shelves after 20 minutes. Remove from sheets and add peanuts if desired.

Victoria R. Frisk (Mrs. Fred M., Jr.)

CHOCOLATE COCONUT BALLS

1 cup sweetened condensed milk
1 cup butter, melted
1 teaspoon vanilla extract
2 (16 ounces each) boxes powdered sugar
2 cups finely chopped pecans
3 cups flaked coconut
1 (12 ounce) package semi-sweet chocolate chips
¾ of a quarter pound piece paraffin

Combine first six ingredients. Blend until smooth. Chill overnight. Shape into nut size balls. Refrigerate until ready to dip. Melt chocolate chips and paraffin in top of a double boiler. Using toothpick dip each ball into chocolate mixture and place on wax paper. Cover toothpick hole with chocolate drip. Keep chocolate mixture very warm and thin. Keep balls cool. Makes 80 to 100 balls. Freezes well.

Brenda B. Jones (Mrs. Laurence G.)

CHRISTMAS HARD-TAC CANDY

2 cups sugar
1 cup water
⅔ cup light corn syrup
Food coloring
Powdered sugar

Flavoring: flavor oils - use 1 to 2 teaspoons
peanut butter - use 3 tablespoons
butter - use 2 tablespoons
cocoa - use 2 tablespoons

Combine sugar, water and corn syrup in saucepan over medium heat. Using candy thermometer, cook, stirring constantly, until temperature rises to 300°; hard crack stage. Add a few drops coloring and flavor of choice. Pour onto waxed paper or greased marble slab. When just cool to touch, cut into strips with kitchen scissors. Cut strips into bite size pieces. Dust with powdered sugar. Makes a nice Christmas gift displayed in a pretty glass jar.

Pamela Ann Hedrick

PEANUT CLUSTERS

1 (12 ounce) package
    butterscotch chips
1 (12 ounce) package semi-
    sweet chocolate chips

3 cups salted Spanish
    peanuts

In top of double boiler over hot water melt chocolate and butterscotch chips. Stir until smooth. (May be done in microwave.) Add peanuts and stir until well coated. Drop by rounded teaspoonfuls onto waxed paper lined cookie sheets. Chill. Makes 4 dozen clusters.

Sharon H. Hall (Mrs. William R.)

MICROWAVE PEANUT BRITTLE

1 cup sugar
½ cup white corn syrup
⅛ teaspoon salt
1 to 1½ cups Spanish pea-
    nuts or pecan halves

1 teaspoon margarine
1¼ teaspoons vanilla extract
1 teaspoon soda

Combine sugar, syrup and salt in a 1½ quart microwave dish. Cook on high 4 minutes. Stir in peanuts. Cook on high 4 minutes. Stir in margarine and vanilla. Cook on high 1 minute. Stir in soda until foamy and light in color. Pour onto a greased cookie sheet. Cool. Break into pieces.

Elizabeth H. Thomas (Mrs. Jeffrey B.)

PEANUT BUTTER FUDGE

4 cups sugar
¼ cup light corn syrup
¼ teaspoon salt
½ cup butter
1 cup evaporated milk

7 ounces marshmallow
    creme
1 cup peanut butter
1 teaspoon vanilla extract

In deep heavy saucepan combine butter, sugar, corn syrup, salt and milk. Cooking over medium heat, bring to hard, fast boil. Boil about 3 minutes. (If using candy thermometer boil until temperature reaches 230°.) Stir constantly. Remove from heat. Add marshmallow creme, peanut butter and vanilla. Beat until smooth. Pour into buttered 9" x 13" pan. Cool and cut into squares.

Dorothy Dean

VANILLA FUDGE

3 cups sugar
1 envelope unflavored
    gelatin
1 cup milk

½ cup light corn syrup
1¼ cups butter
2 teaspoons vanilla extract
1 cup chopped nuts

In large deep saucepan mix sugar and gelatin. Add milk, syrup and butter. Bring to boil over medium heat and cook without stirring until mixture reaches 238° on candy thermometer or soft ball stage. Remove from heat. Pour into mixing bowl and cool 15 minutes. Beat until thick. Stir in nuts. Spread into buttered 9″ square pan.

Virginia Miller

BEER NUTS

1 egg white
1 tablespoon water
12 to 16 ounces salted peanuts

½ cup sugar
1 tablespoon cinnamon

Beat egg white until frothy. Add water. Stir. Add peanuts. Stir until well coated. Blend sugar and cinnamon. Add to nut mixture, coating well. Spread on greased cookie sheet. Bake at 250° for 1 to 1¼ hours. Stir, turning nuts over, halfway through. Let set at room temperature 1 hour or until peanuts crisp up. Break up clumps. Store in airtight container.

Betsie M. Dobbs (Mrs. William F., Jr.,)

SUGAR AND SPICE NUTS

1 egg white
2½ tablespoons water
¾ cup sugar
1 teaspoon cinnamon
½ teaspoon salt

¼ teaspoon ground allspice
¼ teaspoon ground cloves
¼ teaspoon ground nutmeg
1 teaspoon vanilla extract
8 cups pecan halves

Beat egg whites with water until frothy. Add next 7 ingredients and mix well. Fold in pecan halves. Place on baking sheet. Bake at 275° for 55 minutes. Remove to waxed paper. Cool. Break into pieces. Store in airtight container.

Kay A. Smith (Mrs. William W.)

WEST VIRGINIA EXECUTIVE MANSION

The executive Mansion was planned and supervised by Charleston architect Walter F. Martens who was relatively young in his profession at the time and had not undertaken a project of such scope before. Mr. Martens went on to become one of the leaders in his profession throughout a long and illustrious career.

The Georgian Colonial architectural style was selected for the building and the design reflected the style in each meticulous detail. The front of the mansion has a central two-story portico with a dentiled pediment supported by four free standing and two engaged fluted columns of the Corinthian order. The capitols of the columns are decorated with ornate acanthus leaves. The arched entranceway frames a graceful fanlight above the door.

The walls are of red Harvard colonial brick laid in Flemish bond with black headers. A dentiled cornice runs around the building above the second floor below a brick parapet. The roof is Colonial mansard style interrupted with third floor dormers. Columned porches grace each side of the mansion. The east porch is open and the west porch enclosed but both are topped with flat roofs which serve as balconies onto which second floor end rooms open. Delicate open-pattern decorative wood railings enhance the balconies.

Inside the entrance door is a large entrance hall of checkered black Belgian and white Tennessee marble floor leading to dual Georgian staircases. The first floor has the formal drawing room, ballroom, State dining room, a sitting room and a library. Eight bedrooms and four baths, including the Governor's private quarters and family room, are located on the second floor, and the third floor houses two additional bedrooms.

The Executive Mansion was completed in 1924-25 in time for Governor Ephraim F. Morgan to occupy it for one week before his term ended. The enclosed gardens and garage were completed in 1926 and the third floor, although included in the original plan, was completed in 1946.

Photo by George H. Flowers

PICKLES AND PRESERVES

Peony

BREAD AND BUTTER PICKLES

5   quarts cucumbers, sliced
6   large white onions, sliced
2   green peppers, sliced
      (optional)
⅓   cup salt

5   cups sugar
1½ teaspoons turmeric
3   tablespoons pickling
      spices
3   cups cider vinegar

Chill first 3 ingredients on ice for 3 hours. Drain. Mix remaining ingredients. Combine with cucumbers, onions and green peppers. Bring to a boil. Pack immediately in hot sterile pint canning jars. Seal and process 10 minutes in a hot water bath. Yield: 10 pints.

Mrs. Russell Morris

BUTTERCHIP PICKLES

3¾ cups vinegar
3   cups sugar
3   tablespoons salt
4½ teaspoons celery seed

4½ teaspoons turmeric
¾ teaspoon mustard seed
12 cups sliced cucumbers

Mix first 6 ingredients. Bring to a boil. Boil for 5 minutes. Pack cucumbers in 6 sterilized hot pint jars. Pour hot syrup over cucumbers. Seal at once. Process in a hot water bath for 5 minutes.

Mary Lee W. Lilly (Mrs. J.K., III)

FOURTEEN DAY PICKLES

2 gallons cucumbers, sliced lengthwise	2 cups salt 1 tablespoon powdered alum

Days 1-7: Into a clean stone jar, place 2 gallons cucumbers, washed and sliced lengthwise. Regardless of size, they must be sliced or they will shrivel. Dissolve salt in 1 gallon boiling water. While hot, pour over cucumbers. Weight down, cover and let stand.

Day 8: Drain. Pour 1 gallon boiling water over cucumbers. Let stand 24 hours.

Day 9: Drain. Add alum to 1 gallon boiling water. Pour over cucumbers. Let stand 24 hours.

Day 10: Drain. Pour 1 gallon boiling water over cucumbers. Let stand 24 hours.

Day 11: Drain. Combine ingredients below for Pickling Mixture, using only 6 cups sugar. Add to cucumbers. Let stand 24 hours.

PICKLING MIXTURE

5 pints boiling vinegar	6 to 8 cinnamon sticks
9 cups sugar, divided	2 to 5 teaspoons cloves, optional
5 teaspoons celery seeds	

Day 12: Drain, reserve pickling mixture. Add 1 cup sugar to reserved liquid. Bring to a boil. Pour over pickles. Let stand 24 hours.

Day 13: Drain, reserve pickling mixture. Add 1 cup sugar. Reheat to boiling. Pour over pickles. Let stand 24 hours.

Day 14: Drain, reserve pickling mixture. Add 1 cup sugar. Heat to boiling. Pack pickles into hot, sterile pint canning jars. Cover with boiling pickling mixture. Seal at once. Process 5 minutes in a hot water bath.

Selina F. Cosby (Mrs. Lowell)

LAZY LADY PICKLES

7 cups sliced cucumbers	2 cups vinegar
1 cup sliced onions, separated into rings	1 tablespoon salt
½ cup sliced green peppers	1 tablespoon celery seed
2 cups sugar	1 tablespoon mustard seed (optional)

Mix all ingredients. Refrigerate. Full flavor is reached in 3 days to a week. Makes 4 pints.

Mary V. Gray

FROZEN PICKLES

8 cups cucumbers, thinly
   sliced
1 cup onion, thinly sliced
2 tablespoons salt

5 cups ice
2 cups sugar
1 teaspoon celery salt
1 cup apple cider vinegar

In a large bowl layer cucumbers, onions and salt. Cover with ice. Refrigerate 24 hours. Drain. Mix together sugar, celery salt, and vinegar. Add to cucumbers and onions. Divide and place in Ziploc freezer bags. Freeze at least 24 hours. After 24 hours, pickles may be thawed and eaten.

Diana H. Pettry (Mrs. Charles E., Jr.)

PICKLED HOT PEPPERS

2 cups water
  Whole hot peppers,
    enough to fill a quart
    jar

1 tablespoon salt
2 cups vinegar
2 teaspoons cooking oil

Boil water. Set aside to cool. Wash peppers. Place in a hot, sterile 1 quart canning jar. Add salt. Add cooled water and vinegar. Place lid on and seal jar. Sweet peppers may be prepared the same way, cutting peppers in quarters before placing in jar. To serve, take as many as needed from brine. Drain. Slice pepper, remove seeds and cut into bite size pieces. Add 2 teaspoons cooking oil per quart before serving. Yield: 1 quart. May be increased easily.

Mrs. Lena Panzera

SWEET AND SOUR BEETS

2 cups vinegar
2 cups water
2½ cups sugar
2 cinnamon sticks

1 tablespoon allspice
½ teaspoon ground cloves
1 teaspoon salt
3 quarts cooked beets

Combine vinegar, water and sugar. Bring to a boil. Add remaining ingredients and bring to a second boil. Remove from heat. Refrigerate, covered, overnight. The next day bring to a boil. Pack hot beets in sterilized jars. Cover with hot liquid. Seal immediately with sterilized lids and bands. Process in a hot water bath for 10 minutes.

Mrs. J.H. Geffken

MOM'S CORN SALAD

18 ears corn
1 head cabbage
4 medium onions
3 green peppers
1½ teaspoons ground pepper

2½ cups brown sugar
¼ cup mustard
¼ cup salt (or to taste)
2 quarts vinegar

Remove corn from cob. Chop corn, cabbage, onions and peppers. Add other ingredients. Bring to a boil in large pot. Simmer for 15 minutes. Ladle into 5 hot, sterile pint jars. Seal immediately. Process in hot water bath 10 minutes.

Kitty W. Atkins (Mrs. E. Garfield)

SEASONED TOMATO JUICE

Wash, core and quarter ripe tomatoes. Remove any bad places. Cook until soft. Run through food mill or purée. Measure juice. To 10 quarts of juice add:

2 tablespoons black pepper
10 tablespoons salt
1 heaping tablespoon celery salt
3 tablespoons garlic powder

3 tablespoons onion salt
¼ cup Worcestershire sauce
6 tablespoons seasoned salt
4 hefty shakes liquid smoke
   Tabasco sauce, if desired

Heat mixture. Place in hot, sterile jars. Seal with sterilized lids. Process in boiling water bath for 15 to 20 minutes.

Ann Wilcher (Mrs. Claude)

GRAPE CONSERVE

10 pounds Blue Concord grapes
1 pound seedless raisins
8 cups sugar

2 bags liquid pectin (or 1 bottle)
2 cups walnut meats

Squeeze pulp from hulls of grapes. Reserve hulls. Cook pulp slowly until seeds separate from pulp. Rub through sieve. Discard seeds. Combine seedless pulp, raisins, sugar and hulls. Put in a deep kettle to allow room for boiling. Bring to a full rolling boil and boil hard for one minute, stirring constantly. Should not be able to stir down. Remove from heat and add pectin, stirring for one minute.

Add nuts. Stir well. Skim off any foam on top. Ladle into hot sterilized jelly jars. Seal with sterile lids. Process in a hot water bath for 10 minutes. Makes approximately 16 cups of conserve.

Mrs. Clark Kessel

WILD GRAPE JELLY

1 pint wild grapes
6 cups water

1 box Sure-Jell
7 cups sugar

Prepare juice by removing grapes from stems. Wash. Cook water and grapes slowly until seeds separate from hulls. Strain through fine sieve. Discard seeds and hulls. Prepare jelly by bringing 5 cups juice to a boil. Add Sure-Jell or Certo. Stir and bring to a rolling boil. Boil for 1 minute. Add 7 cups sugar, all at once. Stir. Bring again to a rolling boil. Boil for 1 minute. Remove from heat. Skim film off top with a silver spoon. Discard film. Pour hot jelly into hot sterile jars. Seal with paraffin. Makes approximately 6 cups.

Mrs. Clark Kessel

PEACH FREEZER JAM

2 pounds fully ripened
      peaches
5 cups sugar
2 tablespoons lemon juice
1 teaspoon salt

1 teaspoon ascorbic acid
      mixture for fruit
1 (1¾ ounce) package fruit
      pectin
¾ cup water

Prepare five 8 ounce freezer safe or jelly glasses with tightfitting lids. Keep warm. Peel, pit and cut peaches into thin slices to make 2¼ cups of fruit. Place in a large bowl. With potato masher, thoroughly crush peaches. With rubber spatula stir in sugar, lemon juice, salt and ascorbic acid mixture. Mix well. Let stand 10 minutes. In a 1 quart saucepan over medium heat, heat fruit pectin and water to boiling. Boil for 1 minute, stirring constantly. Stir pectin mixture into fruit; continue stirring at least 3 minutes, no less. A few sugar crystals will remain. Pour peach mixture into containers to ½" from top. Cover with lids. Let stand at room temperature for 24 hours or until set. Freeze to use within 1 year or refrigerate to use within three weeks.

Maureen F. Galperin (Mrs. S.H., Jr.)

WILD HONEYSUCKLE JELLY

2 cups packed honeysuckle blossoms
Boiling water

Juice of 1 lemon
1 package Sure-Jell
4 cups sugar

Fill and pack a quart jar with flower blossoms. Cover with boiling water. Cap and let sit 1 to 2 days. Strain liquid, measuring 2 cups by reducing or adding water. Add lemon juice and Sure-Jell. Bring to a boil. Add sugar, all at once. Bring to a boil again and boil hard for 1 minute. Pour into hot sterile jelly glasses. Seal immediately.

Mrs. Laura A. McKenney

SELINA'S PEACH BUTTER

2 quarts peach pulp (about 18 medium ripe peaches)

3 to 4 cups sugar
1 teaspoon cinnamon
½ teaspoon ground cloves

Wash, scald (½ to 1 minute), peel, pit and chop peaches. Bring peaches to a boil. Cook 10 minutes until soft. Add only enough water to prevent sticking. Run through a blender, sieve or food mill. Measure pulp. Add sugar (using 1 cup sugar to 2 cups pulp) and spices. Mix well. Cook 30 minutes or until thick. Stir frequently. Pour into hot, sterile jars, leaving ½" head space. Adjust caps. Process pints and quarts for 10 minutes in boiling water bath. ½ bushel yields 21 pints.

Selina F. Cosby (Mrs. Lowell)

PEPPER JELLY

2 to 3 medium size bell peppers, green or red, with seeds and membrane removed
1 small hot pepper, seeds removed

1½ cups white vinegar
Red or green food coloring, optional
6 cups sugar
1 (6 ounce) bottle Certo

Cut peppers into chunks. Place peppers and vinegar in a food processor or blender, process until uniformly chopped. Add food coloring at this time. Green peppers may need a few drops of green coloring to make a pretty jelly. Enhance golden color of red peppers with red food coloring. Pour into a large pan. Stir in sugar. Bring to a medium boil, boil for 5 minutes. Remove from heat and add

Certo. Bring to a boil again. Remove from heat immediately, stirring constantly. Let rest for a few minutes, stirring occasionally to distribute pepper flakes evenly. Pour into hot, sterile jars. Seal with melted paraffin. Makes six ½ pint jars.

Nancy S. Cerutti (Mrs. John)

RHUBARB STRAWBERRY JAM

¾ pound rhubarb   6 cups sugar, divided
2 pints strawberries

Clean and trim rhubarb and strawberries. Dice rhubarb and place in a large stainless steel or enameled kettle. Mash strawberries and add 4 cups sugar. Mix well. Bring to a boil and cook for 4 minutes. Add remaining 2 cups sugar. Boil hard for 5 minutes. Remove from heat and skim foam off top. Place jelly in hot, sterile jars. Seal immediately with hot, sterile lids. Place in hot water bath for 10 minutes. Yield: 4 pints.

SHELLEY JAM

This jam is started in the spring and completed at the end of summer. Use in succession:

Rhubarb, chopped   Pears, chopped
Pineapple, chopped   Peaches, chopped
Strawberries, chopped   Apricots, chopped
Blackberries   Plums, chopped
Red and Black Rasp-   Sugar
    berries

Place 1 cup rhubarb and 1 cup sugar in a saucepan. Bring to a boil, simmering 10 to 15 minutes. Store in a large covered jar in refrigerator until the next fruit is in season. Each time, use 1 cup fruit to 1 cup sugar and boil 10 minutes. Stir into jar in refrigerator. When jam contains desired amount of fruit, place in a large kettle and boil for 10 minutes. Place in hot, sterile jars and seal immediately with lids. Process in a hot water bath for 10 minutes. May be used as jam or served over ice cream.

Carolyn G. Henshaw (Mrs. Harry P., III)

OLD FASHIONED CROUP REMEDY

"Given to my mother in 1954 by Mrs. C.A. Gross, Elkins, West Virginia."

1 large tablespoon Crisco	1 tablespoon coal oil
1 large onion, thinly sliced	1 tablespoon turpentine
1 block camphor	

Simmer onion and Crisco in an iron skillet until all the juice is out of the onion. Crush camphor in a bowl and strain the onion mixture through cheesecloth into the camphor. Add coal oil and turpentine. Stir well and cool. Place hot, wet cloths on chest to open pores. Apply remedy. Cover with a flannel cloth and leave on overnight. Wash off in the morning. NOT TO BE TAKEN INTERNALLY.

Katherine S. Cooper (Mrs. James T.)

GRANDMOTHER'S HOMEMADE TOILET SOAP

11 cups bacon grease	½ cup sugar
5 cups cold water	½ cup 20 Mule Team Borax
1 can Red Seal lye	4 teaspoons oil of sassafras
½ cup ammonia	

Note: Use a flat enamelware pan and a wooden spoon. If grease is salty, place in a kettle with cold water and bring to a boil. Let stand until cold, dip off grease, melt and strain.

Dissolve lye in water in an enamel pan. Add ammonia, sugar, borax and sassafras. Pour melted grease slowly in a small stream into lye mixture, stirring until creamy. Let stand in a warm place for 24 hours. Cut into squares, wrap in wax paper. Let stand 2 weeks before using.

Caroline C. Nelson

THE TRAIN STATION

Those who remember the days of puffing, cinder-throwing, hard driving steam locomotives must be stricken with an almost unbearable nostalgia when they see this photograph of the Cabin Creek Junction Chesapeake and Ohio Railway Company passenger station.

There is a low-pitched roof with its wide overhang, tall windows, wood siding with corner boards and horizontal banding, and five-panel doors. This station and other visible C. & O. yard buildings reflect a once ubiquitous architectural styling which characterized the railway company buildings.

Seen also is switching apparatus, signal lights, a watering spout, a great steam engine, and the inevitable spur line curving away from the main tracks reaching up the hollow to tap the rich coal resources.

The C. & O. was completed through West Virginia in 1873. Soon coal men were opening coal mines and building towns around the mines. At first the company town was an absolute necessity in southern West Virginia coal fields, since the mines were located in remote areas of rugged mountain country. The miners lived in company houses, shopped in the company store, and attended company churches and schools. The railroad was the only transportation link with the outside world, thus every train arrival was an event and the station was a center of activity.

Life was hard in the old towns but the reminiscences of the people tend not to concentrate on their problems, but on the good things. The company town was a good place to grow up, they say. They did not have much but they learned appreciation. They talk about the games and ballfield, local dances, socializing around the company store, taking the train to a town, going to church, and family gatherings. Miners and their families were engaged in a difficult occupation in a remote corner of the world, and they made the most of it. It is certain that the picture of a little train station at the end of the hollow will bring some smiles.

Photo courtesy of Charleston Newspapers

BEVERAGES

Double T

HOT APRICOT NECTAR

1 cup water
2 tablespoons sugar
4 whole cloves
1 (3" length) cinnamon
    stick

1 (12 ounce) can apricot
    nectar
2 tablespoons lemon juice
    Cinnamon sticks
      (optional)
    Lemon slices (optional)

Combine first 4 ingredients in a saucepan. Bring to a boil. Simmer, stirring until sugar is dissolved. Strain mixture, discarding cloves and cinnamon stick. Gradually add apricot nectar and lemon juice to hot mixture. Heat thoroughly. This recipe may be doubled or tripled. A lemon slice and cinnamon stick may be added to each serving. Serves 4.

Beverly S. McElroy (Mrs. William B.)

CHILDREN'S ORANGE SLUSH

1 (6 ounce) can frozen
    orange juice
¾ cup water
¾ cup milk

1 teaspoon vanilla extract
1 tablespoon powdered
    sugar
7 to 9 ice cubes

Combine all ingredients in a blender. Blend on high until slushy - approximately 1 minute. Serves 6 to 8.

Mary T. Karr (Mrs. George W.)

HOT APPLE CIDER PUNCH

2 quarts apple cider or juice
1 cup apricot nectar
1 cup orange juice
¼ teaspoon ground cloves

½ teaspoon ground cinnamon
Lemon slices
Orange slices

Combine all ingredients except fruit slices. Heat slowly, stirring occasionally. Garnish with lemon and orange slices. Serves 10 to 12.

Beverly S. McElroy (Mrs. William B.)

PAM'S COFFEE PUNCH

14 tablespoons ground coffee
8 cups water
2½ cups sugar
3 quarts half and half

2 teaspoons vanilla extract
1½ teaspoons nutmeg
¼ teaspoon salt
½ gallon vanilla ice cream

Combine coffee (not instant) and water in percolator or drip pot to make strong coffee. Dissolve sugar in 2 cups of hot coffee. Set aside to cool. Make 2 trays of ice cubes from strong coffee. Combine all other ingredients with cooled coffee. Stir until ice cream has completely melted. Add coffee ice cubes to punch bowl just before serving. Serves 12 to 15.

Vicki M. Cunningham (Mrs. Jan)

SPARKLING LIME PUNCH

1 (3 ounce) package lime
   gelatin
3 cups pineapple juice
1 (6 ounce) can frozen
   lemonade, thawed

10 (16 ounces each) bottles
   lemon-lime soda,
   divided

Heat 1 cup pineapple juice until boiling. Dissolve gelatin in boiling juice. Add remaining juice and lemonade. Blend well. Chill. Pour 2 bottles of lemon-lime soda into a ring mold. Freeze to make an ice ring. Before serving add remaining 8 bottles of soda to chilled fruit juice base, mixing well. Serve punch in a large bowl. Float ice ring in the center. Serves 20 to 30.

Bonnie G. O'Neal (Mrs. Richard)

PASTEL SHERBET CREAM PUNCH

2½ cups pineapple juice,
    chilled
1 pint lime, lemon or
    raspberry sherbet

1 pint vanilla ice cream
1 (12 ounce) bottle club
    soda, chilled

Combine juice, sherbet and ½ the ice cream. Beat until smooth; add soda. Just before serving spoon remaining ice cream into punch. Serve immediately. Serves 12 to 14.

Sandra W. Mantz (Mrs. Eric P.)

SPARKLING ICED TEA

2 quart-size tea bags
3 quarts boiling water
½ cup sugar

1 (12 ounce) can frozen
    lemonade
1 quart ginger ale

Add tea bags to boiling water. Steep to desired strength. Add remaining ingredients, stirring well. Stores well in refrigerator for several days. Yield: 4 quarts.

Sally W. Preston (Mrs. James C., Jr.)

TOMATO JUICE COCKTAIL

1 (46 ounce) can tomato
    juice
Rind of 1 lemon, grated
Juice of 2 lemons
3 tablespoons sugar

1 teaspoon celery seed
1 teaspoon salt
½ teaspoon Worcestershire
    sauce

Combine all ingredients. Refrigerate 24 hours before serving. Serves 6 to 8.

Sally M. Rowe (Mrs. C. Tom)

TAILGATE BLOODY MARY'S

1 (46 ounce) can V-8 juice
1½ cups vodka
Juice of ½ lemon

1 teaspoon celery salt
Tabasco to taste

Combine all ingredients. Serve over ice. Can easily be doubled or tripled. Serves 10.

Sara Z. Hoblitzell (Mrs. John R.)

BRANDY ALEXANDERS

1 pint French vanilla ice
    cream
¼ cup brandy

¼ cup créme de cacao
Nutmeg and chocolate
    shavings

Combine first 3 ingredients in a blender. Blend on high until smooth. Pour into champagne glasses. Garnish with nutmeg and chocolate shavings. Serves 4.

GRASSHOPPERS

Following the recipe for Brandy Alexanders substitute créme de menthe for the créme de cacao. Serves 4.

ALMOST HEAVENS

Following the recipe for Brandy Alexanders substitute Kahlua and Amaretto for the brandy and créme de cacao.

Sara Z. Hoblitzell (Mrs. John R.)

INDIVIDUAL IRISH COFFEE

1 jigger Irish whiskey
2 teaspoons sugar

Strong black coffee
Whipped cream

Pour one jigger Irish whiskey into a warm glass mug. Add sugar. Fill glass with hot black coffee, stirring to dissolve sugar. Serve topped with whipped cream.

Paula W. Flaherty (Mrs. Thomas V.)

PEACH BRANDIED CREAM

3 fresh peaches, peeled
    and sliced

1 quart vanilla ice cream
3 to 4 ounces peach brandy

Combine all ingredients in a blender. Process until smooth. Serves 8 to 10.

Sue Hancock Miller

PEACH FIZZ

6 fresh peaches, peeled
  and sliced
1 (6 ounce) can frozen
  lemonade

¾ cup gin
½ tray ice cubes, crushed

Combine all ingredients in a blender. Blend and serve. Serves 6.

Kay J. Morgan (Mrs. Frederick M.)

POLAR BEAR

1 pint vanilla ice cream
1½ cups milk

½ cup Kahlua

Combine all ingredients in a blender. Blend and serve. Serves 4 to 6.

Connie B. Stewart (Mrs. David L.)

HOT TOM AND JERRY
A sweet rum flavored drink

2 (16 ounces each) boxes
  dark brown sugar
½ teaspoon cinnamon
½ teaspoon ground cloves

½ teaspoon nutmeg
1 cup butter, melted
3 ounces rum

Mix brown sugar with spices. Blend in butter and rum. Serve one heaping tablespoon of rum mixture to one mug of hot water. Leftover mix may be refrigerated and reused.

Charlotte D. Stallard (Mrs. Troy F.)

VELVET HAMMER

3 to 4 large scoops vanilla
  ice cream
1 ounce brandy

⅛ ounce banana liqueur
⅛ ounce orange-flavored
  liqueur (such as Grand
  Marnier)

Combine all ingredients in a blender. Process until milkshake consistency. A good after dinner drink that can take the place of a more elaborate dessert at a dinner party. The amounts are easily increased. Serves 2.

Tia C. McMillan (Mrs. Robert A.)

GERMAN WINE PUNCH
Nice for a brunch

2   ripe peaches, peeled and
      sliced
1½ cups strawberries, hulled

¾   cup orange-flavored
      liqueur
½   gallon chilled white wine

Place peaches and strawberries in a bowl. Pour orange liqueur over fruit. Let stand 2 hours. To serve, gently stir in white wine. Serve in wine goblets. Frozen peaches may be substituted. Serves 4 to 6.

Barbara S. Wilkerson (Mrs. Thomas S.)

SANGRIA

1   gallon red wine
      (Burgundy or
      Zinfandel)
1   quart orange juice
1   cup lemon juice
½   cup sugar

½   cup brandy
¼   cup triple sec
1   quart club soda
2   oranges, sliced
2   lemons, sliced

Chill first 6 ingredients. Add soda and fruit just before serving. May be increased for large parties. Serves 20.

Donna L. Dean (Mrs. Rodney D.)

WHITE SANGRIA

1   lemon, sliced
1   orange, sliced
1   lime, sliced
¼   cup sugar
½   cup brandy (optional)

1   cup strawberries, hulled
      and halved
½   gallon Chablis wine
1½ cups club soda, chilled

Combine first 5 ingredients in a large pitcher. With a wooden spoon bruise or mash citrus fruit to release juices. Stir in strawberries and wine, mixing well. Chill 2 to 3 hours. At serving time add club soda. Serves 8.

Nancy S. Cerutti (Mrs. John H.)

SLUSH

1 fifth vodka
4 (6 ounces each) cans
      frozen lemonade
2½ cups water

1 (32 ounce) bottle 7-Up
1 (32 ounce) bottle
      cranapple juice

Combine all ingredients in a large container. Freeze for 2 days stirring several times. Spoon into wine glasses. Serves 20 to 30.

Louise C. Christensen (Mrs. David)

STRAWBERRY PINEAPPLE CHAMPAGNE PUNCH

1 fresh pineapple
2 cups sugar
¾ cup lemon juice
1 (6 ounce) can frozen
      grapefruit juice

1½ quarts ice water
1 quart fruit: strawberries,
      peaches and/or bananas
2 fifths champagne, chilled

Peel, core and cut pineapple into bite size pieces. Combine with the next 3 ingredients. Refrigerate 2 hours. Pour mixture over ice. Mix in water. Add fruit and champagne just before serving. Serves 18 to 20.

Marta D. MacCallum (Mrs. Daniel)

CABIN CREEK QUILTS

"Cabin Creek Quilts Cooperative was formed in 1970 with the help of Volunteers in Service to America (VISTA). In the 11 years since that time, our membership has grown from five to approximately 100 skilled artisans, and the cooperative has achieved national recognition. Our quilts have won national awards, are accepted into the best of American craft shows and juried exhibitions, and are sold in shops from Maine to California.

Still, we remain a rural cottage industry. Cabin Creek Quilts products are handmade by individuals, in their homes, in seven West Virginia counties. Our cooperative is owned and managed by women, and every one of our members takes pride in her work.

Each Cabin Creek quilt is made by two women. The piecing of the top is done by a member who specializes in the particular pattern, and likewise, the quilting is done by another member skilled in "finishing" that quilt. All our quilts have a double thickness of polyester batting, for warmth and durability.

The last and simplest task our members perform when making a quilt is to sign the tag. Look for the signature—we feel it reflects the individuality and pride that goes into every Cabin Creek quilt."

Photo by William J. Wykle

RESTAURANTS

Schoolhouse

BAVARIAN INN AND LODGE

Overlooking the Potomac River in the Eastern panhandle of West Virginia, Shepherdstown's Bavarian Inn specializes in German-Bavarian cuisine. From a small inn established seven years ago, it has grown to seat 300 today. The Inn also offers three new Bavarian cottages with 27 rooms. Entrees are hearty without being heavy, and the prices are moderate. These features contribute to a picturesque place to stay and a delicious place to eat.

BAVARIAN INN'S SAUERBRATEN

4 pound rump roast	1 carrot, sliced
1½ cups red wine vinegar	2½ tablespoons shortening
3 cups water	¼ cup sugar
1 medium onion, sliced	¼ cup flour
3 tablespoons whole mixed spice	2 gingersnaps
1 tablespoon salt	½ cup red wine

Mix vinegar, water, onion, spice, salt and carrot in glass, enamel or earthenware bowl. Under refrigeration, pickle meat in this brine 3 to 4 days, turning several times. Drain meat and wipe dry, reserving brine. Grease heavy roasting pan with shortening. Sear meat on both sides. Add part of marinade, cover tightly and roast at 300° for 1½ hours, basting occasionally. When meat is almost done sprinkle with sugar. Roast 5 to 10 minutes more, turning meat while roasting until sugar is dissolved. Thicken remaining marinade with flour and crushed gingersnaps to make gravy. Pour over meat. Roast an additional ½ hour or until gravy is creamy and thick. Remove meat, cool slightly and slice to serve. Stir wine into gravy, strain and serve over meat. Serves 8.

POTATO DUMPLINGS

3 pounds potatoes	1½ teaspoons salt
5 egg yolks	½ teaspoon grated nutmeg
6 tablespoons cornstarch	1 cup small croutons
¼ teaspoon pepper	½ cup flour

Boil potatoes until soft enough to mash. Peel and let stand in refrigerator overnight to dry. Mash potatoes. Add other ingredients except croutons and flour, mixing well. Shape into balls. Stuff 2 croutons into middle of each. Roll slightly in flour. Cook in rapidly boiling salted water for 15 to 20 minutes. Remove from water. Serve immediately. Serves 8.

BERRY HILLS COUNTRY CLUB

Combining gracious dining with challenging golf amid a spectacular ridgetop setting deep in the hills of southern West Virginia, Berry Hills is a private family-oriented country club chartered in 1950. The golf course is recognized as one of West Virginia's five best and has been the site of numerous West Virginia amateur and professional tournaments, currently playing host to the West Virginia University Classic Golf Tournament.

CHOCOLATE MOUSSE

4 ounces semi-sweet chocolate	½ cup unsalted butter, melted
4 ounces unsweetened chocolate	6 eggs, separated
2 tablespoons plus 1 teaspoon water	2 tablespoons Meyer's dark rum
¼ cup powdered sugar	½ teaspoon vanilla
	3 tablespoons sugar

Melt chocolate and water together in top of double boiler over hot water. Add powdered sugar, then butter. Mix thoroughly. Set aside. Beat egg yolks 7 to 10 minutes until they form a thick ribbon. Fold in rum and vanilla. Set aside. Quickly (time is essential to reduce deflation of egg yolk mixture), beat egg whites until foamy, add sugar and beat until stiff peaks form. Fold chocolate mixture into egg yolk mixture, mixing thoroughly. Fold egg-chocolate mixture into egg white mixture by first incorporating ¼ of the egg white mixture into egg-chocolate mixture and then adding egg-chocolate mixture to egg whites. Take care to fold ingredients lightly; too much mixing can cause a heavy mousse. Pour into individual ramekin dishes. Freeze 6 hours or longer. Garnish with whipped cream and a chocolate leaf or candied violet. Remove from freezer a short time before serving. Serves 8.

SHRIMP A LA CHINOISE

1 pound uncooked jumbo
   shrimp, shelled
¼ cup sugar
½ cup white wine
2 tablespoons soy sauce
1 tablespoon ground ginger
   or to taste

2 cloves garlic, crushed
½ cup sliced water
   chestnuts
1 cup fresh snow peas,
   snap peas or pea pods

Combine sugar, wine, soy sauce, ginger and garlic in large skillet or wok. Heat until boiling and sugar is dissolved. Add shrimp and sauté until shrimp is partially cooked and most of the liquid is evaporated. Quickly add snow peas and water chestnuts. Stir until mixture is heated through, being careful not to overcook. Vegetables should remain brightly colored and crisp. Serve over steamed rice. Serves 4.

COIRE TAIGH

Located in Romney, the Coire Taigh provides diners with warm hospitality in a congenial atmosphere. In a building that also has a natural food store, a book store and a crafts center, the restaurant serves lunch and dinner in a relaxed setting of country decor with local artists' works displayed on the walls.

POPOVERS

4 eggs
2 cups milk
1 cup all-purpose white
   flour

1 cup all-purpose whole
   wheat flour
½ teaspoon salt

Preheat oven to 450°. Butter popover pans and place in oven to heat. Slightly beat eggs. Add milk, beating slightly. Stir in flour and salt. (Note: do not beat excessively; too much air in batter results in poor popovers.) Remove popover pans from oven. Quickly fill pans to ¼" from top, pouring directly from batter bowl. Place immediately in oven. Bake at 450° for 20 minutes. Reduce heat to 350° and bake 18 to 20 minutes more.

Caution: Popovers must be protected from top heat. The batter begins the popping process as soon as it hits the pans, therefore speed is essential. Iron popover pans are the best; do not substitute with aluminum muffin pans.

THE CHILTON HOUSE

Come back to the days of glorious and gracious dining at the Chilton House and its 19th century setting. Listed on the National Register of Historic Places, the Chilton House (c. 1849) is alive with fine cuisine, elegant antiques and museum art offering an ambience that is unsurpassed in the Charleston area.

CLASSIC ITALIAN WEDDING SOUP

This recipe, exclusive to the Chilton House, originated at least 5 generations ago in Naples, Italy, and is a house favorite. Preparation time is approximately 4 hours using homemade stock, 1½ hours using instant bouillon.

CHICKEN STOCK

1 whole 3 to 4 pound fryer
4 quarts water
1 tablespoon salt
1 teaspoon black pepper
1 stalk celery
1 whole carrot
1 onion, halved
Bouquet garni: parsley, marjoram, basil and bay leaf

Place chicken in large stockpot and cover with water. Add rest of ingredients. Simmer 2½ to 3 hours, replacing evaporated water with boiling water. Strain stock. When chicken cools, pick meat from bones, chop into small pieces and return to stock. Keep stock simmering.

FILLING FOR SOUP

GARLIC MEATBALLS

½ pound ground chuck
¼ cup Italian bread crumbs
1 egg, beaten
1 tablespoon minced parsley
2 small cloves garlic, chopped finely
Salt and pepper to taste
3 tablespoons olive oil

Combine all ingredients except olive oil in a bowl. Roll into marble size meatballs. Brown in olive oil. Add to stock.

ENDIVE CHEESE MIXTURE

1 pound curly endive or fresh spinach
1 cup grated Parmesan or Romano cheese
3 eggs

Rinse endive and blanch 15 to 20 minutes in boiling water. Cool. squeeze out excess water, chop fine and add to stock. Whisk eggs with cheese in small bowl until smooth. Add to simmering stock and continue to simmer ½ hour to combine flavors. Serve with crusty French or Italian Bread. Serves 12 to 15.

THE CONTINENTAL KEY CLUB

A part of Tiffany's Restaurant in Fairmont, The Continental Key Club is the domain of Joe Sestito, well-known local culinary expert. The emphasis of Continental Key Club revolves around fine food with an intimate dining atmosphere. One should be prepared to spend an entire evening enjoying the delicious fare which includes many Italian dishes and excellent seafood.

SPINACH SALAD

1 pound fresh spinach	3 slices of cooked, crisp bacon, diced
½ cup cooking oil	¼ cup grated Parmesan cheese
½ cup vinegar	
Dash of garlic powder	¼ cup croutons
Dash of salt	Dash of Worcestershire sauce
Dash of freshly ground pepper	2 large fresh mushrooms, sliced
1 coddled egg*	

After washing spinach thoroughly, dry each leaf with paper towels. Place in large salad bowl. Toss with oil and vinegar. Add garlic powder, salt and pepper. Toss gently, adding egg. Toss with bacon, cheese, croutons and Worcestershire sauce. Garnish with sliced mushrooms.

(*Ed. note: to prepare a coddled egg place egg in boiling water, turn off heat and cover the pan for 6 minutes. Plunge egg immediately into cold water. Peel egg. Very fresh eggs are more difficult to peel.)

BAKED OYSTERS ROCKEFELLER

36 fresh oysters on the halfshell	2 tablespoons finely chopped celery
6 tablespoons butter	½ teaspoon salt
10 tablespoons finely minced raw spinach	10 tablespoons bread crumbs
	2 teaspoons paprika
3 tablespoons chopped scallions	Freshly grated Parmesan cheese
2 tablespoons minced parsley	Tabasco to taste
½ cup dry white wine	Lemon wedges

Melt butter in saucepan. Add spinach, scallions, parsley, wine, celery and salt. Cook, stirring constantly, for 10 minutes. Press through fine sieve or food mill. Place oysters in baking dish with a spoonful of sauce on each one. Sprinkle with bread crumbs, cheese and paprika. Bake at 425° until brown. Serve on rock salt or hot platters with lemon wedges and Tabasco on the side. Serves 6 as a first course.

BOSTON SCROD OREGANA

Olive oil or corn oil
2 pounds fresh fillet of
  scrod, cod, haddock or
  white fish
½ teaspoon salt
½ cup dry white wine
Juice of 1 lemon
2 tablespoons fresh minced
  parsley

1 cup dry Italian bread
  crumbs
1 tablespoon oregano
2 cloves garlic, minced
2 scallions, minced
1 cup water
½ cup butter, melted
Lemon slices for garnish
Salt and pepper to taste

Coat a large shallow baking dish with olive oil or corn oil. Arrange fish in 1 layer in a baking dish. Salt lightly and brush with oil. Sprinkle with white wine and lemon juice. Combine parsley, bread crumbs, oregano, garlic and scallions. Spread over fish. Add 1 cup of water, spooning it over bread crumb coating. Add melted butter over bread crumbs. Bake at 400° for 15 to 20 minutes. Place slices of peeled lemons over fish and dot with butter. Can be served moist or well browned as preferred. Serves 4.

BAKED LEMON SOLE FLORENTINE

1½ pounds fresh spinach
2 tablespoons chopped
  onion
1 garlic clove, crushed
2 tablespoons butter
2 tablespoons chopped
  parsley

Pinch of nutmeg
1 ounce lemon juice
1 cup seafood bisque (or
  mornay sauce), divided
1 pound fillet of sole
⅓ to ½ cup Parmesan
  cheese

Blanch spinach in boiling water for 2 minutes. Drain and chop. Saute onion and garlic in butter. Add spinach, parsley, nutmeg and lemon juice. Continue cooking until spinach is done, approximately 3 minutes. Add ½ cup bisque. Place spinach mixture in a casserole, cover with sole, top with remaining bisque and Parmesan cheese. Bake at 450° for 10 minutes.

COOLFONT RE'CREATION

Coolfont Conference Center, just outside Berkeley Springs, offers a family vacation environment as well as a health spa. A natural wood and stone lodge houses the restaurant. Activities include nature walks, swimming and tennis, as well as a fitness program. In May the annual Strawberry Festival takes place nearby with craftspeople, musicians and fleamarkets. Below are some of their suggested low cal, healthful recipes.

EGGPLANT PARMESAN

1 large eggplant
8 ounces sliced Mozzarella cheese
8 ounce jar low cal, no salt spaghetti sauce

Garlic powder to taste
Onion powder to taste
Low cal Italian dressing
3 tablespoons Parmesan cheese

Peel eggplant and slice in thin slices. Alternate layers of eggplant and cheese in baking dish. Cover with spaghetti sauce and season to taste with garlic powder, onion powder and Italian dressing. Sprinkle with Parmesan cheese. Bake at 350° until eggplant is soft when pierced with a knife. Serves 4.

LOW CAL PIZZA

4 pockets Pita bread
8 ounces Mozzarella cheese

1 (8 ounce) can sliced mushrooms
2 cups Roma sauce

Split pita pockets into circles one layer thick. Cover each with Mozzarella cheese, sliced mushrooms and 3 tablespoons Roma Sauce. Broil until cheese melts and corners of bread are crisp.

ROMA SAUCE

2 (2 ounces each) jars chopped pimento
1 small bay leaf
2 teaspoons lemon juice

1 cup tomato juice
1 (4 ounce) can mushrooms
¼ teaspoon oregano
Paprika to taste

Combine ingredients. Cover and simmer 20 minutes. Remove bay leaf. This sauce is also good combined with 2 cups diced eggplant sprinkled with 2 teaspoons lemon juice. Cover and simmer 20 minutes as above.

COUNTRY ROAD INN

Mrs. E.J. Jarroll, proprietor of the Country Road Inn, calls on her Italian heritage in preparing a wide array of appetizers and homemade pasta. A Civil War era country farm house near Zela is a friendly setting for a leisurely and generously served dinner. Diners are warned not to fill up too soon as dessert brings a tray of homemade pies, cakes and the house specialty—Coffee Tortoni. (The recipe for Coffee Tortoni is included in our first book, Mountain Measures.)

SAUSAGE, ONIONS, AND PEPPERS

1 pound Country Road Inn
   Hot or Mild Italian
   Sausage

½ cup sliced onion
½ cup sliced green peppers
½ cup tomato sauce

Slowly cook sausage in a small amount of water. Drain off fat. Add sliced onions and peppers. Cook slowly with tomato sauce until tender. May be served as a main dish or on a hot toasted bun with cheese. Serves 4.

EDGEWOOD COUNTRY CLUB

High on a hill overlooking Charleston, Edgewood Country Club, chartered in 1898, has the distinction of being the oldest private country club in the state of West Virginia. The elegant white columned clubhouse, built in 1936 after a fire destroyed an earlier building, serves as the focal point for golf, tennis and social activities for many Charlestonians as well as being a popular gathering spot for lunch and dinner.

CHICKEN A LA EDGEWOOD

4 chicken halves
   Dijon mustard
   Bacon bits
1 cup water

2 tablespoons flour
1 chicken bouillon cube
1 teaspoon parsley, chopped
   Dash of thyme

Wash and pat dry chicken halves. Place in baking pan. Brush generously with Dijon mustard. Sprinkle with bacon bits. Bake at 400° for 1 hour or until tender. Remove from pan and keep warm. Strain juices from pan into heavy saucepan. Add 1 cup water to baking pan, strain into separate container and reserve. Add flour to juices in saucepan, stirring to make thin paste. Cook over medium heat one minute. Add other liquid, chicken bouillon cube, parsley and thyme. Stirring constantly, bring to boil and cook until thick. Add more water if necessary to bring to desired consistency. Pour sauce over chicken. Serves 4, allowing ½ chicken per person. Recipe may be increased or decreased easily.

ERNIE'S ESQUIRE SUPPER CLUB

Ernie's Esquire in Charleston, brings to mind fine dining in an elegant and congenial atmosphere. Over the years many individual specialties have been featured: Ernie's Hot Coquille, Sweetbreads and Steak Diane. Recently three new well-received entrees have been added: Veal Esquire, Shellfish with Pasta and Red Snapper Veracruzano.

STEAK DIANE

2 (8 ounce) filets, seasoned with salt and pepper	4 dashes Worcestershire sauce
6 tablespoons garlic butter*	1 teaspoon Dijon mustard
8 tablespoons sliced fresh mushrooms	2 large pats butter
1 teaspoon chopped chives	2 ounces brandy
2 tablespoons chopped green onion	¾ cup Bordelaise sauce**
1 teaspoon chopped parsley	2 ounces dry red wine
	2 ounces cream

*Mix softened butter with 2 to 3 cloves crushed garlic.

Split filets in half. Set aside. In large hot skillet melt garlic butter. Add mushrooms, chives, green onion and parsley. Simmer 2 to 3 minutes. Stir in Worcestershire and Dijon mustard. Move vegetables to one side. Add 2 pats butter and melt. Add seasoned filets, sear on both sides and cook until one step below desired doneness. Add brandy and flame. Move meat to side of skillet. Add Bordelaise sauce and wine. Simmer until hot. Stir in cream to thicken sauce. Move meat and vegetables back into sauce and cook until meat reaches desired doneness. Serve immediately. Suggested accompaniments: blended rice and a sherry glass of sour sherbet. Serves 2.

**(Editor's note: Bordelaise sauce may be made as follows: Simmer 2 minced shallots in ½ cup dry red wine until reduced by ¾. Add 1 cup quick brown sauce made by combining 2 tablespoons butter and 2 tablespoons flour in skillet, cooking 2 minutes until smooth and bubbly. Stir in 1 cup beef bouillon and cook until slightly thickened. Season with ½ teaspoon lemon juice and ½ teaspoon chopped parsley.)

THE GREENBRIER

Recipient of the Mobil 5 Star Award, the world renowned Greenbrier Hotel is located in White Sulphur Springs. The historic resort has a tradition of fine food and excellent service and now offers The Greenbrier Cooking School for guests as part of its wintertime program. A stay at The Greenbrier will become a cherished memory.

CHOPPED CHICKEN LIVERS
A Chicken Liver Paté

1 pound chicken livers
1 cup butter
3 small onions
⅔ cup medium sherry

1 jigger (about 2 ounces) brandy
½ cup heavy cream
Salt, freshly ground pepper to taste

Chop onions and sauté in butter until golden. Add the chicken livers and sherry; simmer on low heat, covered, for ½ hour. Chill until butter is solidified before proceeding to next step. Place cooled ingredients in a food processor; add remaining ingredients and blend until very smooth. Season to taste. Chill again before serving.

It is important to add the brandy and the seasoning after the cooking. "Sherry to stew, brandy to finish," is the adage. The sherry and brandy combine to mellow (take some of the sharpness from the edges) the chicken liver. This is an excellent canape spread on either Melba toast or crackers. You may also put into pastry bag and pipe out to serve as an appetizer with onion and tomato wedge on a lettuce leaf. Yield: 2¾ cups. As dinner appetizer: 10 to 12 servings.

BACKFIN CRAB MEAT MAYO

1 pound fresh backfin crab meat
1 tablespoon lemon juice
Salt to taste
Freshly ground black pepper to taste

½ cup mayonnaise
¼ cup sour cream
Finely grated horseradish to taste

Pick over chilled crab meat. Discard any bits of shell or cartilage. Season with lemon juice, salt and half of the pepper. Gently fold in mayonnaise, sour cream and horseradish. Place in a bowl and sprinkle remainder of pepper over the top. Serve with Melba toast or crackers. Yield: 2 cups.

RACK OF LAMB "GREENBRIER"

2 French trimmed racks of lamb, 2½ pounds for both	2 eggs
2 tablespoons cooking oil	1 tablespoon Poupon mustard
1 pinch rosemary	½ cup butter, melted
1 pinch garlic	1 cup red wine
6 slices white bread with crust removed	1 cup brown sauce*
½ cup loosely packed parsley sprigs	1 tablespoon fresh, chopped tarragon

Heat oil in skillet and brown lamb racks well. Place fat side down, sprinkle with garlic and rosemary and place in 475° oven for 5 minutes. Remove lamb from oven. Place bread and parsley in food processor. Chop to fine bread crumbs. In separate bowl, whip eggs and mustard together; add melted butter slowly while whipping. Dip lamb into egg mixture; loosely coat with bread crumb mixture. (Reserve skillet for use later). Place lamb on a rack in a baking dish. Bake at 400° to desired doneness. Pour excess fat from skillet and deglaze pan with red wine. Reduce to one-half volume. Add brown sauce and tarragon; bring to simmer. Adjust seasoning and serve with carved lamb. Serves 4.

*(Ed. note: A quick brown sauce may be made as follows: Combine 2 tablespoons butter and 2 tablespoons flour in a skillet, cooking 2 minutes until smooth and bubbly. Stir in 1 cup beef bouillon and cook until slightly thickened.)

ROAST DUCKLING WITH BURGUNDY AND PEACH SAUCE

1 (4 pound) duckling, seasoned and trussed	1 cup Burgundy wine
2 tablespoons cooking oil	1 cup brown sauce*
6 tablespoons brown sugar	2 whole, peeled peaches, (sliced thinly)
½ teaspoon red wine vinegar	2 tablespoons brandy

Heat oil in heavy skillet and brown breasts of duck. Place duck in an ovenproof dish on its back and roast for 1½ hours at 400°, basting frequently. When duck is finished, place on warming tray and pour excess fat from skillet. Add sugar and cook to a light caramel color.

Deglaze pan with vinegar and red wine; allow to reduce to one-half volume. Add brown sauce and bring to simmer. Add peaches that have been flamed in brandy. Carve duck and serve with sauce and wild rice. Serves 2.

*(See Ed. note under Rack of Lamb "Greenbrier" for a quick brown sauce.)

VEAL SCALLOPINI MARYLAND

¼ cup butter, softened
Juice of ½ lemon
¼ teaspoon Worcestershire sauce
1 tablespoon chopped parsley
1 tablespoon white wine
½ teaspoon Poupon mustard
8 (2 ounces each) scallopini of veal
¼ cup flour
Salt and pepper
¼ cup clarified butter
2 ounces Prosciutto ham, cut in julienne strips
1 cup backfin crabmeat, picked for shell

Stir together first 6 ingredients. Set aside. Season and flour veal. Heat clarified butter in skillet until butter just starts to smoke. Sauté veal quickly, until light brown color appears. Arrange on a platter. Pour off excess oil from pan. Add seasoned mixture. When hot, add ham and crabmeat. Toss until all is heated through. Serve over scallopini. May be served with Hollandaise or Bernaise sauce. Serves 4.

COLD BOURBON SOUFFLÉ

4 tablespoons unflavored gelatin
1½ cups bourbon
16 eggs, separated
4 teaspoons vanilla extract
Pinch of salt
2 cups sugar
2 cups heavy cream, whipped

Dissolve gelatin in bourbon in top of a double boiler over hot water. Set aside. Beat yolks until they are thick and lemony in color. Add vanilla. Mix in gelatin mixture, slowly stirring constantly. Cook over low flame until mixture coats the back of a metal spoon. Chill mixture until it begins to set. Beat the egg whites with a pinch of salt until foamy. Gradually beat in sugar, one tablespoon at a time, until the mixture looks like marshmallow. Whisk ⅓ of meringue mixture into egg yolk mixture. Fold in remaining egg whites. Fold in whipped cream. Place a 1½" buttered paper or aluminum foil collar around the inside rim of a 2 quart soufflé dish. Add mixture and chill. After mixture has chilled, remove collar and decorate top of soufflé with whipped cream rosettes. Serve with Deluxe Vanilla Sauce. Serves 10.

GREENBRIER BREAD PUDDING

5 slices plain, white bread
½ cup butter, melted
6 eggs
1 quart milk
½ cup sugar
Vanilla extract to taste
1 cup raisins

Cut bread slices into 1" squares and toast in a hot oven. Place in the bottom of a 3 quart casserole dish and drizzle with melted butter. Combine remaining ingredients. Pour over bread. Bake at 350° until custard is firm, approximately 45 minutes. Serve topped with Deluxe Vanilla Sauce. Use ½ cup sauce per serving. Serves 8 to 10.

DELUXE VANILLA SAUCE

2 cups heavy cream	1 tablespoon vanilla extract
½ cup sugar	¼ teaspoon salt
4 egg yolks	2 scoops vanilla ice cream
1 tablespoon flour	

Combine cream and sugar in a 2 quart saucepan. Bring just to a boil. Remove from heat. Beat egg yolks, flour, vanilla extract and salt together. Stir in a little of the hot cream. Then add mixture to remainder of cream in saucepan. Cook, stirring constantly (do not overcook), until just thickened. Remove from heat and add ice cream, stirring until melted. Strain. This sauce may be served hot or cold. Yield: approximately 1 quart.

"THE GREENBRIER" CHEESE CAKE

6 (8 ounces each) packages cream cheese	Pinch of salt
1½ cups sugar	6 eggs
⅛ cup lemon juice	½ cup graham cracker crumbs
1 tablespoon vanilla extract	

Have cream cheese and eggs at room temperature. Combine cheese, sugar, lemon juice, vanilla and salt. Mix until smooth. Add eggs. Heavily grease 10" spring pan or torte pan and line with graham cracker crumbs (pour out excess). Place mixture in pan. Bake at 400° for 25 to 30 minutes or until done. When done, let cool on rack. Do not attempt to unmold until it is cool. Top with blueberries, strawberries or your favorite fruit topping. Serves 8 to 10.

MOUNTAIN VILLAGE INN

Reminiscent of a Black Forest chalet, the Mountain Village Inn is located in Davis, West Virginia. The inn, with its rough sawn, board-and-batten siding and gingerbread decoration, features steaks, seafood and country ham as well as homemade breads, cakes and pies. It is a delightful place to relax and dine among the evergreens with the evening mist rising off Silver Lake.

WALNUT PIE

3 eggs
⅔ cup sugar
½ teaspoon salt
⅓ cup butter, softened

1 cup light corn syrup
1½ cups walnuts
1 9" unbaked pie shell

Beat eggs, sugar, salt, butter and corn syrup together. Stir in nuts. Pour into pie shell. Bake at 375° for 40 to 50 minutes.

WHOLE WHEAT ROLLS

1 cup milk
1 cup water
2 tablespoons sugar
1 tablespoon salt
¼ cup oil

1 egg
1 package dry yeast
3 cups whole wheat flour
3 cups white flour

Scald milk and water. Remove from heat. Add sugar, salt, oil and egg. Mix well. Cool to lukewarm. Sprinkle in yeast, stirring until dissolved. Add 3 cups flour. Beat until smooth. Add remaining flour, or enough flour to handle easily. Knead well. Place dough in greased bowl, cover and let rise in warm place until double in size. Punch dough down and shape into rolls. Let rise until light. Bake at 375° for 30 minutes until done.

1

MULDOON'S

Muldoon's first opened in 1979 and since then a tradition of good food, great service and fine entertainment have been established in this popular Charleston restaurant. Having an extremely varied menu, Muldoon's offers appetizers, salads, crepes, omelettes, sandwiches, entrees, desserts and most recently, Chicago style deep dish pizza. One of Muldoon's goals is to keep pace with a more and more knowledgeable dining public: one being achieved with success.

BROCCOLI SOUP

1 pound broccoli	1 quart water
½ cup margarine	1 teaspoon white pepper
1 medium onion, chopped	1 teaspoon salt
1 stalk celery, diced	1 teaspoon basil
1 carrot, diced	1 teaspoon oregano
1 quart milk	½ cup flour

Cook broccoli and chop finely. Set aside. Sauté onion, celery and carrot in margarine in large saucepan or Dutch oven until transparent. Add milk and water. Stir for five minutes. In small cup combine flour and enough hot liquid to make smooth, thin paste. Stir slowly into soup. Add rest of ingredients. Stir in cooked broccoli. Cook until heated through. Serves 10.

MULDOON'S CLAM CHOWDER

1 medium onion, chopped	1 quart water
1 stalk celery, chopped	1 dash Tabasco sauce
1 carrot, chopped	2 teaspoons basil
½ cup margarine	2 teaspoons oregano
1 (8 ounce) bottle clam juice	½ teaspoon thyme
2 (6½ ounces each) cans chopped clams	4 cups cooked potatoes, chopped in ¾" pieces
1 quart milk	Salt and pepper to taste
	½ cup flour

Sauté onions, celery and carrot in margarine in large saucepan or Dutch oven until transparent. Add all other ingredients except flour. Cook and stir for 5 minutes. In separate cup add enough hot liquid to flour to make a smooth thin paste. Stir slowly into soup. Cook until smooth and slightly thickened. Serves 10.

THE RED FOX INN

Overlooking the Hawthorne Valley near Slatyfork in the midst of West Virginia's ski region, the Red Fox Inn serves guests in an English hunting lodge atmosphere. With an emphasis on native craftsmanship, the dining room features a large fireplace in a room paneled with all native woods and lighting fixtures forged by local craftsmen. Specialties include Mountain Trout, Highland Quail and Venison, as well as steaks, seafood and elegant desserts.

FLORENTINE CREAM SOUP

1 pound fresh spinach	1 stalk celery, chopped
¼ cup butter	¼ cup chopped parsley
½ cup flour	¼ teaspoon salt
4 (13¾ ounces each) cans chicken broth	2 egg yolks
½ cup chopped onion	1 cup heavy cream

Wash, cook, drain and purée spinach. Set aside. Melt butter in large saucepan. Add flour; cook, stirring often for 2 minutes. Add chicken broth; cook, stirring constantly until smooth. Stir in onion, celery, parsley and salt; lower heat. Simmer uncovered for 30 minutes. (Skim off film from surface.) Strain soup; discard vegetables. Add spinach to soup. Beat egg yolks and cream in a small bowl. Stir in about 1 cup soup. Slowly add mixture to hot soup, stirring constantly. Cook over medium heat for 3 minutes. DO NOT BOIL! Serve with croutons if desired. Serves 8.

DIJON BUTTER
An interesting way to spice up your butter.

1 tablespoon Dijon mustard   1 pound butter, softened

Blend mustard well with butter. Place in a decorative mold or a nice country crock. Serve with herb breads.

CRANBERRY GLAZED TURKEY

Prepare stuffing and glaze for each 10 pound turkey wanted to cook. A 10 pound turkey is easier to store, handle and season; and will roast in less time than bigger birds. Sprinkle turkey inside and out with salt and pepper. Stuff the bird just before placing in the oven. Skewer or sew openings. Place turkey on a rack in a shallow roasting pan. Roast at 350° for about 3 hours. If turkey becomes too brown, cover with foil tent. Thirty minutes before the turkey is ready, baste with half of glaze. Remove from oven and place the turkey on a large platter. Spoon remaining glaze on turkey.

STUFFING

12 cups slightly dry bread cubes	1 teaspoon dried rosemary
⅓ cup finely chopped onion	1 cup chicken broth
⅓ cup snipped parsley	6 tablespoons butter, melted
1½ teaspoons salt	2 cups English walnut pieces
1½ teaspoons ground sage	
1 teaspoon dried thyme	

Combine first 7 ingredients. Add broth and butter. Toss lightly to mix. Add walnuts. Use to stuff a 10 pound turkey.

GLAZE

½ cup butter, melted	1 tablespoon cornstarch
1 teaspoon maple flavoring	1 cup sweetened cranberry juice

Mix butter, maple flavoring and cornstarch in a saucepan. Gradually stir in cranberry juice. Cook on low heat until sauce bubbles and thickens. Use glaze as directed above.

THE RED FOX INN'S CHICKEN BREAST SUPREME
"Created especially for Mountain Measures: A Second Serving"

3 whole chicken breasts, split	¼ teaspoon pepper
¾ cup flour	5 tablespoons butter
1 tablespoon lemon rind	1 tablespoon vegetable oil
1 teaspoon rosemary	Water to thin gravy
2 teaspoons salt	½ cup dry white wine
1 teaspoon paprika	1 cup of sour cream

Shake chicken breast halves in mixture of ½ cup of flour, lemon rind, paprika, rosemary, 1 teaspoon salt and pepper in plastic bag. Brown chicken in 1 tablespoon butter and vegetable oil. Place in shallow pan. Pour in ½ cup water and wine. Cover. Bake at 350° for 45 minutes until chicken is brown. Remove chicken to heated platter to keep warm. Pour liquid from pan into 1 cup measure. Add water to make one cup total. Melt remaining 4 tablespoons butter. Stir in remaining ¼ cup flour and 1 teaspoon salt. Cook, stirring constantly, until thick. Stir in sour cream just before serving. Serves 4 to 6.

CREAMED ONIONS

2 dozen small onions
3 tablespoons butter,
 divided
 White wine
 Chicken broth
1 bay leaf

Pinch of thyme
Salt to taste
1 cup heavy cream
 White pepper
2 tablespoons fresh chopped
 parsley

Drop onions in boiling water for 30 seconds to loosen skins. Shave off root ends and slip off the peel. To minimize bursting pierce a cross ¼" deep in the root ends. Arrange onions in wide pan in one layer, if possible. Add 1 tablespoon of butter and enough white wine and chicken broth to come half way up onions. Add bay leaf, thyme and salt. Simmer, covered, for 25 minutes or until just tender when pierced. If liquid has not evaporated, raise heat and boil it off, then add cream. Boil several minutes to thicken slightly. Reheat just before serving, adding a few grinds of white pepper. Fold in 2 tablespoons of soft butter and a sprinkling of fresh chopped parsley. Serves 4.

FRESH GREEN PEAS OUR WAY

4 cups young fresh green
 peas
 Lemon juice
 Salt
1 head Boston lettuce
10 scallions, halved

1 clove garlic, crushed
2 cups water
2 tablespoons chicken fat
 Freshly cracked pepper
1 teaspoon sugar
¼ cup butter

Wash peas well with lemon juice and water. Drain and place in a saucepan. Pour boiling water over peas. Add ½ teaspoon salt and let set 5 minutes. Drain. Quarter lettuce and blanch with scallions and garlic in 2 cups of water. When water comes to a boil, add chicken fat, peas, salt, pepper and sugar. Place in a 2 quart casserole. Cover with wax paper and a lid. Bake at 325° for 1 hour. Remove, stir in butter and serve. Serves 6 to 8.

SQUASH PIE

2 eggs
2 cups milk
¾ cup sugar
1 cup cooked winter squash
 (acorn, butternut,
 Hubbard)
½ teaspoon cinnamon

½ teaspoon salt
½ teaspoon nutmeg
½ teaspoon ginger
½ teaspoon vanilla extract
1 unbaked 9" deep dish pie
 shell

Beat eggs. Add milk and sugar. Mash and strain squash in a separate bowl. Add salt and spices. Combine two mixtures, blending well. Fill pie shell. (A nice pecan shell is out of this world.) Bake at 400° for 5 to 10 minutes. Reduce heat and bake at 325° for 20 to 30 minutes or until filling is thick.

RIVERSIDE INN

Located in an 80 year old two story log cabin situated on the banks of the Greenbrier River at Pence Springs, the Riverside Inn offers diners a step back into the colonial past. Served by waiters in colonial attire, one dines on a six course meal featuring such unique fare as Colonial Game Pie, Roast Goose, Hen and Hare, and the Fruit Stuffed Duckling given below.

RIVERSIDE INN'S FRUIT STUFFED DUCKLING

1 (4 to 6 pound) duckling
1 cup whole grain bread cubes
1 stalk celery, diced
¼ cup dried prunes, diced
1 tablespoon raisins
1 tablespoon browned sliced almonds
2 tablespoons sliced water chestnuts
1 tablespoon dried currants (may substitute white raisins)
½ teaspoon poultry seasoning
2 tablespoons melted butter
2 tablespoons orange juice
2 tablespoons orange marmalade
Orange slices for garnish

Prepare stuffing the day before cooking bird and allow to sit in refrigerator overnight to blend flavors. Combine bread cubes, celery, prunes, raisins, almonds, chestnuts, currants, poultry seasoning, melted butter and orange juice for stuffing. Mix well, cover and refrigerate. Just before cooking duck, place stuffing in breast cavity. Roast duck on rack at 400° for 90 minutes until well browned and done. May need to cover legs with foil tents during last 30 minutes if becoming too brown. Glaze with orange marmalade. Bake approximately 20 minutes. (Watch carefully or it will blacken.) Garnish with orange slices sprinkled with nutmeg, cinnamon and sugar. Serve warm. Multiply stuffing by number of birds needed to stuff to increase recipe. Serves 4.

VALLEY BARN RESTAURANT

Located in the picturesque Greenbrier valley, north of White Sulphur Springs, the Valley Barn has established itself as one of West Virginia's top restaurants. Open only five years, the restaurant is in an actual barn that dates from the 1930's. Beautifully restored, the decor features authentic Victorian antiques. Dining areas are on the second and third floor balconies. Twelve different entrées highlight the menu; one of which is the Navarin of Fresh Bay Scallops, provided below.

NAVARIN OF FRESH BAY SCALLOPS

1 small zucchini	⅓ cup white wine vinegar
1 small yellow squash	Salt and pepper to taste
1 carrot	1 cup cold butter
1 leek	1 pound fresh bay scallops
1 tablespoon minced shallots	

Cut zucchini, yellow squash, carrot and leek into julienne strips. Mix together and set aside. Combine shallots, vinegar, salt and pepper in a small saucepan. Bring to a boil, lower heat and reduce sauce by ½. While sauce is still hot, cut in cold butter until blended. Sauce will thicken as it sets. Steam scallops and julienne vegetables for 5 to 10 minutes. To serve, place scallops in a shallow bowl. Place julienne of vegetables over scallops and spoon sauce over. Serves 4.

THE YELLOW BRICK BANK RESTAURANT

Located in Shepherdstown in a former bank building, The Yellow Brick Bank Restaurant is a casual, friendly place with tables set with bright tablecloths and fresh cut flowers. Featuring sandwiches, quiches and salads for lunch and more specialized dinner entrées, the owners take great care to ensure high quality ingredients seeking out suppliers for red shrimp, mussels and lobster as well as fine wines and beer. Two recipes have been featured in "Bon Apetit's Reader Requests".

SAUTÉED CHICKEN BREASTS WITH COUNTRY HAM

6 chicken breasts, boned	1 teaspoon sage
2 teaspoons flour	½ cup sherry
2 teaspoons butter	6 slices country ham, large
1 teaspoon crushed garlic	enough to cover
1 teaspoon chopped parsley	chicken breasts

Pound chicken breasts to ¼" thick. Flour breasts lightly. Set aside. Melt butter in large skillet. Add garlic; cook until soft. Add chicken and brown on one side. Add sage and parsley. Turn chicken and brown on other side. Add sherry and ham. Simmer 10 minutes until chicken is done. Serve on warm plates with ham covering chicken. Serves 6.

REBELS AND REDCOATS

Highlighted by a large open fireplace, the wood paneled dining room, accented with pewter table settings, creates a tavern atmosphere reminiscent of the Revolutionary War era. Located in Huntington, specialties include Rack of Lamb, King Crab Newburg and Steak Oscar as well as seasonal offerings of rainbow trout and coho salmon.

MUSTARD SAUCE

1 cup sugar	2 egg yolks
2 tablespoons dry mustard	1 cup hot coffee cream
2 teaspoons cornstarch	4 teaspoons cider vinegar
½ teaspoon salt	

Mix sugar, mustard, cornstarch and salt in heavy saucepan. Beat egg yolks. Add to dry ingredients, mixing well. Gradually add hot cream to egg mixture, beating until smooth. Cook over medium heat, stirring frequently until sauce thickens and starch base disappears. Slowly add vinegar, whisking constantly. Cool sauce, stirring frequently. Serve with Alaskan King Crab Claws and Legs or other meat and vegetable dishes. May be served hot or cold.

FAIRS AND FESTIVALS

Tree of Life

THE BUCKWHEAT FESTIVAL

A special buckwheat flour, produced in Preston County, is responsible for the special taste of the Buckwheat Cakes served up at the annual Buckwheat Festival beginning the last September Thursday of every year in Kingwood. The famous cakes, along with the mouthwatering sausage, are served up throughout the four-day event to give festival-goers energy to participate in other activities, among them the annual arm-wrestling competition, arts and crafts exhibits, coronation of King Buckwheat and Queen Ceres, parades, livestock displays, and a carnival.

PRESTON COUNTY RAISED BUCKWHEAT CAKES

1 cake yeast	½ teaspoon baking powder
1 teaspoon salt	2 teaspoons sugar
1 quart lukewarm water	1 cup hot water
3 cups buckwheat flour	1 cup warm water
½ teaspoon soda	

Mix yeast and salt into 1 quart water in a large bowl. Let stand a few minutes. Stir in buckwheat flour to make a stiff batter, adding more flour if necessary. Let stand covered overnight (at least 4 to 5 hours).

Before baking, dissolve soda, baking powder and sugar in 1 cup hot water. Stir into batter. Add 1 cup or enough warm water to make a thin batter. Bake on a hot griddle, turning once.

Save 1 cup or whatever batter is left for the next baking. Batter will keep in refrigerator one week. To renew batter add: 1 pint lukewarm water, ½ teaspoon salt and enough buckwheat flour to make a stiff batter. When ready to bake repeat paragraph 2. Serves **4 to 6.**

CHARLESTON STERNWHEEL REGATTA

The entire city of Charleston turns its attention away from routine and comes together in a celebration of music, the river and life during this ten day festival from the last Saturday in August through Labor Day. Sternwheel races and shoving contests, special river activities of all types, the Charleston Distance Run with over 1000 runners on a 15 mile course and the "Taste of Charleston" when the city's restaurants join to offer a sampling of their tastiest fare are major events. Other events include open air concerts, historic tours, hot air balloon races, street parades and arts and crafts fairs.

FUNNEL CAKES

1⅓ cups flour	¾ teaspoon baking powder
¼ teaspoon salt	1 egg, beaten
2 tablespoons sugar	⅔ cup milk
½ teaspoon baking soda	Cooking oil for frying

Sift first 5 ingredients together in a bowl. In a separate bowl combine egg and milk. Add dry mixture, beating until smooth. Place 1″ of oil in a 10″ frying pan or electric skillet and heat to 375°. Hold a finger over the bottom of a funnel and fill the funnel with batter. Let the batter flow from the funnel opening, making circular motions into the skillet. Fry until golden; do not turn. Remove, drain and sprinkle with powdered sugar. Serve immediately.

CHERRY RIVER FESTIVAL

In Richwood the visitor to the annual Cherry River Festival not only has the chance to taste the traditional Hush Puppies, but can also hear the lore behind the tradition. Richwood's Eva Porter offers her special recipe along with the tale that hunters would quiet their hungry pups with these delights to keep them silent near their prey, thus coining the name "hush puppies". The festival takes place the second week of every August with parades, craft shows, gospel sings, an antique car show and talent contests.

OUR HUSH PUPPIES

2 cups sifted corn meal	1 tablespoon butter, melted
1 cup sifted flour	½ cup chopped onions
1 teaspoon baking powder	½ cup buttermilk
½ teaspoon salt	¾ cup water
1 teaspoon sugar	1 egg, beaten

Combine first 5 ingredients. Stir in remainder of ingredients, mixing well. Shape into balls ¾" thick. Deep fry at 350° for 5 to 7 minutes.

THE COUNTRY ROADS FESTIVAL

In 1862 a farm newspaper published 33 different recipes using corn—and at the Country Roads Festival, held in early September in Pennsboro, corn is celebrated in just as many ways. In addition to the good food, the festival includes community events, a parade, and musical entertainment.

HOMINY IN SOUR CREAM

"Corn in the morning. Corn at night. It was one of the first crops frontier folks planted, and it was the food they were most likely to have when all other food was gone. As a result, the pioneers were always looking for new ways to use corn."

2 tablespoons butter	1 cup sour cream
2 (14½ ounces each) cans golden hominy, drained	½ teaspoon salt
	Dash of pepper

Melt butter in a heavy skillet. Add hominy and sour cream. Season with salt and pepper. Heat through, stirring often. Serves 8 to 10.

THE KING COAL FESTIVAL

Coal is King in West Virginia—and the King Coal Festival held the third week of each September celebrates the industry through a series of events including square dancing, parades, coronation of King Coal, handicrafts, a tennis tournament, and down-home West Virginia food. Truly old-fashioned recipes for Apple Butter prepared the traditional way are fast disappearing, but the following is for nostalgic purists who want to recapture the past in a 16-gallon kettle!

OLD FASHIONED APPLE BUTTER
(16 Gallon Kettle)

4 to 5 bushels apples, peeled, cored and sliced

20 to 25 pounds sugar (brown sugar will make a darker apple butter, but will take less than granulated. Honey or molasses may be used)

½ to 1 fluid ounce desired flavoring. (Cinnamon is most preferred. Cloves, wintergreen, sassafras, vanilla or others may be used)

Put sliced and rinsed apples in a large well-scoured copper kettle. Cook over an open wood fire. Stir constantly and thoroughly until apples have cooked up to become applesauce and have begun to turn red. Gradually add sugar, a small amount at a time. Cook until thoroughly dissolved before adding more. Add sugar until desired sweetness is obtained. Cook until desired consistency and color. Add flavoring, stirring in thoroughly. Remove from heat. Pour into clean, sterile jars. Seal immediately with sterilized lids and bands. Process in a hot water bath for 10 minutes.

APPLE BUTTER NOTES: The open wood fire should be a steady slow-burning fire of constant intensity. Too high a fire increases the chances of burning; too low, cooking time is increased. There should be at least two people present when trying to make apple butter in this method. Someone must stir constantly while the other person tends the fire, adds apples and/or sugar. The second person may also be preparing jars, testing or other odds and ends. The stir must be kept on the bottom of the kettle and that it covers it over and over again throughout the long cooking. Cooking may take the entire day. This is important to keep the apple butter clean and the bottom from burning. Preparation of the apples is also time consuming. The apples should be prepared the day before. Remove all peel, core, bruises and blemishes. Slice into small pieces. Keep overnight in stone or enamel containers. Do not allow the apples to touch metal. If desired, cook the cores and peels in the kettle the day before to help prevent having a copper taste in the kettle. Before cooking the butter the next day scour the kettle with vinegar and salt and rinse well. The kettle must be treated this way before a batch of apple butter is made. Add enough water to cover the rounded part of the bottom of the kettle. Then add as many apples to the kettle as can be stirred. Then lay the fire under the kettle, making sure no wood touches the bottom of the kettle. Do not add sugar until the applesauce has begun to turn red and all lumps are gone. Do not allow the sugar to lump in the bottom as it may cause burning. You may add 3 to 4 pounds at a time. To test for doneness set a spoonful of apple butter in a saucer. If water rises around the edges it needs to be cooked longer. Remove the apple butter from the fire immediately after stirring in the flavoring.

THE MOUNTAIN STATE APPLE HARVEST FESTIVAL

The Mountain State Apple Harvest Festival has been known to delight visitors to the Eastern Panhandle of West Virginia since the early days of this century by offering such diverse activities as an Old English Fox Hunt, Turkey-Calling, a Pancake Breakfast—and, of course, apples. There's an Apple Pie Baking Contest, the Apple Trample (10,000 meter marathon), Apple Butter Making, Corona-tion of Queen Pomona (Goddess of Apples) and a Pie Auction. This slightly different Swiss Apple Pie recipe, which uses a custard filling, is a festival favorite.

SWISS APPLE PIE

"This recipe is a bit different from most apple pie recipes, in that it has a custard in the filling. It is said to have originated in Switzerland, which it could have done—as its taste may start you yodeling."

2 cups chopped or ground raw apples	¼ teaspoon salt
¾ cup sugar	2 eggs, beaten
½ teaspoon nutmeg	1 cup rich milk, scalded
¾ teaspoon cinnamon	1 unbaked 9" pie shell

Combine sugar, nutmeg, cinnamon and salt. Add eggs. Stir in milk. If using chopped apples, place apples in pie shell and pour liquid over. If using ground apples, mix apples with liquid and then pour into shell. Bake at 450° for 15 minutes, then at 350° for 35 minutes. Serve warm or cool.

MOUNTAIN STATE ART AND CRAFT FAIR

Held annually the first week of July at Cedar Lakes near Ripley, the Mountain State Art and Craft Fair is the largest fair of its type in the state. Each exhibitor is required to demonstrate his or her craft during the fair. In addition to craft booths there are open air concerts of Appalachian music, square dancing, apple butter and lye soap making and a juried art show. There are numerous food booths, including those making homemade ice cream, sassafras tea and outdoor barbecued chicken and corn. It is well worth the trip to attend this fair.

GRILLED CORN ON THE COB

Soak fresh corn still in the husk in cold water for ½ hour. Immediately before cooking pull husks back slightly, remove silk, close husks and tie back. Dip in water. Cook on a grill over medium to glowing coals 6″ from heat for 15 to 20 minutes, turning as needed to prevent burning. May also baste the corn with butter seasoned with garlic powder, Parmesan cheese or cayenne pepper after pulling the silk.

David C. Shepler

OGLEBAYFEST AND FARM DAYS

Oglebayfest and Farm Days bring parades, free dances, country fairs, arts and craft tents, special exhibits, an International Festival of Foods Buffet, and amphitheater programs to Oglebay Park in Wheeling (Oglebayfest is in late September-early October; Farm Days take place in late June). In a contest sponsored by the West Virginia Department of Agriculture in 1983, the following chicken recipe emerged winner.

DIPPIN' CHICKEN STICKS

2 whole chicken breasts	1 tablespoon milk
1 egg	1 cup Italian style bread crumbs

Cook chicken breasts until tender. Cool, bone and cut meat into strips. Roll in egg beaten with milk, then in bread crumbs. Mold into sticks. Deep fry until golden brown. Dip into your favorite barbeque sauce.

RAMP FESTIVAL (FEAST OF THE RAMSON)

"If you don't eat ramps, you just can't <u>live</u> here," says a Richwood, West Virginia native, reminiscing about the annual Feast of the Ramson which has glorified the rather odorous plant for more than a score of years. The "feed" takes place during Ramp Season, usually the middle of April, and also offers up complements of corn bread, ham, fried potatoes, scrambled eggs and sassafras tea. All the work is done by community volunteers—from the kids who uproot the ramps to the women's clubs who run the kitchen.

RAMPS AND PORK

Take 3 or 4 pounds of fresh pork ribs. Cook until tender. Remove all the bones. Put ramps through scalding water, then place in a saucepan, cover with the meat and a little of the broth from your meat. Salt and pepper to taste. Put in the oven and roast (approximately 350°) for twenty minutes. Turn meat and ramps and roast until they are lightly browned.

Courtesy of:
Barbara Beury McCallum
Mom & Ramps Forever © 1983

FRIED RAMPS AND POTATOES

Clean as many ramps as you want to cook. Cut into 1″ pieces using tops and all. Peel and slice about same amount of potatoes as ramps. Fry together in bacon fat until done. Break 2-3 eggs over ramps and potatoes and stir through. Let mixture fry a minute or two until eggs are cooked on bottom. Turn and cook several minutes more until the eggs are done. Twice as good served with homemade bread and butter.

Courtesy of:
Barbara Beury McCallum
Mom & Ramps Forever © 1983

THE WEST VIRGINIA STRAWBERRY FESTIVAL

The West Virginia Strawberry Festival is a week full of entertainment and fun for people of all ages. Held the end of May in Buckhannon the fair offers parades, pageants, coronations, strawberry exhibits and auctions, arts and crafts, sporting events, concerts, dances and much more. The recipe below was a first place winner in its division in the 1983 Strawberry Festival Recipe Contest.

STRAWBERRY CREAM DESSERT

1 cup flour
2 tablespoons sugar
½ cup margarine
1 cup chopped pecans, divided
1 (8 ounce) package cream cheese
1 cup powdered sugar
1 (12 ounce) carton frozen whipped topping, thawed and divided

2 (3½ ounces each) packages instant strawberry pudding or flavor of your choice
3 cups milk
2 cups strawberries, washed, sliced and drained

Combine flour, sugar, margarine and ½ cup pecans, blending well. Spread in bottom of a 9″ x 13″ baking dish. Bake at 350° for 15 minutes. Cool. Cream sugar and cream cheese until smooth. Fold in 1 cup whipped topping. Spread over cooled crust. Combine pudding and milk with a mixer. Fold in strawberries. Spread over topping. Spread remaining whipped topping over all. Sprinkle with remaining pecans. Refrigerate 2 to 3 hours before serving. Serves 10 to 12.

VANDALIA GATHERING

Vandalia Gathering's full name is "A Festival of Traditional Arts" and its goal is to celebrate and preserve West Virginia's folklore of yesterday for generations of tomorrow. The serious goal aside, Vandalia is a Memorial Day Weekend full of fun at the Science and Culture Center grounds in Charleston. Highlights include the annual banjo and fiddle contests, ethnic and traditional food booth, clogging and square dancing, storytelling & Liar's Contest, polka and other ethnic dances, quilt exhibitions, craft demonstrations and surprises each year.

BAKLAVA

Submitted by St. John's Greek Orthodox Church Guild in Charleston which has provided a food booth with Greek specialties at recent Vandalia Gathering festivals.

SYRUP

3 cups sugar	½ lemon
3 cups water	¼ orange
1 stick cinnamon	½ cup honey

Combine all ingredients in a saucepan, using whole lemon half and whole orange quarter. These are for flavoring. Bring to a boil and cook about 30 minutes until syrup is slightly thick. Let cool completely before using. Remove orange and lemon pieces.

PASTRY

2½ cups chopped walnuts	2 pounds phyllo dough
2 tablespoons cinnamon	1 pound sweet butter,
1 teaspoon cloves	melted
¼ cup sugar	

Combine first 4 ingredients, mixing well. Brush bottom of a 14" x 20" or a 12" x 18" baking pan with melted butter. Place one sheet of phyllo pastry on bottom of pan and brush with melted butter. Repeat until five phyllo sheets line the bottom of pan. Brush top layer with butter. Barely cover with some of nut mixture. Add another sheet of phyllo, brush with melted butter and sprinkle with nut mixture. Repeat this process until all of nut mixture is used. Finish with five phyllo sheets on top, brushing each with butter. Brush top with butter and cut into diamond shapes. Bake at 350° for 60 to 70 minutes until top is golden brown. Remove from oven and pour cold syrup on hot baklava. Keeps well in refrigerator for a month and in freezer for 6 months. Serves 50 to 55 depending on size of pieces.

WEST VIRGINIA BLACK WALNUT FESTIVAL

The West Virginia Black Walnut Festival means good eating beginning the second Thursday of each October in Spencer. For more than 25 years, the festival has served up black walnut recipes—chosen through an annual bake-off—as well as events like the Black Powder Shoot, Fiddlin' Contest, Chicken Flying Contest, Canoe Race and more. The following recipe won first place in the 1982 Black Walnut Bake-Off.

BLACK WALNUT PANOCHA

1½ cups sugar
 1 cup brown sugar
 ⅓ cup light cream
 ⅓ cup milk

2 tablespoons butter
1 teaspoon vanilla extract
½ cup broken black walnuts

Butter sides of a heavy 2 quart saucepan. Combine sugars, cream, milk and butter. Heat in saucepan over medium heat, stirring constantly until sugars dissolve and mixture comes to a boil. Cook to soft ball stage (238° on candy thermometer), stirring only if necessary. Remove from heat. Cool to lukewarm (110°) without stirring. Add vanilla. Beat vigorously until fudge becomes very thick and starts to lose its gloss. Quickly stir in black walnuts. Spread in buttered shallow pan. Score in squares while warm, cut when firm.

WEST VIRGINIA STATE FOLK FESTIVAL

It's the granddaddy of folk festivals, and old-time musicians travel miles and mountains the third week of June each year to be part of the West Virginia State folk Festival, affectionately just called "Glenville" by those who go—and know. Folklorist Dr. Patrick Gainer began the festival in 1950 with the goal of presenting non-professional, native West Virginia musicians and craftspeople in order to preserve remnants of West Virginia rural life. The festival remains true to its goal today—no organized bluegrass bands are permitted and any electrically-amplified instruments are forbidden. An organized schedule? No. Festival directors believe the best music "just happens". The following apple butter recipe can be found keeping festival-goers full and happy the traditional way.

APPLE BUTTER

1 peck apples
1 gallon sweet cider
6 cups sugar

1 tablespoon cinnamon
½ tablespoon ground cloves

Wash and slice apples. Add cider. Cook until soft, then press through a sieve. Boil the strained pulp until thick enough to heap on a spoon. Add remaining ingredients. Continue to boil until thick enough that no liquid runs from the butter when tested on a cold plate. Pour while hot into hot, sterile jars. Seal immediately with sterile lids and bands. Process in a hot water bath for 10 minutes.

Note: a less rich sauce may be made by using only 1 or 2 quarts cider.

THE HILLBILLY CHILI COOK OFF

Started just a few years ago the West Virginia Hillbilly Chili Cook Off is held annually in August at Snowshoe, West Virginia. The two day affair now draws people from all over and offers mountain music, bluegrass music and arts and crafts in addition to the Chili Cook Off. In charge of the event are Bill and Martina Neely who also have produced the International Chili Society Official Cookbook. The winner of the Cook Off is sent each year to California to compete in the national contest—below is the West Virginia winner from 1981.

BROWN'S HILLBILLY CHILI

6 (¼") slices bacon	½ teaspoon black pepper
2½ pounds coarsely ground chuck	2 (12 ounces each) cans beef bouillon
1½ pounds coarsely ground pork	2 (6 ounces each) cans tomato paste
3 pounds bottom round roast, cut in 1" strips	2 (3 ounces each) cans chopped green chilies
2 tablespoons cooking oil	3 tablespoons chili powder
6 large onions, chopped	½ teaspoon oregano
6 garlic cloves, minced	1 quart beer
2 green peppers, chopped	3 tablespoons honey
4 red cayenne peppers with seeds, chopped	2 tablespoons freshly ground cumin seed
1 tablespoon salt	

Cook bacon in a large skillet. Add chuck, pork and beef strips in batches and brown. Remove meat with a slotted spoon and place in a large stockpot. Discard bacon and fat. Sauté onions, garlic and peppers in oil. Stir in salt and pepper. Add to stockpot. Add remaining ingredients, using only 1 tablespoon cumin. Bring to a boil, stir and lower heat. Cook for 4 hours, adding remaining cumin and extra honey as needed. Makes a large amount; can be frozen.

John H. Brown, Jr.

ITALIAN HERITAGE FESTIVAL

The Italian Heritage Festival is a weekend full of Neapolitan celebration with the wonderful foods of the old country dished up delightfully in Clarksburg, the West Virginia home to many Italian descendants. In addition to the pastas and pastries, the Festival offers Italian dancing, organ-grinders and much merriment during each Labor Day weekend.

ANCHOVY AND PIMENTO

6 tablespoons olive oil
2 teaspoons Italian herbs
1 teaspoon wine vinegar
2 (2 ounces each) cans anchovy fillets, separate and reserve oil
2 (4 ounces each) jars pimento
Juice of 1 lemon
½ clove garlic, minced
1 tablespoon Marsala wine

Combine olive oil, herbs and vinegar. Pull the flat anchovy fillets apart. Add anchovy and oil to olive oil, tossing gently. Slice pimentos thinly and add to anchovy mixture. Add lemon juice, garlic and Marsala and toss again. Serve immediately. Serves 4.

William Neely
Courtesy of: Martina Neely
West Virginia Italian Heritage
Festival Cookbook © 1980

CHICKEN CACCIATORE

3 pounds chicken, boned
⅓ cup olive oil
2 medium onions, thin sliced
2 garlic cloves, minced
1 pound can tomatoes
1 pound can tomato-herb sauce
1 teaspoon salt
1 teaspoon basil, crushed
½ teaspoon celery seeds
½ teaspoon pepper
1 bay leaf
⅓ cup white wine
1 pound spaghetti, cooked
½ cup Parmesan cheese

Brown chicken in olive oil in a large skillet. Remove chicken and set aside. Add onion and garlic to the drippings in the skillet and sauté until transparent. Combine tomatoes, tomato sauce, salt, basil, celery seed, pepper and bay leaf and add to skillet. Simmer for 30 minutes. Add wine and blend well. Add chicken to skillet and cook at low heat for 50 to 60 minutes. Serve chicken over spaghetti. Spoon sauce over chicken. Top with Parmesan cheese. Serves 6.

Walter Neely, III
Courtesy of Martina Neely
West Virginia Italian Heritage
Festival Cookbook © 1980

MICROWAVE MAGIC

QUICK SNACKS

1. Bacon wrapped bread sticks: Wrap a bread stick with ½ strip bacon (cut lengthwise) dredged in Parmesan cheese. Cook on HIGH on a bacon rack for 4½ to 6 minutes for 10 bread sticks.
2. Baked apples: Core apples. Place in each hole 1 teaspoon butter, 1 teaspoon brown sugar and a few raisins. Sprinkle with cinnamon. Bake on HIGH for 8 to 10 minutes for 4 apples.
3. Speedy S'mores: Layer a graham cracker, ½ of chocolate bar and 1 large marshmallow. Cook on HIGH for 15 seconds or until marshmallow puffs. Top with another graham cracker.
4. Quick nachos: Place a slice of Cheddar cheese on a round tortilla chip. Heat on HIGH for 15 seconds until the cheese melts. Add taco sauce if desired.
5. Dessert toppings: 1. Melt a jar of jelly for ice cream garnish. Cook on HIGH for 2 to 2½ minutes.
   2. Caramel topping: Combine 20 caramels and 3 tablespoons liquid (cream, water or rum). Cook on HIGH 3 minutes.
   3. Steve's Super Hot Fudge Sauce - see Dessert Sauces.

MAKING LIFE EASIER

1. Bacon bits: Cut bacon in ½" to 1" pieces. Separate and place on bacon rack in microwave. Cook on HIGH 2 to 3 minutes.
2. Juicier citrus fruit: Fruit is easier to squeeze and will give more juice if heated on MEDIUM ½ to 1 minute.
3. Cracking nuts: Remove nut shells by placing 2 cups nuts with 1 cup water in a bowl. Cover. cook on HIGH for 1½ to 2 minutes. Nut pieces are easier to remove with less breakage.
4. Blanching nuts: Heat nuts in boiling water on HIGH for ½ to 1 minute. Drain and slip skins off by rubbing nuts between a paper towel.
5. No Fail White Sauce: Combine 3 tablespoons butter with 3 tablespoons flour in a glass dish. Cook on HIGH 2 minutes. Stir. Add ½ teaspoon salt, ⅛ teaspoon ground white pepper and 1 cup milk. Cook on HIGH for 3 to 4 minutes. Stir every minute.
   Variations: 1. Add 1 cup grated Cheddar cheese for cheese sauce. Heat on HIGH for 1 to 2 minutes or until melted, stirring every minute.
   2. Add 1 to 2 teaspoons horseradish.
   3. Add 1 cup grated Swiss cheese and 1 teaspoon lemon juice for Mornay sauce. Cook on HIGH for 1 to 2 minutes until cheese melts, stirring every minute.
6. Sauté vegetables for sauces, omelets, soups, casseroles: Place desired amount of vegetables in a glass dish, add a small amount of butter, oil or water and cook on HIGH for 1 to 2 minutes for 2 cups of vegetables.

7. Egg for salad garnish: Poach an egg until set according to your microwave directions. Chop to use in salads.
8. Cleaning your microwave: Place a bowl of water in the oven. Heat on HIGH for 4 to 5 minutes or until oven is well steamed. Wipe with a soft cloth or sponge.

SALVAGING THE UNSALVAGABLE

1. Corn on the cob. Save leftover corn on the cob. Reheat leftovers the second day on HIGH for 30 seconds to 1 minute per ear.
2. Hard brown sugar: Add a few drops of water to the box. Place in microwave and cook on HIGH for 15 seconds until sugar is soft.
3. Quick rising bread: Place yeast bread dough in microwave on lowest setting with dish set in water. Will rise in ⅓ to ½ the normal time.
4. Flaming desserts: Warm liqueurs for flaming in a glass measuring dish on HIGH for 30 to 60 seconds. Flame while pouring over dessert.
5. Hard honey: Decrystallize honey by placing the open honey jar in microwave on HIGH for 1 minute.
6. Overly dry dried fruit: Moisten by adding a few drops of water to the fruit in a small bowl. Cover and heat on HIGH for 30 to 60 seconds.

TOASTING AND DRYING

1. Orange and lemon peels: Place grated peel in a small bowl. Heat on HIGH for ½ to 1 minute or until dry. Stir once. Store in tightly covered bottles.
2. Herbs: Spread 1 cup of a fresh herb in a thin even layer on a paper plate or paper towel. Heat on HIGH for 4 minutes. Crumble herb into a powder and store in an airtight container in a cool, dark cupboard.
3. Toasted coconut: Spread grated coconut on a glass dish. Heat 1 cup for 1 minute on HIGH. Stir. Cook for 1 additional minute.
4. Croutons: Melt 2 tablespoons butter on HIGH for 45 seconds. Pour over 2 cups bread cubes. Sprinkle with ½ tablespoon paprika, garlic powder or celery salt. Spread on glass plate. Cook on HIGH for 3 to 4 minutes. Stir every minute.

EQUIVALENTS

1 POUND

Apples	= 2 to 6 apples	= 3 cups diced
Bananas	= 3 bananas	= 2 cups sliced
Dried beans	= 2½ cups raw	= 5 to 7½ cups cooked
Celery (1¼ lb.)	= 3 cups diced	= 2 cups
Cheese	= 4 to 5 cups grated	
Cherries	= 3 cups stemmed	= 2½ cups pitted
Cranberries	= 4 cups	= 4 cups sauce
Eggplant	= 4½ cups diced raw	= 1¾ cups cooked
Green beans	= 3 cups cooked	
Mushrooms	= 6 ounce can	= 3 cups sliced fresh
Parsnips	= 4 medium	= 2½ cups diced cooked
Peas	= ⅔ cup shelled raw	= 1 cup cooked
Peaches	= 4 to 6 peaches	= 2½ cups sliced
Potatoes	= 3 medium	= 2½ cups diced cooked
Raisins	= 3 cups	
Rhubarb	= 4 to 8 stalks	= 3½ cups diced
Sugar	= Granulated	= 2¼ cups
	= Super fine	= 2⅓ cups
	= Brown	= 2¼ cups
	= Granulated Brown	= 3⅛ cups
	= Powdered	= 3½ cups
Spinach or other Greens	= 2 cups cooked	= 4 cups raw
Zucchini	= 3 to 4 small	= 3 cups sliced raw

1 medium avocado	= 2 cups cubed
1 medium onion	= ¾ to 1 cup chopped raw
1 medium green pepper	= ¾ to 1 cup chopped raw

CRUMBS

Bread	= 1 slice	= ½ - ¾ cup soft
Bread	= 1 slice	= ¼ cup fine dry
Saltines	= 28 squares	= 1 cup
Graham crackers	= 14 squares	= 1 cup
Vanilla wafers	= 22 wafers	= 1 cup
Chocolate wafers	= 22 wafers	= 1 cup
Round butter crackers	= 24 crackers	= 1 cup

SUBSTITUTIONS

1 cup buttermilk:	1 tablespoon lemon juice or vinegar plus whole milk to equal one cup or 1 cup plain yogurt or 1 cup whole milk plus 1¾ teaspoons cream of tartar
1 cup heavy cream:	¾ cup whole milk plus ⅓ cup butter
1 cup light cream:	⅞ cup whole milk plus 3 tablespoons butter
1 lemon:	2 to 3 tablespoons juice and 1½ to 3 teaspoons grated rind
1 teaspoon lemon juice:	1 teaspoon vinegar
1 teaspoon finely shredded lemon peel:	½ teaspoon lemon extract
¼ cup chopped onion:	1 tablespoon instant flakes or minced, or 1 teaspoon onion powder
1 clove garlic:	⅛ teaspoon garlic powder or ¼ teaspoon minced garlic
½ teaspoon cornstarch:	1 tablespoon flour
1 cup sugar:	1 cup brown sugar, well packed or ¾ cup honey and reduce liquid or 1½ cups molasses and reduce liquid or 2 cups corn syrup and reduce liquid or 2 cups sifted powdered sugar
1 ounce chocolate:	4 tablespoons cocoa plus ½ tablespoon butter
½ to 1½ teaspoons dried herbs:	1 tablespoon fresh
1 cup self-rising flour:	1 cup all purpose flour plus 1½ teaspoons baking powder and ¼ teaspoon salt
1 tablespoon prepared mustard:	1 teaspoon dry mustard plus 1 tablespoon vinegar
1 teaspoon baking powder:	¼ teaspoon baking soda plus ½ teaspoon cream of tartar or ¼ teaspoon baking soda plus ⅓ cup molasses or ¼ teaspoon baking soda plus ½ cup buttermilk

INDEX

MOUNTAIN MEASURES: A SECOND SERVING
Junior League of Charleston, West Virginia
P.O. Box 1924, Charleston, WV 25327

Please send _____ copies of **MOUNTAIN MEASURES: A SECOND SERVING** at $11.95 plus $1.50 per copy for postage and handling. West Virginia residents, please include sales tax of 60¢ per copy.

Enclosed is: _____ ☐ check ☐ money order

Send to: _____

_____

_____

Gift wrap available: 50¢ per copy.　　☐ Gift wrap
COMPLETE YOUR SET:
Order the original **MOUNTAIN MEASURES**: $9.95 plus $1.50 per copy for postage and handling. West Virginia residents add sales tax of 50¢ per copy.

Send _____ copies of **MOUNTAIN MEASURES.**

All copies will be sent to same address unless otherwise specified. If you wish to enclose your own gift card with book, please write name of recipient on outside of envelope, enclose with order, and we will include it with your gift.
ALLOW FOUR WEEKS FOR DELIVERY

MOUNTAIN MEASURES: A SECOND SERVING
Junior League of Charleston, West Virginia
P.O. Box 1924, Charleston, WV 25327

Please send _____ copies of **MOUNTAIN MEASURES: A SECOND SERVING** at $11.95 plus $1.50 per copy for postage and handling. West Virginia residents, please include sales tax of 60¢ per copy.

Enclosed is: _____ ☐ check ☐ money order

Send to: _____

_____

_____

Gift wrap available: 50¢ per copy.　　☐ Gift wrap
COMPLETE YOUR SET:
Order the original **MOUNTAIN MEASURES**: $9.95 plus $1.50 per copy for postage and handling. West Virginia residents add sales tax of 50¢ per copy.

Send _____ copies of **MOUNTAIN MEASURES.**

All copies will be sent to same address unless otherwise specified. If you wish to enclose your own gift card with book, please write name of recipient on outside of envelope, enclose with order, and we will include it with your gift.
ALLOW FOUR WEEKS FOR DELIVERY

If you know a store in your area that might be interested in carrying our book, please send us the store's name and address.

Thank you.

_____

_____

_____

_____

_____

_____

_____

_____

_____

If you know a store in your area that might be interested in carrying our book, please send us the store's name and address.

Thank you.

_____

_____

_____

_____

_____

_____

_____

_____

_____

_____

_____

MOUNTAIN MEASURES: A SECOND SERVING
Junior League of Charleston, West Virginia
P.O. Box 1924, Charleston, WV 25327

Please send _____ copies of **MOUNTAIN MEASURES: A SECOND SERVING** at $11.95 plus $1.50 per copy for postage and handling. West Virginia residents, please include sales tax of 60¢ per copy.

Enclosed is: _____ ☐ check ☐ money order

Send to: _____

_____

_____

Gift wrap available: 50¢ per copy.   ☐ Gift wrap

COMPLETE YOUR SET:
Order the original **MOUNTAIN MEASURES: $9.95 plus $1.50 per copy for postage and handling. West Virginia residents add sales tax of 50¢ per copy.

Send _____ copies of **MOUNTAIN MEASURES.**

All copies will be sent to same address unless otherwise specified. If you wish to enclose your own gift card with book, please write name of recipient on outside of envelope, enclose with order, and we will include it with your gift.

ALLOW FOUR WEEKS FOR DELIVERY

MOUNTAIN MEASURES: A SECOND SERVING
Junior League of Charleston, West Virginia
P.O. Box 1924, Charleston, WV 25327

Please send _____ copies of **MOUNTAIN MEASURES: A SECOND SERVING** at $11.95 plus $1.50 per copy for postage and handling. West Virginia residents, please include sales tax of 60¢ per copy.

Enclosed is: _____ ☐ check ☐ money order

Send to: _____

_____

_____

Gift wrap available: 50¢ per copy.   ☐ Gift wrap

COMPLETE YOUR SET:
Order the original **MOUNTAIN MEASURES: $9.95 plus $1.50 per copy for postage and handling. West Virginia residents add sales tax of 50¢ per copy.

Send _____ copies of **MOUNTAIN MEASURES.**

All copies will be sent to same address unless otherwise specified. If you wish to enclose your own gift card with book, please write name of recipient on outside of envelope, enclose with order, and we will include it with your gift.

ALLOW FOUR WEEKS FOR DELIVERY

If you know a store in your area that might be interested in carrying our book, please send us the store's name and address.

Thank you.

_____

_____

_____

_____

_____

_____

_____

_____

_____

_____

- -

If you know a store in your area that might be interested in carrying our book, please send us the store's name and address.

Thank you.

_____

_____

_____

_____

_____

_____

_____

_____

_____

_____